JUST ANOTHER BLOODY YEAR

JUST ANOTHER BLOODY YEAR

(My Life and Other Problems)

VERNON COLEMAN

BLUE BOOKS

Published by: Blue Books,
Vernon Coleman, PO Box 639 Weston super Mare, BS23 9ND, England
First published by Blue Books in 2013 in a limited edition of 500 copies.
This book is copyright. Enquiries should be addressed to the author
c/o the publishers.
Copyright Vernon Coleman 2013
The right of Vernon Coleman to be identified as the author of this work has been
asserted in accordance with Copyright, Designs and Patents Act 1988.

ISBN – 10 1-899726-28-8
ISBN – 13 978-1-899726-28-8

A catalogue record for this book is available from the British Library.
Printed and bound by CPI Group (UK) Ltd, Croydon, CR0 4YY

Books by Vernon Coleman include (in order of appearance):

Medical:
The Medicine Men
Paper Doctors
Everything You Want To Know
    About Ageing
The Home Pharmacy
Aspirin or Ambulance
Face Values
Stress And Your Stomach
A Guide To Child Health
Guilt
The Good Medicine Guide
An A to Z of Women's Problems
Bodypower
Bodysense
Taking Care Of Your Skin
Life Without Tranquillisers
High Blood Pressure
Diabetes
Arthritis
Eczema and Dermatitis
The Story Of Medicine
Natural Pain Control
Mindpower
Addicts and Addictions
Dr Vernon Coleman's Guide To
    Alternative Medicine
Stress Management Techniques
Overcoming Stress
The Health Scandal
The 20 Minute Health Check
Sex For Everyone
Mind Over Body

Eat Green Lose Weight
Why Doctors Do More Harm Than
    Good
The Drugs Myth
Complete Guide to Sex
How To Conquer Backache
How To Conquer Pain
Betrayal of Trust
Know Your Drugs
Food for Thought
The Traditional Home Doctor
Relief from IBS
The Parent's Handbook
Men in Dresses
Power over Cancer
Crossdressing
How to Conquer Arthritis
How To Stop Your Doctor Killing
    You
Superbody
Stomach Problems - Relief At Last
How to Overcome Guilt
How To Live Longer
Sex
Coleman's Laws
Anyone Who Tells You Vaccines Are
    Safe And Effective Is Lying.
Do Doctors And Nurses Kill More
    People Than Cancer?

Psychology/Sociology:
Stress Control
How To Overcome Toxic Stress

Know Yourself
Stress and Relaxation
People Watching
Spiritpower
Toxic Stress
I Hope Your Penis Shrivels Up
Oral Sex: Bad Taste and Hard
To Swallow
Other People's Problems
The 100 Sexiest, Craziest, Most Out-
rageous Agony Column Questions
(and Answers)
How To Relax And Overcome Stress
Too Sexy To Print

Politics:
England Our England
Rogue Nation
Confronting the Global Bully
Saving England
Why Everything Is Going To Get
Worse Before It Gets Better
The Truth They Won't Tell You...
About The EU
Living In A Fascist Country
How To Protect & Preserve Your
Freedom, Identity & Privacy
Oil Apocalypse
Gordon is a Moron
The OFPIS File
What Happens Next?
Bloodless Revolution
2020
Stuffed!

Animals:
Why Animal Experiments Must
Stop
Fighting For Animals
Alice and Other Friends
Animal Rights - Human Wrongs
Animal Experiments - Simple Truths

General Non Fiction:
How To Publish Your Own Book
How To Make Money While
Watching TV
Strange But True
Daily Inspirations
Why Is Public Hair Curly
People Push Bottles Up Peaceniks
Secrets of Paris
Moneypower
101 Things I Have Learned
100 Greatest Englishmen and
Englishwomen
Diary Of A Disgruntled Man
Just Another Bloody Year

Novels (General):
Mrs Caldicot's Cabbage War
Deadline
Second Innings
Mrs Caldicot's Knickerbocker Glory
Tunnel
Mr Henry Mulligan

Bilbury Novels:
The Bilbury Chronicles
Bilbury Grange
Bilbury Revels
Bilbury Pie (short stories)
Bilbury Country
Bilbury Village
Bilbury Pudding (short stories)

Novels (Sport):
Thomas Winsden's Cricketing
Almanack
Diary Of A Cricket Lover
The Village Cricket Tour
The Man Who Inherited A Golf Course
Around the Wicket
Too Many Clubs And Not Enough
Balls

Cat books:
Alice's Diary
Alice's Adventures
We Love Cats
Cats Own Annual
The Secret Lives Of Cats
Cat Basket
The Cataholics Handbook
Cat Fables
Cat Tales
Catoons From Catland

Writing As Edward Vernon:
Practice Makes Perfect
Practise What You Preach
Getting Into Practice

Aphrodisiacs - An Owner's Manual
The Complete Guide To Life

Writing As Robina Hood:
Revolt

Written with Donna Antoinette Coleman:
How To Conquer Health Problems Between Ages 50 & 120
Health Secrets Doctors Share With Their Families
Animal Miscellany
England's Glory
The Wisdom of Animals

Small Print

All opinions, predictions and ramblings in this book are aired in public purely as private entertainment. Readers who act on any of the alleged facts in this book, or who are misguided enough to follow any advice which may have crept, uninvited, onto the pages, do so entirely at their own risk. All alleged facts and opinions should be treated cautiously and with great suspicion. Any apparent advice should be ignored completely. None of the people or places named in this book should be confused with real people or places who or which share the same or similar names. Books can be dangerous objects and should not be thrown, dropped or otherwise projected into areas where people, civil servants, health and safety officials or objects, valuable or otherwise, may be damaged.

Warning To Debutants In The Libel Business

Any person wishing to identify himself, or herself, or any other person, dead or alive, with any character in this book, may do so at his, or her, own discretion. It shall be explicitly stated, however, that no such identification was intended, or called for, by the author. Any person who doubts the author's word for this, and accuses him – in spite of the above explicit statement to the contrary – of having committed a libel by portraying any actual person, alive or dead, will therefore himself commit a libel, namely, that of accusing the author of telling lies, and will thus himself be sued for libelling the author instead of the author being sued for libelling him.

From *The Face on the Cutting Room Floor* by Cameron McCabe, published in 1937.

Dedication

To The Princess, My Antoinette, because when you smile my life is full of sunshine and when you are sad my life is cloudy and grey. In all the years we have been married there has never been a day when I would not have asked you to marry me. And I know that however long I live there will never be a day when I am not happy that you said yes. You are my heroine. I am addicted to you; you have doubled my joy and halved my despair.

CONTENTS

PREFACE

This is not a guide book. It is not a novel. There is no information of practical value in this book. No times of museum opening or details of hidden, wonderful restaurants where the owner's wife cooks bass in claret - the fish caught by her cousin and brought up specially that morning. There are no lists of wonderful shops where you can buy genuine Dior dresses at 10% of their price in the Avenue Montaigne. There are no descriptions of gardens or cathedrals or exquisite buildings. There are, however, goodly chunks of raw life, served up with a sauce of passion. I have always had a penchant for doing things the hard way. If there is a short cut and a long way round I have always chosen the long way round. The only difference between fiction and non-fiction is that fiction has to make sense. This book is non-fiction and is doubtless full of the sort of bizarre confusions and scarcely believable contradictions which beset all our lives. This is the book that the old men who stand on street corners shouting at passers-by would write if they had typewriters. This is a book for people who shout at their television sets.

I used to believe that if I worked hard I could deal with all my problems and live a monkish life of unflustered calm but by the age of 11 I realised that whatever I did the problems would keep rolling in like waves onto a beach. It was, however, relatively recently that I realised that the waves had changed; today they are driven by a storm and the beach is windswept and the sky always angry. The Blairs and Browns and Cleggs and Cables and other supernatural horrors, villains of our time, ride the waves with grinning faces and fiendish, ghoulish whoops of glee as they whip their mounts into ever more fury. I feel, as I always have, like a small boy at the beginning of a new day at a new school. But the future seems ever more terrifying. It's as though I've woke up to find everyone speaking a different language and obeying different rules; as though I've been transported to another world, a different galaxy perhaps. The world has been turned upside down, inside out and back to front and most people don't seem to have noticed.

For some time now no one has voted for anything. Most people have just voted against the party they consider most hateful. The problem is that most people feel hostility towards all the parties, and all the politicians, so most don't vote at all.

The fundamental problem we have is that our politicians are a toxic mixture of milquetoast finicks and grasping feather-merchants. They may be cheaper to bribe than anyone else's politicians but they are still crooks. They make promises they know they can't keep. Not once. Not twice. But every time they want a vote. They lie, lie and lie again so often that in the end I doubt if they think they are doing anything wrong. And, of course, in the manner of small-minded functionaries everywhere, they routinely and persistently fiddle and cheat on the big things (elections) and the small things (their expenses). Really big stories which matter hardly ever appear in the media and if they do they are dismissed. Modern politicians, drenched in cynicism, know that the truth is an unnecessary luxury; it simply doesn't matter. Even plausibility is usually unnecessary as long as what is said is memorable, slickly produced and repeated frequently. If something bad happens it can be brushed out of the public consciousness by providing the media with something more immediately newsworthy. (The 'A good day to bury bad news' syndrome). And if you want to damage someone then you simply accuse them of something that is not only hard to refute but also tends to last in the public consciousness. So, for example, accuse your opponent or critic of rape or sexual assault, especially involving a child or animal. There doesn't need to be any proof or any conviction. Just an accusation and a rumour will do the trick.

Well over half of all stories in newspapers and on television are a direct result of a press release. Cut out the crime stories, the sports news and the stories about the Duchess of Cambridge taking off her clothes (and then expressing surprise and horror when the photographs end up on mugs and table mats) and there is very little left that is the result of old-fashioned journalism. The releases are often printed verbatim. Newspapers print lies and deceit and myths and misconceptions, and truths and legally enforced apologies are hidden at the bottom of page 19, if they get any space at all. Modern journalists are rarely, if ever, objective. Editors take a stance according to their prejudices and their proprietor's prejudices. Opinions which don't fit the guidelines are often blue pencilled out of existence. When I wrote the agony column for *The People* newspaper one editor (the now famous Neil Wallis) inserted the words 'I believe' so many times that the column read like the lyrics for a gospel song.

The modern journalist goes to cocktail parties with politicians, accepts gongs from Prime Ministers and generally behaves like a member of the Establishment. No real writer should be part of the system, be liked by politicians, receive awards or mix with other writers or even publishers. Writing should be a solitary business. My favourite writers were all independent minded and unconsciously eccentric. (It is important not to confuse genuine eccentricity with the sort of forced, faked, attention seeking eccentricity practised by television celebrities. That's exhibitionism. The truly eccentric do not think that their behaviour is in any way odd and they would never dream of describing themselves as eccentric.) The successful modern author is a media celebrity, living in an incestuous pond where he never meets or talks to anyone who isn't a celebrity. Television people need to have lovely hair rather than brains. That's why they tend to pass their view by date so early on in their careers.

British Governments and the submissive media slaves who do their every bidding (with the BBC at the top of the list of course) have done everything they can to destroy the principle of a free press. The phrase 'BBC journalist' is oxymoronic nonsense. At the BBC, hypocrisy rules. (My favourite example of BBC hypocrisy is the way news and feature programmes attack newspaper photographers by showing film of them working - as though the TV cameras were somehow invisible to the person being 'papped'. The BBC, which makes Pravda look feisty and anarchic is a loathsome, traitorous organisation which has consistently betrayed and deceived taxpayers. Yesterday, I found an old diary for 1960. In it I discovered an entry in which I questioned the independence of the BBC. I was just 14-years-old at the time.

Tragically, journalism, once an honourable profession, the scourge of the political classes, has become a mixture of gossip, commercial promotion and half-baked second-hand opinion. It is almost impossible to read a news story that hasn't been contaminated with the opinions of an editor or the opinions of the public relations firm which wrote the original release. Most journalists spend their days regurgitating press releases; they no longer understand the meaning of the word 'news'. Most of the stuff they prepare for their newspapers is either propaganda or opinionated drivel that distorts the truth in the interests of the proprietor or some of his powerful friends or advertisers. Their idea of balance is to bend the stories they write to fit their paper's needs.

And there's more bad news!

Many apparently eminent publications (newspapers and magazines) now readily print advertisements which look like editorial. Even when you know what you're looking for it can be nigh on impossible to tell which articles were paid for and which are appearing because someone paid for them to appear. The days when the word *Advertisement feature* or *Advertorial* appeared at the top of a page are long gone. Finding the wheat among the chaff requires inside knowledge, a cynical eye and the patience of Job.

The absence of real leadership means that our world is now controlled by interfering, politically correct do-gooders who are misinformed, misguided, hypocritical and more often than not just plain old-fashioned bent in a sly Arthur Daley sort of way. While they insist that small children wear eye protectors when playing tiddly winks, and full body armour before even threading a conker onto a shoelace, they plan new forms of deceit. There seems to be no inbuilt sense of right or wrong among the perpetrators (possibly because of the calamitous decline of the power of religion in the Western world) and this absence is exaggerated by the absence of any sense of justice, or even indignation, among the public at large. Moral outrage is conspicuous by its absence. The effect of all this on our so-called leaders cannot be underestimated. Modern political life is littered with Cleggs and Cables, the dregs of human society.

Many of our politicians have intellectual, commercial, political or personal commitments which mean that we cannot possibly trust them to make impartial decisions. The awful Clegg, to take but one nauseating example of the modern political man, is an ex-employee of the European Union and, as such, is in line for a hefty EU pension. It seems to me that this half-witted nincompoop, who would have surely been out of his depth as a school prefect, has a personal interest in supporting and defending the EU. He is currently Deputy Prime Minister of England and it seems plain to me that he should excuse himself whenever the EU is discussed. He won't, and doesn't, of course.

Our politicians take decisions to protect their party's chance of winning power at the next election. The Scottish banks were rescued by English taxpayers, at vast expense, so that the failing Labour Party could protect the seats of Gordon Brown and his chums. We, and the rest of the Western world, now have a banking system which is so corrupt and indebted that it is the major cause of misery in the country. By creating poverty, depression and anxiety, and consequently causing heart disease and cancer, the big banks have killed far more people than terrorists. It seems impossible but they may have even killed more people than doctors and nurses. We should be waging war not on Al Qaeda, but on Goldman Sachs et al.

We have one of the world's biggest arms industries. Around 300,000 people in England earn their living making things designed to kill (mostly innocent) people. We didn't have that many people making bombs when we really were at war. Our Prime Ministers routinely humiliate themselves (and, therefore, us) by doing dirty arms deals with shady regimes. Our foreign policy is designed to keep those 300,000 people in work. What a bloody country. The Minister of Obfuscation and the Minister for Bed Cushions and Scented Candles spend their days making sure that when they leave office they will have some well-paid directorships waiting for them. If corrupt politicians were a saleable commodity there would be a glut and the market price would go so low that it would be necessary to reintroduce the halfpenny. It isn't difficult to argue that we live in a kleptocracy, where the nation's assets are routinely stolen by our rulers. The tradition in fiction (particularly films) is that good things happen to good people and bad things happen to bad people. In the real world, sadly, the opposite is true.   The result is that almost everything is worse than it was yesterday, last month, last year and last decade.

Every good idea must run the gauntlet of criticism and suggestions from taxpayer funded busy bodies who must have their say in order to justify their vast salaries and bonuses but who offer nothing of value and do nothing of use except make themselves look important. Government departments and quangos complicate and damage and add nothing to our lives. As a result the world frustrates and disappoints and frightens me, sometimes all at once. In Victorian England (a time now sneered at) a quarter of the world's population lived under English rule. We spread civilisation, a decent language and cricket to previously unlit corners on all continents. England was the wealthiest nation on earth. Things which bore the stamp 'Made in England' were built to last and the label was accepted worldwide as a mark of excellence. England has been reduced to penury and even possible bankruptcy. We now live in a world where classroom assistants are allowed to teach, milkmen are allowed to deliver the mail and nurses allowed to give anaesthetics, prescribe drugs and perform surgical operations. Playing fields are sold by the dozen so that councils which have become little more than pension funds for overpaid former employees can afford to heat school classrooms in the winter.

Our world has been turned inside out, upside down and back to front by people who cheat and lie for a living and who don't give a fig for our history, our culture, our legacy or our nation's integrity. Common sense is now as rare as integrity among politicians or in the EU headquarters.

It's sometimes difficult to avoid the feeling that the world has gone stark raving mad. Just this morning I heard a council spokesman say that his council was turning off the street lights at night because there aren't as many people around after dark. Another council has closed its public library because people in wheelchairs cannot get up the stairs at the front and, since the building is listed, they aren't allowed to put in a ramp. The EU has allowed millions of Bulgarians and Romanians to come to England to claim benefits. No one in Brussels seems to give a damn that our country is packed to the gunwales with legal immigrants and with immigrants who came to England on the Eurostar train but didn't bother to buy tickets because they travelled underneath the carriage instead of inside it. The additional millions will, of course, immediately be entitled to free health care, free education and the world's most generous benefits programme. The number of households surviving on state hand-outs already exceeds 50%. Thanks to the EU's disastrously stupid policies we're heading for bankruptcy. Before we get there we'll enjoy a rapidly declining standard of living and a rapid rise in resentment, confrontation and disappointment.

We live in a world where people who show signs of loyalty, honour, courage, respect and integrity are classified as either just plain potty or dangerously eccentric. We live in a society in which anyone who threatens the State is considered more dangerous than a mere criminal. So not paying your BBC television licence fee will attract a bigger punishment than killing an old man for the change in his pocket. We live in a world where the simple truths are the most complicated, the most difficult to understand, the easiest to ignore and the hardest to do anything about.

We now live in a world dominated by deceit and incompetence; a world where the medium is far more important than the message and the perception widely considered to be of more importance than reality, meaning or truth. True history is what we remember and what influences our lives, rather than what actually happened. Facts are less important than myths. A widely believed falsehood is, in our world, more powerful and relevant than a little known, artfully suppressed truth.

The media generally (or, in the case of the BBC, exclusively) support the Government and the Establishment. Media people think of themselves as good and honest and fair and objective and idealistic. But they are not. They are deluded, prejudiced and bigoted. Just about everyone working for the BBC (particularly those who are salaried employees), is protecting the interests of the commercial establishment as promoted by politicians and lobbyists. The BBC would endorse the Flat Earth Society if it was supported by the European Union.

There may be more types of media available today but there is very little honest news or original thought in any of it. Original ideas of any kind are suppressed - particularly if they oppose the acknowledged establishment in any way. I have for many years believed that the only original work appears in the work produced by small, independent publishers. More than ever I now believe that to be true. There is much talk about the value of our free press but the English press is highly censored and is, when measured impartially, among the least free in the world.

I worked for tabloid newspapers for many years and I know that a big proportion of the stories involving and exposing celebrities are actually done with the approval of the celebrities themselves. So, for example, a press agent for a homosexual male star who wants to appear heterosexual will pay a girl to spill the beans about an alleged night of passion. The newspaper pays a fee for the exposé (knowing that they won't be sued for libel), the girl receives a fee and some publicity and the limp-wristed star has his sexy image burnished. The story itself will be the usual sort of fiction ('He couldn't keep his hands off me. We were at it for hours. At least five times a night. He was better equipped than a horse.').

Forty years ago I exposed how some medical journals will print articles which are paid for by drug companies. Nothing has changed. Whole issues of magazines and newspapers are devoted to a particular subject in order to attract specific advertisements. In newspapers and magazines and on television and the internet, the line is blurred between editorial and advertisements. Book publishers are no different. Some of the snootiest publishers will publish a book by a company, celebrity or politician if they are paid a fee. This is true vanity publishing but everyone concerned pretends it isn't.

We are drowning in information but real news is stuff that someone, somewhere, doesn't want you to print, and very little of it is appearing in newspapers or on the television (which is largely dominated by dodgy celebrities who are rude, very rude and unbelievably rude and whose sole talents are in thinking up new ways to shock). And if you think you can find news or truth on the Web then think again. If you are conducting a search on the internet then you will find the truth (or something related to it) only if you are already an expert and can pick your way through the propaganda, the commercial exploitation and the censorship. Google is the most dangerous and evil creation in the history of the media. Today, the main problem is not a lack of information but a surfeit of information and a limited amount of time and ability to process all the information and to make decisions.

People who read modern newspapers, watch television news programmes, listen to the radio or surf the internet may think they are keeping up with what goes on in the world but most are simply wasting time, effort and energy on remote, complex, insoluble problems and ignoring real, possibly soluble, problems. They are being manipulated in a way that would have delighted Orwell's Big Brother.

We live in a dark world where millions think only of themselves, where the general sense of entitlement exceeds the sense of community and where all sense of responsibility is constantly overwhelmed by a never ending exhibition of petty authority. (Scarily, most people in England have a bigger television set than bookcase and more DVDs and computer games than books.) It is politically incorrect to remind anyone of Thomas Malthus, who pointed out that *giving* food to the poor encourages them to breed, and thus creates an ever bigger problem. It is even more incorrect to suggest that he might have had a point worth debating.

There used to be a rich stratum of honesty running through Middle England. There have always been high levels of crime among the poor and the rich but the middle classes always used to be honest. No more. The main problem, of course, is the fact that there are now so many rules and regulations that it is impossible for the most law abiding citizen to avoid breaking at least one law a day. Much of this law breaking is a result of ignorance (not even specialists can keep up with the torrent of new laws regulating our every move) but a good deal of it is a result of a not unreasonable feeling of weariness. And once people start breaking the law on a regular basis morality starts to crumble.

Living in England today is, in some ways, worse than living in the old USSR. At least residents of the pre-Gorbachev USSR knew what the rules were and could unite together in their distrust of everything they were told. Here most people still believe what they see and hear on the BBC, the most prejudiced, bigoted, fascist organisation on the planet. Most people do not want to hear the truth and so I, and people like me, can be banned, and silenced, very effectively. Staff at the BBC aren't bright enough to understand that it isn't the anti-immigration nationalists who are the dangerous extremists or that it is the fascist authoritarian pro-EU fanatics who threaten our future and whose activities mean that these will soon be the good old days.

Enough.

Finally, I feel that I must take this opportunity to warn readers that this book probably contains numerous errors of fact, certainly includes many uncorroborated anecdotes and is crammed with personal opinions. I mention these undoubted shortcomings only in order to free myself from the tedious responsibility of having to consider making apologies or corrections after publication.

The scene is set for another bloody year in my life.

Vernon Coleman 31.12.12

JANUARY

1.

The vandals from whom we bought our new house took with them the curtain rails, recycling bins, log burning stove, garden shed, instructions for the burglar alarm, outside lights, telephone directories (it is only when moving into a new house in a new area that you discover how useless the internet is for finding tradesmen), all the manuals for all the fixtures we bought (such as the boiler), the curiously shaped seat cushions that fitted the window seats in two 18th century bay windows, the specialist tools for the AGA, wall light fittings (the wires were left hanging out of the wall and we had to find electricians before we dared do anything), fixed mirrors from the bathrooms, toothbrush holders, bathroom cabinets, plugs from sinks and baths, doorbell chime (they left the bell push so callers think they are ringing the bell but we don't hear anything because there is nothing to hear) and the lavatory seats. Yes, unbelievably, they took the seats off the lavatories. Maybe we should be grateful that they left us the doors. The vendors probably sucked the remaining gas out of the pipes and the electricity out of the wires. I have seen tidier, cleaner, smarter squats.

To be fair, they didn't take everything. On a shelf in a bathroom they left us the contents of one of their medicine cabinets: a small brown bottle with a dozen white tablets and the label 'Aspirin (almost certainly)' and a bottle of medicine that had separated into brown and white layers which bore the label 'stomach bowel and ear problems - also good for removing stains from carpet'. There was a parcel of rotting fish in the freezer (we had to throw the freezer away because it smelt so much) and in the greenhouse there were three bucketfuls of broken glass. And they left us the foundations for an un-built stable block. We don't want any stables so since the foundations are over 60 foot long and 5 foot wide we're going to sprinkle a few bags of grit and small stoned gravel and create our own boule court.

When we collected the keys the estate agent had handed us a huge paper bag full of assorted keys, none of which were labelled. (After many hours I still hadn't found the garage key but had eliminated 27 suspects from my enquiries. In the end we gave up trying to find out which key fitted which lock and simply had new locks fitted almost everywhere.)

Worst of all the water had been turned off. We found, and turned on, three stop cocks but it took us another three days to find the fourth. The estate agents were unable or unwilling to help, they said they had no contact details for the owner who seemed to be in hiding. The surveyor's report, for which we had paid an arm, a leg and a chest of gold, was of little value, telling us merely that the house was supplied with water. Every time I give money to a surveyor I wonder why I'm behaving so stupidly. Past experience tells me that the bastard will write 40 pages of ass-covering nonsense. He will state the obvious, fill pages with pointless and subjective comments on decorations and recommend that we obtain outside advice on the state of the woodwork, the roof, the walls, the electricity supply, the plumbing and everything else. Our survey contained much talk of work 'involving significant costs' and instructions to obtain outside quotes for all repair work before exchanging contracts. There were the inevitable warnings about damp and the usual disclaimers. We ignored everything on the grounds that old houses, unlike new houses, are likely to be still standing in a few decades time. Anything that has remained in the same place for three centuries is probably not going anywhere in a hurry. To be honest, I'm surprised anyone who hires a surveyor ever buys a property in England. It is not surprising that surveyors are as rare as auks in France. I sometimes think that any house buyer would do better with a penknife (to stick in door and window frames), a pair of binoculars (to check out the roof and chimney stacks) and a notebook and pencil to record all their observations.

2.

I found a photograph of my old friend Stuart Roper while clearing out one of my many filing cabinets and waiting for someone at Npower to answer the telephone. (For the record it took them 27 minutes.) It was a

BBC publicity photograph taken when he worked for the local radio station in Birmingham. In the photograph he was grinning broadly.

For twenty years, in the 1970s and 1980s, I toured the country constantly, promoting books and campaigning on a variety of issues, and at one time or another I visited every radio station available. And since there were, at the time, very few doctors prepared to talk on the wireless (for fear of attracting the wrath of the General Medical Council and being accused of advertising themselves) I was the resident doctor at many stations - including the BBC in Birmingham. That was where I met Stuart Roper.

Roper was one of the very best of all local radio presenters. He had a distinctive, friendly style which was ideally suited to community radio. He would sit in the studio with a copy of the local A to Z on the desk in front of him and when he spoke to a caller he would ask them where they lived. He would then look up the name of their street in the A to Z, pretend to think for a moment and then, using the map, talk to them about all the local landmarks - schools, pubs, parks, shopping centres and churches. Callers loved him. And at the time, although I'd been to radio stations everywhere, I'd never seen anyone else do this. Added to a natural charm and easy manner it made him a perfect radio presenter. The listeners felt that he knew them, their neighbourhood and their lives. He soon acquired quite a reputation as the man who knew Birmingham best.

And then a woman presenter broke the spell. For a quick laugh, and the chance to put him down, she told the listeners his secret. 'He just sits here with an A to Z in front of him,' she scoffed.

Roper was appalled. He was broken. He felt shamed and betrayed. The woman's nasty comment wrecked his fragile self-confidence. I wasn't surprised. I knew many BBC radio stations quite well. Unlike the commercial stations, which tended to be bright and full of quick thinking, go-ahead people, the BBC stations were miserable, dowdy places: full of intrigue and political nonsenses. It is often said that the BBC is the voice of the left-leaning political establishment. It isn't. The BBC is the voice of the State. Since the BBC runs all its staff recruitment advertising in *The Guardian* newspaper this is not particularly surprising. It has always surprised me that a national organisation should be allowed to recruit exclusively from a relatively tiny band of heavy breathing panty-waisters and buttinskis who are eager to represent and promote the State.

Roper announced that he was leaving. He had, he said, been offered work in America. He was emigrating to find fame and fortune in a bigger market.

Since I knew him well his producer asked if I would telephone and wish him goodbye during his final show. I said I would do better than that. I drove 200 miles from Devon and when I arrived at the Pebble Mill Studios in Birmingham I telephoned the studio on a pay phone (there were no mobile telephones in those days). I wished him well and then pretended that I wanted to see him in person. 'The show is over in 30 minutes,' he said sadly. 'You'll never get here from Devon.' I promised him that I'd make it. I ran up the stairs and two minutes later I bounced into the studio. After the show had finished we went for coffee and promised to keep in touch.

He rang me the next day.

He was in Exmouth in Devon. He was staying at his parents' home. He hadn't gone to America. There had never been any job there. He had resigned without anywhere to go. He was unemployed. He wanted to know if I could find him some work.

I knew people at the BBC in Devon and at the commercial radio station in Exeter and I helped him get shows at both stations. A friend found him occasional work at an English speaking radio station in Vienna.

But he started drinking heavily. He turned up late for shows. He went on air slurring his words. In the world of radio these are unforgiveable sins. He was fired, fired and fired again. I was cross with him for letting himself down, and for embarrassing me, but our friendship survived. He tried to sell time share apartments but couldn't bear the idea of tricking gullible customers and never sold anything. Then he managed to get a job as a photographer on a local paper in Worcestershire. (He'd been a professional photographer before he'd started broadcasting).

But he didn't stop drinking. He drank more and more. He took blurry photographs at a couple of weddings. He refused all offers of help. He said the drinking wasn't a problem. He shouted at me when I tried to persuade him to get help.

And then, inevitably perhaps, he was found dead, alone, in his tiny flat. Did he kill himself? Did the drink kill him? I don't know. But I know what really killed him.

I dug out a copy of an ancient, dog eared A to Z of Birmingham which I'd used when I'd done some locum work in Birmingham, placed the grinning photograph inside it and cremated them together.

3.

I spent twenty minutes browsing in the WHSmith store in Taunton. You can learn a good deal about a town by looking at the magazines on sale. In Cirencester, just a few of miles to the west of our new home there seem to be endless magazines about horses, horse riding, and hunting. In Gloucester, the Cotswold centre for tattoo parlours and all day breakfasts, I counted 15 different magazines dealing with tattooing. (The variety that involves ink and many regrets rather than the type that involves members of the armed forces.)

And you can learn a good deal about life in general by looking at the warnings printed on the back of perfectly ordinary items. In Smith's, for example, I found this warning on the back of a box of pencils: 'During all creative activity, we suggest that you wear overalls and/or old clothes and that you cover furnishings and flooring.' They were pencils, for heaven's sake.

WHSmith's have, like most chain stores, employed a puzzle designer to put up a series of barriers defining the route customers must follow if they want to interface with a retail sales executive. While wending my way along the defined route in the branch of Smith's in Taunton I found myself stuck behind a very fat man sitting in one of those motorised scooters that were designed for the disabled but which are so popular these days with the indolent and the obese. The oaf had parked his vehicle (about the same size as one of the original Alex Issigonis mini cars) in the middle of the complicated maze-like aisle all shops now favour (the owners will doubtless argue that they were designed and introduced to save the environment and to help protect us from terrorism and money laundering) while he worked out which of his many credit cards to use. He was quite immobile and oblivious to the fact that a queue was developing behind him while in front of him two assistants had nothing to do because no one could find their way past him. Eventually, by squeezing between a bollard and a display box full of chocolate bars I managed to by-pass the hold up and reach a waiting assistant who was eventually kind enough to take a break from chatting to her companion in order to attend to my needs. I had finished the fiscal part of my transaction (allowing the two assistants to resume their discussion about the shortcomings of someone else's boyfriend) and was packing my purchases into my bag (in the bad old days the whole transaction would have taken half the time because the assistant would have placed my purchases into a bag immediately after scanning them) when the oaf in the wheelchair decided that he didn't want to buy anything after all. Naturally, he wanted to leave the store and, equally naturally, he didn't want to wait. 'Move out of my way!' he snarled. 'Can't you see I'm trying to get past. I'm in a wheelchair.' I politely explained that I would be no more than ten seconds. He swore at me and deliberately drove his vehicle against my leg. It hurt. Looking at him I suspected that he was only in a wheelchair because he was very fat. He had no signs or symptoms of ill health. I was terribly tempted to tip him and his vehicle over onto on his side to see if he really needed to be driving through Smith's in what seemed to me a vehicle as big as a small car. I was stopped from doing this only by the thought that I would probably end up on YouTube and, as a result, spend two years sharing a cell with an expense fiddling Member of Parliament. I picked up my purchases and hurried away slightly ahead of the oaf.

Shopping is such a joyless experience these days. I can remember when shop assistants would say 'It's a pleasure' when a customer offered a 'thank you' at the end of a transaction. These days the best you're likely to get in England is: 'It's not a problem'. Why should it be problem to accept money from a customer? In France the shopkeepers do still say 'C'est moi qui vous remercie'.

After leaving Smith's I crossed the road and went into the nearby Marks and Spencer store. They too have little mazes and long queues. I found something that I thought The Princess might like, and was standing in the queue thinking that if I had been able to make constructive use of all the time I've wasted queuing to hand my money to shop assistants I would have been able to learn another foreign language, when I was rewarded with a delightful vignette of modern life.

A fat woman in tight, faux animal skin trousers and a violet cardigan suddenly came into view, running towards the tills with all the eagerness of a keen shopper who had spotted a bargain. But, instead of bearing down on a reduced-price mohair sweater in pink, the surprisingly athletic woman was heading for the sales counter where, I suddenly noticed, someone had left a pair of aluminium health service style crutches. The woman wasn't going quite fast enough to win an Olympic sprint medal but she was moving faster than most folk half her age could manage. She didn't even seem out of breath. When she reached the counter she grabbed her crutches, stuffed one under each armpit and hobbled off, now limping with both legs and moving at a pace that even an arthritic snail would have found painfully slow.

By this time I had reached the top of the queue and the Marks and Spencer assistant greeted me with a cheery 'Thank you for waiting'. It's obviously something they're trained to say because they all say it all the time. I suspect that they say it when they're at home serving hubby his dinner. And for all I know they probably say it at more intimate moments too. It's annoying because it's a meaningless phrase when recited by rote. (Marks and Spencer isn't the only guilty store. It's obviously something retail, catering and banking staff are taught when they're hired.) The other annoying thing they all say is: 'Oh, what a lovely choice.' I bought three greeting cards the other day. The assistant who handled my order said: 'Excellent choices. Lovely cards.' The miracle is that she managed to make this assessment without bothering to look at the cards. It happens in cafés and pubs, too. Order a drink and the waiter will say: 'Oh, that's my favourite!' The implication is that you have good taste. But I'm not sure that I want to share my tastes with a 19-year-old Romanian with dirty cuffs, halitosis and a tattooed dotted line around his neck. My life will be complete when I buy a drain cover at the ironmongery store and the assistant says: 'What a good choice, sir. What an unusual shade of black you've chosen.' The trouble with compulsory corporate niceness isn't that it is utterly insincere but that it prevents voluntary niceness. No one working in a store bothers to be polite or helpful of their own volition these days. They do what they're taught to do and that's it.)

From Marks and Spencer I walked to the HMV record store where I wanted to exchange a Blue Ray Disk which I had bought by accident, intending to buy a DVD version of the same film. Five assistants were standing behind the counter chatting merrily about something important. I said 'excuse me' several times, coughed a few more times and eventually, with an audible sigh, one of the youngest assistants tore herself away and gave me a small part of her attention. I don't think the assistants were accustomed to dealing with customers. Most of the people in the store were browsing and using mobile phones to purchase their chosen items from Amazon and other internet suppliers.

'Receipt?' demanded the assistant, when I had explained that I had picked up the Blue Ray version of the film in error and that since we have only just upgraded from a video recorder we have no intention of replacing all our disks and players yet again.

I handed her the receipt. She examined it minutely, giving it the sort of scrutiny immigration officials give to passports from small African countries.

'Too late,' she said, handing me back the useless disk and the receipt.

'I'm sorry,' I said. 'I don't understand.'

'The transaction took place 26 days ago.'

'You're undoubtedly right,' I agreed. I didn't have my reading glasses on and couldn't read the fine print on the receipt.

'You can't change it now.'

'Could I have a word with the manager, please?'

After another loud sigh she tapped the arm of a man with what looked like a metal puzzle from a Christmas cracker screwed into his nose. I couldn't help wondering if he knew it was there. Perhaps I should mention it. Perhaps none of the assistants dared to say anything. Perhaps it had got stuck to his nose during a hectic game of pass the orange.

'We don't exchange after 21 days,' said the manager in the sort of condescending manner which used to be the exclusive right of civil servants but which is now enjoyed by anyone standing behind a counter and protected from questioning customers by an armoury of legislation.

I didn't move and didn't say anything. I simply put the useless Blue Ray Disk and the receipt back on the counter in front of him. I then stared at him as though he had a piece of a metal puzzle from a Christmas cracker attached to his nose. It wasn't difficult.

'I suppose I can make a special exception just this once,' he said. He sent one of his sulky minions off to exchange the Blue Ray Disk for a DVD.

I thanked him.

I wanted to explain to him that the only advantage that High Street stores have over internet stores is in service and courtesy. I wanted to help him understand that his company's future, already bleak, was dependent upon his ability to persuade customers to find shopping at HMV a pleasurable experience. But I couldn't be bothered.

'I have some advice for you,' I told him.

He stared at me, puzzled.

'When HMV goes bust and you find yourself at the Job Centre I suggest that you look for something that isn't a service industry.'

He continued to stare at me. I think perhaps the phrase 'service industry' wasn't something he understood.

I was exhausted by my shopping expedition and when a grinning chugger stopped me I was in no mood for extortion or blackmail. Instead of just telling him to 'chugger off' I stopped and smiled back at him. 'I am so glad you have stopped me to chat,' I told me. 'I'm a Jehovah's

Witness.' I reached into my pocket as if for a leaflet. 'Do you have an hour or so to spare? We could go somewhere to talk...'

But he was gone.

4.

The Princess and I bought ourselves a new television set. It is, according to the box, a Sony 32 inch LCD digital colour television and we chose it because it was the biggest one we could carry from the shop to the car.

When we opened the box we found a booklet. And when we read the booklet we found this instruction (it was listed as 'item 4'):

Preventing the TV from toppling over:

1. Insert a wood screw (not supplied) in the stand.
2. Insert a machine screw (not supplied) into the TV.
3. Tie the wood screw and the machine screw with a strong cord (not supplied).

The Princess and I always share the work when we buy things and have to complete the construction process and so while she fixed the Sony television set onto its stand and connected it to our DVD player I occupied myself by putting the batteries into the remote control device. (While doing this I lost the small screw which holds the lid in place. From past experience I know that the easiest way to find small, lost items such as screws is to move around the floor on my knees. I found the screw with my left knee much more speedily than I would have found it with my hands.)

By the time I'd found the screw The Princess had finished building our television set, including tying the two screws together with string, and had discovered that the leads which had been sold to us with the television set didn't fit. We had, of course, been sold the wrong ones. The assistant had been so keen to sell us an insurance package which we didn't want (and didn't buy) that he didn't bother to check that he was selling us the right stuff.

The first television set I ever saw was built by my Dad in 1952. I was four and my parents woke me up so that I could see people dancing around on a tiny screen amidst a mass of valves and wires on the kitchen table. My dad subsequently made the cabinet to house his home-made television set. I can remember distinctly that there was no string involved in any of the construction.

5.

I am old enough to remember when a 24 hour plumber used to be a plumber who came out 24 hours day. He would even call around at night.

Everything changed around 20 years ago. I remember ringing a 24 hour plumber and being told that the plumber could be with me the following Thursday. 'But that's four days away!' I said. 'We have water pouring from a leaky tank.' How can you call yourselves 24 hour plumbers?' I probably used other words to make my displeasure clear. In those days you could swear at workmen without them seeking legal advice. 'We are 24 hour plumbers,' said an indignant woman at the other end of the telephone. 'We answer the telephone 24 hours a day.'

Things have got even worse. I rang a 24 hour plumber and found myself listening to an answering machine. 'Please leave your message and one of our executives will get back to you when the office opens.' The second number I dialled found me talking to an incredibly snotty woman who seemed to have more than her fair share of superciliousness. She demanded that I explain to her the nature of our problem. I did this, as best I could, and waited. 'I don't think you are explaining very well,' said the woman. 'You obviously don't know anything about plumbing.' I tried again. The woman sighed the sort of sigh that means 'Why are you wasting my time? I am far too important for this' and told me that if I couldn't explain my problem she wouldn't be able to tell the consultant and so he wouldn't be able to call. By this time I was deeply fed up. 'Is there a man in the office?' I asked her. 'Why?' she demanded. 'I just thought that perhaps if I spoke to a man he might understand a little better,' I said. 'Or maybe if you consult with a male colleague he would know a little more about plumbing and so better able to understand the problem.' The response was a very satisfying scream of abuse and the sound of the telephone receiver being slammed down onto the rest.

Eventually The Princess managed to find old-fashioned plumbers who did house calls. There were two of them and neither of them spoke a word of English. Actually, that's not strictly true. One of them did say 'Cupteayes' and made a drinking motion with his hand and arm. However, it's surprising how little conversation you need with plumbers. I pointed to the radiator that was dripping, they got out their tools and they mended it. When they'd finished one of them handed me a figure on a scruffy piece of paper and although I know the European Commission will be terribly upset about this I handed him the appropriate amount of money in cash.

When they'd gone The Princess said that she felt as though she were the one living in a foreign country.

6.

At St Pancras railway station, on our way to Paris, I saw a huge notice in the window of WHSmith promoting their eBook reader. They were selling it for £69 and, according to the poster in the window, they seemed to be offering a million free books with it. These are, presumably, the ones that Google stole. I never fail to be surprised by the way that bookshops work so hard at putting themselves out of business. Waterstone's have been enthusiastically promoting eBook readers for some time. Barmy. Utterly bonkers.

The whole eBook phenomenon is fascinating. As the world's biggest online retailer, Amazon had a head start in selling eBooks. In 2007, the company launched its Kindle eBook reader and by 2010 it controlled 90% of the entire eBook market. (Just why that didn't attract the attention of the Monopoly Commission is an unanswered puzzle.)

Books appeared to have made a successful transition from print to digital. Publishers were relaxed and confident and enthusiastic. Who wouldn't have been happy? The new eBooks enabled them to make money without actually doing anything very much at all. Amazon still paid the publishers what they wanted. Customers were happy too because Amazon merrily sold many books at knock down prices. The company actually lost money on lots of books.

Unfortunately, the goops, grunts and pipsqueaks at the publishing companies hadn't realised that what had happened to music and films was inevitably going to happen to their industry. It was so obvious that it was painful to watch the way publishers walked into disaster. (My favourite absurdity was the sight of a book wholesaler, setting up an eBook division. A wholesaler, with huge warehouses, was setting itself up to sell eBooks. Surely, another commercial effort worth a prize for lunacy?)

Eventually, the publishers did wake up. And when Apple introduced its iPad in 2010, and built it in such a way that the device could be used to read books, publishers thought they would prevent Amazon from owning 100% of the eBook market by doing business with Apple as well.

There was one problem.

Apple, still run at the time by the late Steve Jobs, didn't want to sell books at a loss. It wanted the same 30% margin that it makes selling magazines, newspapers and games on the iPad.

So a number of publishers and Apple did a deal whereby the publishers could charge whatever they wanted for their eBooks and Apple would be paid 30% for doing the selling. The publishers were doubtless very excited and delighted that Apple had agreed to reduce its cut from 30% right the way down to 30%. That was sharp negotiating on their part.

Brain dead, unimaginative publishers were delighted. But, entirely predictably, things have not gone smoothly.

The USA Department of Justice accused Apple and some of the biggest publishers of colluding to fix prices for eBooks. Three of the publishers, realising that the USA Government has more money than they have, quickly settled (this is a legal term meaning 'rolled over and played dead').

And my guess is that cheap eBooks will come back. And since anyone, anywhere in the world, can buy an eBook from anywhere, there seems little doubt that what the American Government decides will decide the price of eBooks.

The return of cheap eBooks will mean that the price differential between a real book and an eBook will rise dramatically.

And we will, I suspect, see the decline and disappearance of the traditional bookshop and the traditional wholesaler. They have no more of a future than candlestick makers or wheelwrights. As a publisher I can't say I'm heartbroken. I never had much help from either shops or wholesalers. In fact, wholesalers were a menace. I remember once buying £15,000 worth of advertising for one of my books, sending out letters to 1,500 bookshops to promote the book and then discovering that our main wholesaler had failed to put the books they had in stock into their computer. The result was that bookshops which asked for copies (a rare enough event, since most bookshops won't touch books from small publishers) were told that the book was out of stock. Our reputation with the bookshops was wrecked and we were left with several thousand books we couldn't sell. So I won't need a box of tissues if wholesalers all go bust.

Not that publishers have much of a future either.

Amazon is now publishing books.

And you don't need much capital to set up as an eBook publisher.

The rise and rise of the eBook will see the decline and fall of professional authors as well as bookshops and publishers. The problem is that eBooks have little or no cost and are therefore regarded as having little or no worth. They will, therefore, be passed around quite freely. People will send them to friends and once books are on the internet they will, like films and music, be available free to anyone. In just one month in 2011 each of the top ten bestselling books was illegally downloaded an average of 80,000 times. The authors didn't make a penny from those sales. The worst three countries in the world for stealing books are the USA, the UK and China. A recent survey of women aged 35 plus, all eBook readers, showed that one in 8 had illegally downloaded a book compared to 1 in 20 who confessed to downloading music. Book piracy will destroy the global publishing industry. And it will destroy authors too.

Just the other day I read a report in the *Financial Times* saying that Amazon will let users of its Kindle e-readers borrow electronic books from two thirds of American libraries. This is significant because public libraries in the USA have spent several years building up their eBook collections. 'Amazon is working with OverDrive, a leading distributor of eBooks, which makes a catalogue of 400,000 books available to 11,000 libraries. Tablet users who have a library card can borrow eBooks from their local lender without ever visiting it, by logging on to the library's website.'

At the moment libraries are limited to lending an eBook to one reader at a time and some publishers require that its eBooks expire once they have been borrowed from a library a certain number of times. Anyone who expects either of these restrictions to last long, or to be taken seriously, was clearly born on another planet.

Still, it seems that even the eBook is likely to have a short life. People download the things but it has been shown that 99 per cent of the downloaded eBooks aren't ever read. People download them because it's easy to do so but most find whole books too daunting. In Japan four of the recent five best-selling novels were written and read on cell phones. No printing, no shipping, no returns. And no money changed hands.

There is no future for professional authors. In future authors will have to be sponsored and it will not, I fear, be by kindly benefactors but by lobby groups and industry public relations groups. No one will ever write or publish the sort of books I've spent my life writing.

Whether or not that is sad depends upon your point of view, I suppose, though it is worth pointing out that evidence shows that children develop much more quickly, and become much brighter, when they grow up in houses which have at least 500 real books in them - books that can be looked at, picked up, felt and smelt as well as read. Not, of course, that our masters are too keen on the idea of children growing up intelligent and inquisitive.

The Princess popped into the St Pancras branch of Smith's to buy an armful of assorted newspapers and magazines. The counter assistant recognised her from previous visits and they chatted for a few moments. He told her that he is from Sri Lanka. She told him that she was originally from Wales. The counter assistant was very impressed. 'Your English is very good,' he told her with a beaming smile.

7.

We were so tired after our journey yesterday (and, possibly, the fact that we sat up listening to old Dick Barton and Paul Temple tapes until 3 a.m.) that we decided to get up late. When we were woken by the sound of a man on a bicycle ringing a bell to let the world now that he was up and about and ready to grind our knives I picked up the clock, looked at it and discovered to my horror that it was still only 6.00 a.m. Only after I had stared at it for a few moments did I realise that I was holding it upside down and that the time was really 12.00 p.m. It isn't often that we get up at the crack of noon. We had breakfast at 12.30 p.m., lunch at 4.00 p.m., afternoon tea at 6.00 p.m. and dinner at 9.00 p.m. and so in the end everything worked out very well.

After breakfast we spent a pleasant twenty minutes or so blowing soap bubbles out of our window and watching them float up and down the street, occasionally landing on the heads of unsuspecting pedestrians. We gave up only when the wind changed and blew several hundred bubbles back in through our window.

Later in the afternoon we walked to the Passerelle Leopold Sedar Senghor (named for a Senegalese writer). This is a footbridge across the Seine which, on the left bank, starts at the Thomas Jefferson statue on the Quai Anatole France. The bridge, like several others in Paris, including the Pont des Arts, is now festooned with padlocks fastened to the railings and after walking to the middle we added our own padlock to the thousands already there. It is engraved with our names, our wedding date 3.12.99 and the word 'Forever'. We tied a pink ribbon to the padlock and then threw the keys into the river. They just missed landing on a police launch which passed under the bridge at just that moment. Looking down I realised how clean the Seine now looks; certainly much cleaner than most rivers passing through English towns and cities where, too often, the bridges look like staples inadequately joining the two sides of a gaping wound filled with green pus.

We then walked back to our apartment, in freezing but invigorating January chill, along the river. We stood and watched an old lady playing with her adoring dog; a happy, white mongrel. She was kicking a cork down the Quai. The dog, of course, was fetching the cork and dropping it back at her feet. She was too stiff and frail to bend down. But she could kick. I can't remember when I last saw a happier woman or a happier dog. Up above, the plane trees still carried their seed pods. They looked like Christmas trees, still festooned with decorations after the festivities.

A little further along, The Princess and I watched a tramp feeding the seagulls. He had set up camp by the river's edge and had lit a fire in a brazier. He had a huge stock of dead Christmas trees for firewood. I don't think I have ever seen a happier man. He was throwing bits of food up into the sky for the birds to catch. 'It's always the same isn't it,' said The Princess. 'It's the people who can't afford to give who give most generously.'

Finally, close to home, we saw another tramp. He had a black mongrel dog which was wearing an old jumper to keep out the cold. The dog was literally bouncing with joy. The tramp was beaming with pride and happiness.

We were about five minutes from our apartment when what looked like a toilet bowl suddenly crashed onto the pavement directly in front of us. It shattered and the pieces flew in every direction but ours.

Instinctively, we both looked up, though I don't know if this was to see where the toilet had come from or to check that there were no more on the way.

A man in a dinner jacket looked down, waved and shouted his apologies.

'Why did you drop a toilet from your window?' I shouted, rather angrily.

'It was not a toilet, it was a bidet,' he explained.

'It fell so fast I could not tell,' I explained.

'That's OK,' he said with a smile and a wave. He then disappeared back into the room.

'I suppose it would be marginally more acceptable socially to have been killed by a falling bidet than a falling lavatory bowl,' said The Princess as we hurried back home.

We had seen three gloriously happy people and two gloriously happy dogs. We had seen three lonely old people all of whom had, in their own way, found some small delight on a brisk, cold day. And we had closely missed an unpleasant death.

We arrived back at our apartment brimful of happiness. Total cost of all that pleasure? Nothing. Absolutely nothing.

We warmed ourselves up with gloriously smoky lapsang souchong tea and madeleine cakes.

8.

Our French electricity and gas supplier has sent us an easy to remember internet address so that we can drop whatever we are doing and check our energy consumption. It is, they tell us proudly, an aide memoire. Here is our new easy to remember access address: http:/www.economie.gouv. fr/dgccrf/consommation/thematiques/Electricite-et-gas-naturel. Once we have reached this sanctuary all we have to do is fill in our personal details and doubtless answer a couple of dozen security questions.

9.

It rained all day and The Princess and I spent the afternoon in the Deux Magots cafe in St Germain. Buying papers at the kiosk near to Deux Magots I once stood behind a famous fashion designer buying his newspapers. What made this a slightly surreal experience was the fact that most of the papers he and I were buying had his picture on the front page. According to one of the papers he had just gone bankrupt, owing 100 million dollars, or some such extra terrestrial amount. He didn't look like a man who was facing ruin. When he'd paid for his papers he gave the change to a nearby beggar. From the beggar's response it was clearly a daily ritual.

There are few joys greater than sitting comfortably in a quiet, warm Parisian cafe with a large glass of vin chaud on the table, an empty bladder and a good book in one's hands, while outside, inches away through the glass, streams of sodden people are hurrying to and fro in the rain; coats flying, umbrellas inverting and buses splashing. The joy is, of course, so much more intense when the people getting wet and irritable are all foreign and largely French.

I would, of course, never dare admit to any of this in public. Beside opprobrium it would, I fear, draw down upon me the wrath of those authorities whose job it is to stamp on all simple pleasures, particularly those which can be defined as examples of political incorrectness.

As we sat in the café we watched a man walk by pushing a wheelchair. He had a violin case sitting on the chair. A few minutes earlier The Princess had put several euros into his cap as he sat in the chair 'playing' his violin (very badly). He clearly could not play the violin and seems clear that he isn't disabled either.

On the way home we called in at our favourite supermarket (there are nine within half a mile of our apartment) and bought a vegetarian pizza, some fruit, a box of ice cream and two large rolls of black refuse sacks. We paid two boy scouts a euro each not to pack our bag for us. They stand at the check-out counter and pack bags to raise money but they are very bad at it. No one has taught them that it is sensible to put the heavy stuff at the bottom and the light stuff on top. They do the opposite. On the other hand, maybe they think that putting the light stuff at the bottom enables them to save the planet by squashing it and, therefore, cramming more stuff into each bag. The pizza and ice cream are for supper. The black bags are to take back to England. In order to cut down the nation's use of petroleum based products such as plastic, the EU has ruled that we are no longer allowed to use old-fashioned metal dustbins but must pack all our rubbish in plastic bags and put the plastic bags inside large plastic containers. I have no doubt that this makes sense to EU parasitic bureaucrats. (The phrase 'parasitic bureaucrat' is, of course, tautological.) But then they probably believe that the EU deserved the Nobel Peace Prize. We have been told that we are entitled to have two black rubbish bags taken away by the council but although the instructions tell us that the bags must be black no one has said what size the bags must be. So, although the council delivers tiny little bags we throw those away and use our own black sacks, which we buy in a supermarket in Paris and import. They are huge and will hold four times as much as the council issue bags.

As we tottered back home we were both nearly knocked down by a couple of hugely obese Americans driving along in those large disability scooters which resemble the sort of golf carts used in Florida. They shouted at us to get out of their damned way, as Americans do, and we just managed to save ourselves. The Americans who visit Europe are a self-selected minority who think they are superior to everyone else (including other Americans) because they have passports and two pairs of shoes and because they know that France is the one with the cute metal tower and England is the one with the Queen. They are a shapeless people who have as little style as they have morality or manners. They invariably dress in garish clothes, usually wearing the American national costume of checked shorts and checked shorts (two different checks of course). ('There are lot of Americans in Paris at the moment,' said The Princess as we drove from the Gare du Nord recently. 'How do you know?' I asked. 'I've seen a lot of fat, badly dressed people wandering about.') I used to think that Americans must take lessons in bad dressing but recently I have come to understand that it is something that comes naturally because they are a new and still culturally backwards people. When they want to walk the obese Americans climb off their golf carts, leaving them in the middle of pavement, and wheeze along bumping other pedestrians out of the way without any concern. They walk with hips pushed forward in a swaggering sort of way; as though they are pushing their bellies ahead of them which, in a way, I suppose they are. There is no doubt that the Americans have a natural sense of self-satisfaction which makes them appear arrogant and insensitive. This is not as bad as it sounds, however, because the vast majority of Americans are arrogant and insensitive and so the image they portray is a true one. The only thing that can be said in favour of Americans is that they are entertaining to watch. To observe Americans at a railway station or in a café is to watch another species. And even if they have been in another country long enough to buy clothes and get their hair cut locally, Americans are always identifiable as Americans. If they could keep their mouths shut (something most Americans do only when their lips are actually stapled together as part of a medically approved dieting programme) they would still obviously be American.

10.

'You can't wear that shirt!' cried The Princess. 'I haven't ironed it.'

'It's fine,' I told her.

'It's all wrinkled,' she said, trying to grab the shirt to take it away from me.

'It's ok,' I insisted. 'I'm wrinkled too so it will fit nicely.'

We strolled up to Les Invalides this afternoon so that we could walk around the cloisters (my favourite spot on the planet) and then take a look at the beautiful red and black firebugs under the lime trees in the park nearby. On our way back we watched groups of men playing boule (surely the only sport which is widely played without anyone bothering to keep score) and walked around the Eiffel tower. We were approached by at least a dozen men trying to sell us small metal models of the tower. By the way they were all looking over their shoulders they were probably illegal immigrants. In Paris female illegal immigrants end up working in the Rue St Denis as prostitutes while men end up working around the Eiffel tower selling cheap metal trinkets. I don't know which is worse.

The Eiffel tower is a wonderful creation with an extraordinary history. During the First World War the French put trained parrots onto the tower in the hope and belief that the parrots would give advance warning of incoming aircraft and enable anti-aircraft gunners to shoot them down. The plan was abandoned when the French realised that the parrots couldn't discriminate between Allied aircraft and German aircraft and that although they were very good at announcing the imminent arrival of the 11.43 from Dusseldorf they were unable to differentiate between that and the 11.44 from Lyon.

Finally, we fed the birds and the ducks in the lake beside the tower with a loaf of bread we'd taken with us. We have, in the past, tried feeding them with all sorts of good, wholesome food. The experts, who are supposed to know about these things, complain that bread is not good for them. We've even bought them special bird seed from a pet shop. But neither the birds, nor the ducks, have read what the experts say and they all prefer bread.

11.

I went to the freezer shop and was standing in the queue when another till opened. Although I was next in line the woman in front of me had bought enough food to feed the Premier League and so I moved across to the new till. But before I could get there a French couple pushed their way in front of me. I had only one item. They had enough frozen food to feed Algeria. I glowered at them and muttered (in English) something about the French being rude and not understanding the principles of queue forming. 'You are not the French liking?' demanded the husband, a round fellow with a red face and eyebrows large enough to vote. 'No!' I told him firmly, though I confessed that I did have a secret admiration for the people who voted in vast quantities for the political candidate who had bulldozed a branch of McDonalds to the ground. 'Then why you come at France?' he demanded. 'I love Paris,' I explained with an English shrug. 'Ha!' he cried, despair and disappointment written all over his face in 30 point. He looked like a four minute miler who has just seen someone run a three minute mile. 'You is like all the English. You love Paris and hate the French.' 'Exactly!' I responded, delighted that the ignorant Gallic fool knew how the English feel about the French, delighted that he had realised that I am English and not American and, I confess, quietly pleased that I had done my little bit for the day to further improve understanding between our two nations. Wonderful. I was far too pleased to worry that I was the victim in what was clearly a racially inspired attack on a member of an ethnic minority. As we parted I merrily waved two fingers, although I suspect that he did not understand the historical significance of the gesture. The V sign was first used by English archers at the battle of Agincourt in 1415. If the French captured English archers they used to cut off their two bow fingers to stop them taking part in any more fighting. The English waved those two fingers to show that they still had them.

I always like talking to the French in my language because they are usually no more capable of speaking English properly than are the Scots or the Americans. It comforts me to know that however bad my French is (and they are always eager to tell me how bad it is), it is probably no worse than their English. Letters, menus and even posters provide evidence for their inability to learn our language. Just today we saw a poster which invited passers-by to attend an *Alone Man Show*.

The French never speak slowly when speaking to people struggling to speak their language and so, in retaliation, I always speak as quickly as one of those voiceover specialists rushing through the small print on an insurance company advertisement on television. And I try to mix up the accents a little too. Sometimes I speak in a broad Somerset accent, sometimes in a Liverpudlian accent and sometimes in my own version of Cockney. Occasionally, I throw in a sentence or two in a Glaswegian accent.

(I find, incidentally, that the Scots are increasingly incomprehensible. Many years ago I travelled to Scotland once a week to make a television programme. I spent two hours a week entombed in taxis with Scotsmen who talked incessantly. I never understood one word any of them said. There is a woman who appears on a discredited BBC programme called *Newsnight* who might as well be speaking Serbo-Croat for all I can understand of her. Why we are expected to pay a massive licence fee for programmes we cannot understand is beyond me. How do we know just how prejudiced the BBC has become if we cannot understand a word the presenters are saying?)

12.

While we've been in Paris I've been studying the career of Jacques Tati, the great French clown, mime and film maker. Tati wanted to control everything himself and worked alone and quite apart from the French film industry. This was, apparently, much admired at the time. He wrote, starred in and directed his own movies. He also produced them and stuck up the posters.

As an artist Tati was a cross between Harpo Marx and Tommy Cooper with a large dose of Orson Welles and touches of Flanders and Swann and the Bonzo Dog Doo Dah band. He was one of the most innovative of film directors. In his films he plays a character who wanders through life in something of a confused daze. However, Tati's real life was a fairly endless series of ultimately damaging misunderstandings.

For example, at a garden party in Paris, Tati waited in line to meet General de Gaulle. When he finally arrived at the head of the queue, de Gaulle's secretary whispered 'Jacques Tati'. Suddenly, realising that the General had no idea who Jacques Tati was, the secretary tried to help by whispering 'Mon Oncle' (the name of one of Tati's most famous films). The General smiled, nodded and congratulated Tati on having such a charming and brilliant nephew.

Some of the misunderstandings damaged Tati's career quite badly. In Rome, at an audience with Pope Pius XII, the Pope was handed the wrong cue card when he met Tati and as a result the Holy Father talked exclusively about the gas fitting, plumbing and electrical trades. Outside the Vatican, when asked what the Pope had talked about Tati accurately answered 'he spoke about gas and electricity'. This was perceived by Italians as heretical. Tati's distributor claimed that the star lost 40% of his Italian audience with that one remark.

In America, the boss at the Warner Brothers studio offered Tati unlimited financing if he would make a film called *Mr Hulot Goes West* with Sophia Loren. Tati's reply was: 'No, sir. Mr Tati Goes East.' Tati meant that he was going home to France but it was understood to mean that he was a red and as a result no further offers came to Tati for the rest of his career. His films weren't shown in America because he was considered to be a communist.

As the years went by Tati got into more and more trouble for no fault of his own. He was accused of being anti-Jewish and banned by Jewish producers (though his only arguments with them were as a result of his claiming that he wasn't being paid enough money) and his mime of a traffic policeman directing vehicles in Italy was described as racist.

(I am always slightly bewildered by the way many Jews describe themselves by giving their religion first and whatever it is they do second. 'I am a Jewish mother.' 'I am a Jewish doctor.' Everyone else I know does things the other way round. A mother and a Catholic. A doctor and a Presbyterian. A Frenchman and a Christian. Religion does not define anyone - not even a Muslim - in quite the same way that it seems to define a Jew. A man who is a surveyor, father, husband, son, fisherman and golfer will think of himself first and foremost as a Jew. I wonder why this is. Is it a sense of elitism? A feeling of exclusivity? Jews often complain that people treat them as different but couldn't that be because they think of themselves as being different; some seem to me to behave as though they are members of a special clique and have a tendency to look down their noses at those of us who are not Jewish. When I wrote my two books about America (*Rogue Nation* and *Global Bully*) I got into terrible trouble with Jews. Although the books were about the USA and not Israel a number of Jews wrote vicious letters accusing me of anti-Semitism simply because I had dared to criticise the illegal invasion of Iraq. They regarded an attack on America as nothing more than a slightly veiled attack on Israel, which it most assuredly was not. More significantly a number wrote angry letters demanding that newspapers and magazines refuse to accept advertisements for the books and a number of those publications did as they were told.)

Gradually, towards the end of his life, Tati found it increasingly difficult to raise money for films. His own circus pals rallied round and helped him make a film but in the end the splendid isolation slowly morphed into fearful solitude.

13.

Our local supermarket in Paris has installed a row of those horrible self-service tills which are now so unpopular in English supermarkets and chain stores. In an uncharacteristically techno-friendly moment I thought I would try to make the thing work. I pressed the button confirming that I wanted to pay for my shopping (presumably there is an alternative option for those who prefer to just take away their shopping without paying for it) and a voice told me to put my bag in the bagging area. I put my bag in the bagging area and a voice immediately told me that before going further I should remove the unauthorised item from the bagging area. This sort of nonsense is clearly built into these machines which are undoubtedly programmed by impoverished Chinese peasants who are directed by their Government to do everything they can to weaken dastardly foreigners by raising their stress levels. However, I have found a solution. Whenever there are no executive sales assistants in sight and I am forced to use one of these damned tills I simply put something heavy down on the weighing scales and leave it there. This causes a pre-recorded voice to scream abuse at me. There are sometimes bell and whistle noises too. And in the more expensive supermarkets a red light flashes. I ignore the instructions and stand there looking elderly and helpless (this is not difficult). Within a minute or so an assistant will come over and operate the machinery for me. I was delighted to see that when I did this in Paris the same thing happened and my technological needs were attended to by a Gallic executive sales assistant. (I refer to her as Gallic but I suspect that her birthplace was nearer to Bucharest than Paris.) Unfortunately, I had to wait a while because all the available executive sales assistants (ESAs) were running hither and thither attending to all the other customers trying to pay for their shopping and their running hither and thither was impeded by a cluster of people collecting money for charity. The whole scene reminded me of something by Brueghel. It transpired that the French have not quite got the hang of this new technology because much of their merchandise is sold without a barcode. For example, fruit and vegetables are still displayed loose and must be selected and bagged by the customers. And baguettes, sold in the customary long thin paper bags, don't have a barcode either. Since every French shopper buys fruit, vegetables and at least one baguette the predictable result was chaos. The ESAs were having to take bags of apples, tomatoes, lemons, potatoes and so on to the back of the store, weigh them, work out the prices and then return to the self-service tills at the front of the store, use their personal key and secret code word to by-pass the barcode readers and then input the information manually. Only the French could create such a circus out of a labour saving device. It took me thirty minutes to pay for my small selection of groceries and compared to other shoppers I did rather well. Still, things will improve soon. The assistant who dealt with my purchases apologised profusely and assured me that the managers (doubtless safely cocooned in an office block in Lyon, Dijon or Toulouse) have been informed of the glitch and have found a solution. 'We are being given more staff to help us operate the self-service tills,' she told me proudly. They have also put up a sign advertising 'Friendly service with a smile'. Unfortunately, we will have to wait until these luxuries are in season. The French claim to have a sophisticated sense of humour but only the English really understand irony. As I left I saw a young girl of about seven reluctantly handing back the notepad she had intended to buy. The price was five euros and 75 centimes and she only had a five euro note. I wanted to hand over the extra 75 centimes and would have gladly done so but was stopped by the realisation that if I did so in England I would undoubtedly be arrested, vilified and labelled a paedophile or, worse still, a member of UKIP. I'm not sure how barking the French have become about this sort of behaviour but I reluctantly decided that I had better play safe and keep my change in my pocket. What a sad, sad world the politically correct have created for us all.

As I left the supermarket, hurrying back to our apartment where The Princess was making dinner, a woman pushing a pram the size of a small Citroen banged into my legs from behind, nearly knocking me into a large display of seasonal vegetables. Why do pram pushing women the world over always assume that they always have the right of way? They should be forced to take pushing tests. I struggled back to the apartment with arms aching, legs hurting and brain whirling.

When I had taken my medication (a glass of Cardhu) and had recovered from this exhausting experience we watched Carol Reed's film of Graham Greene's novel *The Third Man* for the umpteenth time. Joseph Cotten and Trevor Howard are magnificent and the film will always be in my Top Ten but the movie is, of course, stolen by Orson Welles playing a black marketeer. Hitchcock was wise not to hire Welles to play the wicked spy with the missing finger in *The Thirty Nine Steps* for if he had done so Welles would have stolen my other favourite film too. Even Steve McQueen could have taken lessons on scene stealing from the master. (The traditional advice should have been: 'Don't play in films with children, animals or Orson Welles.')

Despite being American (and, therefore, at a huge cultural disadvantage) Orson Welles was one of the most talented men of the 20th century. Sadly, he peaked too early and neither he nor anyone else found it easy to cope with the peaking. He was, however, what Arnold Bennett would have referred to as a 'card'. Once, when lecturing at a women's club in Santa Monica, so few people turned up that the lady who was due to introduce Welles fled into the safety of the powder room (a term which always reminds me more of Guy Fawkes than ladies taking the shine off their noses). Unflustered by the absence of his hostess Welles steamed on and introduced himself to his tiny audience by saying: 'I am a director of plays. I am a producer of plays. I am an actor. I write, direct and act on the radio. I paint and sketch and am a book publisher. I do many other things.' Then he leant closer to his tiny audience and said, in that wonderful, sherry-rich booming voice: 'Isn't it a shame that there are so many of me and so few of you?' They don't make them like Orson any more.

14.

Back in London, we met a tramp outside St Pancras railway station. The authorities no longer allow tramps into public buildings, probably because they're a threat to national security and the banking system and the stability of the European Union, so they have to hang around outside in the rain. The Princess always gives money to tramps who look to be over the age of 55. She knows that most of them will spend it on booze but, as she says, if you give people money you can't tell them how to spend it. Besides, if alcohol helps them forget whatever it is they're running away from then it's medicine. I have a theory that when God makes people He has barrels full of stuff to put into them - kindness, sensitivity and so on. One Friday evening God had most of a barrel of sensitivity left over and knowing that it would go off if not used He put it all into The Princess. And so she became too sensitive. When one of the angels warned Him what would happen He just smiled. 'It will be nice for the world to have a really sensitive and kind person around.' The result is that The Princess is a delicate primrose in a world of heavy boots.

This particular tramp was sitting on the pavement with a religious placard resting beside him. I can't remember the exact words - something about the wrath of God and the end of the world.

'What are you going to do if the weather gets really bad?' I asked him. The forecasters were talking about freezing temperatures, snow and ice. He looked at me, thought for a long, long while and then replied with one word: 'Vicissitudes.'

He spoke very softly and I didn't quite catch what he had said, though this may have been because it was not an answer I had expected.

'I beg your pardon?' I said, leaning closer.

'Vicissitudes,' he repeated. He shrugged lightly. He looked tired. He clearly didn't have the energy for a proper shrug.

'Do you have a date?' I asked him. 'For the end of the world.' I wasn't being funny, I really wanted to know.

He looked at me and I knew he was trying to tell if I was taking the mickey. He could see that I wasn't. He shook his head. 'It's in God's hands,' he said. 'He will decide when. I could guess. But it is not wise to give a specific date when predicting the end of the world,' he said. I got the impression it was the longest speech he'd made for quite a while.

I waited for him to continue.

'If the date is near and you are wrong then you will be discredited,' he explained. 'People will laugh. No one will take you seriously.' He licked his dry, cracked lips with a sore, smooth, tongue. You didn't need a laboratory to tell he was vitamin and iron deficient. 'If you give a far-away date then no one will care.'

I nodded and waited but he had finished. I put a bank note into his hand. 'Do you want us to take you to hospital?' I asked him. He shook his head. Wise man.

We left him.

'I hadn't realised just how tricky the wrath of God business can be,' I said quietly to The Princess.

15.

I thought lists of criminals went out with John Dillinger (who was famously Public Enemy No 1) but the Americans still publish a list of their most wanted criminals. I know this because someone called Vernon Coleman, the last remaining free member of America's Black Mafia Gang, is on the American Most Wanted list and frequently a member of the Top Ten. I wonder if there is kudos among criminals who make it into the Top Ten. Does number 9 consider himself to be socially superior to, say, no 11? Can number 16 move up a couple of places by knocking over a small bank in Ohio?

16.

We took a pile of books to a local charity shop which raises money for a hospice. We took two huge black sacks of paperbacks and two large boxes full of hardbacks (mostly first editions which were duplicates of books I had on my shelves). We said 'good morning' but the woman in charge of the shop that day, who was sitting reading a book, couldn't even be bothered to turn her head, let alone bring herself to greet us or to waste breath muttering 'thank you'. A fortnight ago we took the same shop some books and a bag full of DVDs. 'There aren't any videos in that bag are there?' demanded the woman. 'No, they're all DVDs,' said The Princess. 'I'll check,' snapped the woman. She ripped open the bag and insisted on emptying it onto the floor to make sure that we were only donating DVDs. When she was satisfied she grunted something, presumably to let us know that we could go. We won't be taking any more donations to this particular charity shop. Maybe we shouldn't expect a 'thank you'. But a little ordinary courtesy wouldn't seem a lot to ask.

On our way out I couldn't help taking a peep at the books they had on their shelves. I picked out three and moved towards the till.

'Do you really want to buy those?' asked The Princess.

I looked at the books I was holding. 'I've read them all and I used to have copies but I don't think I have copies now.'

'Those three were among the books we bought here two weeks ago,' she pointed out quietly. I looked at her. She smiled and shrugged. 'I just thought I'd mention it.'

I looked at the books more carefully. They were, indeed, the very same books that I'd donated. I put the books back on the shelf.

17.

The hot tap in our lovely new kitchen doesn't work. I have discovered that five years ago a builder who did some 'improvement works' put the pipes into the space between the stone walls and then compounded the problem by putting four large airbricks into the outside wall. The result is that the air around the pipe is freezing cold. I have no doubt that the air bricks (huge things, as ugly as social workers) are there to satisfy some daft regulation thought up by a team of quarter-witted Belgians and enforced by equally dim and petty-minded English bureaucrats. (Just for the record I would like to point out that this book would have been finished in half the time and with considerably less effort and expense without the assistance of these malignant posses.) I confess that what worries me more than the number of rules which now exist is the number of people who seem to love applying them with enthusiasm, even when they must surely know that the rules are stupid. We are the only country in the EU who takes any notice of the rules from Brussels. (The French love rules, because their existence gives them the joy of ignoring them.

Without rules you cannot be a rebel and the French always consider themselves to be rebels. They are rebels with a thousand causes: some wise, some just and some absurd. In what city other than Paris would lawyers go to the streets and protest en masse about something no one could quite understand?) England is now full to the coastline of sanctimonious self-important cretins and I am full up of worries: I really don't have any room left for new worries. The next self-important prat who tells me I must do this or do that will just have to wait until I've got rid of one of my worries and have some space available.

The temperature fell to minus eight last night when the hot tap froze and so this morning I went outside and screwed four squares of thick carpet over all four airbricks. I am confident that this will solve the problem. I also discovered that our conservatory is freezing cold because a huge air brick which some lunkhead of a builder has stuck in the wall is letting in vast draughts of freezing cold air. I cured that problem by filling the inside of the airbrick with cotton wool then covering over the inside grille. There was a note on the airbrick saying 'Do Not Cover' but I don't give a fig. I assume that the people in Brussels are worried that without their intervention we may run out of air. Well, much of our new home is over 200-years-old (the larger part of the modernisation was done in 1750 when planning regulations were just a smirk on some serf's poxy face) and it doesn't need air bricks, thank you very much. The outside air can get in all by itself. Two of our keyholes alone are big enough to get a hand through (the keys are solid iron and a foot long) so I don't think we'll suffocate.

18.

I've been re-reading George Gissing's *The Private Papers of Henry Ryecroft* (a fake diary by a retired writer). In the book Gissing (as Ryecroft) writes 'They tell me we are burning all our coal, and with wicked wastefulness. I am sorry for it, but I cannot on that account make cheerless perhaps the last winter of my life. There may be waste on domestic hearths, but the wickedness is elsewhere - too blatant to call for indication.' He goes on to say:'...hold by the open fire as you hold by whatever else is best in England. Because, in the course of nature, it will be someday a thing of the past (like most other things that are worth living for).'

Gissing himself was a great fan of an open fire and wrote warmly of his preference for a real fire over heating circulated through radiators and other systems. At the time when he wrote *The Private Papers of Henry Ryecroft* there was a coal shortage throughout Europe. Coal prices soared to 40 shillings a ton in 1900 just three years before Gissing wrote the book and three years before he died at the age of 46.

I too am a great fan of open fires (to me the words 'log on' means that the fire needs feeding) and believe that the size of a problem can be measured by the number of logs it requires to sort it out. (A five log problem being quite a challenge.) Sadly, these days, thanks largely to the efforts of the politically correct and the health and safety brigands, fireplaces everywhere are being blocked up and hearths replaced with fake fires fed by electricity or gas. Pubs and country hotels all over England have got rid of their fireplaces, doing away with log fires on the grounds that central heated lounges and bars are cleaner, healthier and safer. They are undoubtedly correct. But, on a cold winter's day, there is nothing quite as cosy and welcoming as a pub with a log fire burning. From half a mile away the smell of the smoke rising from the chimney is a sign of delights to come. Some pubs and hotels still have log burners but they're a poor substitute for the real thing.

But when the oil finally runs out, and the lunatics in charge of our energy policies realise that the production of electricity requires other energy sources such as oil, coal or gas, those who want to keep warm will suddenly revive their interest in open fires. And then they will rediscover the joy of flame watching.

A real open fire uses fewer logs and gives more heat. And the aesthetic value of flames dancing on a log is beyond price. We now have a new log burner in one of our fireplaces (to replace the one the previous owners carted away) but we always leave the doors open. When I told the installer that I intended to do this he was appalled, insisting that such a practice would use more wood, be a fire risk and do more damage to the environment. I told him I didn't much care about the amount of wood we use (we grow our own), that the risk of a fire starting in a stone fireplace or on a flagstone floor was pretty slim and that we would do far less damage to the environment than if we burnt oil or heated our rooms with electricity.

19.

I received a rather snooty letter from a journalist complaining that self-published books aren't proper books and don't deserve to be reviewed.

She told me, rather stiffly, that no decent author ever published their own books. She obviously doesn't understand much, if anything, about books or authors.

Books can, could and should have power and influence for good but now that the international conglomerates are in charge they don't, can't and won't because controversial issues are rejected as not suitable for the list (the lawyers wouldn't allow it or the board wouldn't like it). If in doubt the marketing and financial people who decide which books to publish will just say 'no'. No one in publishing ever got fired for saying 'No'. For years now, publishing companies have been getting bigger and bigger and more out of touch with books and readers. There are now many layers of bureaucracy between reader and writer. That's why I publish my own books. Many of my books (including some that would have been considered huge bestsellers if they'd been published by the official industry) would have never seen the light of day.

I sent back this reply: 'The following authors all published their own books and you may have heard of one or two of them: Gertrude Stein, Virginia Woolf, Walt Whitman, Horace Walpole, John Galsworthy, Rudyard Kipling, Walter Scott, Thomas Paine, Mark Twain, Edgar Allan Poe, Upton Sinclair, W. H. Davies, Zane Grey, Robbie Burns, Tobias Smollett, William Carlos Williams, Alexander Pope, Lawrence Stern, Ezra Pound, Norman Douglas, Anais Nin, Robert Lewis Stevenson, James Joyce, D. H. Lawrence, Evelyn Waugh, Lord Byron, William Morris, Jane Austen, Harry Crosby, Caresse Crosby, Robert Graves, Beatrix Potter, J. M. Barrie, Frank Harris, Henry Miller, T. S. Elliot, Bobby Fischer, J. L. Carr, Susan Hill, Jill Paton Walsh, Timothy Mo, Honore de Balzac, Jonathan Swift and Enid Blyton. Many of these did it frequently, repeatedly or exclusively. William Cobbett did it all his life. (He should be a hero to any self-publisher. During his life he wrote and published 30 million words without a computer or a typewriter. (Not having a computer would have been worth 25 million words in productivity. Because I have run out of old computers able to cope with DOS and Word Perfect 5.1 I have recently had to start using the latest version of Microsoft's graphic based word processing software. Windows is slow, clumsy and seems to me to have been designed by people who hate writers.) Cobbett, who averaged around 3,000 words a day, was sensitive enough to be a writer and tough enough to be a publisher. In addition to writing and publishing, he ran a farm, campaigned for a zillion causes and wandered around the world by boat and horse. Of course, he didn't have to sort his rubbish into five separate containers or fill in VAT forms online. Lewis Carroll self-published *Alice's Adventures in Wonderland* and Edward Lear did *Book of Nonsense* himself. The Brontë sisters self-published and the first book they did sold two copies. Beatrix Potter published *The Tale of Peter Rabbit* and *The Tailor of Gloucester* herself. William Blake, who even made his own ink and printed his books himself, got Mrs Blake to sew on the covers. *Lady Chatterly's Lover* was first published privately by D. H. Lawrence and T. E. Lawrence self-published *Seven Pillars of Wisdom*. Graham Greene published himself. Jerome K. Jerome, Balzac and Dickens all ran their own magazines and Scott and Twain all ran their own publishing companies. John Buchan, Grant Richards, T. S. Elliot, Frank Swinnerton and Alec Waugh all worked in publishing. John Grisham self-published his first novel and sold copies from the boot of his car. Some of these authors referred to what they did as 'self-publishing', many referred to it as 'privately printing' but they all did it because they had something to say and were damned well going to say it whatever the cost and the inconvenience. I suspect they may have shared my own simple publishing philosophy: 'I will publish whatever I damned well please and I don't give a fig whether agents, wholesalers or bookshops like it'.'

I doubt if my correspondent will be convinced. Self-publishing has (as a result of manipulative opposition from the publishing industry) come to be regarded as a sin greater than putting your bottles in with your cardboard and failing to bring your wheelie bin back in on time. And it has, of course, been the publishing establishment which has worked hardest to marginalise self-publishers. They have good reason to worry. Self-publishers have, in recent years, shown that they can survive without the industry parasites.

Doing it yourself has always been popular in other areas of creative activity. Charlie Chaplin paid for his own movies to be made. Harold Lloyd financed his own movies. Woody Allen has effectively self-published films throughout his career. Tom Cruise produces films he stars in.

In almost any other area of creative human endeavour, doing it yourself is considered laudable. Make your own film or record and you are regarded as brave and innovative, mould breaking, striking a path away from the hideous commercial leeches who turned creative artists into conveyor belt producers - obeying the predictable whims of marketing men in sharp suits rather than the urges of the muse and ignoring the fact that artists are people who live life out loud not because they choose to but because they can see no other way. Indie film producers and indie record makers are regarded as being at the sharp end of their respective industries. But publish your own book and you will attract nothing but derision and contempt. (The name says it all. Make your own film or record and you are an indie producer. Make your own book and you are a self-publisher or, worse still, a vanity publisher. Many people in the industry like to pretend there is no difference. The irony is that those immensely snooty publications *The Guardian* and *The Independent* are now losing so much money that they are, in reality, nothing more than vanity publications.) There is a very good reason for this. No one making their own film or CD can possibly compete with, or threaten, the giants. These are complex industries. But book publishing is simple. Anyone can do it just as well as the so-called professionals. Moreover, it isn't expensive. You can have your own book printed and delivered to your garage for the price of a small car. Try making a movie for that. Publishers know this, of course, and they are terrified - utterly terrified - that authors (particularly successful ones who make big money for publishers) will find out. The industrial publishers know that if word gets out that publishing is a doddle and anyone can do it then the whole publishing edifice will come tumbling down. Editors, agents and all the rest will have to get proper jobs and since most of them have no skills outside their own conceits they will probably find life in the real world rather hard going.

Mention self-publishing to anyone in the orthodox world of publishing, and their nose will rise several inches into the air. Publishers (and just about everyone else involved in publishing) hate self-publishers: largely because self-publishing is a major threat to the cosy, out-dated world of orthodox publishing. Successful self-publishers prove that orthodox publishers are parasites. Everything they do can be done better by authors.

The simple-minded drones in the publishing world - agents and publishers - are scared stiff self-publishers will put them out of business. They deliberately confuse self-publishing (or indie-publishing) with vanity publishing but the reality is that modern publishing houses often only exist because they are protected and subsidised by other parts of the industrial conglomerate in which they sit. Hot shot authors often fail to sell enough books to cover their advances. One large American publisher recently wrote off about $35,000,000 worth of unearned advances while another wrote off close to $80,000,000 worth.

Why do publishers hand over vast sums on books they should know won't sell? Sometimes, it is because they misunderstand the value of celebrity and pay huge sums for books by individuals who are famous but have nothing much to say. Back in 2005, the *Financial Times* reported that: 'In today's competitive publishing world, always on the lookout for the next new name, youth and ethnicity can be an author's most valuable assets.' Publishers are hiring teams of 20-year-old footballers to write autobiographies and they are hiring platoons of semi-literate girlfriends to write novels, cook books, fashion guides and, quite possibly, political treatises. ('Don't worry about the writing stuff, love, we'll find someone to do all that for you. We just put your name on the cover. No, of course you don't have to read it if you don't want to.')

And sometimes it is pay-back time to politicians who have done favours. Publishers pay huge fees to politicians for memoirs which no one with functioning brain tissue expects will sell more than a handful of copies. So why do they hand over so much money for books that aren't really expected to sell? Payment for services rendered or payment for services to come? Of course. The situation is confused even more by the fact that publishers and agents drool at the idea of having long lunches with big-name politicians. I once knew a very pushy literary agent who represented a number of well-known politicians. When I asked her why she bothered to represent such literary disasters she looked at me as if I were mad. 'They're not just famous,' she told me. 'They're so powerful!' She looked as though she was having a multiple orgasm at the very thought.

The sad truth is that many orthodox publishing houses have far, far more in common with vanity publishing than do successful self-publishers. Overheads at big publishers are vast. There are huge salaries and expense accounts, expensive premises in central locations, expensive sales conferences in five star hotels, long lunches, big bonuses, etc. All this means that there is no money left for publishing daring books. It has been estimated by American publishers that there are no more than 100-200 authors in America who can earn a living from writing books; the rest have to moonlight by working at other day jobs. So how many professional authors are there in the UK? Considerably less than 100 I suspect. And as the internet grows in size, and copyright theft becomes more widely approved, and newspapers and magazines continue to expect articles and serial rights for free, the number will decline still further.

For many years as an indie publisher I paid more tax than many big publishing companies made in profits. The biggest problem I faced was that as a writer I needed a thin skin but as a publisher I needed a thick one.

Sadly, the advent of eBooks and the dramatic rise in print costs and the cost of postage mean that there is no more of a future for proper self-publishing by professional authors than there is for any other type of publishing.

And that is a real tragedy.

20.

The Princess and I had been packing books all day. We were exhausted. 'I'm going to light a fire, pour myself a large glass of Laphroaig and read a couple of chapters of my book,' I announced after dinner. I was reading, and much enjoying, a copy of *A Great Man* by Arnold Bennett which I'd picked up for £1 in a second hand bookshop. I looked around the cluttered room. I looked everywhere but couldn't find it. Every available surface in the room was covered with books, padded bags, stamps and sticky tape. 'Have you seen my book?' I asked the Executive In Charge Of Literary Product Insertion Procedures. 'The one I was reading.'

'Where did you put it?'

'I left it over there,' I said, pointing to a table by the door.

'What did it look like?'

'Hardback. Yellow background with a picture on the front of a living room with four people in it.'

'It was on that table?'

'Yes.'

The Executive In Charge Of Literary Product Insertion Procedures (aka The Princess) looked at the table and then at me. 'I packed everything on that table.'

I looked at the row of five large, grey sacks lined up by the door. Each sack contained around 40 parcels, all stamped and ready to go. One of those parcels contained a copy of *A Great Man* by Arnold Bennett.

'I'll just have the whisky,' I said.

21.

This afternoon I received an e-mail offering me a goodly number of dollars for my website - including all the content. This is a puzzle. I regularly receive (and turn down) requests to take advertising on the site but none of these requests has involved sums of more than a thousand dollars or so and I really cannot believe that www.vernoncoleman.com is worth so much money. And then it occurred to me that whoever is offering the money probably wants to close the site down - and remove my articles from the internet. It is the only thing that makes sense.

22.

We tried to find an odd job man to do some small tasks around the house. We wasted thirty minutes searching the local directories, and the internet, for an odd job man. Eventually The Princess found two. One described himself as a multidisciplinary contractor and the other described himself as a household specialist. I assume that both are, in reality, odd job men who can do useful things with taps, plugs and broken bits of wall.

Because the work people do is, by and large, so dull, repetitive and pointless bosses get round this by making all jobs sound important. Everyone is a consultant. Nail clipper operators become digital keratin cosmetic manipulators. The woman who works at the counter in a record store calls herself a 'home entertainment consultant'.

And since, despite the nomenclature, the jobs are dull and unsatisfying, most people don't spend their days doing what they want to do, instead they do jobs they don't like and they do them just for money and so they have to spend to make themselves feel alive. And much of the money is spent on needs for their jobs (suit, travel, expensive lunches) so they really aren't going anywhere; they are in jail, self-imposed exile from real life.

And they fight for leisure time which they spend polishing cars, cutting grass and going shopping for things they don't need or even really want. They then need more money to buy cupboards to contain the things they have bought but didn't need. And they have to rent storage lockers for the stuff that won't fit in the cupboards.

23.

Napoleon Bonaparte, when he was first consul of France, and as big a cheese as there ever has been in France, reckoned that nine out of ten letters he received would answer themselves if left. And so he opened letters only after six weeks, by which time not many still required an answer. Coleridge, the English poet, was reputed to have developed an even more effective solution to dealing with mail. He opened none and, therefore, never had to answer any. Neither Napoleon nor Coleridge would, I suspect, have had much time for e-mail. I'm not in the slightest bit surprised to see that more and more companies are deciding that e-mail is an inefficient tool for internal communication. They prefer people to talk, telephone or send physical notes to one another. Astonishingly, most people now receive more than 100 e-mails a day and feel under pressure to answer them quickly. That's not surprising since most senders expect a reply to their e-mails within an hour or two at most. The result is that most people constantly check their e-mail. (I confess I do understand this need for instant gratification. I check my e-mail every week unless we're away or I am very busy.) And, of course, a seemingly endless supply of e-mail newsletters and promotions pour into the average inbox and need to be dealt with.

My Dad, who at one point in his life ran a medium sized factory employing several hundred people insisted that he always left his mail for a week or two 'to mature'. 'If it had got lost in the post I wouldn't have been able to answer it,' he said, with perfect logic.

These days Napoleon, Coleridge and my Dad would have all been in trouble because of the new habit governments and large companies have of introducing absurd new policies by default. So, Royal Mail wrote recently to tell us that unless we object they will, if we are out or fail to answer our front door within 0.01 seconds, leave our mail with a neighbour. To make life more fun for everyone they won't bother to tell us which neighbour they've left it with. Since one in six people in England now has a criminal record this means that there is a one in six chance that they will leave important parcels and packages with our local, neighbourhood thief. Anyone who wants to opt out of this absurd policy has to ring up and ask for a special sticker to put on the front door.

In France, everyone is now assumed to have a television set and so everyone is assumed to owe the Government a licence fee. When the Government sends along a tax demand it adds on the fee for the licence. Anyone who doesn't watch television and doesn't want to pay the licence fee has to apply to be considered exempt. The default state is always confiscation. This is inertia mugging. 'Unless you take the trouble to do something that will take time and trouble we will do something nasty to you.' Even changes to pension legislation are made by default. If you don't notice what is happening (and say 'no') all sorts of terrible things can happen to your pension fund. The authorities know, of course, that most people cannot possibly keep up with all the new information being thrown at them. And they know, too, that even when people do know about something that is about to happen they won't have the time or the energy to take action. And so it goes on. Everywhere we look these days we find that unless we are constantly alert, suspicious, and wary terrible things happen to us by default. (It has also become exceedingly difficult to spot the important news in the constant hail of material with which we are drenched.) We are in a constant state of war; a stage of siege. Every day brings new laws, new demands, new orders and new difficulties. I cannot be the only one who finds it impossible to keep up. Only those dependent upon the State (and in receipt of regular cheques) are immune (their votes are essential and whichever party is in power is kept there by the zombies.) It sometimes seems that we are living in a world of change for the sake of interference.

One problem with the information storm is that most people are appallingly bad at making decisions and judging risks. And most don't understand that you can't really do the former without being able to do the latter. If you don't take risks you never get anything done. The trick is to quantify the risk and then decide if the risk is worth taking. But there is a risk in not doing things and that, too, has to be taken into account. All decisions and actions, however apparently insignificant, have consequences, and all failures to make decisions (or take action) produce equally irreversible consequences.

24.

We drove to Bilbury two days ago, and yesterday afternoon a friend of ours called Dalby Barrington came to stay with us in our cottage there for the night. He is slightly obsessional and extremely polite. He is, indeed, so polite that I have heard him say 'thank you' to an automatic cash dispenser. Dalby always carries a furled umbrella but never unfurls it. Once, when walking down Charing Cross Road in the pouring rain I asked him why he didn't open up his umbrella. He said he had to keep it tightly rolled because he knew that he would never again be able roll it so that it looked quite so elegant. He said he had unrolled the umbrella once but that afterwards, when he had dried it off with a series of handkerchiefs, he had taken it back to the shop in New Oxford Street and had it re-furled. Looking elegant was, to him, far more important than keeping dry.

Dalby is an expert on English piers and came to North Devon to study and photograph Bilbury pier. It was, as he quickly discovered, a wild-goose chase. Bilbury is half a mile from the sea and there is not, nor ever has been a pier. This morning, as he was about to leave he burst into the kitchen in quite a panic. 'I've lost my reading spectacles!' he announced. 'I must get a pair made. Is there an optician in the village?'

I pointed out that there is no optician in Bilbury but told him that there are several in Barnstaple.

'Can you take me there? I can never find my way round. I'll be lost for hours if I drive there myself.' I sighed silently for I was not feeling entirely up to the mark. The Princess woke me three times last night to see if I was still alive. Apparently, I breathe very quietly when I am asleep and she worries that I might have died. Stricken by anxiety she bangs me on the head and rocks me to and fro to find out whether I'm still entitled to claim my winter fuel allowance. Being fast asleep I had no knowledge of any of this until I was woken. 'You didn't seem to be breathing,' she explained. 'And you seemed to be a funny colour.' 'How could you see what colour I am? It's pitch black.' She said she just knew, or thought she knew, and that I should be pleased that she loved me enough to wake me up to see if I was dead or not and eventually I agreed that I was very grateful and I thanked her. So I was tired. But I drove Dalby into town and waited while he persuaded an optician to make him up a pair of glasses that would be suitable.

'They aren't quite right, of course,' he said. 'But the optician said they're pretty close to my prescription. They'll do until I get back to London.'

We then drove back to Bilbury where The Princess gave us both a very late salad lunch. He then unfastened the largest of his three suitcases and put the new spectacles inside.

'Don't you need them for the journey?' I asked. 'In case you need to look at the map or something?'

'Oh I won't need those,' he said. He then took another spectacle case out of his jacket pocket. 'I'd rather use these. They're better than the ones I picked up this morning.'

I honestly didn't understand. 'I thought you'd lost your spectacles,' I said, grasping for the plot.

'Oh, I did, I lost one pair,' he said. 'These are my spare pair.'

'But we drove into Barnstaple to get you a spare pair.'

'Yes, those are my new spare pair. These are my old spare pair. I always travel with two pairs.'

'But you could have used your spare pair. We didn't need to go into Barnstaple at all.'

'Oh we did. If I use my spare pair I obviously don't have a spare pair. And I must have a spare pair for emergencies.'

'But this was an emergency.'

'Absolutely. But there might be another emergency. I might break or lose the original spare pair. And if I didn't have a new spare pair I wouldn't have a pair at all.'

I don't usually drink alcohol in the morning. But occasionally exceptions must be made. I was so exhausted that I went out into the garden to sit and do absolutely nothing. The Princess kindly said she would come with me to help.

25.

I read a book by someone claiming that England isn't a country and the English aren't members of a nation because England is populated by a mixture of Celts, Danes, Romans, Angles, Saxons, Jutes, Normans and goodness knows what else. What utter nonsense. What about America? The USA is a young nation made up of people from every part of the world and yet no one dares say 'American isn't a nationality'.

26.

Doctors love treating blood pressure. It is one of the most profitable of all diseases for drug companies because once a patient has started taking tablets to bring his blood pressure down he will probably never stop.

When I first started work as a GP I found that my predecessor had put nearly all patients on pills to lower their blood pressure. For some reason known only to him he had decided that any patient with a systolic reading of over 100 was hypertensive. (A normal systolic is usually said to be around 120 so he was treating vast swathes of perfectly healthy people.)

Not surprisingly, most of these patients were constantly calling into the surgery complaining of dizziness. I solved their problems by telling them that their medication had cured them and that they no longer needed to take it. I told them that the dizziness was a sign that the pills had worked. They all praised my predecessor and I agreed that he had been exceedingly clever in dealing with their problem so effectively.

I took my own blood pressure this morning. (The Princess had bought herself a new self-measuring device which I was testing.)

To my horror I found that my blood pressure was dangerously raised. I couldn't understand why.

I'm not overweight. I don't smoke. I don't eat a lot of fatty food. I take gentle exercise.

And then I had a thought.

I had a lot of intestinal wind at the time (I suffer from that much underestimated problem Irritable Bowel Syndrome) and I wondered if the wind could be pressing upon arteries around my kidneys and elsewhere and forcing up my blood pressure. (On a previous occasion, wind in my intestines caused kidney bleeding which nearly led to my having a kidney ripped out.)

'Hug my teddy bear,' suggested The Princess. 'It might help.'

It wasn't a daft suggestion. I have long argued that anxiety can make blood pressure worse. (Indeed, I got into terrible trouble when I was a young doctor for suggesting that there might be a link between stress and blood pressure. Several members of the medical establishment publicly suggested that I be struck off the medical register for voicing such an outlandish thought in public.)

So, I hugged the teddy bear and took my blood pressure again. This time it was down.

'There you are!' said The Princess, delightedly. 'My teddy bear has cured you.'

I was quite prepared to accept this and then it occurred to me that while hugging the bear I had sat up very straight and had changed position. By moving around I had taken the pressure off my aorta and renal arteries.

So I tried a simple experiment.

When I was slumped in the chair my blood pressure was high. When I was sitting up it was normal.

I now believe, quite firmly, that intestinal wind can cause intermittent high blood pressure. If I hadn't wriggled around, changed my position and proved the link to my satisfaction I might now be taking potentially dangerous blood pressure medication. The medical profession won't accept this association, of course. It's far too simple. And it would cost the pharmaceutical industry (and, therefore, the medical establishment) untold billions.

27.

The Princess went shopping for new curtains this morning and wisely suggested that instead of hanging around saying things like: 'These red and orange ones look fine' and 'What's wrong with these blue striped ones' I might like to wander along to the local golf club for an hour or two.

I gave up playing golf several years ago when I was thrown out of a club for leaving my old Bentley S1 in the Lady Vice Captain's parking spot. (My excuse, that it was the only available spot in the whole car park, was dismissed as irrelevant by the prosecution.) However, I am still a member of one club and I go there very occasionally, partly because they have a good selection of malt whiskies and partly because as a professional people watcher I find the people in golf clubs provide tremendous entertainment. The members at this club are surely the most gullible people on the planet. On one occasion I told a fellow member, a headmaster of a private preparatory school, that I had hit a ball so high that, while waiting for it to return to earth, my partner and I had gone ahead and played the next hole before returning to await the fall of my ball at the previous hole. On another occasion, when conversation in the clubhouse had, for reasons which are now long forgotten, turned to Hitler, I asked an accountant whose name I have forgotten if he had heard that Hitler's body had been found in a bunker. When he said he had heard this. I told him confidentially that although it isn't widely known outside certain circles, Hitler's body was actually found in the bunker just short of the green on the fourth hole at the Berlin Golf and Country Club and that that particular bunker had been modelled on the bunker to the left of the 17th on our course. The accountant was astonished at this piece of news and rushed home to tell his wife who was, apparently, quite an enthusiastic viewer of the History Channel on television.

I was sitting at the bar enjoying a quiet Cardhu when a fellow called George Barraclough clambered rather clumsily onto the next but one stool and placed the folded newspaper he had been carrying on the bar in front of him. He nodded, I nodded and we exchanged a few cordial words of greeting.

'Don't often see you having lunch here, George,' said the barman who was the only member of staff to ignore club protocol. He called everyone, regardless of their position in the club, by their Christian names. He leant forward across the bar. 'Not planning a little assignation are you, sir?' he asked rather cheekily, with a wink.

'No,' said George, who was studying the bar menu. 'Actually I had to come out for lunch because I lost Deidre, my wife, this morning.' He shrugged. 'One minute she was there. The next minute...gone.'

The barman turned ashen, muttered apologies and polished the glass he was holding so hard that I feared he might rub right through the glass. 'I'm sorry to hear that, sir,' he said. He lowered his voice to a more suitably funereal tone. 'What would you like for lunch?' he asked. 'Or would you prefer just a drink? Don't suppose you feel much like eating, do you?'

'On the contrary, I'm feeling rather peckish. I think I'll have the steak and kidney pie,' replied George. 'With roast potatoes. Lots of 'em.' I glanced across when I heard this. I knew that Deidre always kept George on a short leash when it came to food. I had heard that at home she fed him almost exclusively on food that was green. She had a pet theory that anything brown or white was bad for you. George was clearly not losing any time in restoring the colour balance of his diet.

'Right you are, sir,' said the barman, who seemed to regard George's healthy appetite as a good sign. Perhaps he had remembered that Mary Queen of Scots enjoyed an excellent game of golf after the murder of her husband.

'And turnips, sprouts and peas,' continued George. 'No. Forget the sprouts and peas. But I'll have double carrots. Followed by a large portion of spotted dick and custard.'

'Certainly, sir,' said the barman, who was noticeably cheering up as he realised that George was not exactly in mourning and that he was, therefore, freed from any requirement to remain funereal and respectful. It is probably fair to say that no one in the club actually liked Deidre; a self-important woman with an exaggerated sense of her position in life. Most people simply avoided her or ignored her whenever they could. George, on the other hand, was pretty widely liked.

'Make that a large helping of spotted dick, please,' said George. He thought for a moment. 'With double custard,' he added.

'Right you are, sir.'

Deidre, I thought, would have never approved of spotted dick. Or custard.

'And a half carafe of the club's claret,' added George. He thought for a moment. 'Oh damnit, let's push the boat out a bit. Make that a bottle of decent stuff.' He studied the wine list which was printed on the back of the menu. The list was short enough and unchanging enough for most of the members to know it by heart but George had rarely ventured further down the list than the club claret; a thin, pale red imitation which was served in nasty little glass carafes which had long ago turned opaque in the club's aged industrial dishwasher. 'A bottle of St Emilion,' said George, splashing out on the most expensive item on the list.

The barman, whose pallor had now disappeared, scribbled furiously on his pad, nodded and backed away. 'Right away, sir,' he murmured. He took two paces, paused, thought about saying something, reconsidered, took another pace, paused again, reconsidered and half turned. 'May I just say how pleased I am to see you in such a good state,' he added. He seemed in awe; his admiration inspired by George's lack of false sensitivity. George was behaving like a man who, having just been released after a long prison sentence, walks into a pub and celebrates his freedom by ordering a pint of everything available.

In response to the barman's congratulations, George, who had folded his newspaper to the back page and had been studying the crossword, looked up. He seemed slightly puzzled. 'Thank you,' he said. 'Don't forget to bring the mustard.'

I sipped at my whisky until the glass was empty, and then quietly stood up. 'I'm so sorry to hear about your wife,' I murmured as I prepared to leave.

George looked up at me and frowned.

'Losing your wife,' I said, in case he'd forgotten.

'Oh, she'll turn up,' he said.

It was my turn to frown.

'With any luck she's not noticed I'm missing yet,' said. 'We were supposed to meet in Debenhams,' he explained. 'But the damned place was crowded out. Sale on, I suppose. She'll be busy buying more shoes I expect.' He grinned. 'It'll cost me a few hundred quid but I get a couple of hours off and some decent food for a change.'

28.

Each week seems to bring more revelations about the death of bin Laden. The American military say that they were suspicious of a house in Pakistan because the people living there paid cash for their purchases. And they burnt all their rubbish. Very suspicious. The original official story was that the military raided the house and there was a gunfight.

They said that soldiers shot bin Laden as he hid behind his wife. They later admitted that this wasn't true. They executed him. He was unarmed. He didn't hide. He was in his bedroom. They shot his wife too. But how did they know it was him? How did they identify the body? It seems from one report that they knew that bin Laden was 6 feet 4 inches and the body of the man they'd shot seemed about that height. But they didn't have a tape measure or anything else with which they could measure the cadaver. So one of the soldiers who was around 6 foot 4 inches tall lay down beside the corpse. That's how they knew the body was bin Laden. A dead, foreign looking bloke who was around 6 foot 4 inches tall. They then threw the body into the sea so no one will ever really know the identity of the man they killed.

29.

I have learned the hard way in life that initiative is never rewarded. Indeed, at school and in the army, doing well in an initiative test can be positively dangerous.

When I was at grammar school I was forced to be a member of the Combined Cadet Force. I loathed it. I loathed the itchy uniform almost (but not quite) as much as I hated the discipline. We were sent out on an initiative test one day. A coach dropped us in the middle of a great stretch of moorland waste known as Cannock Chase, near Wolverhampton. At the start of the day's exercise we were given a long questionnaire full of detailed queries about local beauty spots, graveyards, architectural wonders and the like. The idea was that we would trudge around the neighbourhood searching for clues and answers.

I didn't know where I was but I could see a village nearby so I headed in that direction. Once in the village I headed straight for the village shop where I bought a bag of sweets and asked a very nice lady behind the counter if she could help me with my questionnaire. It was the sort of shop where you could buy shaving brushes, potted shrimps, caraway seed, propelling pencil leads, corn plasters, catapult elastic, candles, radio valves and tiger striped bulls' eyes. The questionnaire was full of daft questions such as 'Who is the organist in the local church?' The shop was one of those establishments where a few years ago, the proprietor always used to be female, middle aged and rather on the plump side of overweight. I've always regarded such corner shops with great affection, ever since my schoolboy days when they played a great part in my education.

They'd sell you anything at the shop that was nearest to the school I attended. You could buy one marble or one liquorice stick. Or one cigarette if you were daring enough to ask for one.

Delighted to help a customer, and with nothing else to do, the woman took the form from me and filled in all the answers in less than five minutes. This freed me from the tedium of wandering around looking for signposts, gravestones and so on. I then found a comfortable spot in a nearby wood and there I sat, ate my sandwiches and sweets and watched the birds and the squirrels (there were red ones in those far off days). When the coach returned at the prescribed time I climbed aboard and handed my form to the officer in charge.

'You're the only cadet to have all the answers right,' he told me forty five minutes later. 'You've got twice as many marks as anyone else. How did you manage that?'

'I asked the village shopkeeper to help me,' I replied with naive honesty.

The officer went puce and disqualified me for cheating.

'But you didn't say we couldn't ask for help!' I told him.

'You wouldn't have been able to ask for help if the shopkeeper had been foreign,' replied the officer. 'Not if you'd been in enemy territory.'

'But you didn't say we were in enemy territory,' I pointed out. 'And she wasn't foreign.'

'This was supposed to be an initiative test!' complained the officer bitterly. 'You've spoilt it for everyone by cheating.'

I still think I had been using my initiative.

The oddities of my ageing memory mean that although I can remember all this very well I cannot remember what triggered the memory.

30.

A well-meaning author whose name you would probably know has written to me to suggest that I might be able to sell more books if I were to follow his example. 'I always carry copies of my books in my car boot,' he said. 'Wherever I go I try to sell copies of my books to people I meet. I rarely go out of the house without selling one or two books.'

I shuddered when I read this letter. I am so shy that I cannot imagine going up to people and trying to sell them copies of my books. I have on many occasions been invited to give talks at public events such as literary festivals and been told that I can cover my expenses by having a table stocked with my books at the back of the hall. The thought makes me go cold.

Another writer once told me that he regularly visits bookshops, finds copies of his books on their shelves and offers to sign them. He says that the 'beauty' of this is that the bookshop cannot return books which have been signed. He suggested that I would sell more books if I followed his example.

I feel myself going even colder when I think of doing this.

When I was young I had books in the official bestseller lists a number of times and on a couple of occasions I succumbed to pressure and agreed to visit bookshops so that I could sign copies of my books. It was awful. I remember sitting at a desk at the front of a shop in Nottingham, Leicester or Derby with a huge pile of books in front of me while in the absence of real customers, members of the staff constantly paraded in front of me inviting me to sign books for them. Can you imagine anything worse? Bookshop signings really only work for film stars and major celebrities.

Many years ago I used to speak at literary luncheons and dinners. I remember speaking at a *Birmingham Post* literary dinner and then sitting between Arthur Marshall and Ned Sherrin, waiting for people to ask us to sign their books. The three of us spent the evening chatting and watching in astonishment as a television news reader called Jan Leeming furiously signed endless copies of one of those books that television personalities write for the Christmas market. Towards the end of the evening Arthur Marshall, Ned Sherrin and I all signed books for one another and retired to the bar, leaving Ms Leeming scribbling furiously.

31.

We went to Taunton and took with us some leftover bread for the ducks. I pride myself on being able to land a bill sized piece of bread within two feet of any selected duck within a forty foot range. This enables me to ensure that the shy and sensitive ducks are as well fed as the greedy and aggressive ones. The ducks were so hungry, we went to a nearby Morrisons supermarket and bought four large white loaves which we proceeded to tear into pieces. By the time we'd finished we were feeding around 70 ducks and nearly 20 swans (and, inevitably, a few seagulls). I half expected some jobsworth to tell us that what we were doing was illegal but none did.

February

1.

I heard today of the death of Hugo, an old chum of mine. I hadn't seen him for years. We met when we both applied for a job as house surgeon in Leamington Spa. He was the scruffiest and most accident prone person I've ever known but a kind and warm-hearted fellow. His car was so full of bits of food that I used to kid him that if he ever got stuck in snow he would be able to survive for a week on the bits of biscuit, old sweets and 'harmburger' droppings. I liked him very much. I'm sad that our lives took us apart.

As a young man he was a doctor in the RAF. I went to visit him once and he told me with considerable delight that the base where he worked was being visited by some of the RAF's senior officers. 'All the officers have to be on parade,' he said with considerable pride. Like most doctors in the armed forces Hugo had no idea how to march or stamp his feet or do any of the things that forces personnel do when they are being inspected.

'You're going to be on parade?' I asked him, hoping that I'd managed to keep the surprise out of my voice. I couldn't help noticing that his RAF uniform was stained with dried egg and brown sauce. There were clumps of cigarette ash clinging to the lapels.

'Oh yes,' he insisted. 'I'm looking forward to it.' I don't think he ever thought of himself as scruffy. He believed that just wearing a uniform made him smart.

'Don't you have to be able to march about?' I asked him, wondering if it would be possible to wangle a ticket so that I could watch. In addition to being scruffy Hugo was innately clumsy. He was the only person I knew to have cut himself putting a plaster onto someone else. He had been trying to cut a piece from a strip of sticking plaster and had nicked himself with the scissors. He also once lacerated his scalp trying to pick apples in his small orchard. Unable to reach the highest apples he put his children's trampoline under the tree and tried bouncing up and down on it so that he could grab at apples and toss them to his wife. He became increasingly angry at the fact that his wife kept dropping the apples he threw down (and therefore bruising them just as much as they had fallen naturally from the tree) and as a result he lost concentration and hit his head hard on a stout branch. He needed six stitches and told everyone at the hospital that he had hit his head on a low doorway in his local pub.

I next spoke to him a week after the RAF inspection had taken place.

'How did you get on?' I asked, hoping that he hadn't turned the wrong way, saluted with the wrong hand or buttoned up his tunic inaccurately.

'It was brilliant, absolutely brilliant!' said Hugo. 'The Group Captain wanted me to feel part of the whole thing so he put me in a plane. We flew over the airfield at 2,000 feet.'

And now he's sitting on a cloud.

When we're young we honestly believe that we're all immortal. Only if we live long enough does it ever dawn on us that we're not.

2.

I was trying to cram the contents of three sacks full of parcels into a double mouthed red post-box when an old lady (actually, to be honest, she was probably younger than I am) approached with two letters. She thrust the letters at me clearly expecting me to take them from her. With one hand I was holding a grey sack and trying to keep it off the dog shit ridden pavement and with the other hand I was feverishly feeding parcels into one of the openings. It was raining and I was keen to get the parcels out of the rain before the stamps were washed off. 'You can pop them into the other opening,' I told her, helpfully. 'What a rude man,' she snorted. 'I shall complain to the Post Office and write to the *Daily Mail*.' Still clutching her two letters she stalked off. It was only later that I realised that she must have thought that I was a Royal Mail employee. Just why she thought a postman would be busy putting mail into a post-box I do not know.

3.

The Princess and I went to an auction in Prinknash recently and, for no good reason other than that no one else wanted them, I bought a box of old postcards. I was sorting through them this afternoon when I found a card which had been written by my mother almost fifty years ago when we lived in a village called Inkpen, near Newbury. The card had been addressed to Mrs Pearce, a lovely woman in the village who used to 'do' for my parents. (What this meant, in practice, was that my mother would rush around the house with the vacuum cleaner and duster and then give Mrs P a cup of tea and a plateful of biscuits when she arrived.)

On our way home we stopped at a wonderful, old-fashioned looking country bookshop. It was the sort of shop which sells 'proper' books rather than television tie-ins; a genuine delight for those who enjoy 'previously enjoyed books'. There was a handwritten sign on the door which announced: 'Established a long time ago'. An elderly couple were arguing quietly when we went in. 'My wife keeps tidying up the books,' said the man, a genial looking fellow with gold rimmed half-moon spectacles perched precariously right on the very tip of his nose. 'I tell her that people like a bit of a jumble in a second hand bookshop – makes them think they'll find a bargain.' His wife, twice his size in width and the best part of a foot taller, looked at us, and raised an eyebrow but said nothing. We were obviously expected to comment. I hate interfering in domestic discussions. 'An organised jumble is probably best,' I said diplomatically. They both laughed and left us alone to browse. Actually, to be precise, she laughed and he chuckled. The chuckle is a rare and probably endangered beast these days (hounded out of existence by sniggers and titters) and always a pleasure to encounter. An hour later we left carrying a first edition of *Jeeves and the Feudal Spirit* by the incomparable Wodehouse in its dust-wrapper (at £7.99 it was the same price as a modern paperback), a first edition of Evelyn Waugh's *Unconditional Surrender* (again in an excellent dust wrapper) and a first edition of his *Officer and Gentleman* (again with a wrapper), and an illustrated early Edwardian edition of R. S. Surtees' books based on Ackerman's 1843 edition (the original marked price was £80 but the set had been knocked down to £18). And I bought two books by the extraordinary William le Queux. I spotted, but did not buy, a book of *Quotations by Women*. Why would anyone compile or publish a collection of quotations by women? It seemed sexist and patronising to me, as though women don't say or write things which are worth putting in a standard book of quotations.

It was a joy to spend some time in a well-stocked bookshop run by kind and warm-hearted folk. They'd been so friendly that as we left I was reminded of the contrast with a shop I once visited near to Ilfracombe. The shop was open but the proprietor, who looked to be at least 150 years old and who was standing in the doorway, wouldn't move to let me in. 'What do you want?' he demanded. 'Do you have any fiction?' I asked. 'No. No fiction,' he barked. 'Any non-fiction?' 'I don't sell non-fiction. I'm too old to sell non-fiction.' I shouldn't laugh. If I ran a bookshop I would probably be just as unwilling to part with any of the stock.

On our way back we saw a man by the side of the road digging a hole with a shovel. Four men wearing yellow jackets were standing watching, as though they had never seen anything quite like it before. They probably hadn't. We had a good view of this unusual scene as we crept past at 5 mph. There was no danger of triggering the attention of the average speed cameras. When I was a boy I used to love the *I Spy* series of books. A modern version would award at least 100 points for the sight of a workman doing something constructive by the side of the road. A few miles further on we saw a sign which said 'Slow Work Force In Road'. There was no comma after the first word. We saw a man washing traffic cones by hand. He was using a piece of rag but there was no sign of a bucket of water. Out of 29 men we counted on his stretch of road he was the only one doing anything. The rest (all 28 of them) were asleep, reading the paper, chatting on the telephone or standing chatting.

We spent so long crawling along the motorway that we took a side road, found a café and stopped for something to eat. This is something of a rarity for us. We don't like eating food which has been fondled by strangers and so we don't usually eat out. We ordered tomatoes on toast, thinking this would be fairly safe. A waiter, a waitress, two chefs, the owner and the owner's wife all stood around trying to work out how to satisfy this apparently unprecedented request. In the end they brought us each a slice of dry toast upon which lay four slices of fresh, cold tomato. The sight of this unappetising meal reminded us why we tend to eat in these days. Disappointed we decided to fill our stomachs with fluid instead. The Princess ordered a cup of Earl Grey and I requested a black coffee. The waitress seemed much more at home with the idea of serving coffee. 'Would you like a shot of expresso with water or a cup of our new filter coffee?' I said I'd try a cup of their filter coffee. 'Medium roast or full roast?' I said I thought I'd take the full roast. 'Cup or mug?' I opted for the mug. 'Medium mug or large mug?' Feeling exhausted by all the decisions I mumbled 'medium'. 'And would you like milk with your black coffee?' she asked. I looked at her and raised an eyebrow until she realised what she'd said, blushed with embarrassment, and went away.

4.

Three dogs belonging to neighbours of ours are constantly in our garden. Although they are kept as pets they are unpleasant, aggressive dogs. They bark, they threaten and, not surprisingly, perhaps, they have acquired the habit of using our lawns as a lavatory. The dogs are unwelcome visitors, their bowel-emptying habits will make cutting and strimming the lawns a deeply unpleasant task and they will frighten away, or kill, the wildlife we hope to encourage. And so we're having a fence erected all around the garden. This will cost us several thousand pounds but since our neighbours are unwilling to control their dogs there seems to be little alternative.

5.

We were woken early this morning by the birds singing. One of these days I'm going to pop outside at midnight and make as much noise as I can to wake up all the birds and let them know what it's like. There is far more noise in the countryside than most people realise. Even if you ignore the manmade sounds of chainsaw, tractor, church bells and pheasant shooting there are always noises, and silence only really comes just after a heavy snowfall. The wind rustling through leafy trees, the cooing of courting pigeons, the twittering and tweeting of the tits, the bubbling of our stream and the distant sound of a cow calling for her calf or a ewe for her lamb. In the daytime there are robins, blackbirds and finches, magpies, jays, crows and a tireless woodpecker and at night the owls seem to hoot tirelessly. We have at least three living among our trees and they call incessantly to one another. And, of course, there is the noise of the squirrels scampering across the roof. (It is a tribute to the marketing and presentational skills of squirrels that we would be a good deal more worried if it were rats we were hearing.)

A couple of decades ago, together with a friend, David Freeman, I recorded a relaxation tape. The plan was that one side of the tape would include a discussion about stress, and the need to relax by a method I called 'daydreaming', while the other side of the tape would include countryside sounds recorded by David on a piece of high tech equipment which he'd borrowed from a chum. The problem was that when we played back the countryside sounds they were anything but relaxing. Birds were calling, lambs were baaing, the wind was rustling, a nearby river was making the sound that rivers make and a distant church clock seemed to be constantly chiming. A recording made in Piccadilly Circus would have been more calming. David had to edit out the more intrusive sounds to produce a sanitised, bowdlerised version more suitable for our purposes.

6.

When the Second World War began, my Dad was in a protected occupation (he was an electrical engineer) so he resigned from his job and joined the Royal Navy. At the time he had never even seen the sea so this was a jump into the unknown with his eyes shut. Most people with a little curiosity would have slaked their thirst for knowledge by taking a day trip to the seaside and a wander along a pier. But my Dad joined the Navy. Moreover, because he wasn't allowed to join as a volunteer he had to sign up for twelve years.

In his later years he spoke often about his experiences during the War. He was as proud, or prouder, of his naval adventures as he was of the things he had invented or his successful business career. He even wrote two books about his war years. I lost count of the number of times the ships he was in were torpedoed and sank but he seemed to spend a good part of the early 1940s swimming around in the middle of the Atlantic.

Because I knew of his interest in things nautical I used to buy him books on the Navy and I still find myself spotting volumes he would have liked. Today, I found two he would have loved if the damned doctors hadn't succeeded where the Germans had failed. *The Ships of the Royal Navy,* which was published in 1942, lists all the Royal Navy's ships, and all the ships sunk up until the point of publication. The book gives the sizes, weight, guns, speed and crew details. I imagine the Germans must have bought up thousands of copies and handed them to submarine captains so that they could use them like I-Spy books and tick off the ones they'd sunk. *Warships at Work,* first published in July 17 1940, and reprinted in November of that year, contains precise details of such ships as The Hood and Repulse (our battle cruisers). The book includes precise details of the ships' armaments. The Hood, for example, had eight 15 inch guns, twelve 5.5 inch guns, eight 4 inch AA guns, four three pounders and four above water torpedo tubes. The Germans would undoubtedly have been interested to know that the armour plating over primary target areas was 15 inches thick but between 5 inches and 12 inches 'at sides amidships'. Top speed was 31 knots. I wonder how many copies of that the Nazis ordered.

I bought both books to stop them falling into enemy hands.

7.

Researchers who have spent years studying sheep have come to the conclusion that they can detect minute changes in the 'baas' other sheep make and can identify individual sheep by the sounds they produce. Shepherds have known this for years, of course. If you watch sheep and their lambs in a big field you will see mother and child finding one another by sound from some distance away. (Sheep are also able to recognise humans by their shape, face and voice and will run towards people they trust and away from strangers. One of the sheep I kept as a pet was terrified when men came to shear her. She kept running away and could not be caught. They were astonished when I called her over. She walked straight up to me and I stroked her head and talked to her while they sheared her. She was fine. Afterwards the shearers admitted that they were absolutely astonished and would not have believed it if they hadn't seen it.) When ewes are shorn and their shaggy fleeces removed their lambs are confused for a while, bewildered by the alteration in visual appearance, but they quickly recognise their mother by her smell and sound.

Sheep have an unjustified reputation for being stupid. When threatened they run away together and ill-informed observers assume that this is through stupidity. In fact, it is the opposite. Sheep have no way of defending themselves from predators other than their speed and agility. And so when they are alarmed they run. The truth is that sheep are considerably more intelligent than horses, so why do people worry about eating horses but not worry about eating sheep? Sheep can undo knots in ropes and as I have shown in previous books they have, over the years, proved themselves capable of original thought. When sheep want to escape from a pen one will stand by the wall to allow others to climb on their backs and climb over the wall. Sheep will remember where to get out of a field and know to get back in when they see someone coming.

When the Government was endeavouring to find and kill sheep because of the foot and mouth outbreak inspectors from the Ministry of Agriculture and Fisheries twice called to see if we had any sheep. The sheep knew that they had to keep quiet and so they stayed absolutely silent until the inspectors had gone. Not a baa. They didn't move. (There was no way the Government was going to kill those sheep. I had lawyers on stand by and bought two sizeable areas of land in case I needed other hiding places.)

No mentally healthy individual could eat lamb if they had ever spent any time watching sheep and their lambs. I am always appalled when I read that farmers allow their children to keep lambs as pets and then encourage them to eat them when they've been killed. No wonder farmers are such a soulless lot. Farmers say they are sad when their lambs die but this is just commercial disappointment; they breed their ewes in January and leave the lambs out in the freezing cold without any shelter. Then, when they are a few weeks old and have known a life of rain and cold, they tear them from their mothers and send them to be slaughtered. I was even more appalled when I read that teachers at a primary school had allowed children to keep a lamb which was then killed to eat. If I ever become exceedingly rich I will make a one minute film of lambs gambolling in a field in April. I will then add, at the end, a voiceover announcing: 'When you eat 'lamb', this is what you are eating'. I will then put the advertisement on television stations and broadcast it at dinnertime.

Showing respect for animals, and behaving well towards them, is a vital part of moral human behaviour. If we don't treat animals with kindness and respect how can we ever be expected to behave well in dealing with people? Our treatment of animals is an example of our society's selfish decadence.

8.

'Have I been with you longer than anyone else?' asked The Princess. 'Definitely,' I told her. 'By miles.' 'Gosh,' she said thoughtfully. 'I must be very tolerant mustn't I?' She then danced out of reach.

9.

'I have swallowed a stamp,' I said to The Princess.
    'What sort was it?'
    'One of the pound stamps that you have to lick.'

'Can you bring it up?'

'No. It's gone too far.'

We were packing books and had been doing it for six hours To be more accurate, The Princess spent six hours packing books. I spent six hours 'helping' in that unhelpful way that children 'help' their mothers when they're cooking and 'help' their fathers when they are doing stuff in their sheds. Though, I did stick on the stamps.

'Where's the book I was reading?' I asked when we'd finished. I'd stupidly put the book down and forgotten where.

After a twenty minute search among the wrapping detritus we gave up. 'I'm sorry, I must have packed it,' said The Princess.

I looked at the 140 parcels, all stamped and ready to go. One contained a copy of an Adam Hall novel.

'I'll order another copy,' I said.

This is the second time I've done this.

I wonder which reader received the surprise book this time.

10.

I was out in the garden taking a look at our new fence when a rotund, belligerent looking fellow approached. He wore green wellington boots and a Barbour gilet but had snakes tattooed on his bare arms. It struck me that he was the sort of fellow who hasn't worked out the difference between looking the part and looking a prat.

'What's that?' he demanded.

'What's what?'

'That fence thing?'

'It's a fence.'

'Why have you put that there?'

'To keep out the dogs which wander around,' I explained.

'Bloody stupid thing to do,' he snarled. 'If you don't want the dogs in your garden just send them home.'

'Not quite that easy,' I said. 'For one thing they don't take much notice of anything anyone says. And for another, I really don't want to spend my life looking out of the window and rushing outside to shout at dogs.'

'Bloody townie!' snarled the prat, storming off.

'Good fences make good neighbours,' wrote Robert Frost. Clearly, Mr Frost had never met our neighbour and our neighbour had never read Mr Frost.

11.

I fell into our pond. It was a very graceful fall, with hardly a splash. I was standing at the edge of the pond, with my boots in six inches of mud and one foot of water, trying to dig out weeds which were growing out of control. I lifted a forkful of weed and mud and, with my feet firmly anchored, the forces of action and reaction, combined with the irresistible temptations of gravity, sent me reeling very slowly backwards. I knew what was happening but could do absolutely nothing to stop myself falling. Both feet were fixed as though in concrete. It took me several minutes of splashing to free myself from the pond's clutches. It occurred to me as I fell that I am probably too long in the tooth to be playing in water and mud.

12.

I told The Princess that I was feeling tired.

'You don't think you could have leukaemia do you?' she asked. 'Are you breathless, does your spleen hurt?' She rapidly reeled off all the possible symptoms of leukaemia.

I was impressed and told her so. 'How come you know so much about leukaemia?'

'I'm a hypochondriac,' she reminded me with a shrug. 'I've had leukaemia dozens and dozens of times.'

The Princess was not exaggerating.

I believe she knows more than most doctors and all nurses about medical ailments. And she is forever checking for signs of illness. She doesn't suffer from high blood pressure but nevertheless she keeps a sphygmomanometer on her dressing table so that she can check her blood pressure and pulse at regular intervals. She loves pharmacies like I love bookshops and stationery shops.

13.

We are still finding the tradesmen we need to do work on our house in the Cotswolds. The search has, inevitably perhaps, become something of a nightmare. In the 18th century it was believed that the commonest cause of madness was moving into a new house. I suspect that is still true but these days the mad days don't end when the boxes are unloaded from the removal van. There are a number of generic problems. First, no one ever writes anything down any more. One builder who came to give a quote walked round with us and nodded emphatically every time we pointed out some work that needed doing. He didn't make a single note. I assumed that he must have been a waiter in a Parisian café and acquired a phenomenal memory. I was wrong about that. His quote, when it came, missed out most of the work we wanted doing and included a good deal that we didn't want doing. The second problem is that, thanks to Mr Berners-Lee's wretched invention it is now fairly easy for tradesmen to find out how much we paid for our house. They then adjust their quote accordingly. It seems that means-testing has hit the private sector. The third problem is that builders in the Cotswolds are very picky about what they will and won't do. We invited two painters to give a quote for painting our rather large Victorian greenhouse. The first wouldn't walk up the garden to look at it because it was raining. And the second shook his head and turned the job down because 'there's a lot of glass, a lot of narrow bits of wood and it's quite high isn't it'. He also confessed that he didn't like the smell of the fumes paint gives off. 'Why did you pick that one?' I asked The Princess. 'He had a lovely advertisement in the local paper,' she replied. 'It had flowers round the border.' One tradesman (who described himself in his advertisement as a multidisciplinary consultant) graced us with a consultation (to see if he could fit us into his busy schedule) but warned us that he didn't do anything requiring power tools because he hadn't got any, that he didn't work overtime, weekends, Thursdays or during the Cheltenham Festival, that he didn't do plumbing or electrics and that he didn't work after dark in the winter. The fourth problem is that Godot arrives more speedily and reliably than builders in the Cotswolds. Waiting for them to turn up is enervating. When tradesmen enter your life you are always waiting. Waiting for them to quote, waiting for them to turn up, waiting for them to come back and waiting for them to finish. And, naturally, since we live in an out-of-the-way spot, they always get lost. And when, after two or three telephone calls, they do arrive they moan endlessly about the difficulties they've had. Few things in life are as rare or as welcome as a competent, friendly, reasonably priced workman who brings his own flask of tea, turns off his mobile telephone and has a capacious bladder. I have learned two things about builders. The first is that one should never allow them to get on first name terms with you. They all go to a special training school where they are taught to get on first name terms with their customers. It's much harder to refuse requests for pots of tea and platefuls of sandwiches when they call you by your Christian name. The second thing I've learned is that there is no point in getting upset with them when they do silly things. Builders all have their brains removed at birth by a secret Government department which prepares babies for work in the building trade. One lot of builders The Princess and I once hired finished painting the outside of a house and then announced that they were going to remove a lintel which needed replacing. When I asked why they hadn't replaced the lintel before doing the painting they stared at me as if I were entirely mad. I honestly believe that if builders found themselves with a supply of gloss paint but no undercoat they would apply the gloss paint and put on the undercoat later.

14.

We've now acquired a new problem. Dog walkers who drive down our lane to take their dogs into the woods are using the car parking space outside our house. We came back from the shops and, having unloaded the car, were unable to park. This is the third time it's happened in the last ten days. The only answer is to get the fencing people back to put up a couple of white poles and a 'No Parking' sign. I hate having to do this but I really cannot think of any alternative.

15.

Three men turned up to erect a garden shed which we have bought from a garden centre. It took them all day and when they had finished one of them, the leader, handed me a huge bag of screws. 'Do you want these?' he asked. Puzzled, I accepted the bag. 'They're left over,' he said, hurrying off to his new Audi. He'd told us earlier that he and his girlfriend were off to New York for a few days. When they'd gone I discovered that they had fastened the shed together with staples. I spent two hours putting in some of the leftover screws.

16.

One of our new neighbours is a foreigner and like all foreigners he desperately wants to be mistaken for an Englishman. And why wouldn't he? This one wears a hacking jacket and plus fours. I expect he would wear plus sixes if he could find them anywhere. But, sadly, our neighbour will always be a foreigner. Foreigners don't understand this but the English are never foreign, wherever they might be. When he is abroad an Englishman is merely an Englishman abroad. Foreigners may become British but they can never become English.

Our neighbour will never be English, or even pass for English, not simply because he will never ever master the nuances of our language but because he doesn't understand the first thing about our nation.

The English are a mass of contradictions. We always respect the underdog, we believe that emotions are for foreigners and women and we always play by the rules (as long as we made them in the first place) but we don't like being told what to do. We can be the most polite people on the planet but also the rudest. We believe in moderation in all things except things we enjoy and we have an unmatched ability to put up with discomfort. We have a sense of humour which marries irony with the absurd. Only the English could have selected as their patron saint a man who was not a saint, not English, not a dragon killer and not really called George. We are proud of the fact that our weather and our plumbing have always been more full of surprises than anyone else's. We are proud of our stiff upper lip and our ability to hide our feelings but although we don't like making scenes in public we are perfectly happy to make fools of ourselves if the time seems appropriate. We are stoic, unpredictable, modest and creative. We invented all the sports the world has ever known but never bothered about being particularly good at any of them. We believe that showing off is unacceptable, we apologise for things which aren't our fault and we say please and thank you without ever really meaning either. We say things like 'We've had a wonderful time', 'We must do this again soon' and 'We will speak later' without meaning any of them. We ask people how they are and are shocked and dismayed if they have the effrontery to tell us. We are never happier than when forming a queue but we despise people who stand in line. The English class struggle is never between people in different classes but always between people within the same class (just as those in campaigning societies will always fight one another with far more ferocity than they fight the people they are supposed to be opposing) and we regard foreigners in the same generous way that we regard dogs, cats and budgerigars.

How can foreigners ever understand any of this?

I realise that some of this may sound a little patronising but it isn't meant to be. The big problem is that foreigners are, well, foreign and nothing can be done about that. The other problem is that there are so many of them. Foreigners are no laughing matter these days. Because they breed incessantly there are more of them than the English and they can be found in vast quantities absolutely everywhere

17.

This morning, while clearing out a filing cabinet, I found an old letter from an American nursing magazine asking me to help them set up a Medical Olympics in the United States of America. The request was inspired by a spoof I wrote for *Nursing Times* in which I described how doctors and nurses in England had organised and taken part in a Medical Olympics. Events included such delights as throwing the syringe and needle, bandaging contests and tossing the gallstone. The Americans thought all this had really happened, were desperate to organise their own version and wanted to hire me as a consultant to help them set things up. Unfortunately, I can't find my reply.

I've been involved in several dozen spoofs over the years. I put out a press release once reporting that an entirely imaginary golf course in Devon had installed under-course heating so that players would never again have to worry about bad weather interfering with their play. Several publications printed that one. When cigarette companies were allowed to issue coupons with their product I hoaxed several national newspapers by reporting that one company was offering heavy smokers a chance to have a State funeral. A story that major football clubs were transferring supporters as well as players was printed on the sports pages of several newspapers. When I worked for a radio station in Birmingham I performed open heart surgery live on air, explaining all the time what I was doing. The idea was that listeners could perform the same operation at home. The broadcast was stopped when a senior station official burst into the studio in terror. I spoofed numerous West Country newspapers by reporting that the hill path between Lynton and Lynmouth in Devon was being used by our Winter Olympics team as a practice toboggan run. I also once persuaded several publications that the Open University was conducting a medical degree course and that students could take delivery of a dead body at their homes so that they could study for their anatomy examinations in their kitchen. And I wrote a book on aphrodisiacs which included much material (particularly about the aphrodisiacal qualities of chocolate) which I made up but which seems to have been accepted as fact and is now widely quoted in magazine and newspaper articles.

But my favourite spoof concerned the golf club in Westward Ho!. I was a member at the time and became increasingly irritated by the heavy-handed rules about acceptable clothing which kept appearing on the notice board. The Princess and I crept into the clubhouse one evening and put the following notices on the notice board.

1. Shorts and Hairy Legs

Men who insist on wearing shorts (and who, therefore, risk being punished by the security guards) must have their legs shaved. Men who wear shorts and exhibit hairy legs will be punished. Their legs will then be shaved before they are allowed back into the club house.

Your alternative committee would like to make it clear that it considers men with hairy legs to be a horrid sight.

2. Clothing Rules for Women Members

A number of regulations have recently been introduced for male members. In order to ensure that the club complies with Sexual Discrimination Laws your Alternative Committee has decided to introduce new dress code regulations for women members. The following items of clothing will, in future, not be allowed: tweed skirts, trousers (of any kind), skirts which go below the knee, jumpers or sweaters, tights, socks, boots, girdles and sensible shoes. The following items of clothing will be allowed: stockings (compulsory), micro-skirts, see-through blouses, skin tight tops (with lots of cleavage showing), PVC/Rubber wear (must be skin tight), peephole bras (especially worn with see-through blouses), thigh length boots and high heeled shoes.

Women will not be allowed into the clubhouse if not wearing make-up. Women who take size 18 and over will only be allowed to play golf during the hours of darkness and then by prior arrangement with the committee.

Not surprisingly, the Committee immediately launched an enquiry in an attempt to find out which member had dared to place these spoof notices on the notice board. They never did find out, though various newspapers (including *The Times*) reported the story of the spoof clothing requirements and the club's response. Most committees have a collective IQ slightly lower than the IQ of the most stupid member and this particular committee included one individual who had the IQ of a pickled walnut.

The Princess and I resigned from the club a little while later. We told the secretary that we didn't want to be members of a golf club which had attracted such notoriety.

18.

The elderly lady in front of us at the till in WHSmith's was holding two magazines and a small bar of chocolate. The two magazines were both shrink wrapped. She was frail and walked with a stick which she clearly needed. Her clothes were threadbare but neat. The cashier scanned the three items and told the elderly lady the price. She blushed and looked embarrassed. 'The magazines are free,' she said nervously. She pointed a shaky finger at the word 'free' which was printed in huge letters at the top of both magazines. 'There's a free catalogue with each magazine,' said the assistant impatiently. 'You have to pay for them. Do you want them or not?' The old lady fumbled with her purse, looked at the price on the till, looked back at the magazines and, with regret, shook her head. 'No thank you,' she said. She apologised, paid for her small bar of chocolate and shuffled away. 'I'll take the two magazines,' said The Princess, picking up the two magazines the old lady had left, and adding them to our own purchases. She paid for everything and then hurried after the old lady. 'Excuse me,' she said. 'I just bought these by mistake but then realised that I already have copies at home. It seems a pity to throw them away. Would you like them?' The old lady's face lit up. 'Are you sure?' she asked. 'You'll be doing me a favour,' said The Princess.

19.

Cloud computing is the new hula hoop. The new Bakelite radio. The new doll that wets itself. I cannot believe that human beings with brains are having anything to do with this nonsense. The cloud involves storing data remotely via the internet and in fact there is nothing new about it since people have been doing this for years. (Interestingly, I was reading William Haggard's novel *The Antagonists* recently and noticed that he used the word 'net' to describe a system used for sharing communications back in 1964.) Even Steve Wozniak, the technical genius behind Apple (Steve Jobs was the marketing genius) thinks the cloud is a disaster waiting to happen. 'I want my work in progress where I can see it and secure it.' The cloud is as useless and as reliable as a Scottish bank. Those who use it will find that people they don't know (and probably wouldn't like and certainly wouldn't trust) can capture all their private information and will be able to steal and deface everything they write. Mind you, I also believe that anyone who uses internet banking either needs counselling, or will need it later when they find that their bank account has been emptied by a band of 14-year-old Romanian hackers who have spent all the money on sweets and computer games.

20.

Our insurance company has told us that they will no longer insure us. Someone in the company's offices recognised my name. 'You have written books which sell on the internet,' said a 17-year-old girl somewhere in Asia. 'You are too famous.'

21.

The fencing people have put up our 'No Parking' sign and erected three thin, white posts. Our hope is that this will make it clear that our car park isn't just a piece of scrap land, available to anyone who wants to use it.

22.

At the start of our journey to Paris this morning, the Princess sat on a railway station bench waiting for a First Great Western train driver to find his way to the station. An old man in a shabby suit sat down next to us. He was carrying an old-fashioned leather carrier bag which he placed carefully on the bench next to him.

'My wife is coming home today,' he told us. 'She's been to see her relatives.' He paused. 'Sickness in the family,' he added. 'First time we've been apart.'

'You've obviously missed her,' said The Princess.

'Oh yes,' said the old man.

There was then a silence for a while. The station announcer told us that the train we were expecting would be another fifteen minutes. And she thanked us for our patience and understanding. They usually do. The phrase annoys me more than the delay.

'She's a lovely girl,' he said. 'Sprightly. A lovely dancer. We used to dance all the time. She moves like a dancer. Doesn't look her age.' He took out a large handkerchief and blew his nose. 'She has lovely hair,' he said. 'Brunette.'

I assumed that he must have married someone much younger than himself.

We sat together, the three of us, for a little longer and then the train pulled alongside the platform. The Princess and I stood up, ready to board. We said goodbye to the old man. He had now taken a small bouquet of garden flowers out of his shopping bag. He was holding it in his right hand.

As we boarded I looked back and watched as the old man watched his wife get down from the train. She was about his age and had grey hair; it was almost white. She moved with great difficulty, as though she had bad arthritis in both hips. They moved slowly towards each other. He touched her cheek. They kissed. He gave her the flowers and took from her the small blue case she was carrying. She admired the flowers and linked her arm with his. They then hobbled off slowly towards the exit.

23.

The French always honour their great men by naming streets, buildings and Metro stations after them. Walking around Paris it's impossible to avoid the name of Felix Faure who not only has more streets named after him than anyone else but also has his very own Metro station. He even has a requiem, of course. A little investigation in our collection of French history books shows that Faure was a successful industrialist who became President of the French Third Republic until his death in office. In the formal history books his death is simply described as 'sudden'. But the less formal books report that he died seated at his official desk wearing a frock coat and a high starched collar. Nothing unusual so far. But he wasn't studying affairs of State. Just before he died he had a naked girl between his legs and his hands were caressing her head. When he reached orgasm he had a heart attack and died with his fingers fastened in her hair. The poor girl could only be released by having some hair cut off. When the news hit the streets Felix Faure immediately became a national hero. Citizens who had regarded him without much affection immediately clutched him to their collective bosom. And Faure became the best remembered politician in French history.

There is no doubt that the French are different to the rest of us.

As we wandered around we couldn't help noticing that Paris is looking unusually scruffy these days. At the Louvre the water feature beside the glass Pyramid has broken and looks dreary and very worn. At the Beaubourg Centre (aka the Pompidou Centre) the massive forecourt, which was originally intended as an arena for jugglers, fire eaters and musicians now smells of urine and the entertainers have all gone, driven away by health and safety regulations.

Still, there are always unusual delights for those who keep their eyes about them. Outside the cathedral of Notre Dame we watched a Chinese tourist guide walk briskly along while holding up a closed, red umbrella as a beacon for her flock. The trouble was that she had no flock. She only noticed that she was alone when she stopped to give her next abbreviated lecture. Horrified, she realised that she was quite alone. A pied-piper with no children following her. Only after a momentary panic and a frantic five minute search did she discover that they were mistakenly but innocently following another tourist guide, this one Japanese, who was using a similar red umbrella as a guiding beacon. This accidental confusion reminded me of a day in London when a medical student friend of mine used a similar device to hijack a flock of 36 assorted American tourists. He took them for miles through Soho and abandoned them in a rather seedy area. Since there were no mobile telephones in those days they probably had quite a job getting back in touch with their leader. On the upside they probably saw a part of London that they might otherwise have missed.

And just a short distance from home we spotted a pub called 'Au Bureau'. In England I know of pubs called 'The Library', 'The Potting Shed' and 'The Surgery' so it's good to know that the French have caught on to this piece of mild trickery.

24.

There are many, many things about which I know next to nothing. An alphabetical list would begin with astronomy, beekeeping and campanology and end with yachting and zoology. My ignorance is extensive and, as the world acquires new information, my ignorance enlarges hour by hour. By the end of every day I know less, as a percentage of man's knowledge, than I knew when I had breakfast.

But in order to keep my brain topped up to the brim with knowledge I keep a notebook in which I jot down curious bits and pieces of information. Here are a dozen (admittedly not entirely useful) things I've learned this week:

1. Che Guevera was rhythm and tone deaf. He could be seen dancing a mambo while everyone else was dancing a tango. No one ever told him. (Well, would you tell Che he was dancing the wrong dance?)

2. When Queen Victoria spotted pieces of lavatory paper floating in the river Thames she asked an aide what they were. She was told that the bits of paper were small printed notices telling her subjects that swimming wasn't allowed. It's also true that Victoria famously did not believe that lesbianism existed. And she signed a reprieve for a woman accused of having sex with a dog - on the grounds that despite the evidence she simply didn't believe it could possibly have happened. A sweet lady and a great monarch.

3. When men toasted a lady's health in ancient Rome they would drink one glass for each letter of the woman's name.

4. The gate posts of country houses often have stone balls balanced on top. They are there because in ancient times it was the custom of the victors in battle to decorate their doorposts with the skulls of the vanquished. The stone balls are there as a civilised representation of the skulls.

5. Charlie Chaplin once came second in a Charlie Chaplin look-alike competition. Graham Greene once came second in a competition to 'write like Graham Greene'. (In Greene's case the winner was his brother, the then Director General of the BBC).

6. A Mr Thomas Wedgewood, who was a friend of Coleridge's, suffered from restlessness and irritability. He opened a butcher's shop in the belief that the affronts and disputes to which he would inevitably be exposed might be beneficial to his health.

7. Wallpaper was banned by Oliver Cromwell who regarded it as frivolous.

8. An oyster's heart continues to beat for half an hour after it has been swallowed.

9. Isadora Duncan's death is well documented (her scarf caught in a car wheel) but her husband's is less well known. Duncan was married to the Russian poet Serge Essenin who cut the veins in his wrist and wrote a farewell poem in his own blood.

10. In February 1912 Britain's Committee of Imperial Defence, an organisation set up to advise on the military strategy of the British Empire, was staggered to hear the chairman of Lloyds testify that if German ships were sunk by the Royal Navy, Lloyds would be honour bound, and legally obliged, to cover the losses.

11. 'Just what the doctor ordered' was an advertising slogan for a brand of cigarettes in the 1950s.
12. When Ian Fleming, the creator of James Bond, was told by his doctor to give up drinking he talked his physician to allow him one drink a day. After the doctor had agreed that Fleming could have one fluid ounce of alcohol each day the novelist did some research and found that Green Chartreuse contains the most alcohol per ounce. And so that was what he drank for the rest of his life. One fluid ounce of Green Chartreuse per day.

25.

Pigeons are as much a part of any city as the people and maybe they have just as much a right to live there. Do they do harm? Of course they do. They defile buildings and vehicles (and occasionally pedestrians) and they undoubtedly carry some diseases. But they contribute a great deal too. They add life and companionship for many who would otherwise be alone. Personally, I find dogs an infinitely greater hazard than pigeons and no one has yet had the temerity to suggest banning the walking or feeding of dogs in cities.

From time to time The Princess and I are told off for feeding the pigeons. Irate citizens shout at us and berate us. The law is doubtless on their side for I understand that, as it is in London, it is now against the law to feed the birds in Paris.

Outside, in the parks, our excuse is that we aren't feeding the birds but that we are simply messy eaters. But it is more difficult to make the same argument when we feed the pigeons from our top floor apartment. We feed them when they land on the ledge below our windows. In the mornings the pigeons gather on the ledge of the building across the street and, when they consider it breakfast time, go to our bedroom window (the one with the shutters drawn) and coo. If there is no response to that then they move to another window and peck loudly on the glass. They are noisier than an alarm clock, though they like to be fed before I would normally like to get up. As soon as they hear movement inside the apartment they flock to the window from which I usually feed them and the sparrows which follow. When they have finished feeding the birds all return to the ledge across the street to chat and dance and court and do what pigeons do to while away the morning.

Last night another resident in our building, a tenant of a lower apartment, banged on our door and protested about our feeding the pigeons. She had a fierce face that looked as if it had known much anger. Unlike many continental women she was pretty well clean shaven though this was probably a result of her having invested in a small shaving device. As she berated me she became almost hysterical. I smiled at her and said: 'I don't understand but thank you for the invitation.' I spoke in English as I often do when I don't want to be understood. I find that the ploy works well in both France and England. I then shut the door. Unfortunately, this move was not entirely successful for the pigeon hater returned ten minutes later with an interpreter.

'You want me to feed the pigeons more often?' I asked, deliberately misunderstanding the protest. When it became impossible to pretend not to understand any longer I shook my head and nodded and tutted and agreed wholeheartedly with his objection to the feeding of the pigeons. 'We were feeding the wild parrots of Paris,' I explained. 'We had heard that there are many rare and beautiful parrots in this wonderful city.' I shrugged. 'But, sadly, only pigeons came.'

Our callers went away desperately confused but I have no doubt that they will, like the television licence gestapo, return.

The Princess reminded me that much the same thing happened a few months ago when a caller berated me for feeding the pigeons. On that occasion I shook my head and told her we didn't want cable television, thank you very much. When we went downstairs the next day and opened the front door the angry woman was looking out of her window. She glowered at us. With appalling timing the pigeons that had been waiting on the ledge across the street saw us and reacted instantly. The credibility of my obfuscation faded a little in believability when we were immediately surrounded by a crowd of delighted pigeons who had decided that here, perhaps, was a chance to say 'thank you' and maybe enjoy a little mid-morning snack. We walked briskly away up the street, followed closely by a cooing cloud of noisy birds.

26.

Friends of ours who live in the north of England are moving house so we sent a postcard to their new address in the Lake District. I wrote the card and put 'Sir and Lady...' before their names. 'Why have you put that?' asked The Princess. I explained that postmen always read postcards and that when their local fellow saw the title he would be bound to tell all the neighbours. 'There will be much fawning and lending of cups of sugar,' I pointed out. 'They will be warmly welcomed to the bosom of their new community.'

27.

We headed back to England.

The Gare du Nord in Paris used to be an exciting and romantic railway station. No more. Catching a train there today is something of a nightmare. There is never room for a taxi to park and so our driver simply stops in the middle of the road. We have to get out, thrust notes into his hand, grab our baggage and then dodge through the traffic and the Romanian beggars to the pavement. On the pavement there are more beggars. They guard the entrance like stony faced militants on a picket line. The only difference is that these pickets jostle and pick pockets. (Paris is now the world centre for pickpockets. They are as skilful as they are shameless. The other day The Princess had her bag opened inside the cathedral of Notre Dame.) The beggars are all graduates of the International School of Begging. They whine, roll their eyes, hold up their borrowed babies, point to their rented dogs and hold out grubby hands. They invariably carry small pieces of crumpled cardboard which contain a message in English. (They only attack the English. Foreigners just boot them out of the way.) The Princess recently learnt a few words in Romanian and these days I leave the beggars to her. I don't know what she says to them but they smile, bow their heads and back away so it must be something good and obviously isn't just 'piss off'.

Inside the station, which now appears to be run by a committee with absolutely no common sense, there are queues galore. There's a queue to pass through the ticket barrier. There is a queue to pass the French customs post. (This is laughable. The Princess and I once mistakenly went through this one holding each other's passports. The official on duty let The Princess through on my passport and allowed me through on hers.) And then there's a queue to get past the British passport officials (who are ruder and more arrogant than the worst doctors' receptionists) and finally there is French baggage security. Baggage and coats must be placed on the usual filthy dirty conveyor belt and then collected at the other end. The officials hired to look at the X-ray pictures are usually chatting and looking the other way. You could get a suitcase packed with rocket launchers past them. Everything is made much worse by the fact that the French seem incapable of travelling light. They firmly believe that it is possible to 'get away from it all' but when they go to the country or the seaside they take it all with them.

28.

I read an interview with one of our Olympic athletes. I see that in her 'team' (everyone worth their salt has a 'team' these days) she has two coaches, a physiotherapist, a soft tissue therapist (I wonder if this is what used to be a masseur?), a bio mechanist, a psychologist, a physiologist and an agent. She doubtless has a manager, an accountant and a tax adviser too.

Ah, even I can remember the days of amateur athletics. I remember working as a postman one year when I was still at school and finding that an Olympic runner was also delivering letters. I was told he was earning extra money by running round the streets of Walsall delivering Christmas cards so that he could compete in the Olympics.

The Olympic movement has become absurdly expensive and self-important. The 1948 London Olympics cost £750,000 and the athletes were, of course, amateurs. Allowing for inflation that works out at about £23 million in today's money. The original budget for the 2012 Olympics was £2 billion and the final cost was considerably more than £10 billion - not counting the billions of pounds worth of volunteer labour. An astonishing £270 million was spent building a swimming pool. How on earth can a pool cost that much money? You dig a big hole, tile it and fill it with water. There's the pool. You then add a few plastic seats around the sides so that very keen relatives can sit and be bored witless for hours on end. What did they spend the other £269 million on?

When it's all over the athletes who won medals will expect gongs from the Queen. Win a gold medal and you get a knighthood. Win a bronze and you get an MBE. What nonsense all this is. This was all fine in the days when athletes were amateurs and were winning medals for their country. Today's athletes run and throw things for a living. And to be honest it's a pretty easy life. They are paid hugely well by the taxpayers and those who win can make millions out of advertising foods that rot teeth and cause heart disease. (Would anyone really be surprised if eating competitions, sponsored by a well-known chain of 'harmburger' restaurants, were introduced into the Olympics?) For all the talk about 'stress' and 'pressure' those who enjoy sport for a living have a pretty easy time of it. Running, jumping and throwing things are just hobbies that have got out of control. Those who can make a living out of doing these things are damned lucky. I don't see why they should expect to be honoured as well as paid.

Mind you, I don't see why civil servants, pop singers and industrialists should be honoured either. Most do what they do because it's a way of making money. They do it for themselves. They don't shuffle paper, make records or build widgets for their country's sake. Today's honour system is as absurd as the one which rewarded pirates and harlots with honours and huge estates.

Honours should be distributed only to people who do things to help their community and their country and who don't get paid for what they do. Volunteers and campaigners deserve to be honoured. Swimmers, cyclists and people who row boats for a living don't deserve anything other than a bit of plated metal.

MARCH

1.

Three weeks ago a woman who lives in Canada wrote and complained that she had been sent a catalogue for my books but that she had never heard of me and wasn't interested in any of my work. When The Princess checked she found that the woman had bought three copies of *Alice's Diary* and that we had received a letter from her telling me that *Alice's Diary* was her very favourite book. However, because my name doesn't appear on *Alice's Diary* as the author (we like to suggest that Alice herself wrote the book) the woman had no idea that I had written it. Because her letter praising *Alice's Diary* had been so fulsome I sent back a note explaining the situation. Today I received an indignant letter from the woman. She agreed that she had bought and enjoyed copies of Alice's books but said that she was very cross that I was pretending to have written them. 'These books are clearly written by Alice herself,' wrote the woman. 'If I hear again that you are claiming to have written her books I will report you to the authorities.' She didn't say which authorities. We gave up and deleted her name and address from our simple database.

I received two other letters relating to *Alice's Diary* this morning.

The second letter was from a reader who said: 'On the inside front flap of the dust cover you claim that *Alice's Diary* contains 'an insight into what its really like to be a cat' but this is a gross error and entirely unacceptable.' She rightly pointed out that its should have been spelt it's. This reminds me that last month I received yet another letter complaining that there is a grammatical error somewhere in the book. 'I realise that the book is written by a cat,' complained the letter writer. 'But that doesn't excuse bad grammar.' I refuse to change a word of *Alice's Diary*. Since she died many years ago it does not seem right to fiddle with her grammar without being able to obtain her permission. Before I tossed the letter into the bin I wrote back to say that most people are impressed that a cat was able to write a book at all - and that they were, therefore, prepared to overlook the occasional grammatical slip.

The third letter was from a woman offering to ghost write more Alice books for me. 'I could do much better illustrations than you have at present,' she added.

2.

At a bookshop in Nailsworth I bought a huge collection of old magazines from the early part of the 1900s up until the 1950s. The magazines included *Lilliput, John Bull* and *Everybodys*. It's fascinating to see just how good the articles were in those days. For example, *Everybodys* was very much a mass market magazine but, in addition to all the usual magazine 'furniture' (crosswords and letter page) the contents of the February 2nd edition of 1952 included: an article about the economy entitled *Who Will Wield The New Axe?,* an article *When Royalty Flies* (describing the aircraft used by H.M. the Queen), a piece about humorous barristers, a description of an actress Wagner had loved, *Quo Vadis* (the serialisation of a book by Henryk Sienkiewicz), an article about baboons entitled *Funny Old men of the Kopjes* and a piece entitled *On the Field of the Cloth of Gold* (a description of the rivalry between Henry VIII of England and Francis I of France). There were articles entitled *Tavern of the Seas (a history of Cape Town and Table Mountain), Two Toms and a Joe* (a biographical piece about Wordsworth and the two poets called Warton). Finally, there was a piece headed *Down Dimbleby's Way* (about television), an article headed *Old Buddha* (about China's last empress), a beautifully illustrated piece called *Beware of the Horse* (about thoroughbreds who were dangerous and difficult to ride) and an article about sport called *Football Immortals,* written by the cricket legend John Arlott. These were all long articles (1500-2000 words on average). All that for just four old pennies.

3.

We both jumped out of our skins at midnight as the silence of a moonless night was shattered by a series of violent explosions. Since we have no near neighbours and there are no passers-by at night we don't bother to draw the curtains so we peeped out through the living room window to see if we were being attacked by terrorists firing rocket launchers, noisy burglars announcing their arrival or little green men saying hello.

Fireworks.

It wasn't a bad display. There were some spectacular rockets, showering multi-coloured sparks across the sky, and after a few minutes silence was resumed.

This morning I was putting out our black bags for the rubbish collector to pick up (we live in such an inaccessible spot that there is no room for wheelie bin collecting vehicles and so we are excused rubbish sorting) when Baskerville, one of our distant dog-owning neighbours, drove by in his gleaming limousine. He slowed down, lowered the passenger side window and looked across at me. 'Hope my firework celebrations didn't annoy you!' he said, clearly hoping that they had.

I looked puzzled and shook my head. 'You must have bought the quiet ones,' I said. 'That was very kind of you.' I thought for a moment. 'I suppose it's only the big expensive ones that make a lot of noise.'

'Mine made a hell of a lot of noise!' he insisted. 'They were the best you can buy. Professional quality.'

'Were you celebrating a special birthday?' I asked, feigning interest. 'For a fireworks display I suppose it must have been one with a nought at the end. Gosh it wasn't your 70th was it?'

'Seventy!' he protested indignantly. 'Do I look 70?'

I leant forward and examined him closely. 'A youngish 70.'

'It was my 60th!' he snarled. He put his foot down and sped off up the lane, skidding on the loose gravel in a frost damaged stretch of tarmacadam and scraping the side of his beloved motor car on an untidy branch. He slowed, almost to a stop, and I could see him trying to decide whether to get out or not. And then he speeded up again and disappeared into the distance.

I love teasing the neighbours but Baskerville is such an easy target that he really isn't much fun.

4.

Some director in America is making a film version of Sherlock Holmes with a woman playing the lead. Inevitable. She will be known as Shirley Holmes. The Princess and I spent a jolly few minutes thinking of other classic stories the Americans might spoil. We came up with *Romeo and Julian, Jim Eyre, Monsieur Bovary, Larry Doone, Marvin Poppins* and *Mr Marple*.

We won't be watching the Shirley Holmes film. But we are currently re-watching the old Basil Rathbone and Nigel Bruce films. We're working our way through the series. Rathbone and Bruce were the greatest of chums in real life (Rathbone was terribly cut up when Bruce died) and just as screen chemistry works between a male and female star so it is needed between Holmes and Watson. With Rathbone and Bruce the friendship seals the screen partnership. Never before or since have there been two more quintessential Englishmen who weren't born in England. Rathbone was born in South Africa and Bruce was born in Mexico, though only because his parents just happened to be on holiday there when he arrived. The series stopped when Bruce died. Rathbone, who hated Holmes for a long while, refused to make any more without his friend Nigel beside him. (Rathbone, now remembered mainly for his Holmes, made a goodly number of excellent films. He was the Sherriff of Nottingham to Errol Flynn's Robin Hood and always claimed that he could have beaten Errol Flynn in a fair swordfight. He probably could have too. He must have fought more onscreen swordfight battles than any other star - even including Douglas Fairbanks Jr - and was forced by circumstances and plot to lose all but one of them. And Bruce, of course, played one of the cricket mad buffoons in Hitchcock's *The Lady Vanishes*. No man ever played buffoons with more honest enthusiasm.)

Watson, not Holmes, was of course Doyle's greatest invention. (Though, I think Mrs Hudson is pretty important too.) Just about every detective writer now uses the same trick of having an assistant or amanuensis - someone the great man (or woman) can tell what is happening, someone to record the great man's work and someone to listen with admiration while the great man explains what has happened. Even cowboys have their Watsons. Where would Hopalong Cassidy, the Range Rider, Kit Carson or the Lone Ranger be without their Dr Watsons? (If the Scots get too uppity about Doyle it is, of course, possible to argue that Watson is merely a reincarnation of Daniel Defoe's Man Friday.) Watson was Doyle's genius.

Doyle, who was, in real life, prone to say things like 'the game's afoot' when involved in adventurous activities, was a rare man: a man who had more than one flash of genius. His second flash of genius was of course in creating Mycroft - Sherlock's cleverer brother. The creators of *Frazier,* the spin off series from *Cheers,* seemed to me to do something similar by creating Niles, the even pottier psychiatrist brother of Frazier. And the third flash of genius was creating Moriaty, the recurring nemesis, the hater of all things Holmes. 'Holmes the meddler, Holmes the traitor, Holmes the lickspittle.'

Rathbone *was* Sherlock Holmes. He even looked like the illustrations in the early *Strand* stories. The only possible competition for Rathbone and Bruce might have come from Peter Cushing and Roger Livesey.

But Jeremy Brett was the most entertaining Holmes. He played Holmes as though he were acting on stage, ideally something pantoesque in the Edwardian era, and he played the Great Detective, variously, as gay, vain, and mad. He was constantly posing and trying, in vain, of course, to capture the famous and inimitable Rathbone profile. (Rathbone was once described by Dorothy Parker as two profiles pasted together). Brett started his 40 odd episodes sensibly but was wildly and was gloriously over the top before the end, by the time he was so ill that he had to sit in a wheelchair between takes. (One big mistake was when he walked arm in arm with Watson down Baker Street. Two men walking down the street like that in Victorian times would have attracted a crowd of small boys and a good many rotten tomatoes.) Brett took Holmes to new heights and it always seems to me that the directors must have told all the other actors to play it straight and to leave Jeremy to play the part as though he were playing the bad Baron in a version of Cinderella in Cleethorpes.

The Princess and I agree that the series Brett made for Granada suffered from the two Watsons. They're workmanlike but the truth is that I feel that Brett needed a more dramatic Watson. Basil Rathbone played Sherlock Holmes straight and without emotion but his version would not have been anywhere near as good without Bruce to play the buffoon with such zest. Brett needed someone with more oomph. Ray McNally or Michael Gambon would have both played Watson with tremendous strength and given Brett's Holmes more verisimilitude.

Conan Doyle was many things (it is not widely known but he introduced skiing to Switzerland) but he was primarily a plotsman and his characters do tend to be rather thin occasionally. Jeremy Brett was warned by his close friend Robert Stephens (who played Holmes in a rather curious film made by Billy Wilder) that he shouldn't try to play Holmes because everyone who had done so had had a breakdown (except Rathbone). The problem was that Holmes was never a clearly defined person (in modern parlance there was no 'back story') and Brett, like many previous actors, ended up putting too much of himself into the part. (With the result that occasionally viewers were treated to a surprisingly fey, not to say gay, detective.)

Producers will doubtless keep making versions of Sherlock Holmes for as long as there are actors and audiences. There will, undoubtedly, be politically correct directors who want to portray Holmes as a black, wheelchair bound lesbian and Ms Watson as her lover. But there will be good versions too. Robert Downey Jr has made two excellent editions. Downey Jr seems to us to be much like Patrick McGoohan in these films: soft voice, staccato, even speaking out of the side of his mouth occasionally. And McGoohan would have made a fine Holmes.

5.

A reader has sent me a video of a speech I made in Trafalgar Square in 1997, before Labour's narrow victory. I'd forgotten all about it. It was at an anti-hunting rally and I am proud to say that I can be seen persuading an audience of around twenty thousand to chant with me 'You can't trust Tony Blair'.

Like millions of others I am constantly appalled that Blair is trying to re-establish a position of influence. I've read that he would like to be Prime Minister again. Harold Shipman, Ian Brady and Fred West all killed 'retail' and as a result they were all reviled and punished. Tony Blair killed wholesale and is now a millionaire with far more homes than principles. I hope to live long enough to see him serving a life sentence as a war criminal.

6.

I bought a hat, a fairly ordinary slouch hat, from Bates the Hatter in Jermyn Street. It cost as much as my first three cars put together. That's a pretty good example of inflation.

Last weekend I found a small black and red notebook from my days at medical school in the 1960s. I see that I received £32 per term as a grant and my parents gave me £15 a month. My basic annual income was £276. Out of this I had to pay for rent, food, clothes, stationery, travel and books. I even had to buy a skeleton. (I bought it for £11.10.00 and sold it back for £11 a year later.) I was rich by student standards because I also earned money by writing columns and drama reviews. The *Birmingham Post* paid me thirty shillings a night to review plays. (But having to write a review of 300 to 500 words in less than 30 minutes taught me to write quickly and succinctly.) When I reviewed books the literary editor allowed me to choose as many books as I could carry. I received three guineas a week for writing a magazine column and thought that was absurdly generous. I was as rich then as I am now. That is my definition of inflation.

7.

A reader wants to know if the questions which appear in newspaper agony columns are real. They aren't. At least mine weren't. I've written agony columns for six national newspapers and magazines and all the letters were made up. And I know that Marje Proops, the well-known agony aunt of the *Daily Mirror,* made up letters for her column. She had a slick answer to the question: "Do you make up the questions?" She would reply: "If you saw the amount of mail I received you wouldn't ask that!" The real letters were too long, too rude, too complex or too boring. Besides, I always thought it dangerous and impertinent to try to offer advice through a newspaper. And having made up the questions I could be as rude as I liked since no one could be offended or hurt.

8.

I have always loved piers. I can't remember where it was but when I was a boy I once saw a one-legged man perform an extraordinary act on a pier. He used to set fire to himself and jump into the sea. That was the act. It wasn't clever, or innovative or anything very much really. It was stupid more than anything. But it was a piery sort of thing to do.

The Princess and I walked on the pier in Weston super Mare. In front of us walked a family of three: father, mother and bored daughter. The daughter was about 12-years-old. She was wearing ripped jeans and her hair was dyed green. As she walked she looked at herself in a small hand mirror. She was, I think, examining her spots. And then I saw her notice two 14-year-old boys. They both wore baseball caps with the peaks at the back. They stared at her and nudged one another. She sneered at them to let them know that she was interested.

'Would you like a ride on a donkey?' asked her dad, who hadn't noticed the boys. He also hadn't noticed that he no longer had a little girl who liked ribbons and ice cream and dolls.

The girl gave her father the sort of black look only teenage girls can give. It made my blood go cold. It is a relief that girls lose this skill as they mature. Very few grown women can muster the sort of malevolent look a teenage girl can manage with such ease.

9.

Two days ago The Princess told me that she had read that singing is good for the health. 'It releases endorphins,' she told me. 'It will make you feel jolly. You should sing every day.' And so for two days I have followed her advice faithfully. I can never remember the words to proper songs so, instead, I have been singing nonsense songs which I've been making up as I went along. After the first day she came home with rubbery yellow plugs which she stuffed into her ears every morning. When I asked her if my singing was annoying her she said that she was wearing the ear plugs because of the noise the neighbours were making. I haven't heard any noise at all and the nearest neighbours are half a mile away but maybe I am going deaf. Today, The Princess told me that she has discovered new advice showing that singing too much can cause laryngeal problems. 'It can,' she warns me, 'cause permanent damage.'

10.

'Where's your husband?' demanded an uninvited visitor.

'He's busy with a new book,' answered The Princess.

'I wish I had time to sit and read at this time of day,' said the visitor.

'Er no, he's writing one not reading one,' explained The Princess.

'Can't see much difference,' said the visitor sharply.

11.

The trouble with the Cotswolds is that instead of being populated with straw-in-the-mouth yokels, and descendants of W. G. Grace, it is now stuffed to the edges with people who have sold their semi-detached bijou residences in Fulham for a million quid and used the proceeds to buy themselves a little something in yellow stone. Their only quality is an over-reaching sense of self-importance. Having worked for decades as a senior regional manager for a utility company or the Libor fiddling desk at Barclays Bank or the Department of Culture And Ethnic Sensibilities in Whitehall they strut around expecting nature to behave itself and bow before them. There are more snotty bastards per square mile in the Cotswolds than in any other part of the country. Most are so full of their own sense of self-importance that they won't speak to their own wives or husbands, let alone their neighbours. These truculent, hypocritical bastards think they are saving the planet if they put the four wheel drive into two wheel drive occasionally. They clearly believe that owning a large, barky dog and a pair of coloured Wellington boots with little straps at the top turns them into country gentlemen. It may well be true that the meek shall inherit the earth but for the time being the snotty and sanctimonious are in residence.

Three days ago I answered the front door to find a short, round fellow standing there. He was red-faced and looked like a 'before' advertisement for an indigestion remedy. 'I've scratched my car on your hedge,' he told me.

I stared at him. I didn't have the foggiest idea who he was or why he'd shared this piece of news with me. He looked the sort of strutty, fussy man who buys posh luggage, wraps it in a special bag for the journey and then takes it out of the bag just before he arrives at the hotel reception.

'It was a piece of bramble, dangling dangerously into the road,' he told me.

'They do that,' I said. 'Unruly sometimes.'

'You should trim your hedges more often,' he instructed me. 'It's going cost me £200 to have that scratch repaired.'

'Why not just leave it?' I asked him. 'These lanes are so narrow that our cars have scratches all over them.'

He stared at me as though I'd asked him if he would like to take out a subscription to the *New Statesman.*

'Disgraceful!' he snorted. And marched off. Actually, it was more of a whinny than a snort.

This morning the indigestion advertisement came back.

'You must cut your hedge,' he told me. 'It is too high. And very untidy.'

I looked around the garden. 'It looks fine to me,' I said.

'The top of it is very straggly,' he said. 'My wife isn't happy with it. It could be a lot neater.' He had one of those pink breast cancer ribbons pinned to his lapel. It was a large one so that people wouldn't miss it.

I said I was very sorry to hear that.

'And are you going to leave your truck parked on that piece of land by your garages?'

I said it seemed a good place to park it because it wouldn't fit into the garage. 'We'd bring it into the house and park it in the living room,' I said. 'But the wheels always seem so muddy.'

'We can see it from our kitchen window,' said the man.

'Ah,' I said. 'You must live in the house near our garage.'

'It's very dirty and we can see it,' said the man, as though this settled the matter. 'Besides, if you park your truck there we have nowhere for our visitors to park.'

I stared at him, hardly able to believe my ears.

'It's your land, of course,' he said. 'If you want to park on it you can.'

'Thank you,' I said.

'But it's very inconvenient.'

I didn't say anything. Actually, I couldn't think of anything to say.

'Perhaps you could give it a wash?' he sniffed. There was a long and deliberate pause. 'If you must leave it there.'

I told The Princess about this extraordinary conversation. We realised that we still don't know their names. But it doesn't matter. We will call them Mr Spick and Mrs Span.

12.

The Princess had a rather upset telephone call from our friends in the Lake District. She was told to ask me not to put 'Sir and Lady' on any more correspondence. Apparently the neighbours aren't speaking to them (assuming, so our friends suspect, that they will be snooty and snobbish and that he probably received the title for selling hand grenades to Bosnians) and all the local tradesman are quoting prices that are twice as high as they should be. Oh dear. It's so easy to put your foot in it when you're trying to be jolly and helpful at the same time.

13.

I was appalled to read that another bunch of wimpy, greedy, policemen are suing taxpayers for compensation. The policemen claim that they are suffering from post-traumatic stress disorder because of unpleasant experiences they had while doing their jobs. Pfui. Many years ago I worked as a police surgeon and in the course of that work I unwrapped a woman who had been murdered by her husband, wrapped in plastic, put into a supersize plastic bag and left out with the rubbish (the dustmen called the police because they couldn't lift the bag), certified a man burnt to a crisp (you could smell the burning flesh half a mile away) and dealt with the remains of a man and his dog who had both been bludgeoned to death by two killers (I then examined the two killers, alone, in a police examination room, with the door shut). And so on and on. The point is, I was doing what I was paid to do and even though I still remember these incidents I cannot for the life of me imagine why I should be entitled to sue anyone for compensation.

14.

I see that, as I predicted in my book *2020,* the authorities are planning to force journalists to have licenses. This is a scary idea because it means that if a journalist writes something which makes the authorities feel uncomfortable then there is a risk that their licence will be taken away. Still, I'm not surprised. Some journalists scoffed when I wrote *Living in a Fascist Country.* I wonder if they are still laughing.

15.

Our local council is talking about putting up a sign welcoming careful drivers. They are telling us this as part of their 'community awareness and consultation programme'. I have written to tell them I don't think their planned sign will do any good at all. I have suggested that, instead, they erect a sign which says: 'Drive slowly or we will chase after you and when we catch you we will tear off your limbs and stuff them down your throat.' The Princess said she doesn't think they will accept my suggestion. I told her that if the sign is too long I will cut it to: 'Drive slowly or we will chase you and when we catch you we will tear off your limbs'.

16.

Because they are always in a hurry people who live in towns and cities tend to get to the point quite quickly when they are sharing an anecdote, telling a joke, reporting a piece of news or passing on an item of gossip. To them the message is everything. The method of its telling is of no account.

But life in the country is different. The pace of life is slower in almost every respect; there is a far smaller sense of urgency about things.

This afternoon I tottered up the village shop to buy a loaf of bread and a paper.

'Do you want today's or yesterday's paper?'

'Today's would be good,' I said, thinking this was a joke.

'Well I'm afraid you'll have to come back tomorrow,' said the woman behind the counter. 'The delivery van hasn't come with today's papers. He broke down.'

I thought for a moment. 'Well, in that case,' I said. 'I'll take a copy of yesterday's.'

'They're all much the same aren't they?'

I don't know why but I looked around to make sure there was no one else in the shop. 'Actually,' I admitted, 'I only want it to light the fire.'

17.

A friend of The Princess's has children at school. She has been struggling to help them with their homework, which they are expected to do with the aid of research work conducted on the internet. 'I'm not convinced that the information is accurate,' said The Princess's friend a couple of days ago. 'Some of the sites seem to be heavily sponsored.' The Princess agreed with her, told her that to find information on the internet you really need to know exactly what you are looking for, and to be something of an expert in the subject so that you can differentiate between the reliable and the suspicious. 'Why not visit the reference section of the public library,' suggested The Princess. Today the friend rang. 'That was a fantastic idea!' she said. 'Thanks! We did my daughter's homework in half the time using the library.' My own feelings about children are somewhat akin to those of the late W. C. Fields but I do feel sorry for the little mites, struggling to thrive and survive in an internet dominated world.

18.

A woman in the street coughed all over me and I have developed the flu. Chest pains, shortness of breath and a temperature. It is scary to realise that many people my age now die of pneumonia. It is probably because the bugs we catch are much stronger, and drug resistant, because they originate in badly run hospitals. If I die I will have been murdered by a careless stranger who couldn't be bothered to put her hand over her mouth when she coughed. I find that I think about death too much at the moment. My life has gone by so fast. There are so many things left to do. So many frustrations and disappointments to be reversed. And most of all I don't want to leave The Princess. How will it all end? And when? Stroke, cancer, pneumonia, run over by a bus?

19.

'I went to Keith Yates's funeral this morning,' said Thumper Robinson, a good friend of ours.

I'd never heard of Keith Yates. Thumper explained that he is famous locally for a sixty year old feud which he and his brother Harry sustained through illness, bereavement and the usual mixture of good and ill fortune. Country dwellers of all shapes and sizes hate their neighbours more than they hate the council or the Chancellor of the Exchequer. They are invigorated and kept alive by feuds about fencing and disputes about boundaries. Nothing keeps them young more than discord over a shared access. They defy their doctors' most pessimistic prognostications thanks to a multi-generational quarrel. Nothing keeps a true countryman alive more than the determination to get one over the farmer on the other side of the hill.

No one could remember what this particular feud was about but for half a century both brothers had been driven exclusively by a desire to spite one another.

'Was Harry at the funeral?' I asked.

'He was,' said Thumper. 'But he was in an absolutely foul mood. He told me he was convinced that Keith had died first deliberately so that he could leave Harry out of his will.'

It seems that Harry's solitary remaining ambition in life had been to die before his brother so that he could have the pleasure of knowing that he had left his brother absolutely nothing in his will.

Thumper had, however, managed to cheer Harry up considerably by pointing out to him that by living longer he had really managed to get the best of his brother.

'He left the funeral with a big grin on his face and a spring in his step,' said Thumper. 'I've never seen him look so cheerful. So, in a strange sort of way I suppose I did my good turn for the day.'

20.

A reader whose Christian name is Leslie wrote to me putting (M) after his name. I suppose it must be quite confusing to have a Christian name which is used for men and women. And when you think about it a good many names are interchangeable between the sexes. Ruby, Ronnie, Paige and Sam are four that spring to mind. A good many male authors had names which are usually associated with women: Evelyn Waugh, Vicki Baum, Beverley Nichols, Joyce Carey for example. Carol Reed the film director was a bloke. As was Marion Morrison (who worked as John Wayne). A man called Shirley Brooks was the second editor of *Punch* magazine and Florence was Ziegfeld as well as Nightingale.

21.

Our new bed and bedroom furniture were delivered at last. There was, inevitably, a good deal of fuss. The driver of the lorry bringing it tele-phoned every five yards in hysterics. 'I'm stuck!' he cried. 'I'll never get out of here!' We constantly reassured him and eventually he reached our home. He was perspiring, red-faced and probably palpitat-ing. It has taken us a couple of months to find anyone prepared to deliver furniture. Several companies refused point blank. When we asked if delivery men would wait at the top of our lane while we trans-ferred our purchases to our truck we were told that this would not be possible. 'The driver will unload and leave your stuff on the road,' we were told. 'But he won't wait for you or help you put the furniture on your truck roof.' No one would deliver a fridge or a freezer either. In the end we brought both home (separately) in our truck. And we pulled, dragged and lifted them into the house ourselves. So we're grateful to get a delivery at all.

The delivery man told us that our wardrobe should be polished with beeswax every two weeks and given a bowl of water to help it settle in. The Princess asked if we would be expected to take it for walks. He then told us that we must turn our bed mattress once every month and laughed when he reported that he had once met a couple who admitted that they had never turned their mattress. Not once. He grinned and shook his head as though this were the craziest thing he'd ever come across. He couldn't have been more shocked if the people concerned had worn the same socks for a month. The Princess and I exchanged silent, guilty glances and then laughed with him. We said we always turned our mattress at least once a week and that it was one of the things we looked forward to most in life. He nodded approvingly at this and told us that we didn't need to turn it every week once it had settled.

It seems that these days everything comes with instructions. The carpet man, the curtain woman and the rug man all gave us complicated instructions. The man fitting the replacement log burning stove gave us a fifteen minute lecture on chimneys, flues and carbon monoxide poisoning. The man who swept the chimneys gave us a form for our insurance company. Every device that comes with a battery comes with instructions warning us that used batteries must not, under any circumstances, be tossed carelessly into the general rubbish. Apparently we must contact our local council before disposing of so much as a torch battery.

When the furniture delivery guy had gone we went back into the bedroom and stared at the mattress. 'Should we turn it side to side as well as top to bottom?' asked The Princess. I said we should try just moving it. We managed to drag it half off the bed but could get it no further. We then dragged it back into the same position it had enjoyed minutes before. We promised each other that we'd enrol in a Mattress Management Guidance Group or purchase a DVD giving instructions on mattress turning.

'I'll get some water,' said The Princess.

'Great!' I said. I was exhausted.

But when she returned she was carrying a dish which she placed beside the wardrobe.

22.

Telecom vans have been blocking our lane for most of the day.

'Are you having trouble with your phones?' asked the postman.

'Not that I know of,' I told him. 'We haven't reported anything.'

'They've been here half a dozen times,' said the postman. 'They're always working on your overhead lines. They've even been trimming tree branches and doing stuff to the poles. They're the lines to your house so I thought you must be having trouble.'

He handed me a bill and six pieces of junk mail, got back into his little red van and drove off down the lane. If they hold a round of the World Rally Championships in our area he would win by miles.

I didn't like to tell him but whenever we move house the telephone engineers are never far behind. They like to keep the lines clear so that the boys and girls at Special Branch can make good recordings. We regard it as a perk of being spied upon.

23.

Every time a tradesman calls he finds some reason to terrify us.

We made the mistake of asking a firm of electricians to install a couple of new lights. 'We could check your electrics for you,' said the jolly one. 'It's compulsory now so you might as well let us do it before we start work on the new lights.' When they'd finished checking, the team of smartly suited electricians gave us a six page list of important things that needed to be done if we were not to be in breach of EU regulations. 'Your insurance company will want you to have all these done,' said the straight man. 'You almost failed some of the tests,' said the jolly one, though it didn't occur to me until later that since we had only almost failed then we hadn't actually failed. So The Princess and I gulped, gasped, held hands and told them to get on with it. It took them four days. The bill was huge. We could have equipped an aircraft carrier with that much money. It was only when they'd finished, and we'd paid them, that we realised that we still didn't have the new lights we wanted fitting. (They did, however, fit a chandelier for us in one of the bedrooms. Unfortunately, they left the chandelier hanging so low that every time I go into the room I hit my head. The two electricians who fitted it were very short.)

A locksmith who came to fit new locks on those of our doors which aren't fastened with keys which are over a foot long (we decided to leave those as they are) told us that in order to satisfy the regulations (from guess where) we had to have locks fitted onto our windows. He said the insurance company would require it. But when he examined the windows he found that they had mostly been built in the 17th and 18th century and none of the window locks that were available would fit. So we had to have window locks specially designed and specially made. We were not in the slightest bit surprised when they turned out to be just ever so slightly more expensive than the ones sold in the local ironmongery store.

Today, we had the boiler men in the house. It was my fault. I thought it would be a good idea to have the boiler serviced. I really should know better. At our last house it took two weeks to get our boiler working after a yahoo from a local company did the servicing. In the end we had to call in an expert from the manufacturer. He told us that the clown who'd done the servicing had put in something upside down.

Anyway, the company we'd called this time sent around four men in two vans. 'It'll be quicker with four of us,' said the leader. He didn't mention anything about it being more expensive. He then got out his telephone and rang his head office to find out where they were going next, and to tell them that it had taken them ages to find our house. Another of the men asked us where the lavatory was, one of them went back to the van and started eating sandwiches and the fourth, a teenager who didn't look old enough to be using matches let alone playing with boilers, asked me to show him to the boiler room and direct him to the situation of the nearest heated water outlet. I told him I could show him the boiler room but that I didn't know whether we'd even got a heated water outlet. 'Hot tap,' he explained. I thanked him for the translation and showed him both.

After forty five minutes of eating sandwiches, making telephone calls and using our various lavatories the head boiler man came into my study. He looked very grave. 'Your boiler isn't working,' he said.

'It was working fine before you came!' I told him.

'Maybe,' he admitted. 'But it isn't working now.'

'What's wrong?'

'Not sure,' he said. 'We need to bring in one of the experts from Gloucester. But he can't come until next Wednesday.'

'But we'll freeze to death by then!'

'They're forecasting nasty weather for the weekend,' he agreed. He then looked down at the clipboard he was holding. 'We've found another problem,' he said. 'You haven't got an inspection hatch in your flue.'

I stared at him. I had no idea what he was talking about.

'It's a new EU regulation,' he said. 'Flues must have an inspection hatch. You haven't got one.'

'What flue?' I asked. 'The flue from the boiler goes straight outside.'

'Not that flue, the flue from your AGA. It goes up through a bathroom and there's no inspection hatch in the flue. It's an EU law. You have to have one.'

Most of the time my brain is stodgy, like porridge which has been left in the pan overnight, but occasionally, probably once every two or three years, I have a brainwave. 'Do you have to put inspection hatches in chimneys?'

He frowned and looked puzzled. 'Just flues.'

'That's OK then,' I told him with absolute certainty in my voice. 'The pipe from the AGA is a chimney not a flue.'

He looked at me, opened his mouth but said nothing and then nodded. 'A chimney?'

'Definitely,' I said. 'It's a chimney.'

'Oh.' He sounded terribly disappointed. 'Well that's OK then.'

'Don't bother with the expert from Gloucester,' I told him as I ushered them out of the front door. 'I'll get someone else to sort it out.'

'You need four carbon monoxide alarms fitted,' he shouted as he left. 'We could fit them for you.'

When they'd gone I telephoned their head office, told the startled woman who answered the telephone that if they dared to send a bill I would sue them for something, and rang someone else.

The new guy arrived an hour later. It took him approximately nine seconds to get the boiler started. It might have been ten. It wasn't more than ten seconds. He pointed to a switch. 'Someone had turned that off,' he said. He spent a few minutes looking around inside the casing and then closed it again. 'These modern boilers don't need much attention,' he said. 'They're electronic. There isn't much anyone can do unless something needs replacing.'

'Do you have your boiler serviced?' I asked him.

He looked at me and smiled, thought for a moment and then shook his head. 'We've had our boiler for seven years,' he said. 'And I've never even looked at it – except to check the water pressure every few months. You can do that yourself.' He showed me the gauge I needed to check and the tap I needed to turn.

I paid him what he asked for in cash. Workmen like cash, not because they want to cheat the taxman but because there are no delays, no charges and no risk of the bank going bust.

'I'll tell you something,' he said, lowering his voice. 'A fifth of all boiler breakdowns take place immediately after a service.'

24.

I purchased a carbon monoxide alarm. It came with 32 pages of instructions. There was a warning in red on the front of the box. 'Must to be installed by a competitant persons.' But, nevertheless, I managed to do it. All I had to do was pull a little plastic tab and the battery started to work. I assume that means that I must be 'a competitant persons'. This is quite a thrill.

25.

The water with which we are supplying our new wardrobe has been disappearing at a remarkable rate. 'You don't think we've got a wardrobe monster, do you?' asked The Princess. I said I didn't think it likely.

And then we saw the mouse droppings.

We have removed the water.

The wardrobe will have to manage without.

26.

Chris Cairns, a former New Zealand cricketer, has won £90,000 in damages for a libel which appeared on Twitter. Hoorah. I hope he sues in another 100 countries. His success will, hopefully, mean that the internet will no longer be a free for all medium for intellectual thugs and it will become easier for people who are defamed on the internet to take action.

I really do find it difficult to feel any enthusiasm for this silly idea. I gather that the Twitter thing enables millions of people to write daily, and endlessly, about their eating habits and their latest bowel movements. (I suppose we cannot be too surprised by this. Today's twats grew up watching pitiful and desperate nonentities washing, eating and arguing in the Big Brother House.) This is all sad. Even sadder is the fact that people read this stuff (they are, I believe, known as 'followers' and, if they leave, as 'unfollowers' which would have given Orwell a thrill). Children need limits, structures and hierarchies but these days they are all mouth and tweet, all hubris and Facebook. Look at me, I'm the best. Unbelievably, even British Gas has Twitter followers though I struggle to imagine what sort of human being would want to be regularly updated by British Gas about anything. Bloggers, twits and Facebook aficionados have all the knowledge and style and reliability of doodlers and graffiti specialists. It's typing not writing. Do the people who commit their thoughts to these sites realise that Twitter owns everything ever said on it, and that Facebook (which also claims to own everything put on its site) exists to sell advertising? (I heard recently that in America the Library of Congress is so enamoured of Twitter that they are planning to archive every twittle sent by an American. Since American twits send around 400 million a day that's an awful lot of rubbish to store.)

Does anyone really believe that these social media sites are run for the good of the stupid people who use them? (Actually, some probably do. The world is packed with people who believe what they are told.) There is irony in the fact that Web users demand everything free (free books, free music, free films), regard copyright as theft and then allow the biggest, richest corporations to own their copyright so easily? Who, in future, will pay for the production of books, music and films? Even if writers, musicians and filmmakers will all be amateurs someone has to pay for the ink (or the electricity), the instruments and the cameras. (Back in the early 1990s I tried to charge for material on websites. It seemed a good idea at the time. But the principle that everything on the internet must be free had already taken hold. I doubt if it will ever really be possible to charge a decent, commercial fee for original, creative material on the internet.)

I am comforted by the knowledge that it won't be long before Facebook and Twitter will die. These companies rely on making money through advertising and an increasing amount of evidence shows that internet advertising simply doesn't work - either because users are immune to the adverts and ignore them or because they don't bother to click on them. In addition, why would companies pay to have an advertising presence on these sites and to be roundly abused by internet trolls? Without adverts these wretched social media sites will die. (Incidentally, most internet trolls either have a commercial axe to grind because they represent a competitive product or they simply have inferiority complexes because they are inferior.)

The death of these sites will improve all our lives. And make us safer in many, many ways. For example, the internet is a boon for criminals. In the year 2011, 70,000 national heritage sites in England were hit by criminals. The legal director of English Heritage blamed the internet, pointing out that Google Earth helps thieves and vandals go trophy hunting. The thieves can use the internet to work out what they want, where to find it and how to plan their getaway. What is true for heritage sites is, of course, also true for private homes.

And, in the meanwhile, there will doubtless be a good many more lawsuits. I wonder how many twits and Facebook aficionados realise that a writer can be sued for libel in just about any country in the world for anything they write on a blog, a tweet or a Facebook addition. No one should mess around on the Web unless they are confident that they know the criminal and civil laws in every country of the world. Ignorance and prejudice will not be accepted as an excuse.

(I have noticed, incidentally, that computer bullies and hackers (who often cause enormous distress, inconvenience and cost) invariably claim (if they are caught) that they are mentally ill and, therefore, cannot be held responsible for their actions. The favourite diagnosis is some variety of autism. Autism is such a vague diagnosis that it is, of course, possible to argue that almost anyone is suffering from some variant or other.)

27.

We arrived home after a trip to the garden centre to find an anonymous note pinned to a tree near our car parking space. The semi-literate writer of the note accuses us of being territorial and urbanising the countryside because we have tried to protect our car parking space by putting up two poles and a small notice. Anonymous notes are always unpleasant and this one, written in block capitals on a scrap of cardboard, is no exception. Not surprisingly, The Princess is upset by it.

28.

We met a man in a pub just outside Nailsworth who has a donkey living in his garden. He says the donkey earns its keep by eating the grass. 'Better than a goat,' he told us. 'Goats eat all the trees and bushes.' He told us that the donkey is called Hoti. 'That's an unusual name,' said The Princess. The man in the pub just grinned. 'Donkey Hoti,' he said.

29.

We met an editor in London. I noticed that he was wearing a rather splendid looking watch. 'It keeps perfect time,' he said, admiring it. 'Wonderful watch. This is an heirloom.' He looked at my wrist. 'And I bet my dad paid less for it than you paid for yours.'

'He probably did,' I agreed. 'When did he buy it?'

'Thirty years ago,' said the editor. 'He bought it for £2 in Istanbul.'

I didn't have the courage to tell him that the one on my wrist, a genuine version of the same watch, cost considerably more and keeps terrible time. I should have bought the cheap version.

30.

The internet, damn it, is very good for finding books you know exist but cannot find in bookshops, but it is no good at all for browsing.

Here's a list of twelve books I've recently picked up in old bookshops and junk shops recently. I would not have found any of these joys without good old-fashioned browsing. All of these books are out of print and difficult or impossible to find. I paid no more than £1 for any of them. Several are first editions.

1. *Duveen* by S. H. Behrman

Duveen was an English art dealer in the first half of the 20th century. He became the world's greatest art dealer and helped a number of very rich Americans build up hugely impressive art collections. Inevitably, he spent much of his life moving art from Europe to America. Many of the paintings and statues which he sold became significant items in major museums.

2. *Helio-Tropes or New Posies for Sundials*

Published in 1904 this is a reproduction of a book first published in 1625. The book consists of nothing but sundial inscriptions. The original volume was written by John Parmenter and my edition was edited by Percival Landon.

My favourite sundial inscription in the book is: 'Munda Solaria dant, sed cor Saloria Mundum.' Underneath this Mr Landon has written: 'This motto is, I think, incapable of adequate translation. The meaning is that while ground rents provide the smart and mundane things of this world, sundials by their admonition lead men to purity of heart. But I cannot render into equivalent English the double and daring play upon the words.'

The Princess and I have decided that we have to buy a sundial so that we can have this posy inscribed upon it. (Incidentally, I bet there isn't a kindle edition of *Helio-Tropes*.)

How the hell would you ever know this book existed unless you found it in a box of jumbled books at an auction or behind a cupboard in a junk shop?

3. *One Day and Another* by E. V. Lucas

Lucas produced some wonderful books and this collection of essays and stories was published in 1909. My favourite story concerns a new born baby. Fairy godmothers turn up with all sorts of gifts. One gives determination, a second gives self-confidence, a third gives indifference to public opinion, a fourth gives the baby a good memory for faces and a fifth gives a knowledge of men. They all agree that with this array of gifts the baby will be enormously successful. And then another fairy godmother turns up. She is angry at not being given the date of the birth and, determined to destroy the child, she gives him a sympathetic heart.

'He is ruined!' cry the other fairies.

This was never more true than it is today. I doubt if there is a leader in the world who isn't a full-bloodied psychopath. In our strange new world the sensitive and sympathetic stand no chance.

4. *American Notes* by Charles Dickens

Dickens was probably the greatest travel writer of them all. Here's a sample: 'In all the public establishments of America, the utmost courtesy prevails. Most of our Departments are susceptible of considerable improvement in this respect, but the Customs house above all others would do well to take example from the United States and render itself somewhat less odious and offensive to foreigners. The servile rapacity of the French officials is sufficiently contemptible; but there is a surly boorish incivility about our men, alike disgusting to all persons who fall into their hands, and discreditable to the nation that keeps such ill-conditioned curs snarling about its gates.'

Dickens is remembered as the best novelist the world has ever known. He has left us the greatest cast of characters ever invented. But his travel books are a joy. He stands above even Sterne, Smollett and Twain. His description of his journey across a stormy Atlantic is worthy of Jerome K. Jerome at his very best. Even bearing in mind Benjamin Disraeli's comment ('Like all great travellers, I have seen more than I remember, and remember more than I have seen.') Dickens's adventures are both hair raising and hilarious. Bill Bryson eat your heart out.

How did Dickens manage to write so much really good stuff? Maybe the absence of a typewriter or a computer helped him write faster. No software to clunk, no ribbon to jam. The Princess pointed out that Dickens also had no telephone to slow him down and far fewer forms to fill in. Servants were cheap and although travel was time consuming most things in life were less complicated.

No, it still doesn't make sense.

I have no idea how he wrote so much, so consistently well, in such a short lifetime.

5. *Journal 1929* by Arnold Bennett

I hadn't read any Bennett for years until I picked up this cheap paperback of his diary for 1929. In addition to being a great novelist Bennett was, like Charles Dickens, a terrific travel writer. He always saw the little human things and had a great eye for the funny and the curious. He was never afraid to admire what he saw and to enjoy the places he visited and the people he met. On every page there is always a sense of privilege and wonderment and a vein of mischief. One of the joys of discovering (or rediscovering) a great author who has a great oeuvre is that there will be more delights to come. As soon as I'd finished reading Bennett's journal I bought copies of every other book of his I could find. (In his book *Truth about an Author* Bennett wrote this about his first book: 'My profits from this book exceeded the cost of having it typewritten by the sum of one sovereign. Many a first book has cost its author a hundred pounds. I got a new hat out of mine.')

6. *The Riders of High Rock* by Louis L'Amour

I love cowboy films but I had never read a cowboy book before I picked up this book by Louis L'Amour. This one is about Hopalong Cassidy.

L'Amour wrote over 120 books and sold over 300 million copies. He left home at 15 and worked as a seaman, lumberjack, elephant handler and miner. He was an officer in the transportation corps during World War II. L'Amour circled the world on a freighter, sailed a dhow in the Red Sea, was shipwrecked in the West Indies and stranded in the Mojave desert. He fought as a professional boxer and won 51 of his 59 fights. He collected rare books and when he died he left a library of 17,000 volumes. His cowboy books have been translated into 20 languages and nearly 50 of his novels and stories have been made into films. (A figure which must take him close to Georges Simenon.)

7. *We Were Young and Carefree* by Laurent Fignon

Laurent Fignon was my first cycling hero. I've been a fan of the Tour de France since I was a boy and admired Fignon's romantic style. His intelligent, ruthless analysis of his own attitudes, motives and ambitions (not to mention his behaviour after winning his first Tour in 1983) make this the best sporting autobiography I've ever read. It is far removed from the usual sort of self-serving, superficial tat served up in this genre. Fignon was a two time winner of the Tour de France (he famously lost a third race by eight seconds on the final day) and wrote: 'Bad luck plays no part in anything I do. I never lose my morale. I don't complain, even if things go against me. Ill fortune does not touch me.' He describes how in the first of his winning tours he ate too much sugar too quickly. The insulin came in so fast that he suffered a hypoglycaemic reaction. I was genuinely sad when Fignon died in his 50s.

8. *Gilbert of Gilbert and Sullivan* by Andrew Crowther

W. S. Gilbert viewed life as a constant battle waged between himself and the rest of the world and I sympathise with him. He was alienated and full of resentment and either because or, in spite of this, he wrote the most marvellously biting lyrics. It is disappointing to realise that there are people who have never listened to Gilbert's librettos. The world would be a much happier place if everyone was obliged to listen to G&S operas during dinner, watch Basil skewering Holmes after dinner and enjoy almost anything by P. G. Wodehouse at bedtime.

9. *The Lionel Bart Story* by David and Caroline Stafford

This is not just an excellent biography but a brilliant account of the music world in the 1960s. It describes how a man who touched the hem of greatness and grabbed a great chunk of it in his fist, then lost virtually everything. It is a story of hubris more than anything.

10. *Festival at Farbridge* by J. B. Priestley

The only Priestley I could remember reading was *Good Companions* - a marvellous account of traveling music hall acts, back in the days before television brought an end to live entertainment. But this novel is just as good. I immediately bought everything else I could find by him (including *Lost Empires* and *Bright Days.* Priestley is unfashionable these days but his books are a delight and his affection for variety artists is tangible.

11. *The Life of John Law* by H Montgomery Hyde

Law is described on the frontispiece as an 'honest adventurer'. Born in 1671 he was 34 when he published his banking reform plan *Money and Trade Considered* in which he proposed a central bank for manufacturing money as pieces of paper, rather than as cumbersome gold and silver coins. Law was the first of many incompetent and crooked bankers and economists and far more influential than his countryman Adam Smith who nicked everything from William Petty, an Englishman. France tried Law's scheme in 1716, when he founded the Banque Generale which was authorised to issue bank notes. Things went wrong when he combined the bank with a company designed to develop France's North American territories, particularly part of Mississippi. After the disaster of the 'Mississippi bubble' Law fled to Venice where he died in poverty. It surely cannot be a coincidence that, like the proponents of many modern banking disasters, Law was Scottish.

Hyde's biography of an extraordinary man is what used to be called a 'thumping good read' and it merits the description 'unputdownable' as well as anything I've read for a long time.

12. *Fifty BAB Ballads* by W. S. Gilbert

For several years Gilbert (of Gilbert and Sullivan fame, of course) wrote what he called Bab Ballads for the magazine *Fun*. Fifty of the best were collected for this tiny volume, and given the subtitle: *Much sound and little sense.* I'm surprised the ballads aren't better known. They're a joy.

31.

On the train I jotted down these six things I've learned:

1. Never argue with a fool, or a man with a gun, and definitely don't ever argue with a fool with a gun.
2. Never sit in the front row of the ballet. If you do the beauty of what you see will be ruined by what you hear. (Grunts and wheezes and stomping on the boards.)
3. The unexpected works. Hannibal went over the Alps not because he wanted to take the scenic route but because it was a route that everyone else thought impossible.
4. Don't attend meetings or sit on committees. People go to meetings to impress, to be the most important person in the room and to ignore everyone else. Men and women who yearn for companionship, support, authority and a sense of self-importance love meetings, especially if they can call meetings over which they can preside. And most meetings are called not to do business but to give the impression that something is being done. The meeting becomes a substitute for action. As far as the participants are concerned the meeting is the action. They feel that men and

women of such importance cannot possibly get together without something important being achieved. The meeting is the deed in the way that the medium is the message. Moreover, meetings enable the voters to be convinced that things are being done on their behalf; that culprits are about to be punished and causes dealt with. G7, G10 and G20 meetings are perhaps, the perfect example of meetings of which nothing is expected and which invariably satisfy those expectations. (I have it from an unreliable source, by the way, that Gordon Brown was convinced that these meetings all carried the prefix 'G' in recognition of his global importance.)

5. When staying in a hotel, make sure you don't take a room on either of the bottom two floors (they are too easy for burglars) or above the 6th floor (because if there is a fire you'll be trapped). And to avoid legionnaire's disease, never shower in a hotel.

APRIL

1.

The Princess and I have decided to organise our own Olympics in the village. We both believe that we can make athletics far more appealing to spectators by making some mild changes to the traditional regulations.

Here are some of our planned rules. We intend to offer these to the Parish Council at the earliest possible opportunity.

1. Javelin throwers will be awarded bonus points if they succeed in spearing another contestant. Double points will be awarded to contestants who manage to spear an official. The treasurer should look into the possibility of renting a few unemployed bankers to use as targets.
2. Synchronised drug injecting is an obvious event. We intend to invite leading sports pharmacists to help with this event and chemists will be entitled to win medals if their drug cocktails proved particularly effective.
3. To cater for older villagers there will be a knitting event. Competitors will be given a pair of needles and a ball of wool and invited to knit a pair of mittens. The first to finish will win.
4. Throwing playing cards into a hat is a traditional English sport and it is outrageous that this event has never been incorporated into the other Olympics. It should be in ours.
5. Running events need livening up. We intend to do this by allowing the Baskervilles to use their dog as a starter. Contestants must start running when the dog barks. After five seconds the dog will

be released. We could also ensure more entertainment by insisting that all contestants run in rubber Wellington boots.

6. Events involving the use of conkers and marbles must be included. Apple hurling, another traditional English game, should be considered. Pooh sticks, maypole dancing and non-synchronised Morris dancing will be essential.

7. Jumping events should have some added sense of danger. So, the long jump should be a jump across a pond filled with piranha fish and contestants in the high jump should be expected to jump over a solid brick wall.

8. As currently organised the marathon is a tedious race. It would liven things up considerably if officials were to shoot the last runner to pass every mile post. To avoid too much trouble with the authorities the runners could simply be shot in the leg.

9. In order to enable contestants to succeed in gaining genuine world records all events involving distance should be measured in imperial measurements. So, for example, athletes could contest the '102 yard scurry' and the 'mile and a little bit' wheeze and limp.

10. To avoid the embarrassing sight of successful contestants parading around the village with medals around their necks we suggest that all medals be edible. It should be possible to arrange for a manufacturer of seaside rock to prepare suitable awards.

2.

We went to the Cotswold Wildlife Park which is exactly what it says it is and where you'd expect it to be. Brilliant. We watched rhinos courting (with loving nudges that would have sent a double decker bus flying) and a burrowing owl which was clearly terrified at the sight of an approaching Labrador (why do they allow dogs into wildlife parks?) and siamang monkeys reaching through the bars of their enclosure to grab and eat bamboo leaves growing just outside. We stared in astonishment at two vultures watching while a thrush, a robin and two great tits ate their dinner (or some of it), saw a red panda asleep in the fork of a tree and several large pigs asleep and snoring loudly and, for a while, watched as a giant tortoise tried to make a break for it. The whole experience was spoilt only by the damned school trips. The teachers are far noisier than the children and a good deal more objectionable. On our way back we stopped in Lechlade and bought a glazed oak bookcase and a silver plated tray for less than £100. And by late afternoon we found ourselves in Tetbury, which has excellent charity shops and splendid hostelries. I like charity shops. Now that the quality of merchandise has plummeted they are the best places to buy decent products. (Stuff is so badly made these days that if we find something we like we go back immediately and buy six because before long the first one will have broken or stopped working and the manufacturer will, by then, have stopped making them.) I am as addicted to charity shops as I used to be to junk shops (and as I still am to second-hand bookshops). I go in with an open mind and come out with arms full of things I cannot possibly want or use and certainly don't need but which I have found irresistible. A week later I put them into a box and take them to another charity shop. I much prefer buying shirts which come without pins or four acres of cardboard and cellophane. Prince Charles and the Duchess of Cornwall live a couple of miles away, when they're feeling rural, and they have a shop in Tetbury, though I understand they're too busy opening things to spend much time behind the counter. The antique shops aren't so good since they price their stock for daft Americans who cannot operate currency converters, or who like to think that the dollar has parity with the pound. I parked outside Tetbury post office for a moment while The Princess and I popped two armfuls of parcels into their post-box. Although I wasn't causing an obstruction, or in anyone's way, an officious man with dyed hair and jowls told me that I couldn't park where I was. 'Me big chief illegal immigrant asylum seeker with two dogs,' I told him, beaming happily. 'Can park anywhere.' I waved an arm about to illustrate the remark. He stared at me in terror and confusion and scurried away back to his black hole. The look on his face was worth a cream filled éclair of anyone's calorie allowance. The Cotswolds are wonderful but some of the folk can be a bit uppity and think that having green Wellington boots entitles them to push ordinary folk around.

3.

Is it just me or is the number of annoying things increasing daily? I really can't work out whether it's me or the world. I'm glad I don't have a gun. I made a note of all the people I would have shot if I had been carrying a gun. I'd reached 56 by teatime. Here are some of my pet hates:

1. I hate it when I'm on a train, or at a railway station, and some smooth, supercilious voice says: 'We thank you for your understanding and for your cooperation.' I hate it because I probably don't understand why there is a six hour delay and I almost certainly don't want to cooperate. I do and say nothing because if I stand on my seat and scream, or I thump one of their complacent, genuinely uncaring employees, six policemen in riot gear will shoot me with dum dum bullets. I wish they'd forget about the thanks. Just be plain rude to me please, then at least I can feel justifiably resentful and retain my self-respect.

2. I hate it when people suddenly stop at the top of an escalator so that they can look around and decide which way to go next.

3. I hate it when people in hotel or railway lounges talk loudly on their mobile telephones so that no one can else can concentrate on whatever it is they're trying to do. I hate it even more when people take part in video-conferences on their laptops.

4. I hate it when people in shops pay for something cheap with their credit card. And I hate it more when they can't decide which card to use before they pay for their magazine or bar of chocolate. Haven't these people heard of cash?

5. I hate it when the TV licensing thugs start writing to me. I know that whatever I do they will harass and threaten me for months.

6. I hate it when someone demands that before I can perform some simple, basic function I must first hand over my passport, a recent bank statement, my driving licence, one utility bill (original only please) and a signed statement from a neighbour in good standing, who has known me for at least three years.

7. I hate those agreements that appear so often on the internet. (Apple recently sent me a new iPhone agreement for me to read. It's 54 pages long.) If you want to download anything on the internet you are usually required to perjure yourself by agreeing that you have accepted the company's terms and conditions. One year, as an April Fool's Day prank, a video game retailer called Gamestation put up spoof terms and conditions on its website requiring customers to sell their souls. Around 7,500 customers made a purchase from the site and every one of them ticked the box claiming they had read and accepted the conditions. The internet in particular makes casual liars of us all. Terms and conditions (allegedly there to protect us) are incomprehensible and so

lengthy that no one ever reads them. In a world where regulations lie so thick on the ground that none of us can possibly know them all it would surely make sense to have a standard terms and conditions agreement for internet companies to use.

8. I hate the dummies at Special Branch who tap our phone and fax machine and I wish they would be quieter and cause less trouble. Every evening our telephone and fax machine make a curious clicking noise as they suck off details of all our messages and faxes. And when they break into the house to see what's on my laptop I wish they would leave things the way they'd found them.

9. I hate people who say 'There's no need to worry about privacy if you've got nothing to hide.' As each day goes by it becomes increasingly difficult to preserve any privacy in our mad, internet run age. (My own e-mails go out with this note stuck at the bottom: 'Official warning: e-mail messages are public and not private. This e-mail is monitored by the security services. This means that a sweaty, overweight, malodorous moron will scrutinise this message.')

10. I hate workmen who use whichever loo is nearest to them - even if it's in a bathroom - instead of using the one loo they've been asked to use.

11. I hate it when people say: 'We can't do that - what will people think?' or 'We'll get used to it in time.'

12. I hate people who drive around with a Baby on Board sticker on the back window of their car but have no baby in their vehicle. This should be a criminal offence with a mandatory life sentence. A friend of ours who is an ambulance man once risked his life searching a wrecked and burning car for a non-existent baby.

4.

We had a rotten journey on the Eurostar train to Paris. An aggressive and rude granny groper at the station ordered me to lift up my arms so that he could give me a body search. It took me nearly three minutes to persuade him to say 'please' and so, in revenge, while he was patting my chest I handed the coxcomb a small card. 'I suspect you'll need this,' I told him.

'What did you give him?' asked The Princess, as we walked away. 'Details of the Government's official website for job seekers,' I told her.

On the train a quartet of fat Americans (are there any other sort?) sat near us and regaled the entire carriage with their dull boasting. Americans tend to behave in small groups in the same way that they behave as a nation: loud, noisy and arrogant. Since America is a staunchly matriarchal society the women are invariably the noisiest and most troublesome. (If you ask a European couple something the woman will look at the man and the man will answer. If you ask an American couple something the woman will answer, without hesitation. The man just keeps quiet.) Today's quartet included a harridan who complained, with apparently genuine rancour, when the steward failed to open up her napkin and lay it across a small portion of her vast lap.

Eurostar should have non-American carriages in the same way that trains used to have non-smoking carriages. Actually, it would be best to have carriages without Americans, children, noisy eaters, football supporters, mobile telephone users or talkers. We always book the quiet coach but it hardly ever is. I hate noisy people and intend to write to Eurostar telling them that I suffer from hyper-augmented social phobia syndrome and that I cannot share a carriage with boisterous travellers.

When we arrived in Paris the Gare du Nord was festooned with the usual crowd of drivers holding up signs for the travellers they were due to meet. One of them was for someone called Coleman. We knew the driver wasn't waiting for us but I instantly remembered an understandable mistake my father made half a century ago when he arrived at Frankfurt airport, saw a similar sign and assumed that the driver had been sent for him. He wearily and gratefully handed over his suitcase, followed the driver to the waiting car, climbed in and fell asleep.

Three hours later he was shaken awake and found himself staring at a man he'd never seen before in his life. There had been a terrible mistake. My father had got into a car intended for someone else with the same name. The stranger took one look at my father, scowled, muttered something in German, turned away and dismissed the driver and car. It was dark and my Dad didn't have the foggiest idea where he was but he was clearly miles from anywhere. Eventually, he managed to find himself a taxi. He told the driver to take him to the nearest railway station which turned out to be 90 miles away. The whole episode took half the night and cost a small fortune in taxi and train fares.

Things like that were always happening to my Dad. He was brilliant but very forgetful. He invented miniature circuit breakers (those things that replaced fuses) but once arrived in Madrid wearing carpet slippers and without a passport. When I was four he built a television set on the kitchen table. In the 1960s he managed to fit a 13 amp socket into the back of a half wooden mini traveller, so that I could play music on a reel to reel tape recorder plugged into a three pin socket. I probably had the first car in the world with a built in tape recorder. It worked brilliantly and even coped with potholes with equanimity. But even when he was young he would walk past his own car and forget where he had put it.

He was a brilliant inventor, endlessly creative with hands and brain, and when he died I found a huge pile of patents in a filing cabinet. He had signed away all the rights to his employers. He told me once that one Christmas, when he was a boy, he desperately wanted a huge, top of the range Meccano set which he saw in the window of a local toy shop. His parents couldn't afford it. Instead, they bought him a fairly ordinary torch. The day after Christmas he met a friend and they compared presents. The friend, whose parents were well off, and who had been given the Meccano set coveted my Dad's new torch. So they swapped gifts. 'The Meccano set must have cost a hundred times more than the torch,' said my Dad. 'But we were young lads. Neither of us thought of that though I suppose his parents must have done.'

He believed very much in the power of drugs, believing that they would always work immediately and always be safe. I once suggested that he try taking Saw Palmetto for a prostate problem. He rang me the next day to complain that it hadn't helped. Tragically, his trust in doctors went too deep and he died when he was given a contraindicated drug. (There is no little irony in the fact that although one of my bestselling books is called *How To Stop Your Doctor Killing You* both my parents were, in my view, killed by incompetent doctors.)

He never accepted that he was old or frail or even mortal. I tried to turn the conversation several times to practical matters. Funeral arrangements. Burial. Where stuff was kept. What he wanted me to do with his things. He looked at me as though I were mad and impertinent. Death? No, never. He didn't even leave details of his e-mail passwords and as a result neither I nor the solicitors handling his estate could access his e-mail account. His online presence just sort of died with him.

No one in the so-called caring industry seems to care much about the elderly and to many of them he was, it seemed, just an old, powerless citizen past his sell-by-date; he was just another plain old guy wrapped in various shades of beige. No one saw the inventor who had made their lives easier. No one saw the man who had volunteered for the Navy during the Second World War, and signed up for twelve years, because he was in a reserved occupation. He was just another wheezy old man with a bad back and striped pyjamas. Millions of good people are ignored by the people we pay to care; just because they are old.

In Paris the taxi driver who took us to our apartment was a wimp. He stopped to let other cars pull out. He stopped to let buses pull out. He even stopped to let pedestrians wander across the road. He then made a silly mistake and took us into one of Paris's dark subterranean underpasses; an underworld populated by tramps, vagabonds and the sort of people who earn their living filling empty plastic Evian bottles with water from the Seine and then selling them to tourists who aren't bright enough to check that the seal on the top is still intact. (Since there is no outlay the profit on this small example of entrepreneurial activity is vast and an afternoon's work will produce enough profit to purchase an armful of decent wine.) He had the unnerving knack of picking the slowest moving line of traffic and then switching lanes just as the neighbouring lane slowed and our present lane got going. He took twice as long as usual to reach our apartment. The end result was that the fare came to 35 euros instead of the usual 20. He would only take 25, refusing the rest and saying that the long hold up in the underpass was his fault and that he should pay. The Princess and I decided that he could not possibly be French.

Still, he was probably better than the taxi driver we had the last time we were in Paris. This one had a satellite navigation device which was constantly making noises and a dispatcher who never stopped talking. As if that wasn't enough he spent the entire journey with a mobile phone clamped to his ear with one hand while holding a cup of coffee with the other. And he kept racing alongside a chum in another taxi so that they could chat whenever they had to stop at traffic lights. I have never seen one man do as many things at once. He would say something on his mobile phone, swerve round a bus, chat to his dispatcher, curse his satellite navigation system, take a slurp of his coffee and dodge round a woman with a pram who had been foolish enough to venture onto a pedestrian crossing. And all the time, while busy with these other activities, he somehow managed to keep up a steady stream of invective directed at other drivers. And those who believe that hand signals have died out would have been impressed by his repertoire of signals, though I suspect that none of them is to be found in the French version of the Highway Code (if there is one).

We were most impressed that he managed to do all this reasonably successfully and to get through a 25 minute journey through central Paris, in the middle of the day, with only one collision. Moreover, the motorcyclist he hit wasn't even knocked off his bike. And, to be fair, that collision wasn't entirely our driver's fault. In any case the motorcyclist wasn't seriously hurt and dents and scratches are badges of honour to Parisians so no real harm was done.

This was the second time we had travelled in a taxi which collided with a motorcycle. On the first occasion the driver got out of the cab and started a fight with the motorcyclist. However, he made the mistake of trying to punch the motorcyclist in the face. It was a good blow but the motorcyclist was still wearing his helmet. I examined the man's fist and couldn't find any signs of broken bones but he was clearly in a considerable amount of pain and he had to stop at a café and buy a medicinal brandy before he could continue. He was crying when we had to leave him to catch our train, though this may have been as much a result of the size of the brandy as of the injury to his hand.

Taxi drivers in Paris are a peculiar lot. This is undoubtedly due to the fact that unlike London taxi drivers the ones in the French capital don't seem to have any training. There is no French equivalent to 'the knowledge'. We have, in the past, simply told a driver to head for the Eiffel Tower since that is within walking distance of our apartment. (It is fairly easy to find your way across Paris when you realise that the most recognisable buildings, the Eiffel Tower and Sacre Coeur, are both visible from almost anywhere. Once you know where they are situated it isn't difficult to find your way around.) He had absolutely no knowledge of the city and seemed quite unable to read street names. This is not uncommon. Nevertheless, French taxi drivers are masters at finding the long way round. And if you leave them to their own devices they will take you to the Place du Tertre and try to sell you a painting or take you to the Rue St Denis and try to sell you a girl. In London the taxi drivers are professionals and the waiters are amateurs. In Paris it's the other way round.

Apart from the ignorance of the drivers there is one other problem with taxis in Paris. There aren't enough of them. There are 25,000 proper taxi cabs in London and just 15,000 in Paris - the same number that there were in the 1937 when the limit was originally laid down. When the French Government tried to increase the number of licensed taxis, the drivers went on strike and so the Government backed down (as French Governments always do). Finding a taxi in Paris is always something of a nightmare and in wet weather furious matrons with armfuls of shopping can regularly be seen wrestling for the right to commandeer an empty taxi. Tracking down a taxi by telephone isn't any easier. The last time I tried I spent 30 minutes listening to the Rolling Stones singing *I Can't Get No Satisfaction.* The French, like other foreigners, have no sense of irony.

5.

America, the nation of violence and theft, is paradoxically, full of prudes and snitches. According to American newspapers, which I bought at WHSmith in the Rue de Rivoli, several American schoolchildren have been suspended for jumping in puddles, one was referred to a drug awareness programme for accepting a breath mint from a friend, a six-year-old in Delaware was suspended and threatened with reform school for taking to school one of those camping utensils that serves as spoon, fork and knife, a nine-year-old was questioned about a plan to fire a paper pellet with a rubber band (he had to undergo psychological counselling before he was allowed back into class) and a 12-year-old girl in New York was led off in handcuffs for scribbling on her desk with an erasable pen. This is America. Land of slaves and thieves and hypocrites. Those who feel I am being harsh might like to know that after the First World War, the USA was known throughout Europe as Uncle Shylock. Here's what Winston Churchill said about America after the end of that war: 'She (the USA) has by her hard treatment of the Allies accumulated probably nearly three quarters of the public gold in the world.' It was American greed during and after the First World War which caused the Germany currency to collapse, the subsequent rise of Adolf Hitler and the Second World War. The Americans then made a trillion tons more money out of that war – during which they sold armaments to Germany as well as to England. Modern America is wealthy because they robbed everyone else blind during the twentieth century's two big wars. There are undoubtedly many good things that can be said about America but generosity and compassion are not two of them.

6.

We live in a quiet street in Paris, opposite an embassy. There is, generally speaking, little traffic or noise. Except. At 1.00 a.m. on most mornings the peace of the night is broken by the annoying, high pitched whine of a 50cc motorcycle being ridden up the street at full speed. It is, presumably, a waiter from one of the cafés in the arrondissement taking a short cut home. Last night The Princess and I decided to take action designed to persuade the motorcyclist to take another route back home. I filled a bucket with water and then spent a little time working out the height of our building and estimating how far the noisy motorcyclist would travel in the time it would take for an object thrown out of our window to reach the ground. It worked like a dream. One minute the motorcyclist was whizzing along in the dry and a split second later he was whizzing through a thunderstorm. Perfect. Soaked, he stopped and looked around. But he didn't see us. The Princess and I were so delighted by our success that we stayed up celebrating until dawn. This is the second time we have successfully used water to drown out unwanted noises. And the beauty is that if the motorcyclist should complain to the police the evidence will soon disappear.

7.

Paris is surprisingly well stocked with shops which sell books in English. There are, of course, the obvious ones such as Bretano's in the Avenue de l'Opera and WHSmith and Galliano's in the Rue de Rivoli. The now legendary Shakespeare & Company opposite Notre Dame is the best known of the smaller shops but there are many more and it is still possible for the enthusiastic collector to find forgotten bargains on the shelves of many. Quite a few of the wooden bookstalls along the banks of the Seine also contain English books, which are often under-priced. Today I managed to pick up a first edition of Elliot Paul's masterpiece *Springtime in Paris;* this is one of the very best books about Paris and infinitely better than Hemingway's overrated *Moveable Feast.* Paul also wrote other forgotten masterpieces including *The Last Time I saw Paris.*

As we walked back home we found ourselves on the wrong side of a solid sea of cars heading for the Place de la Concorde. We managed to thread our way through the unmoving vehicles but then a woman driver in one of those indistinct, indefinable little grey cars that the Parisians always drive, realising that we were about to walk through the two foot gap between the front of her car and the back of the car she was following, deliberately moved forward to stop us getting through. Parisian motorists always do things like this. When they want to get out of their cars they don't park them they just stop and jump out, parking across pavements and pedestrian crossings without a thought for those they will inconvenience. The Princess and I were now trapped. There was no way forward. And behind us a long queue of pedestrians were lined up in the tiny spaces through which we had already passed. There was only one option. I climbed onto the bonnet of the car and helped The Princess up behind me. We then jumped down the other side and carried on wriggling our way through the traffic jam. The long line of pedestrians following us all did the same. The woman driver was incensed but she could not get out of her vehicle because the cars to the left of her and to the right of her were stopped only inches away. All she could do was open her window and shout at us to stop. Red in face and loud in screech she shouted things at us which were, I suspect, not entirely complimentary. There are times when I consider it an advantage to be linguistically challenged. Naturally, no one took any notice. Other motorists either concentrated on staring at their knuckles or continued to examine themselves in their driving mirrors. As we finally stepped onto the pavement we could still her shouting at us and we still couldn't understand a word she was saying.

On our way back to the apartment we were reminded just how awful English people with children can be. We sat in an empty café for a quiet cup of tea, and an English woman with four very noisy and badly behaved brats in tow burst in and deliberately chose the table right next to us. We didn't say a word but simply moved our teas to another table. Clearly offended by this the woman immediately got up and moved herself and her toxic brood to a new table, again right next to us. I couldn't help noticing that, like Duchess Fergie, she walked like a woman wearing Wellington boots which were three sizes too big for her. When the children started to throw food at each other we left. As we went I told the waiter that the children had mumps and that he should keep well away from them.

Reluctant to risk another café we celebrated our victory over the motorist by buying two large chocolate covered meringue and cream concoctions which used (in pre-politically correct times) to be known as Têtes du Negres but which are now called, rather prosaically, Meringue au chocolat. We ate them in the park near to the Rond Point. They were excellent and well worth the indigestion they will doubtless produce.

8.

We have an English friend in Paris who lives, with his French wife, in a duplex apartment near the Montparnasse tower. He has a model railway laid out on the top floor and for over a decade he has run it like a proper railway. There are several lines, three stations, three passenger trains, three goods trains and many points. For years he has not been able to go to bed until he has run the last train of the day. He has a timetable pinned to the wall and he sticks to it far more fervently than any British rail company honours such a commitment.

For some weeks now he has been very ill. He is dying. We visited him yesterday and at regular intervals his wife would apologise, leave us with him and then go upstairs. Moments later we would hear one of his trains running around the track he built himself. Although he was barely conscious he would smile and nod contentedly.

'If I don't run the trains on time he gets very agitated,' his wife explained when we left. 'He knows the timetable off by heart and even though I don't think he can see the clock any more he knows if his trains are late.'

She said that she too had grown to enjoy the routine and the responsibility and that running the trains gave her life a strange purpose which she could not easily explain.

'He knows he is dying,' she said. 'The other day he asked me if I would continue to run the trains after he had gone. I told him that I would run the trains for as long as I am able and then I will hire a man to run them for me.' She told us that there is a man they know who lives nearby and who ran the trains for them when they were away once at the funeral of a cousin. They have not had a holiday for twenty years because of the trains. 'Jean-Jacque will follow the time table if I fall ill,' she said. 'He can also repair the trains and the track if there are any problems.'

9.

A curious thing happened this morning. Two days ago we had arranged for a security firm to put a new steel door on our cellar in case anyone wants to steal the rubbish and the mice droppings we keep down there. The workmen were supposed to turn up this morning at 9.00 a.m. By 10.30 a.m. they hadn't turned up so, feeling rather angry, I rang up the shop. (Workmen in Paris are usually on time. They are difficult to pin down but usually on time once you've got things arranged.) The guy at the shop was very affable. 'Oh, we did it yesterday,' he said. 'We had time so we got it done for you. I have the new keys here.' So I went to the shop and fetched the keys and took a cheque.

Occasionally, French workmen do rather surprise us. On another occasion we were having problems with a slightly leaky chimney so we rang a building company. The boss came round in a smart suit and climbed out onto the roof to take a look. He gave me an estimate and sent his men round the same afternoon. They did the job very efficiently. When I received the bill it was for less than half the estimate. I queried this (thinking it was a ploy to rebill me later for more money). 'Oh it wasn't as difficult as I thought,' said the boss. 'So I reduced the bill.'

And when our ceiling needed some repair work, and the prospective paperwork looked like taking for ever, we hired some jolly but smelly Russians who came in a huge team, worked like mad and finished the job in two days. We couldn't understand a word they said and they couldn't understand a word we said so everything went very smoothly. I remember being quite miserable about the fact that I couldn't understand anything they said and then being enormously cheered when I discovered that they weren't speaking French. We communicated by sign language and it was efficient and speedy.

I was reminded of these workmen today. The Princess is learning Russian and yesterday she told me that the Russian word for railway station is pronounced 'Vauxhall', though it is of course spelt very differently. To get the full effect of the word you have to use lots of throat, a la Oskar Homolka who was, although born in Vienna, my favourite screen Russian. I'm told that when Russian engineers came to England to look at our first railway stations they were taken to Vauxhall and thought that was the English word for railway station. (The world's first railway station was actually at Euston but that's another story.) So, in the same sort of way that the French borrow many of our words, so the Russian language has been enriched with a little English. The Princess, who is using one of those tapes which are sold in very expensive packages, and which guarantee to produce fluency within 90 days, learnt to say (in Russian, of course) 'This is not a bank but it is a railway station'. I spent some time trying to work out ways in which this could be of practical value on our planned trip to Russia but decided that this sentence must be the modern equivalent of those now infamous phrase book sections giving advice about ostlers, feeding the horses and finding a room for the maid. Still, I can now say more than just 'yes' and 'no' in Russian and I can't wait to try out my new word next time we hire workmen. They will no doubt be impressed (if, perhaps, slightly confused) by my ability to tell them that they are in a railway station rather than a bank.

10.

I went to the pharmacy to buy an eyebath and when I got there I realised that I didn't have the faintest idea what the item I wanted was called in French. I created much amusement when I asked for 'un petite bain pour mes yeux'. The assistant rather snootily told me that I wanted an 'oiellière'. I felt very embarrassed by the hoots of laughter but since I'd got what I wanted I left.

The French language isn't anywhere near as extensive as English (we have 500,000 words and they struggle along with 100,000) but they do, I admit, have some rather fine words.

A flaneur, for example, is someone who saunters through the streets without any particular place to go. A dépaysement means a feeling of being somewhere odd and of having no point of reference. The phrase demi-vierge means a professional virgin. And the French even have a proper word ('le machin') for 'thingy'. The curious thing is that although they have nicked a good many of our words ('le weekend' and 'le picnic' for example) the one word they have given us (brassiere) is something of a joke. In French the word means a baby's vest. The piece of expensive lingerie used to support a woman's superstructure is known as a soutienne gorge.

But the real problem is that the French do tend to take their language rather too seriously. They are always quick to correct a foreigner's pronunciation and never slow to tell you if you use a word in the wrong way. The natives of other countries are always enthusiastic if you try to speak their language. Not the French. The last time I had a conversation in French, and thought I was doing really well, it turned out that the people I was talking to were English. And they were just as impressed by their linguistic skills as I was by mine. The joke is that when the French do try to speak English they usually make a real hash of it. Even the professional linguists sound more Maurice Chevalier than they think they do. If you've ever listened to tapes recorded by Michel Thomas you'll know precisely what I mean. To me the guy sounds like the third baddie in a Gerard Depardieu film.

The Princess and I have decided that we are no longer going to bother with the sexes of nouns or the finer points of irregular verbs. We don't want to write poetry. We just want to buy groceries and deal with the plumber (who will, in any case, probably be Polish). In future we will be content to speak French like natives, even if not natives of France. And we always cheer ourselves up with a thought from our friend Thumper Robinson who once pointed out: 'In France even morons can speak French.'

And when we can't make the French understand us we will switch into English and make them struggle to understand us.

11.

Our French heating service company sent a man round two days ago to point a screwdriver at our French boiler. After five minutes of pointless but noisy activity he told us that we are in breach of a new regulation. Naturally, this comes as a huge surprise. He tells us that our cooker hood has to have an exit pipe in a separate room to our central heating boiler. He told us sternly that he will be reporting us to the authorities and that we have a month to rectify this serious breach of the regulations. It is, apparently, a serious threat to national security, global warming and money laundering activities. In addition I think the bureaucrats in Brussels are worried that the cooker fan will suck all the air out of our 19th century apartment and asphyxiate us. Obviously, only a cynic would suspect that the bureaucrats might be acting on behalf of an expanding industry looking for reasons to do unwanted things and sell unnecessary stuff.

Pretending not to understand what he was saying I thanked him for pointing out that the cooker is in the same room as the boiler. I told him that we had not previously noticed this and that we much appreciated his kindness in sharing his discovery with us. I smiled a lot and shook his grubby hand. He muttered a good deal of sotto voce stuff, gave us an official looking leaflet, picked up his tools and left. (I then scrubbed my hand in a strong antiseptic solution.)

Sadly, I know that this modest victory is as hollow as a politician's promise. The French national motto may be 'See a notice, take no notice' but this is clearly an EU law and even the French are nervous about ignoring the dictates of our masters in Brussels - especially when there are good profits to be made. When they were making up their own laws the French did so with the enthusiasm of people who knew very well that they would ignore them. These days things are different.

According to the leaflet the boiler man has left behind, the problem seems to be that we have two extractor fans in the same room. I decide that there is an easier solution than knocking a huge hole in the wall between the kitchen and the living room: the extractor fan over the cooker doesn't work so if we have it removed we will satisfy the rules.

We won't have an extractor fan over the cooker and so we won't have two fans in the same room. Bingo.

This morning I telephoned a local building firm and asked them to come and remove the offending piece of equipment. Two hulking brutes were with us within minutes, which should have warned me that something bad was going to happen. They looked like extras in an old Alain Delon film. The sort of baddies who get shot within the first ten minutes. They told me that it would cost 763 euros to remove the hood. I threw my hands in the air and shook my head. They brought the price down to 360 euros and agreed that they would take away the malfunctioning hood and leave it on the pavement downstairs where the official refuse lorry would take over and remove it. The whole job took them less than five minutes and involved removing four holding screws and disconnecting the electricity supply. I could have done it myself. Nick Clegg could have probably done it. They then held out their hands for the money.

I got my own back. I didn't tip them. Not one cent.

When they'd gone we managed to get a taxi to the Gare du Nord where we caught the train back to London.

12.

In Hereford we met a man in a park. He was selling copies of a booklet he'd written and published. It was the story of his life. I bought one. The man had a dog with him. A very old Alsatian. As I took the booklet from him I noticed that the man had three fingers missing from his right hand: the index finger, middle finger and ring finger were all gone.

'What happened to your hand?' I asked him. 'How did you lose your fingers?'

'Circular saw,' said the man.

'Couldn't they sew them back on?' I asked.

'The dog ate them,' he said, looking down at the Alsatian with more affection than I might have expected.

Later we went to a café for a cup of coffee. The café was crowded and an elderly woman came over and asked if she could sit at our table. She was very smartly dressed and very proper. She told us that her name was Molly. We moved our cups around so that she could put down her tray. Without further ado she told us that she had met her late husband in 1935 and first kissed five and a half months later. 'I was considered rather fast in my set,' she confessed. She was a substantial woman. If she'd been a ship she'd have been a tanker rather than an Americas Cup contender. She had clearly been built for stability, not speed or manoeuvrability. She confessed that she had been fat even when she was a girl. At school she had played Miss Muffett in the Christmas pantomime and one of the parents had been heard to remark that if she had sat on a tuffet she would have squashed it flat. She laughed a lot when she told us this.

She was eating a meat pie, potatoes, carrots and something mushy and green that I couldn't identify but which didn't look like peas. She told us that she was 85 (children and people over 80 always like to tell people their age) and looked at me rather quizzically. 'I recognise you, don't I,' she said. I said it was unlikely. 'You used to work in my bank,' she said. I shook my head. 'I remember you,' she said. 'Barclays. You were the manager.' She was very definite about it so I didn't argue. Who knows, maybe she was right and I've forgotten a great chunk of my life. She asked us if we lived locally. We said we didn't. She asked us where we'd come from that day. We said we'd come that day from Weston super Mare and that we'd driven up the Wye Valley, past Chepstow race course, Symonds Yat and Ross on Wye.

'During the War I used to hitch-hike from Yeovil to Weston super Mare,' she told us. 'There were dances on the pier. Five of us used to go. The two prettiest stood out front and the other three hid behind a hedge.' She blushed when she told us that despite her size she was always one of the pretty ones out front. 'We were picked up by all sorts of people,' she said. 'We were picked up by top brass once or twice.' Remembering more, she blushed a deeper red. 'Once, we were picked up by a meat lorry. We stood in the back hanging onto the meat hooks.' She put her hand in front of her face and laughed. When she moved her hands away we could see that the surfacing memories had made her blush. 'I always behaved myself, mind you,' she said. 'I was a married woman by then, of course.'

She didn't look like the sort of woman who'd ever stood in the back of a meat lorry, hanging onto a meat hook. But you can obviously never tell.

13.

We bought several packets of wild seeds to scatter along English verges. But on the back of each packet of seeds there is a warning which says: 'Even though they are wild flowers these seeds should not be scattered in the wild without the authorisation of your local Nature Conservation Trust.' Now, the seeds we are planning to scatter are all native to England. So, what do we do? Oh dear. After microseconds of agonising we finally managed to come to a decision. Bugger the quango. Plant the seeds.

14.

Last night The Princess sent an e-mail to a local shop which we often drive past. It's a small shop, in a fairly run down area, but it has three large windows and there is always such a display of beautiful dresses that I slow down so that we can see them more clearly. The displays change regularly. In her e-mail The Princess congratulated the shop owner and told her how much she appreciated the beautifully organised windows. The shop owner e-mailed back today. She was clearly very happy. The Princess is always good at finding ways to make strangers happy.

15.

I collect books, stamps, old toy racing cars, lead soldiers and other people's odd sayings. One of the joys of travelling and sitting in cafés is the opportunity provided to eavesdrop. I don't deliberately listen to what strangers are saying, but some people speak loudly and it's impossible not to hear what they say to one another. If people talk loudly in public places then they must expect what they say to be written down for the entertainment of others. Here's a recent collect of my eaves-droppings (I've sometimes quoted two people speaking):

1. 'She's been engaged more often than a public lavatory in central London.'
2. 'English beer is like a fresh cowpat – brown, flat and warm.'
3. 'You're 20 minutes early!' 'Put it on my account, I'm bound to be 20 minutes late sometime.'
4. 'Was there *anything* to your satisfaction this evening?' (A waiter in a restaurant in London, talking to a customer who had complained about everything.)
5. 'Does my bum look big in this?' 'Darling, your bum looks big in anything.'
6. 'Don't wear a blue swimming costume in England or people will think you're bathing in the nude.'
7. 'Thank you for the lovely tablecloth.' 'Actually, you're supposed to wear it.'

8. 'She could have been slimmer of the year for three years running – and she'd have still needed to lose weight.'
9. 'Since we fought World War II to save Poland you'd think they'd give us a discount when they do our plumbing.'
10. 'She works at the airport and at Christmas all her relatives get penknives and nail scissors as presents.'
11. 'I don't like surprises unless I'm ready for them.'
12. 'If I wake up and I'm still here I know it's already a good day.'
13. 'That's enough about me and my new job. What do you think about my new job?'
14. 'There's no future in history books.'
15. 'Come on, the sell-by-dates will be up by the time we get this stuff home.'
16. 'These will do as my flirty knickers. I'll wear these when he's going to be lucky.' 'By the time he sees them he'll *know* he's going to be lucky.'
17. 'I never give money to fat beggars.'
18. 'I bet you I can give up gambling before you can.'
19. 'No, he wasn't bitten by a dog. He was bitten by a German farm worker.'
20. 'I was so embarrassed. I hadn't got anything on under my clothes.'

16.

Our lane is a favourite spot for local dog owners to 'walk' their dogs. This is, of course, a euphemism. They really bring their dogs into the country so that the animals can open their capacious bowels and deposit their unwanted food residues on our doorstep instead of their own. Occasionally, the dog owners obey the signs which the council has pinned to the trees and take home these unwanted offerings. For this purpose they usually bring a little plastic supermarket bag which, when full, they tie at the neck. Clearly, the idea is that when the procedure has been completed the bag is taken back home and disposed of in some unspecified but hygienic way. Alas, many of the dog walkers who parade along the lanes of our bit of the Cotswolds have only got the hang of the first part of the process. Once their hound has filled the plastic bag they tie the neck and fling it into our garden. I confess that I never quite know what to do with these donations. However, if I ever catch anyone hurling their doggie bag onto our land I will know exactly what to do. I live in hope.

17.

I received a note telling me that a pleasant sum has been paid into my bank account for the photocopying of my books in schools and colleges. It would, of course, be far cheaper, easier and less wasteful for teachers to buy copies of my books rather than to photocopy them but the cost of photocopying comes from a different budget to the cost of buying books. And so teachers regularly photocopy whole chapters so that students can study them. They don't seem to give a damn about how much money this wastes. After all, it isn't their money they're wasting.

At one point my books were being photocopied so often that one printer I know suggested that I put my books into spiral binding and print 'suitable for photocopying' on the front cover.

Sadly, this useful income is about to come to an end. I read the other day that the Government is planning to eradicate the remuneration that authors receive from schools and colleges. In the future teachers and lecturers will be able to photocopy articles and books without any payment being made to the author.

The whole principle of copyright is being challenged in a number of ways. Websites (and their users) now frequently argue that 'copyright is theft' and that authors who insist on being paid for their work are doing something anti-social if not actually downright criminal.

I've received a number of letters over the years from people demanding that I give my books away and I have long since given up trying to stop people stealing and reproducing my work on the internet.

In the bad old days, when thieving was done largely by men in masks and striped jerseys, I used to earn a modest living from the fees I received for the reproduction of articles and book chapters. The fees weren't much by themselves but £50 here and £100 there soon added up. For some reason or other extracts from my work often appeared in textbooks and the fees for those reproductions were very welcome. I haven't received any such fees for years. These days people just help themselves to whatever they want to steal. In recent years the whole concept of copyright has been given a good kicking. Whole articles of mine have been stolen and have appeared in magazines or online. Chapters have been taken from my books and miraculously appeared in other books. ('I have a photographic memory,' was the excuse of one thieving author.) On the Web I have sometimes been credited as the author (though not paid of course) but more often another 'writer' has claimed credit for my work and simply lifted my piece and put his or her name on top of it. On at least one occasion a whole book of mine has been stolen, retitled and sold on the Web. The new Web-happy generation seem to regard copyright as an outdated concept, rather irrelevant. It isn't irrelevant to me. I earn my living as a writer. Someone who steals from my website is stealing just as surely as if they steal from my home. Earning a living is pretty difficult for iconoclastic authors these days.

When I first started writing professionally I learned very quickly that it is unwise ever to sell copyright. The creator of the Wombles, Elizabeth Beresford, is reputed to have sold the copyright in her Wombles scripts for £50 each. She apparently received nothing from the television shows, from the repeats, from the cuddly toys or the other merchandise. Ian Fleming is reported to have sold rights in his James Bond books for £100,000, which doubtless seemed a lot at the time but which, if true, now looks to me like a darned good deal for someone else and a pretty poor deal for the late Mr Fleming.

I always found that holding onto my copyright often made a vast difference to my earning capacity. I've always refused to sell my copyright, insisting on a royalty rather than a fixed fee. In the 1980s I recorded a vast series of taped advice lines for a service known as *The Telephone Doctor*. People could ring up a special number and listen to my advice on a whole range of medical topics. Within months the Royal Society of Medicine, the British Medical Association and the Royal College of Nursing had all found doctors to write and record their own scripts but I'm pleased to say that my lines beat off all the competition. It seemed that not many people wanted the 'official' advice. At its peak around 30,000 people were ringing *The Telephone Doctor* every week. (A friend of mine who found out how many people were ringing in said: 'Gosh, I wouldn't like to do that. How on earth do you answer so many calls?') When the entrepreneur who set up the service was looking for a doctor to record the lines he talked to three doctors. The other two media doctors (whose names were exceedingly well-known at the time) both preferred to take a hefty fee to record the lines. Like them I was offered £2,500 (a decent sum in the 1980s) but I said I didn't want a fee but would take a royalty on every call. The guy who was setting up the business preferred my choice because it meant I had more involvement in the project, and because it meant he didn't have to fork out a big chunk of money upfront. The scripts took me a week to write and I spent another (very exhausting) week sitting in a studio recording them all. The lines ran for quite a number of years and in the end millions of people used them and were, I hope, helped by the advice. Because I had retained the copyright I received a decent royalty on every phone call. In the end I earned several hundred times the fixed fee I was offered. I was able to use the money to help take risks when publishing and advertising books which threatened the establishment.

But now the principle of copyright is threatened. Web thieves and governments everywhere seem to be opposed to the payment of fees and royalties to the originators of new material. Actually, I can understand governments not approving of copyright. If they aren't able to earn a living from their work authors won't be able to write books. And whatever the bloggers and twits might claim the book always was, is, and will be, the most potent influencing force in the media. The Central Intelligence Agency is on record as saying that books are a more powerful influence on society than films, television, radio, newspapers or anything else.

18.

I went downstairs this morning and found The Princess kneeling on the stone floor in the dining room. I didn't need to ask her what she was doing. She had found a dying woodlouse and was trying to keep it alive by transferring it to a piece of damp tissue before taking it outside to put into a comfortable spot in a pile of logs.

The Princess is writing a book about our garden, and the small creatures with whom we share it, and has spent several weeks poring over rare and difficult to find volumes about woodlice, wasps, butterflies and other garden glories.

Apparently, woodlice are crustaceans and have far more in common with lobsters than spiders. They need water. Like spiders they come into the house when they know the weather is going to be bad (they are a much more accurate and practical source of weather information than the Meteorological Office which today warned us all that bad weather is coming and that we must protect ourselves against falling branches and against our roofs being torn off, without giving any advice about how we should do this) but, because of the central heating, they soon start to dry out and before long they become seriously ill. When they are too dry, and desperately need a little water, some varieties curl up on their backs into a ball as a prelude to dying.

Because we live in the middle of a wood we share our home with a constant stream of woodlice and spiders. The spiders can look after themselves very well but the woodlice need almost constant attention. Our downstairs rooms contain innumerable intensive care units where recovering woodlice can be seen reviving themselves on pieces of damp tissue paper.

19.

Our Government seems to have plenty of money to spend on putting stupid concrete barriers down the middle of our motorways, for planting chicanes in perfectly straight roads and for interrupting our pavements with pimply red slabs which pose a real hazard to wobbly pedestrians. (All these are, inevitably, a result of orders from Brussels.) Oh, and turning perfectly decent sections of motorway into 'managed motorways'! (This means creating endless traffic queues by pointlessly limiting traffic to 40 mph. I am convinced that 'managed motorways' were created by communists who want to destroy our society by damaging our economy and pushing up our oil consumption. Traffic congestion costs the British economy £4.3 billion a year. Around £4 billion of that is a direct result of unnecessary speed regulations on motorways.)

But we don't have any money to mend potholes. (The bureaucrats in Brussels obviously don't care about potholes.) And yet potholes don't just lead to a bumpy ride. They are dangerous. People drive round them and crash into one another. We drove into one this afternoon that was so large people were living in it.

One of the problems is that repairing a pothole in England costs as much as building a block of flats in Germany. Repairing a pothole isn't difficult. A man with a degree in brewing sciences digs out the hole a bit more. And a man with a degree in art history fills it in with some black tarry stuff. A man with a degree in economics then drives a small steamroller over it. It's not even as difficult as reading the news and that's one of the easiest damned jobs on the planet. (With the possible exception of being a clothes model, for which narcissism and no brain at all are the only requisites.) And we could use the income from our speed cameras to pay the cost of the navvies and the black tarry stuff. But that won't happen. The money from the speed cameras is already earmarked for paying bonuses to incompetent civil servants in some quango somewhere. And the only way that things are going to change is that next year the potholes will be even bigger.

20.

An advertising agent wants to know if I want to start buying advertising again. He suggests that I might consider advertising direct to bookshops. No thanks. When the film of *Mrs Caldicot's Cabbage War* came out I wrote to every bookshop in the country. I sent them all a cover of the book, and I offered posters, photographs and promotional leaflets. I gave very specific details of exactly how they could order without effort from their usual wholesalers. I bought full page advertisements in *The Bookseller* (described as 'the organ of the book trade'), pointing out that the book could be ordered through all wholesalers or direct from Publishing House. I told bookshops I was buying display advertisements in five major national newspapers (*The Guardian, The Independent, The Daily Telegraph, Daily Mail* and *The Times*).

I should have saved my money. Not one bookshop took any copies of the book and so as far as I am aware none sold any. Not one. And even if I had been able to persuade the shops to take some copies (on sale or return) they would have probably been tucked away in some hidden corner of the shop. It was reported recently in *The Times* that Waterstones, the bookshop chain, was allegedly charging publishers £7,000 for a book to appear on their Paperback of the Year list. Publishers have to pay a fee if they want their books displayed in the window or on the table at the front of the shop.

The truth is that the bookshops wouldn't touch the book of *Mrs Caldicot's Cabbage War* because it was self-published. They weren't interested in the fact that very few major films are made from novels, or that no other self-published novel has ever been turned into a film. Bookshops don't like independent publishers. And that's one of the many reasons that they are dying. (Incidentally, having a film made of a novel is one of the few win-win situations in life. The author, who has nothing whatsoever to do with the film, cannot lose. If people like the film he can take the credit. If people hate the film he can blame the director, the screenwriter, the producer, the stars and the man who operates the clapper board.)

For the first 15 years of my career as an author I could go into any bookshop in the land and find my books on the shelves. There were sometimes whole shelves of my books on sale. But since I started publishing my own books I have hardly seen a copy of any of my books in a bookshop. And yet during that time I have sold more books than ever, and made more money from my books than I ever did when I was writing genuine best-sellers for London publishers.

Just about the only books of mine that did force their way into book-shops were *England Our England* and *Gordon is a Moron*. I remember that one week I sold 2,500 copies of *England Our England* to bookshops in England. That's damned good for a book on politics.

Naturally, neither book featured in the official bestseller lists. How-ever many books a self-publisher sells he or she will never get onto the bestseller lists.

Surprisingly, you don't need to sell all that many books to get onto the hardback lists in England. The lists aren't compiled according to the num-ber of books that are sold but according to some mysterious measure which ensures that only bookshop sales count and a book will only appear on the lists if it has been 'registered'. For many years I sold thousands of copies a week of hardback editions of books such as *Alice's Diary, The Village Cricket Tour* and *The Man Who Inherited a Golf Course* and I know that the sales of these, and other books, were higher than the sales of many books which were sitting proudly in the official lists.

Still, my books had a good long life. Today, most bestsellers now have the shelf life of dairy produce. Book shops return books in the after-noon if they haven't sold well in the morning. And that's the end of it.

21.

There are visitors staying at a nearby house which is usually rented out to holidaymakers. We can just glimpse the house through the trees but yesterday we could hear a good deal of noise coming from that direc-tion. When I walked to the greenhouse to water the plants I looked across and saw a group of six or seven young men standing around. The men all looked to be in their twenties. One of them was holding a bad-minton racket. I watched as he repeatedly hit a shuttlecock high into the air. I was puzzled because I couldn't see what he was trying to do. And then the other young men gave out a great cheer. One of the men placed a long and very rickety ladder against the side of the house and climbed up to the guttering. The house has three floors and is very high at this point. After a surprisingly long search the man on the ladder pulled the shuttlecock out of the guttering and threw it down. There was another loud cheer. And then the game started again. That's all they did. All day. One man would hit a shuttlecock up into the air until it became stuck in the guttering. A second man would then climb up a very dodgy ladder and rescue the shuttlecock. They seemed to find this aspect of the game to be hysterically funny for they laughed a good deal as the ladder was climbed. When it got too dark to see what they were doing they stopped and went indoors. But early this morning the game started again. I couldn't understand who could makeup such a pointless and dangerous game and then be amused by it for ten hours at a time. I couldn't understand why a group of men should rent a house in the country and spend all their time in such a bizarre way.

'Who are those men who hired the house just up the way?' I asked a local who knows everything that happens in the area.

'They are foreign,' he said. He shrugged and pulled a face. 'German,' he added, as though this explained everything. And, on reflection, I realised that it does, for the Germans are a strange people with a peculiar sense of humour.

22.

We were walking in lanes just a mile or two from our house when we stopped to admire an old-fashioned cottage garden. There was, inevitably, a mass of birds about and The Princess, whose study of wildlife has become a serious hobby, suddenly touched me on the arm and said, out loud: 'Look at that pair of great tits!' Moments later a red-faced woman rushed into and out of view, heading for the house. She was fastening a bikini top as she ran and had clearly been sunbathing. We hurried on our way. I once compiled a list of collective nouns and, as we fled, I asked The Princess what she thought one should call a concatenation of great tits. 'A bosom?' she suggested.

23.

I was quite unable to buy ordinary second or first class postage stamps anywhere. Every retail outlet (apparently the new term for 'shop') had sold out and assistants told me that the Royal Mail had refused to provide fresh supplies. Even Post Offices had sold out. There were no stamps on sale anywhere. And so I couldn't post any letters. I couldn't pay my bills. I couldn't reply to readers. The Royal Mail was abusing its monopoly position in this outrageous way because wise citizens (mostly people running small businesses) had realised that by buying stamps before the 30th April (when the price is due for a massive, inflation busting rise) they could save a little money and, perhaps, stave off bankruptcy for a little longer. Royal Mail has stopped printing stamps because they're frightened that awful members of the public might buy a few of the old stamps at the old price. And so we cannot post off any parcels. I sometimes think that the Royal Mail is redesigning itself to reduce the amount of work it has to do.

'Do you have any brown brogues in size 12?' I asked one counter clerk. She was the sort of person who only feels really comfortable when wearing a label, one of those plastic covered identity cards carrying her name and title, dangling on a cord round her neck or pinned to her lapel. She had a chest like a pouter pigeon.

'What are those?' she asked, looking genuinely puzzled.

'Shoes,' I replied.

She considered this for a moment. 'We don't sell shoes,' she said eventually.

'I thought I'd try,' I said. 'You don't sell stamps so I thought you might sell shoes.' I smiled, bade her good day and hobbled off.

I tried to ring to see if anyone knew where there might be a stash of available stamps for ready money. It was, of course, a futile exercise.

If you ever want to taste eternity try telephoning Royal Mail. Almost any of their numbers will do but I do particularly recommend ringing your local sorting office where it is almost certain that no one will ever answer the damned telephone. Maybe they don't know what it is. They hear it ringing (just above the sound of the television) but aren't sure what they're hearing. It's easier to get hold of MI6 than it is to contact the local sorting office. They make GPs surgeries look accessible.

I have, however, managed to acquire details of the new pricing structure and I've discovered that to post a copy of my *Diary of a Disgruntled Man* to Australia will cost just under £15 (not counting the cost of typing out the label, sticking on the label, buying the padded envelope, putting the book in the bag, sticking on the stamps and taking the parcel to the post-box. The Royal Mail has exclusively killed our export trade. And it has, I suspect, also destroyed the chances of *any* publisher or bookseller selling books to foreign buyers. Bravo Royal Mail. Destroying our export trade is just the way to bring the nation out of the deepening and lengthening (and oft-denied) recession.

It is often said that Edgar Allan Poe was inspired by the catastrophes which affected his life to write *The Murders in Rue Morgue, The Fall of the House of Usher, The Pit and the Pendulum, The Black Cat* and many other horror stories. It's a good job poor old Poe didn't have to deal with Royal Mail, the Post Office, British Telecom or British Gas or heaven knows how depraved and terrifying his stories might have been.

24.

A huge tanker was parked in the lane. It stank. It wasn't difficult to see why. On the sides of the tanker were painted the words: *Septic Tanks Emptied.* And underneath was the single word *Guaranteed* and underneath that were the words *Money Back If Not Satisfied.* The driver, a small man in a brown boiler suit, was leaning against the bonnet smoking a cigarette.

'How can you give a guarantee on septic tank emptying?' I asked the driver. 'How would people know?'

He thought about this for a moment. 'Dunno,' he replied, with a toothless grin. 'But if anyone is unhappy with our service we give 'em back their money and everything we sucked out of their tank - all delivered to their door with our compliments.'

It took a moment or two for this to sink in. I shuddered at the thought. 'Do you have many unhappy customers?'

'Not one!' said the driver. 'Not one complaint in 30 years.'

25.

When I was at medical school the half-wits who ran the place introduced a system of continual assessment. Instead of taking examinations at the end of the year we were to be tested at regular intervals throughout the year by filling in multiple choice questionnaires. The very first test we were given was designed to award marks for correct answers and to take away marks for incorrect answers. We were given one mark for each correct answer but had five marks deducted for every incorrect answer. It seemed to me that the way the system had been designed almost everyone would score a negative final total and so at the end of the examination I handed in a blank paper. I duly came top of the class with nought. I had done well by doing nothing. When she was a young girl The Princess had a similar experience with an examination in the English language. The tutor had created a scheme whereby students lost marks for putting punctuation in the wrong places but gained no marks for putting it in the right place. She rightly and sensibly realised that the best solution was not to put in any punctuation at all.

And it now occurs to me that this must be the philosophy being followed by Royal Mail. If they make life intolerably difficult for their customers they will have less mail to deal with and instead of making a big loss every year they will make a small loss, break even or, by concentrating their efforts on a few profitable areas of their business they may actually make a profit.

I can see this philosophy proving popular with all sorts of people. Rail companies who don't run any trains can never be accused of failing to meet expectations. Councils who do nothing can't be accused of doing a bad job, or letting people down.

26.

I've spent ten days filling in my tax return. They've simplified it. Ten whole productive days gone. That's two working weeks for a bureaucrat. Actually, given their working hours and mine it's probably four working weeks for them. Eight.

Part way through the mind numbing process I found the half-pints at HMRC had sent me the wrong supplementary forms. I rang up and asked a clerk to fax me the right forms so that I could get on with filling in the forms before my mind atrophied. 'We can't do that,' she said. 'We don't send forms by fax.' So I asked to speak to a manager. He said the same. 'OK,' I said, 'then in that case I wish to register a formal complaint. You've sent me the wrong forms and now you're refusing to put things right.' There was a slight pause. 'Oh,' said the manager. 'Well, under the special circumstances...' The forms were faxed within two minutes. Yet more evidence for my argument that when dealing with any Government department (but particularly HMRC) an aggressive approach pays off. I rang the pensions agency the other day and my first words were: 'I want to make a formal complaint.'

'What about?' asked the person on the other end of the line. 'I don't know yet,' I replied. 'You haven't told me anything yet.'

'What will I do if you go senile?' asked The Princess. 'I can't possibly fill in the tax forms.'

'Don't worry,' I told her. 'I'll continue to fill them in. They'll never notice and I won't care.'

27.

I received a letter from a reader in Durham who has a pet cockerel called Gregory. She explains that he is named after her hero Gregory Peck. I have written back and confessed that the plant on my study window-sill is called Robert, after the lead singer of Led Zeppelin.

28.

A couple who live nearby but come from Norfolk have three daughters and a pug dog. They are the sort of people whose photographs regularly appear on the crowded society pages of those county magazines that no one ever reads but that people buy to put on the hall table next to their telephone. The daughters are known to us as the Norfolk broads. The father scowls at everyone. The mother sneers. The three daughters, who have clearly inherited these characteristics, all scowl and sneer. I swear that the dog is by far the most handsome of them all.

29.

We bought the first *Downton Abbey* television series a few days ago and today we watched the first few episodes. We were both very disappointed. It may be critically acclaimed but to us both it seemed dull, predictable and hackneyed. The characters seemed to us to be two dimensional clichés, the plots straight out of a soap opera and the dialogue certainly not sharp or witty. It seems to have been designed for undemanding but supercilious Audi drivers and doesn't compare with classics such as *Brideshead Revisited, Reilly: Ace of Spies* or *Raffles.*

The building they use for the Abbey is Highclere near Newbury (which is also used in some of the excellent Jeeves and Wooster programmes that were made some years ago with Stephen Fry and Hugh Laurie). I recognised the house because I delivered fish there when I was a medical student. I had a job with a local fishmonger for two weeks during my first year's summer holiday. I remember driving up to the front door and being told to take my small parcel of fish to the gun room at the side of the house.

30.

The village shop employs a girl whose name is Olivia. But everyone calls her Lisa. I asked the owner of the shop the origin of this pseudonym. 'She's always moaning,' explained the shop keeper. 'And so we call her Moaner Lisa.'

MAY

1.

A friend had a pet duck which was eaten by a fox while sitting on her eggs. Surprisingly, the fox did not eat the eggs. Our friend then persuaded a pet hen to sit on the duck eggs until they hatched. When the young ducklings were old enough to waddle to the pond the hen went mad with panic, clearly frightened that her brood would drown. For the next two years the hen had her own chicks which did not go near the water. But in the following year the hen was again given duck eggs to sit on. This time, when they hatched, the hen flew straight to a small island in the middle of the pond. She stood there and called for the ducklings to follow. They, of course, could not fly. They had to paddle across to her. The hen's actions could not have been a reflex; it was a complex, learned action. We assume animals aren't intelligent because they don't, and can't, do the things we do. But all animals are more intelligent than we suspect.

2.

While reading a copy of *Fanny by Gaslight* by Michael Sadleir (published in 1940) I found this quote. 'By trade Warbeck was a book publisher, who did a little writing on the side. He was seldom shocked by the things which shocked the British public, but often found either painful or disgusting things in which that public took delight. Consequently his tastes and theirs were apt not to coincide. Further, his instinct for novelty outran the normal; and he had not even yet learnt to make allowance for the reaction time - seven to ten years - which was common form among his compatriots when faced with any new idea in the practice or appreciation of matters of the mind. As a result, he published books far ahead of any possible acceptability, failed to sell them and was duly chagrined when, years later, his competitors published others of similar character and got away with them. Further again, he refused to admit that political conviction justified an author in distorting truth or lapsing from literary integrity - a prejudice which lost him many opportunities for profit, but in return won him no particular esteem.'

Apart from the fact that I am an author who does a bit of publishing on the side (rather than the other way round) I have, I think, found my fictional alter ego.

The ego has landed.

3.

We met an old friend of ours. He had written to let us know that he would be in London and so we took the train to Paddington so that we could meet him. We are, as always, shocked by just how dirty and scruffy London has become. There are very few rubbish bins and the streets are constantly littered with unwanted paper and plastic. In Paris there are rubbish bins every few yards and there is very little rubbish on the pavements or in the gutters. I wonder if there could be a link?

Jimmy, our old friend, used to be a photographer on a local newspaper. He did well and at the age of 27 he gave up his job and became a freelance, working for several national newspapers. He made good money and in the 1970s he borrowed £35,000 from a bank, added to it the £15,000 he had saved and bought a street of houses in Lancashire. A whole street. He then borrowed another £7,000 (with no other security other than the houses he had just bought), did them up and rented them out. The rents he received more than covered the amount he had to pay the bank each month.

Twenty years later he sold the row of houses to a property company and netted £1,800,000 after tax. He used a quarter of the money to buy a beautiful house in the French countryside and invested the rest. He lives well and is now worth a small fortune.

Jimmy told me that he nearly didn't make it.

'When I worked for the local paper I was told by the editor to get as many people as I could into every picture,' he told me. 'In those days local papers made much of their money by selling prints of pictures that had been in the paper.'

'When I managed to get my first chance with one of the nationals I was merely a stand-in for a regular guy who was away on another job. I had to take a picture of some politician whose name I've forgotten. He was opening something. As instructed I took a whole roll of film. But because I was used to taking pictures for the local paper I did the same as I always did - I made sure that I'd got lots of people in every shot. When I put the undeveloped roll of film on the train to London I thought I was a really big cheese. A few hours later I didn't think I was such a star. The picture editor rang me and tore my head off. 'There are 27 people in every picture,' he complained. 'And if I look very hard I can just about make out the Minister!' The picture editor had to use an agency picture.

Jimmy was lucky; he had a second chance and took pictures for what used to be called Fleet Street for a good few years. 'I'm glad I got out when I did,' he confessed. 'I had the best years. These days there's no money to be made. Every kid has a mobile phone with a camera in it. The papers get their pictures in seconds. There's no need for freelance professionals. There's no need to put a roll of film on the train. And there's no such thing as an exclusive anymore.'

He said he'd been back to his row of houses in Lancashire. 'I just wanted to see what they looked like. Surprisingly, they look exactly the same as they did when I tarted them up. Nothing has changed.'

He admitted that he had the best years for making money out of property too.

'I was lucky,' he said. 'I was born at the right time.'

There was more than luck to it, of course.

Lots of people were born when he was. But not many of them did as well as he has.

Afterwards we spent an hour or so sitting in Hyde Park having a picnic. Within five seconds of our sitting down a foreigner who didn't speak any English had appeared in front of us demanding money. I assumed he was a representative of the local council and gave him £4.50 - the rental fee for sitting in three deckchairs for one hour. We had a good view of the lake, though the endless stream of joggers and power walkers was rather irritating. Sadly, we had to leave our deckchairs well before our hour was up. The park is full of untethered dogs which wander thither and hither without restraint. The local constabulary, sitting in their motor car, seemed not in the slightest bit interested in this clear breach of the by-laws.

A genuine fear of loose, marauding dogs is a healthy default condition and The Princess and I decided to leave the park while we still had our preferred number of limbs and digits. It is sensible to be afraid. It is the ruthless, reckless dog owners who have a problem: many are, or behave like, psychopaths. The Princess and I used to love walking but these days we rarely wander out on country trails or in public parks because we know that if we do we are almost bound to come face to fangs with platoons of uncontrolled, aggressive dogs and their aggressive owners. We would love to go walking in places like Westonbirt but what's the point? When you have to pick out a couple of large sticks before you set off for a gentle stroll it seems much more sensible to stay at home. (One of the advantages of old age is that one can carry a stick without attracting critical comment. Walking sticks are excellent, not just as aids for crumbling limbs, but also for poking people with.) The vast majority of the dogs out in public are off the lead (even though this is against the law) and the rest are often on those damned extendable leads. With the dog pulling ahead and the owner struggling along behind it is clear who is in charge; the dog is the pack leader and this is always dangerous. Pack leaders eat babies. And the smaller the owner the bigger and more aggressive the dog is likely to be. The Barboured hooligans who breed so well in the Cotswolds measure their social status by the size of their dog.

Over 6,000 people a year are admitted to hospitals as a result of dog bites. And as foreigners and beggars discover that they can claim extra benefit payments if they have a dog or two so that figure is increasing rapidly - at the moment it is more than doubling annually. That's a big drain on the NHS in particular and the economy in general. (In addition, 5,000 postmen are bitten every year - resulting in 15,000 sick days.)

Many of the owners of all the fashionable Rottweilers, bull terrier cross, Alsatians, Dobermans, pit bulls and so on don't bother to buy a dog licence, don't pick up after their dogs and abuse non-dog owners or the owners of other dogs who dare to protest. (Why on earth would any sane human being have a pit bull as a pet? Once they have their jaws around something soft and human these creatures only ever let go in order to get a better grip. Crocodiles would make more sensible pets.) It is people, not dogs, who need licences.

Instructions to muzzle aggressive animals are simply ignored. Dangerous animals are allowed to roam wild and the police are not in the slightest bit interested. The number of stray dogs has soared by 70% in the last four years, and will doubtless continue to rise. People buy dogs for all the wrong reasons (to make money or as weapons) and when they discover how expensive a dog can be they just let them loose in the road. When animals fall sick, and require expensive vet bills, they are simply abandoned.

Cycle tracks are taken over by dog walkers who always let their dogs off the lead (dogs chase bicycles) and parks are too dangerous for children to play in. Dog owners make a huge fuss when there is talk of not allowing dogs to be let off the lead in public parks used by children. I once wrote an article describing the number of children who had been savaged in a local children's park and the attitude of aggressive dog owners was: 'There's a hospital nearby, what's the problem?' When I wrote a column about children being made blind by toxocara an eminent dog lover wrote publicly admonishing me. 'This only affects about 50 children a year,' she wrote. She was absolutely right, of course. 'Only' 50 kids a year go blind because of toxocara. This doesn't mean that those kids go blind temporarily. Or a bit blind. They aren't just blind on Wednesdays or for two weeks. They are blind for ever and ever amen. As The Princess points out they will never see their Christmas presents, never see patterns in clouds in the sky, never see a daisy chain, never see a kitten with a ball of wool, never catch a leaf in autumn and never see a dog catching a Frisbee. All because some bastard dog owner was too bloody selfish and lazy to behave responsibly.

None of this is the dogs' fault, of course. The Princess and I don't blame them for a moment. It's the damned owners, as tight as Kelsey's nuts, who should be hung, drawn and quartered and then, just to make sure they really suffer, subjected to a full HMRC audit inspection.

Our dog troubled afternoon in Hyde Park was followed by a pleasant walk back to the station through the Islamic hinterland that is now Paddington.

I used to enjoy going to Paddington before the powers that be decided to bugger things up. The authorities never seem able to leave a London railway station alone for more than five minutes. The new St Pancras station looks quite pretty from the outside but inside it is a shambles. Once a Eurostar train is announced there is a mad scramble for the escalator and there is more pushing and shoving than you would expect to find at a Debenhams's January sale. But the lunacy has reached new heights at Paddington where Brunel's magnificent and conveniently designed station has been reorganised by planners with all the style and good sense of blind squirrels. In the good old days the taxi rank was an easy walk from (and to) the trains. Today, tourists need hiking boots and a compass to find the taxi rank and sensible and experienced travellers simply walk out into Praed Street and pick up a taxi there. Every taxi driver I've spoken to regards the changes as making life more difficult for everyone. I can only assume that developers and the (in my view) mortally pompous, irresponsible, patronising, incompetent, contemptuous, arrogant buffoons at English Heritage (surely the worst of our 476 million quangos) have got together to make their mark on our lives by using their seemingly unending supply of taxpayers' money to turn an efficient and good looking public facility into something I now regard as ugly and inefficient. I wonder if anyone working at English Heritage has ever had a proper job, or if they have spent their working lives cocooned in a taxpayer-funded world of luxury and waste, where they can specialise in ineptitude, impracticality and a total disregard for the value of other people's money?

Of course, it isn't just London which has been reorganised by idiots. The Gare du Nord in Paris was once a station people actually visited even when they didn't want to travel. The restaurant there, as at all French mainline stations, was renowned. Today, travellers wanting to reach the Eurostar terminal need stout shoes and determination. And it's necessary to allow an extra thirty minutes to navigate your way through the numerous obstacles which interfere with the route from the station entrance to the platform.

4.

Here's an odd thing.

The price of new books has been falling steadily for years. Although all costs have rocketed books are now much cheaper (in actual prices) than they were twenty years ago.

When I first published *Alice's Diary* in 1989 I sold it for £9.99 - which was the sensible price for a small hardback. I still sell the book for the same price but now it seems expensive. And yet the cost of printing the book is at least twice what it was. And every other cost imaginable has soared. Twenty years ago I could charge £1 for postage and packing of any book and be confident that the fee would cover the cost. Today, it costs me £7.22 in postage to send a copy of *Diary of a Disgruntled Man* to France and around £15 to send the same book to an address in Australia. With those sort of postage costs it is impossible to make a profit out of selling books to foreign readers. So, having spent years trying to build up the 'export' side of my publishing venture I have had to pretty well abandon selling books abroad. (I did discover one thing, however. Far fewer of the parcels we sent abroad went missing after we started writing 'contains a book' on the outside. One can only assume that customs officers and postmen aren't much interested in stealing books. I keep meaning to get a rubber stamp made to use on parcels posted to destinations within the United Kingdom.)

But (and here's the irony) old Penguin paperbacks which originally cost 2/6d are now sold in Oxfam shops for a smidgeon under £3. That means that old paperbacks have been the best investment anyone could have made. If you'd filled a warehouse with old paperbacks in the 1960s you would have made a fortune. (The dear old orange and green Penguins were a perfect size to carry in a pocket or small bag. It has only been in recent years that publishers have started producing paperbacks the size of tree trunks.)

The collapse in real book prices has recently been speeded up by the internet, of course. But I have a suspicion that when real books come bouncing back into fashion (as they will) the prices will soar simply because at the moment relatively few books are being printed (and many authors are simply being allowed to go out of print).

5.

A reader who lives in the far north of Scotland has written to tell me that she calls her bowels 'the willows' because they are always full of wind. I have suggested that she contact the Government in the hope that someone in the natural energy department may be able to work out a way to take advantage of her stormy condition.

6.

My collection of eaves-droppings continues to grow. Here's the best of the latest batch:

1. 'I didn't have any breakfast, and by the middle of the morning I was ravishing.'
2. 'She bought a book called *How to train your dog* but she left it on the sofa and the puppy chewed it to bits.'
3. 'If he started a rock garden even the rocks would die.'

4. 'When asked to name the four seasons one of the kids said: salt, pepper, mustard and vinegar!'

5. 'I can't afford to travel first class any more but I always walk down the carriages and get out of the first class in case anyone I know sees me get off the train.'

6. 'He's one of those people who says: 'I always speak my mind' and then takes offence if anyone else speaks theirs.'

7. 'He rented a car and washed it before he took it back.'

8. 'Mummy, is this the fat, thieving bastard Daddy was talking about?'

9. 'Napoleon just gave the world a silly hat. Wellington gave the world really useful boots.'

10. 'He said he wanted to paint the sea and I said I'd always quite liked the colour it was.'

11. 'I can eat anything I like. It's only afterwards I have problems.'

12. 'Women have better memories because they have memory glands.'

13. 'I sometimes wish I were older just so that I'd know I hadn't died young.'

14. 'I call my in-laws Fred and Rose. After the Wests.'

15. 'It fell into the back of our lorry.'

16. 'Does he paint 'Oh, look, it's a…' or 'Are you sure it's the right way up?'

17. 'When the world ends there will be a Dormobile and a shopping trolley left and my brother-in-law will own them both.'

18. 'Do you think it's a coincidence that 'age' rhymes with 'beige'?'

19. 'He's chairman of the local malevolent society.'

20. 'He carries a screwdriver so that he can even steal stuff that's screwed down.'

7.

I discovered this morning that one of our drains was blocked. For nearly an hour I poked around with sticks trying to clear the blockage. I couldn't budge it although I did succeed in disrupting the blockage enough to release some pretty malodorous fumes. I had pretty well resigned myself to calling in the professionals when a chap who works on one of the nearby farms came trundling along the lane on his tractor. He saw me, stopped and came over to see if he could help. When I had explained he did not hesitate. He knelt down and stuck his bare arm into the pipe, rummaged around for a few moments and then pulled out a large handful of brown, glutinous material.

He deposited this on the ground nearby and then plunged his hand back into the pipe. He did this half a dozen times until the blockage was cleared. I thanked the Good Samaritan profusely and then, before I thought what I was doing, I held out my hand. He rubbed his hand on his trousers and we shook. When he had driven away I rushed up the garden and rinsed my hand under the garden tap for five minutes. I then opened the back door with my left hand and asked The Princess to pour half a bottle of Dettol into the sink. I scrubbed my hands until they were almost raw.

8.

A retired banker we know vaguely, who lives in a large house nearby, has a huge gravel driveway. Every time a visitor drives on the gravel and leaves wheel marks he rushes out with a rake to make everything look smooth again. One deliveryman tells us that he always leaves with a lot of wheel spin. He says he doesn't feel at all bad about this because the man is condescending and rude.

9.

'Why do you always wear a hat?' asked a man I know. He is a small, mean-mouthed man with the eyes of a guilty ferret and the pallor of a professional invalid. He speaks in a reedy voice and offers firm judgements on all subjects with the confidence of a man who believes he has been given privileged access to the truth. He never allows ignorance to interfere with his certainty. He is a sidesman at a local church, treasurer of several local societies and a member of his golf club committee. He is famous there for having introduced a 48 page dress code for members and visitors. Professionally speaking he is something big in sewage and it is tribute to his total lack of any sense of humour, or indeed the absurd, that when asked about his profession he invariably replies, in the utmost seriousness, that he is big in sewage.

'Wearing a hat will make you go bald,' he said.

When I asked him if he had any evidence for this claim he explained that if you wear a hat you stop the rain getting to your hair. 'If you cover up your lawn the grass will die,' he said. 'The same thing happens to hair.'

I thanked him for his advice but said that since the damage is done and I am already balding I will continue to wear hats because I like to keep my head warm.

10.

Belatedly, we visited our local surgery to sign up with a new doctor. It has taken us quite a while to find the doctor with whom we are forced to register. I wrote to the Primary Care Trust but got nowhere. I made numerous telephone calls and no one even knew the names and addresses of local doctors. Since the previous owners of our house took the telephone books with them we can't use them to help us. Eventually, I managed to find the name of the practice we have to join.

And so we turned up at the appointed surgery.

We were, inevitably, given forms to complete. 'And we'll need your passports, your National Insurance numbers and two utility bills each,' said the receptionist.

'You can look at some utility company paperwork to prove that we live in the area,' I told her. 'But you can't make copies.'

'Oh, we have to make copies,' she said. 'We're told that we must - by the Health Authority.'

'What do you do with them?' I asked.

'We store them,' she said, nodding behind her to an open filing area. 'They're kept quite safe.'

'I'm afraid you can't copy them,' I told her. 'You can look at our utility bills – though heaven knows why you want to – but I won't allow you to photocopy anything. Moreover, there are no laws which entitle you to copy private documents.' I didn't realise it at the time but they were breaking health service rules in asking for proof of residence of any kind.

'I need to see passports,' she said.

'We don't have them,' I told her honestly (just missing the words 'with us' from the end of the sentence).

She wasn't happy about that but I glowered more than she did and eventually she gave in and registered us as new patients. There was no 'welcome' and we weren't given any introductory leaflet containing phone numbers and surgery opening hours. The Princess's health problems are still the same as they were when she was investigated so thoroughly (and with such little sympathy and so few useful results) a year or two ago. Scarred by her previous experiences of health care in England she does not want to see more doctors and I do not blame her. Today's experience has not changed our view of the modern medical profession. Indeed, they have confirmed and strengthened our disillusion and distrust.

What a dismal world we live in.

11.

Back in the 1980s I used to go on book promotional tours for three or four weeks at time. It was a strange business. I once ended up on my way to East Anglia and genuinely forgot where I was going, why I was going there and who I was. Every radio and television station in every town I visited was talking about me and my book. You eventually begin to think the world is talking about nothing else but you and your darned book. As I approached each town I would tune in to the local radio station to see how they were promoting me. And as I left each town I would listen to the continuing discussion I had sparked. By the time I lost the signal for the one station I would be approaching the next and the whole process would start again. In the evenings there were interviews with local reporters. That's the distortion being on television can create. I shared sofas with film stars and drank bad wine with famous drunks in television green rooms the length and breadth of the nation. And, having spent a considerable amount of time with some real celebrities, I've learned that genuine star quality, charisma, is made up of some almost indefinable qualities. In my view danger, unselfconsciousness, confidence, talent and vulnerability are the essence of real stardom. Real stars are never vain or conscious of their status. And, most of all, perhaps, they have the genuine capacity to surprise. To give a simple and rather obvious sporting example: David Beckham is undoubtedly famous but it seems a plastic, manufactured sort of fame and although Beckham may make more money I don't think he will ever be as charismatic as George Best or Alex Higgins.

When I wasn't promoting books I did endless radio and television programmes. A few decades ago television and radio programmes used to pay guests chunky fees to appear on news and current affairs programmes. (Back in the 1980s it was not unusual to be paid £750 plus very adequate expenses to appear on a local television discussion programme.) I did so much television that I had an Equity card for a few years. I was paying union dues to four organisations separately representing authors, journalists, doctors and performers until I realised that I really wasn't that much of a joiner. (Shyness and a feeling that it was rude to approach strangers and ask them questions meant that I wasn't much of a journalist either.) I resigned from them all and replaced them with membership of the Desperate Dan Pie Eaters' Club run by the publishers of the *Dandy* comic. These days television producers want guests who will appear free of charge, and even pay their own expenses. The result is that the only experts who can afford to broadcast are the ones with proper jobs and well-paid alliances and consultancies with industry lobby groups. And so the only words broadcast are those supporting the industry point of view. Eventually, even the presenters begin to believe the party line. And anything which questions the perceived reality must be suppressed. I sent out over three hundred review copies of my book *Anyone Who Tells You Vaccines Are Safe And Effective Is Lying. Here's The Proof.* It says on the cover of the book that I am a registered and licensed GP. You might imagine that someone, somewhere would be interested - even if only to try to tear me to shreds. But not one radio or television station wanted to interview me. And not one newspaper or magazine published a review. Indeed, on the contrary, many of the books which were sent out were returned. Instead of flogging the book on Amazon or eBay, editors and reviewers actually paid to send the book back. Revolting figures of the Russell Brand ilk are deemed controversial and banned for twenty minutes. I've been banned very effectively for well over a decade. Too much trouble, you see. I have found trying to tell the truth in general, and about medical matters in particular, to be an ultimately frustrating and dispiriting business.

Most media outlets, but particularly those involving television and radio, have become unhealthily incestuous. A select number of self-aggrandising egocentrics interview one another on their own programmes, write books (or have them written for them) based on their television programmes, write (or have written for them) newspaper columns in which they talk about the people they have met while presenting their programmes, present radio shows on which they discuss their television programmes and work with people who also have radio or television shows where the cycle can be perpetuated. A remarkably small number of people constantly appear and reappear.

There are occasional guests, of course. When a particular subject is in the news previously unheard of talking heads will appear. The problem is that the vast majority of these will have been put forward by lobby groups of one kind or another. They will have been prepared, polished and paid in order to promote a particular point of view.

People who have something useful to contribute because they have impartial knowledge, or well-formed original opinions, are excluded because they don't represent an industry or a lobby group with a product or a viewpoint to promote and because television and radio researchers are far too lazy to find them.

However, there are always occasional exceptions and a reader of mine who has written several well-researched pamphlets has written asking for my advice on how best to survive a television interview without making an ass of himself. 'I'm not a great public speaker,' he confessed. 'I am nervous about being interviewed on television but I am determined to put forward my point of view, which I believe to be significant and widely overlooked.'

I'm damned sure I wasn't much good on television (I am naturally shy and had to send along a spiritual doppelganger) but I presented and appeared on enough programmes to know how things work, how television and radio programme makers stitch people up and how to counter their crafty little moves. I also discovered just how self-obsessed, ruthless and uncaring people in television can be. When I presented TV programmes I never missed a show but on one occasion I had to go to hospital for a scan because I had suspected kidney cancer. As soon as the scan was done (and a friendly radiologist had given me the all clear) I drove up the motorway like mad to get to the studios. I got there bang on time. 'You're nearly late,' said the director. 'I had to have a scan to see if I'd got kidney cancer,' I told her. She looked at me, clearly worried. 'You're not going to miss any shows are you?' She was much relieved when I assured her that I wasn't. She didn't ask how I was or what the scan had shown. She was concerned only about the show. Television numbs us all and as the years go by so the programmes have to get tougher and nastier to titillate and shock. Just compare Eastenders with Dixon of Dock Green.

Here's the advice I sent my reader:

1. Assume that the presenter will try to stitch you up. Do not trust anyone working for a television or radio company. They will tell you lies in order to disarm you and make you easy prey. It is wise to assume that the programme is being biased in favour of a particular point of view. And it is almost certain that the point of view being presented (and protected) will have originated with some establishment body. Contrary to popular opinion nearly all broadcasters represent and defend the status quo. Before a programme appears the researchers and assistant producers to whom you speak will assure you that they are on your side. They will ooze sympathy, understanding and support. This is all fraudulent, frothy nonsense designed to put you at your ease and make you easy prey. No one in the studio is your friend.

2. Do some research about the programme and the presenter. When I used to appear regularly on television and radio I was constantly surprised by the number of presenters who would, before we went on air, admit (almost boastfully) 'I haven't had time to look at any of your books. Can you tell me what sort of thing you do?' If an appearance on a programme is important to you (and if it isn't then why are you appearing?) then you should do a little research. Find out as much as you can about the programme maker and the presenter. Try to watch or listen to a few of their interviews. Study their style and the style of the programme.

3. Try to ensure that you only ever appear on live programmes. It is very easy for editors to turn your wise and thoughtful pronouncements into demented gibberish. If the programme's aim is to promote a particular, establishment point of view then that's what they will do. Anyone who opposes that viewpoint will be given airtime (so that the programme can appear fair, balanced and unbiased) but their words will be cut so that they look foolish, ignorant and even dangerous. If you do make a recorded programme ask for a copy of the pre-edited tape to take home with you.

4. Once you enter a studio you must assume that everything you say will be aired. Never assume that cameras aren't working or that microphones are 'dead'. Many neophytes assume that cameras are only 'live' when the red light shows but it's easy to cover up or turn off the red lights. Never ask for advice, never look around for support, never say anything you don't want broadcasting.

5. Remember that the presenter makes programmes for a living. That gives him an edge. But it also gives you an edge. His job is on the line - yours isn't. Where is it written that the presenter has to be in control? A few years ago I saw a well-known trade unionist being interviewed by a tough interviewer. When the interviewer asked a particularly nasty question the trade unionist looked him fair and square in the eye and said: 'Before the programme you told me that you didn't want to discuss this issue. I'm surprised and disappointed that you lied to me. But since you've asked me the question I'll answer it.' The interviewer went bright red, looked enormously embarrassed and completely lost control of the interview.

6. If you intend to make an important point which you can support with published evidence do take the evidence with you and

hand it to the presenter when you make your point. I once saw James Goldsmith destroy two television interviewers by producing documents which substantiated the points he was making. I was once interviewed by Edwina Currie on television. I guessed that she would attack my credibility so I took with me a copy of *Hansard* which included a statement she had made when she was Minister of Health. When, as expected, she said something derogatory I replied by taking the *Hansard* out of my inside pocket and reading a statement she had made in which she had announced that she always read my columns and that the Government had taken action as a result of articles I had written.

7. If the interviewer makes a mistake - however small - make sure that you correct him. Do it politely but firmly and at length.

8. Don't be frightened to answer the question you want to answer rather than the question you've been asked. If you feel that an interview is heading the wrong way turn it around by mentioning something that you want to mention.

9. If the presenter interrupts you and asks a new question just go back to what you were saying before. Tell him that you will gladly answer the new question but that you'd like to answer the previous question first.

10. Never get cross. Don't lose your temper on television unless you are faking it and totally in control. But if you can make the presenter cross then you are winning. Marshall McLuhan's analysis of television as a 'hot' medium is as accurate now as it was in 1964. The presenter may deliberately try to make you angry. Don't rise to the bait. Don't allow yourself to be pulled into a shouting match. If you do then you will look bad and you will lose.

11. Learn to breathe in mid-sentence (as Margaret Thatcher did). Once you can do this you can speak for as long as you like. For the interviewer to interrupt you he will have to speak over you. And that will make him look rude.

12. Ignore the hospitality they may offer before a programme. In the minutes before a programme starts they will probably offer you food, chocolate, coffee or alcohol. Don't accept any of it. The food will make you feel full and lethargic, the chocolate will make it difficult to speak clearly, the coffee will make you want the loo and the booze will dull your mind.

13. Once you have answered a question, and said what you want to say, close your mouth and stay silent. Presenters all use a very old trick: they keep quiet when you think you've finished speaking in the hope that you will want to fill the silence by saying more - and probably saying something foolish. Just keep quiet. It is the presenter's job to keep the programme moving and so he will have to break the silence before it becomes uncomfortable. (I long ago learned the value of the silence. In the mid-1980s an editor rang me to ask if I would write a feature for his magazine. It was a major, weekly woman's' magazine. He had just dumped a big feature for the next week's issue and needed something writing quickly. He wanted 3,000 words delivered by fax in 24 hours. He asked me what fee I wanted. I asked him what he was offering. He said he could pay me £1,500. I didn't say anything. I was thinking about whether or not I could write the piece. I was also thinking what else I would have to postpone or cancel. I was thinking that I would probably have to work through the night. I was thinking it sounded a decent fee. But the editor didn't know I was thinking all this. He thought I was hesitating. 'I can go to £3,000,' he said with a sigh. 'But that's the best I can manage.' 'OK,' I said. A friend of mine, an erudite man who has degrees in French and Russian, and a PhD in European history, and who works as a postman once told me, when I asked him why he said so little, that he believed that one should not say anything unless one had something pertinent and kind to say.)

14. Find out beforehand how long the interview is going to be. If you know that the interview will last two minutes then you will know that you must say whatever is important to you very quickly and succinctly. If the interview is lasting twenty minutes then you will have all the time in the world to make your point.

15. If you have something you really want to say, and the interviewer isn't giving you a chance to say it, begin a reply by saying: 'Before I answer that let me just say...' Politicians (who are trained in media work and who have, as a breed, mastered the art of the interview) will say 'I am glad you asked me that' and then, without blushing, talk about something completely different. Another trick is to end a reply with 'I suppose you will now want to know...' and to segue into an answer to the question you have effectively asked yourself. The importance of television is now impossible to over-estimate. Even in the world of Facebook and

Twitter, television still has the power. Television is all that matters as far as politicians are concerned. It is the beginning and the end. Reagan, Clinton and Blair all became 'leaders' because of their television skills. (Brown would never have been elected Prime Minister. He obtained the post without bothering to trouble the electorate.) The new television age produces bland, dangerous nerds like Clegg and Cameron who wear nice clothes and look reasonably smart in a cheap and tasteless insurance salesman sort of way but who, like fast food, contain nothing of any value and nothing of any real substance. (I'm trying to find a manufacturer to produce loo brushes with a picture of Nick Clegg printed on the bristles. It would, I feel sure, be a huge commercial success.)

16. Always speak in a low, normal voice. Don't allow yourself to be hurried. (Speaking more urgently can work, however, if you are talking on the radio and want to make sure that the listener's attention is captured.)

17. Before the programme starts make sure that you set out the points you want to make. And then make those points, regardless of the questions you are asked.

18. Don't ever look surprised at anything you asked. Long before you go into the studio you should try to think of all the nasty things that could happen. What tricks is the interviewer likely to try? What surprises could there be? Be a boy scout: be prepared.

19. Remember to smile (whenever appropriate). Viewers like people who smile a good deal (that's why a war criminal like Blair can stay in power). When I regularly made television programmes the other presenters and I would remind one another to 'Sparkle!' before the cameras started to work. Television in particular tends to be a slow business. There is much sitting around. It is easy to relax too much. Reminding yourself to 'Sparkle!' is a good way to remember that you're entering the entertainment business.

20. Be prepared to be tricked. Before the programme begins the staff will be very friendly. When they talk to you they will be patient and encouraging. If there is a rehearsal they will give you plenty of time to discuss your point of view. But the questions you are asked in the rehearsal are unlikely to be the questions you will be asked when the programme goes live. The presenter wants to put you off your guard. If the programme has a hidden agenda (to promote a particular point of view) they will want to make you

look edgy, nervous, ignorant and incompetent. At the same time they will want to make the establishment's hired hand look wise, benevolent and independent. He or she will be given freedom and time and will be treated with respect.

12.

I have been invited to speak at the annual dinner of a golf club 200 miles away. 'Don't worry, our expectations aren't particularly high,' I was assured. 'You were our seventh choice for speaker this year.'

'Why did the others turn you down?' I asked.

'Oh, all sorts of excuses,' said the fellow from the golf club. 'But we had to say 'no' to four of them.'

I was puzzled.

'They wanted expenses,' explained the man from the golf club.

I haven't done any public speaking for a long time, and, indeed, the last time I spoke to strangers two thousand of them were armoured policemen and a helicopter was hovering overhead for the whole of my speech. But, over the centuries, I have learned that there are two basic rules that should never be ignored. First, always make sure you know the quickest way out of the room. Second, check with the organisers that only soft bread rolls will be served (the crunchy ones hurt too much). I did once ask for all diners to be equipped only with plastic cutlery, explaining that I wasn't over-keen on the idea of speaking to several hundred people all armed with knives, but this request was rejected out of hand. I mentioned these requirements.

'Oh, we can't control the catering,' I was told. 'Hard rolls, soft rolls, we eat what they give us. But the catering people are very good. Last year they gave us meat balls bunkered in mashed potato, served with greens.'

'Can they do vegetarian food?' I asked.

'Good heavens, no!' said the man from the golf club, extremely shocked. 'Our President owns an abattoir. He doesn't hold with all those leftie nonsenses.'

I politely declined, citing a prior engagement.

13.

An opinion leader (who is, I suspect, the sort of person who always agrees with the last person to state an opinion) claims that the internet is the greatest invention of all time. Really? I think I'd rather have electricity than the internet. (And I would think it's rather difficult to have the latter without the former.) I bet most people would choose the washing machine and the vacuum cleaner rather than the internet. The internet has changed our lives. But has it changed our lives for the better? I don't think so. And in terms of the overall contribution it has made to our lives the internet comes 987th - just above the toaster and just below safety matches. Chimney brushes, the abacus and bicycles all far more useful than computers or the internet. (The bicycle is the only device that gives back more than you put into it. It is the world's only free lunch.) The internet may have been a decent idea but it is now infested with dribbling, drivelling trolls; petty, incompetent and driven by jealousy, and only too aware of their own inability to create anything original, they drive out the brave and the good and deface everything honest and honourable with pustulent, self-righteous, sanctimonious spite. Both the internet and computers are, in the real world, about as much use as a pair of rubber spanners.

Computers, more about the medium than the message, enable us to do things we have lived our lives never doing and never wanting to do, they have introduced more deceit and confusion into our lives and they have legitimised rumour and destroyed the quality of research and education. People who work in government departments and for large companies love computers because they can blame them for everything that goes wrong. Problems made by public sector employees are always blamed on computers, even though computers virtually never make mistakes and public sector workers frequently do. (Thumper Robinson, a good friend of mine, is always dismissive when computer freaks boast about the ability of computers to play chess. He says that he will be impressed when they can also play table tennis and tickle trout.)

The internet is dominated by nasty, nerdy, malignant youths who defame, steal and destroy with impunity. They can do this because they, and they alone, know how to manipulate search engines.

Artificial fertilisers have had a far, far greater effect on our lives than anything with a plug on the end of it or a battery inside it. The telegraph, the motor car and the train were much more important inventions. The washing machine freed women to go to work, started the consumer revolution and helped destroy domestic service (14% of the workforce in England was in domestic service in the years between 1850 and 1920). It also changed the relationship between men and women and changed the nation's economy. Oil rigs, piped water, sewage services, central heating and satellite communication - the list of great and useful inventions goes on and on. And the computer never appears. Let alone the internet.

It is now widely and generally argued by governments and large companies that the internet must be used and revered by all. A big chunk of the population still has no internet access and has never visited a website and the Government's response to this impertinence is to force people online by making it impossible to live without using the damned internet. The reason for this is simple: the internet saves the Government money and it provides them with information which gives them power.

America has taken over the internet. (It is, of course, an English invention but that sort of thing has never given the Americans pause for thought.) And, having stolen the concept, they are now busy ruining it in a typically brash, greedy American way. Our Government and our multinational corporations are merely doing things the American way.

The establishment enthusiasm for the internet is repeated ad nauseam by newspaper columnists who like to think they are trendy and in the fashion. But the truth is that the internet has improved life only for governments which want more power over us and for large companies who want to accumulate information about us which they can use to help them market their products more efficiently and, therefore, more profitably. When I hear that a company is planning to 'improve' its service my heart sinks - especially if their improvement involves the internet. I know that things are going to be chaotic. I know that the changes are going to require hours of effort from me. I know it is going to be more expensive. And I know that things are never going to work as well again.

Internet use is now compulsory in the UK (not just for anyone who is VAT registered or who employs even one person but often for those who pay utility bills and want a receipt). As a result it should surprise no-one that the UK has the highest online spending in the world and that consequently our towns and cities are being ruined faster than anywhere else. The UK makes up 11% of entire global internet retail sales. Around 10% of all retail sales in the UK are now done through the internet.

It is hardly surprising that the internet has adversely affected productivity and growth (both of which have fallen consistently and fairly dramatically since the internet was introduced). As productivity has fallen so, inevitably, has growth. People started to use computers in the 1960s and it wasn't long before productivity fell. Between 1972 and 1996, as more and more businesses introduced computers, productivity fell dramatically. This was no coincidence. In the mid-1990s the internet was introduced and between 1996 and 2004 there was a small increase in productivity. But that didn't last. Since then the internet had provided very few jobs but has destroyed many businesses and created massive levels of unemployment. (It has not helped that employees have started spending most of their time sending out e-mails, updating their Facebook pages and twittering to other twats.) A small bunch of young billionaires have made money out of the internet but most people's lives have been ruined by it. Even those who have remained in employment have suffered because the internet has helped push down incomes. And investors and pensioners have suffered because company profits and dividends have fallen too. Clearly, enthusiasm for this absurd, over-promoted toy is misplaced. The internet is time wasting nonsense. We would all be much better off if we put it back into the box and screwed the lid down firmly. The internet has not improved my life in any way (in fact my life would be a good deal better if the internet had never been invented at all) and I strongly suspect that this is true for most people if they think about it. The Government could, of course, use the internet to help us and save the nation a fortune. For example, if they put up a website containing constantly updated information about road closures, accidents and delays, motorists would be able to avoid traffic jams and save petrol. But the Government only uses the internet when the Government and civil servants benefit directly.

Finding ways to use coal and oil had an infinitely greater impact on our lives than the discovery of the internet, which is no more than a self-serving, ego buffing vanity publisher and mail order machine. Oil gave us riches beyond our dreams whereas the internet has done more to destroy our society than any other single invention in history. (England would have remained a major force in the world, despite being impoverished by America during two World Wars, if the Treasury hadn't been so damned mean at the start of the 20th century. England could have bought the concession to the Saudi Arabian oilfields for £20,000 in sovereigns. That was what King Ibn Saud wanted. However, the Treasury refused to give the necessary exchange control permits and the confession went instead to Standard Oil of California and the Americans.)

Despite all this evidence, the internet's supporters love it blindly. Idiots are providing computers to countries in Africa where there are no roads, no food and no electricity. (These doubtless well-intentioned buffoons are almost as daft as those uninformed benefactors who insist on sending vaccination teams around the world, not realising that instead of spreading good health they are spreading illness and disability.)

The internet is just a gimmick, a hula hoop with a plug on the end (and no exercise value). It is useful for governments and large companies who want to cut their costs and spread propaganda. It helps them distract us and feed us an endless supply of misinformation. The internet is intrinsically corrupt. You will only find the truth if you are already an expert in a subject and you know precisely what to look for, what to ignore and what to accept. Our growing dependence on the internet has altered our lives and even our brains. The whole damned thing encourages hurried, distracted reading (all those adverts flickering away). It is all so damned superficial. We don't acquire knowledge. We browse. Information has become entertainment; a diversion. The internet is full of stuff that is there forever but most of it shouldn't be there at all. Nothing ever gets erased and very little gets corrected. Lobbyists and crooks ensure that the internet is a worthless research tool. The internet land is peopled by semi-literate quarter wits who are obese with opinions but skeletal with knowledge. The internet is very useful for bigots, terrorist groups, paedophiles, confidence tricksters, pornographers, fraudsters, religious nutters and political parties. But who else? I recently saw a claim that the internet is unique in that it enables businesses to know more about their customers than traditional businesses. What nonsense. Anyone who has ever run a mail order business will know just as much about his customers. By and large the only people making money out of the internet are the people who are selling books on how to make money out of the internet.

Among the young the internet has done nothing much except encourage narcissism. Moreover, hundreds of thousands of children are, it seems, addicted to internet pornography. With the exception of pornographers and computer nerds we would all be much better if it had never been invented and if Tim Berners-Lee had invented something genuinely useful (such as a non-drip teapot) instead.

The internet is making people poorer and more miserable, more anxious, fearful and self-centred. Our world is packed with so much information that it is increasingly difficult to separate the wheat from the chaff. Most people find it difficult (or impossible) to differentiate between independent advice and sponsored propaganda. Global growth has actually fallen since the internet was introduced.

The people who are enthusiastic about the internet are determined that it will take over every aspect of our lives. Its use has become compulsory in many unavoidable areas of life. It has become an evil monster, a time waster, chewing up minutes, hours and lives. It is a tired and broken creation, producing tired and broken people. It encourages energy wasting in every sense of the word. Notebooks and paper diaries can be more effective, more reliable, simpler to use, cheaper and far, far more private.

I live in hope that the internet will turn out to be a fad, like hula hoops, platform heels, the Spice Girls and CB radio. I wonder how many people remember CB radio. It nearly took over the world not all that long ago.

14.

I have, more by accident than design, acquired three copies of Hesketh Pearson's excellent biography of Sydney Smith, called *The Smith of Smiths*. Pearson was the best biographer of the 20th century. I love this quote from Smith: 'I write for three reasons: first, because I really wish to do good; secondly, because if I don't write, I know nobody else will; and thirdly, because it is the nature of the animal to write, and I cannot help it. Still, in looking back I see no reason to repent. What I have said ought to be done, generally has been done, but always twenty or thirty years too late; done, not of course because I have said it, but because it was no longer possible to avoid doing it. Human beings cling to their delicious tyrannies, and to their exquisite nonsense, like a drunkard to his bottle, and go on till death stares them in the face.'

15.

The Princess has been reading a book about English prisoners held in Japan during the Second War. The prisoners building the infamous Bridge over the River Kwai were paraded through the streets, naked and starving. The Japanese jeered at them. It started to rain. And much to the astonishment of the Japanese, the prisoners began singing the famous Gene Kelly song from *Singing in the Rain.*

This reminded The Princess that when bombs went off in London a few years ago the television news people broadcast one of the emergency calls reporting the bomb which killed many commuters in London. 'I'm sorry to bother you but a bus has just blown up,' said a quiet, calm, polite, apologetic English voice.

And it reminded me of the Duke of Wellington's aide who, during the battle of Waterloo, turned to the Iron Duke and said calmly: 'I think I've lost my leg.' Wellington turned and looked. 'Begad sir, so you have!' he replied.

16.

Our local post office has a postcard in the window advertising a course entitled: *Empowering Women Through Embroidery And Poetry.* I am tempted to put on a frock and turn up to find out how this works.

17.

Here are a few bits of late news I've recently collected:

1. When the first bestseller list was introduced in the USA in the 1890s, seven of the first top 10 books were pirated books written by English authors. (It is ironic that the Americans are complaining about the Chinese not respecting their copyright rules).

2. Talleyrand suggested that in order to see what sort of person we are we should imagine that we look out of a window and see a fight between two groups of people. 'Do you,' he said, 'instinctively help the losing side, wait till you see who is winning and then join them, or find the cause of the fight and then support the morally correct group.' (Talleyrand didn't consider doing nothing at all an option.)

3. An actress spent the last years of her life living alone and unrecognised in a New York apartment building which she owned. She hadn't been forgotten but most people thought she was dead. One day she was standing on the kerb, waiting to cross the road, when a young man stood next to her. It was raining. The old woman had no umbrella, just a headscarf. Something made the young man look at the frail old woman. 'I've seen all your films,' he suddenly said. 'But I still can't decide which is my favourite.'
   She looked up at him. 'How did you know?'
   'Your eyes. And the cheekbones.'
   She nodded. A slight smile appeared.
   'May I photograph you?'
   She thought for a moment. And then nodded again.
   Greta Garbo.

4. In the early days of the BBC, at the times listed for the broadcasting of the news, radio news announcers would sometimes say: 'There is no news today'.

5. The drummer with the rock band Def Leppard was involved in a road accident. He lost an arm. 'You'll need a replacement drummer,' the band was told. The band shook their collective heads. 'We'll wait for him,' they said. 'He can play with one arm.' They did and he does.

6. Iconic, Bristol born film star Cary Grant did everything he could to protect his image (and to protect his fans). Film director Peter Bogdanavitch's daughter was a great fan of Cary Grant's movies. When Bogdanavitch asked a frail and elderly Grant if he would meet her, Grant said he would not and that he would rather she remembered him as he was in the films.

7. When Adrienne Brown (wife of the deservedly legendary soul singer James Brown) was stopped in Georgia for driving under the influence of drugs, for speeding and for criminal trespass, she instructed her lawyer to file for diplomatic immunity on the basis that her husband was the Ambassador of Funk. To support her argument a lawyer found a speech by US representative Douglas Barnard of Georgia, who, speaking on James Brown Appreciation Day in Augusta, had announced that: 'James is indeed our number one ambassador'. Sadly, it didn't work. But what a try.

8. When Carole Lombard was making a film she suddenly told the cameraman to stop. 'There is a light missing,' she announced. She was right. There were 70 lights directed onto her face at that moment. One bulb was out. She had noticed the change in the amount of heat on her face.

9. Marlon Brando could never remember his lines. Sometimes he had them pasted onto the faces of other actors. But some other actors weren't too keen on this so later he had an ear piece with an assistant prompting him with his lines. This worked well until Brando's ear piece somehow got hooked up to the local police radio. The actress who had said: 'Darling, I love you,' must have been surprised when Brando replied: 'There's been a collision at the corner of Benedix Street and Aspen Avenue'.'

10. And here's a favourite quote from John Fothergill, my favourite innkeeper: (Visitors) 'ask for the menu or what is for dinner, which I always feel to be rude and inquisitive. Having become polite of necessity, much fun is withdrawn from my life.'

11. In his quarter final heat of the Amsterdam Olympic Games in 1928, Australian rower Bobby Pearce stopped for a moment to

allow a family of ducks to paddle across his lane. He still won by 20 lengths and went on to win the gold medal.

12. When Sir Pelham Warner wrote his history of Lords cricket ground (*Lords: 1787-1945*) in 1947 he invited Viscount Ullswater to contribute a chapter describing the pictures and photographs which hang in the Pavilion's famous Long Room. Ullswater made one or two errors in his chapter but Sir Pelham refrained from correcting the mistakes which were described as minor and 'of infinitely less importance than good manners'.

18.

It's my birthday and I am even older than I was yesterday. Today I am 969 years old, matching Methuselah. I began the day by singing 'I'm feeling rather weary, though I guess it's just my age. It really won't be long before I'm dressing all in beige.' One minute I am struggling to make a First World War biplane out of Meccano and the next I am fighting to persuade Scottish Life to release the pension for which I've been giving them money for decades. I suppose I've done well to get this far. There were some close calls. I woke up once driving at 70 mph on the central reservation of the M6. I was driving south after three nights on call at a hospital in Birmingham. I'd fallen asleep and my mini was about twenty yards from a concrete bridge when the bumping woke me up and I swerved back into the fast lane. (There were no barriers in those days). Half an hour later I put the car into a ditch near Stow on the World. A pal and I on a holiday in Italy were swept out to sea when bathing on the beach at Piza. We were both young and fit but a vicious undertow wouldn't let us back onto the beach. We floated round the coast and eventually managed to swim to shore. Many years ago I had an anaphylactic shock reaction to a typhoid vaccination. But now, at last, I'm old enough to know that however lucky I might be, however careful I might be, however good my genes might be, I will one day die. It's curious, isn't it, but one never really believes this until one is over 60-years-old. We believe that death is something that happens to other people.

I have decided that if I reach my 75th birthday I will start smoking a pipe. I love the paraphernalia associated with pipe smoking. The metal prodders and pokers. The pouches full of tobacco. The pipe cleaners. The pipes themselves, all sat neatly in a wooden rack. Officious men and women will rush up to me in public places when they see my pipe. I will tell them that my pipe isn't lit and they will remain indignant as they try to work out what the law is about unlit pipes. What fun. Best of all, any doctors and nurses it is my misfortune to see will be appalled. Pipe smoking will definitely add a little je ne sais quoi to my deteriorating years.

More importantly, The Princess and I have decided that within the next year or two we will have to leave England. The problem is a simple one: I am too old to live here for much longer. All my life I have listened to older people telling me that things were better when they were younger. I never believed them, of course. But now I believe that things were better than they are now. And now I know that I am right. I cannot think of any aspect of life that is better today than it was in the 1970s.

It is now perfectly legal for doctors and nurses to kill old people in National Health Service hospitals. If I need to go into any health service institution they will starve me to death, kill me by withholding treatment or simply kill me with an overdose of something. The NHS is a new branch of murder incorporated; it's become the National Homicide Service. Anyone over the age of 60 who isn't a member of the Royal Family or a senior politician and who enters an NHS hospital does so at great personal risk. The doctors and the nurses kill people to clear the beds and to save money; they behave like civil servants because they are civil servants. (If you are paid by the State then you work for the State. And if you work for the State you are a civil servant. Indifference, contempt and arrogance follow with predictable inevitability.) Worse still, many doctors claim that they are starving pensioners to death, and denying them fluids, because it is the humane thing to do. Mengele would have felt right at home working in an NHS hospital. In the old days (now so derided by all and sundry) the elderly were regarded as providing society with a human reservoir of wisdom and experience; a reservoir which vastly increased the intelligence of each community. Today, the elderly in England are merely regarded as an expensive nuisance; an unproductive luxury no longer to be tolerated.

The Government encourages this mass slaughter because it reduces the cost of providing pensions. (English governments hate the elderly - who are regarded as an unnecessary expense and who have been targeted with endless new taxes, lower interest rates and pension grabs for those not working for the State. One legislative change made by Gordon Brown cost pensioners £100 billion. A flick of the Scotsman's pen impoverished generations of non-governmental employees.)

It is hardly surprising that doctors are regarded as somewhere between estate agents and tax inspectors in the social pecking order. The traditional respect has been replaced by contempt.

The more you know the more it is clear that everything is worse than it was. There is no medical care at weekends or at nights. And I guarantee that services are going to get worse and taxes are going to go up. The only certainty in life is that our so-called leaders will continue to do bad and stupid things.

And so it will soon be time to leave the country.

Where do we go?

There's a good deal of choice.

Countries all around the world are now desperate to attract people who have a little money. It is possible to purchase citizenship for remarkably little outlay. It's called 'citizenship by investment' and governments everywhere are selling passports to people who have a little money. (Even our Government does this. Foreigners who want British citizenship and a British passport can buy one.) It is, of course, possible to become a citizen of one of those little countries which do not demand that the new citizen pay any taxes. A number of people do this every year. They spend five months living in France, five months living in Switzerland and two months somewhere else. They may spend a week or two in England, just to see how bad things have become. And so they are not liable to pay tax anywhere.

But it isn't the taxes we want to avoid.

And so the simplest solution may be to continue to pay tax in England but to move ourselves to a country where the elderly aren't regarded as a nuisance and treated as disposable; to a country where the elderly aren't sneered at and derided and regarded as rather less important than our weekly recyclables. (You can recycle an empty yoghurt carton but what can you do with an octogenarian?)

Meanwhile, it is my birthday and I feel every minute of my 969 years. If I am not that old then I have been cheated because that is the age I feel.

Only children and old people are ever proud of how old they are but I don't feel proud so I can't be either. I have never been quite this old before and so I am not entirely sure what to expect. How much creaking is normal? How much suggests that parts are malfunctioning and may need attention? Do I care about the creaking? It seems merely inconvenient but is it a sign of more fundamental damage? When I go out into the cold my toes and fingers go white. What on earth happened to my circulation? In my mind I am six and want to play outside. But my body is 66 and won't countenance such nonsense.

The future offers little more than rheumatism, deteriorating senses and developing dementia. I was 24 and then the next day I woke up and I was 66. What happened? Where did it go? What happened to my hopes and dreams and ambitions? I've been running as fast as I could but I'm still in the same place. Why have I spent so much of my life dealing with petty irrelevances that the dreams have been pushed aside?

I can't help feeling that the world has deteriorated massively during my lifetime.

Life was better when I was paid in guineas, when old ladies fed the pigeons without being arrested and when the grass at Lords was green and not covered with painted slogans. (As an MCC member I was told recently that some members of the MCC want to sell part of Lord's Cricket Ground to developers who want to build yet more flats in St Johns Wood. There is talk of a £50 million cheque. But what good is £50 million when the ground is ruined? The club might as well sell the whole ground for £1,000 million and then share out the cash. After expenses we would receive around £50,000 each. We could then all go and watch cricket at the Oval.) I have always been aware of the risk of nostalgia: the essence of history as we remember it; bowdlerised and cleansed of sadness and misfortune, viewed through sentimental eyes and cannibalised for our delight. But these are bad, bad times. It is not surprising that computer games and programmes, events and publications which remind us of happier days are increasing in popularity. Millions who enter these other worlds are unwilling to return to the one in which they are supposed to be living.

The older I get the more I become aware of the fragility of the human body. I no longer take quite so many risks. Which is odd. You'd think that as one got older and had less to lose one would be more willing to gamble with what life there was left. But it doesn't work that way. As I get older I become more aware of the joys of being alive, more protective of what days I have left and more aware of the endless ways in which it can all be ended.

As I become older I become increasingly aware that I need to take full account of whatever time I have left. I am aware that not everyone sees things quite like this. My desperate urge to make the most of what I have left means that I become increasingly impatient with the world and intolerant of time wasting nonsense. I now work harder than ever. Or, at least I try to work harder. Time is running out and I have so many things left to do as the clock tick-tocks remorselessly onwards.

For decades I cherished the prospect of acquiring the sort of respectability and gravitas that would make me feel as if I belonged to the right clubs. I obtained membership of those clubs (easy enough to do) but I never felt that I belonged. I never fitted in; my anger, my sense of injustice would never allow it. Only in the last few years have I realised that I am a born outsider. I have filled my life with worry and anxiety by spending too much time in the future and not enough in the present. Things have got so bad that now if I'm going to worry about something new I have to stop worrying about something that is already taking up worry space. I'm full to the brim with anxiety and haven't got room for new worries - even small ones must wait their turn. I've seen the future and it has exhausted me. Additional regrets and recriminations have been generated by spending too much time in the past and worrying too much about what might have been. Long ago, I learned to anticipate problems; to be proactive. But that was a mistake. Our lives now are so full of real problems, and we are daily besieged with so many new hazards, that it is pointless to try to plan ahead. (Not that I have ever been any good at planning ahead. I have always admired and respected people who could think things through, and then plot their lives years ahead. But my life has been a sequence of occasionally serendipitous and frequently un-serendipitous incidents.) The carefully and imaginatively crafted solution to one problem will be rendered pointless by another completely unpredictable hazard.

What have I learned now that I am as old as Methuselah? I have learned that nothing unsettles any part of the establishment more than an original thinker. I have learned that telling the truth always causes pain and is unpopular with the majority. I used to believe that by writing books I could help change the world. I no longer believe that is possible. The system is now too powerful to be changed by mere words. It is hope-crushing to realise that things now progress out of control, led by corporate and bureaucratic forces which are outside all human control. And, of course, we all have to remember that if we're not in control of our lives then someone else must be.

I have learned that our lives are defined by the opportunities we take and the ones we are offered but reject. Many decisions are completely out of our control and are a consequence of incidents over which we have absolutely no control.

I know that it is not what happens to us in life which determines the outcome but how we respond to what happens. I know that we tell the truth as much as we dare, and we grow more daring as we grow older. I suspect that my mind has been hijacked and put into an old person's body. I have a support bandage on my right knee and one on my right elbow. If I were a motor car my fan belt would be a pair of tights and a piece of string would be holding my exhaust pipe off the ground. I've learned that I am more crippled by shyness and lack of self-confidence than I realised when I was younger. I've learned that being old makes us fragile in two ways. First, things are wearing out and we become weaker. Second, we become more aware of the general fragility of life and the many ways in which it can be taken away. I've learned that too often the big decisions we make, the ones which influence our lives in the most dramatic and enduring ways, aren't decisions at all. Things happen. Sometimes we feel driven to do this or that. Sometimes we are directed by accidental happenchance. Sometimes we go in a particular direction because of momentum and habit and custom and the expectations of others. That, at least, is my experience. Others, I know, are more directed. They set their targets when they are still teenagers, they unfold their life-map and then they resolutely follow their designated route.

Chaos and injustice are an increasingly inevitable part of life. I used to hope that I could one day reach the end of a day, a week a month or a year and have all my problems sorted. But it has taken me until now to realise that at no point in life am I going to be able to clear the 'in tray'.

I've learned that life is like eyeing a fancy cake on a plate and deciding to keep it until later. And then, later, you find that you're so full that you can't eat the cake. And you keep it until tomorrow. And when tomorrow comes you find that the cake has gone stale.

My personal hopes, ambitions and expectations have all evaporated, boiled away by the fiery disapproval, prejudices, condescension and arrogance of the establishment (in all its forms) who, threatened by anything new, do everything they can to oppress and suppress humanity, originality and the sort of wisdom that used to be known as common sense.

I feel exhausted by even the simplest activity. The most exhausting thing I've done today was to take the lid off a jar of marmalade and to do that I had to use one of those plastic and rubber devices designed for the weaker paralympians. (I did attempt to invade the vacuum with a kitchen knife but abandoned that when I nearly lost one of my favourite fingers.) Most of my physical skills have diminished. The only thing I am better at these days is dribbling and I can do that in my sleep. Damnit, I have even lost my ability to whistle. Where has my whistle gone to? What peculiarities of the ageing process have removed my ability to whistle?

I look back on my life and see little but failure and disappointment. And, inevitably, the real feelings of failure and disappointment concern the times when I didn't have the courage to try, when I didn't accept the challenge, when I didn't put myself to the test. I have at last learned to accept the inevitability of random and serial and continuous disappointment.

As we get old, our hopeful future becomes a frustrating present and a disappointing past. It is difficult not to slide into resentment and weariness and to waste the days just moping around in front of the television. I suspect that I will know the decline is dangerous when I start to think that the programmes on daytime television are worth watching and that the scheduling seems innovative, exciting and worth getting up early to view. When I look forward to watching the sort of awful programmes I used to make then I will know it's time to call it a day.

Henry David Thoreau, one of my great heroes, was described by E. B. White as torn between the gnawing desire to change life, and the equally troublesome desire to live it. I know the feeling only too well. I have spent much of my life screaming like an Old Testament prophet. Readers who probably know me as well as I know myself have sent me many generous letters and have fed my rage with an endless diet of clippings and tidbits of information.

All my life I have argued with pompous, overbearing representatives of the establishment. I'm doing it with increasing frequency these days and this morning I wondered if I was becoming less tolerant. I honestly don't think I am. On the contrary, I rather suspect that I am mellowing with age and staying silent when I would previously have made a noise. I try hard to ignore the little difficulties with which life tries so hard to tire us out.

The problem, I believe, is that the establishment now employs more overbearing representatives than ever before and they are ever more intrusive and demanding and increasingly pompous.

I have learned that the urgent tends to crowd out the important and that as a result the urgent seeming crap tends to take precedence over the truly important; like some ever-growing parasite the crap expands to fill all the time available, greedily pushing aside all the important, valuable and, heaven help us, fun things we might otherwise do with our time. It is not the big crises or even the real day to day challenges which do the damage to our minds and souls; which erode our spirits and leave us broken and without hope. Even our spiritual lives have been asset stripped. It is the endless torrent of irrelevant, trivial crap I resent; the daily dross, the annoyances and the time wasting paperwork caused by the incompetence, the greed, the laziness, the stupidity and the bloody mindedness of State and corporate employees. The State is now every-thing and we are nothing. The eurocrats are (with their usual contempt for democracy) doing everything they can to protect the mortally wounded euro even though their efforts are destroying stability, growth and employment prospects within their territory. The survival of the State, the Superstate, is now all that matters to them. It is no wonder that so many people now believe that we live in a kakistocracy. We waste our lives on an accumulation of pointless red tape and regulations and as a result we never get round to doing the stuff that matters. A hundred tiny pieces of crap, when pooled together, become a huge cloud of the stuff. The crap spoils everything. We were due to go to London yesterday but neither The Princess nor I could face the journey or the inevitable prob-lems. As I threw our expensive, reserved tickets onto the fire I thought of Dr Johnson; who said: "A man who is tired of London is tired of life." The trouble is that, for us, England's capital has lost something. London is, in my heart, gothic buildings covered in soot and pigeon shit; dramatic vistas with surprises round every corner and more nooks and crannies than a thousand 17th century pubs. But the city is now filled with inter-lopers, visitors, strangers without passion or style who don't live there and who care nothing, absolutely nothing, about London or its history. The invaders occupy the place. They don't live in it. And, as an English-man, I no longer feel that London belongs to me.

I am constantly amazed by the fact that with so much unavoidable crap spoiling our lives there are millions of people voluntarily wasting their days on social networking sites such as Twitter, Facebook and Linkedin. Haven't these people got anything worthwhile to do with their time?

The real problem is that stress is cumulative. Crap causes as much frustration and anger (vital causes of stress) as other, bigger, far more important events. After all, Dr William Harvey, the 17th century physi-cian who discovered the secret of the circulation of the blood, was not exaggerating when he predicted that his life was at the mercy of any petty bureaucrat. He died not long afterwards of a stroke induced during a hospital management meeting.

'Don't sweat the small stuff', they say. But that's not so easy.

I rang the garage to order some tyres for the truck.

'What's the number on your current tyres,' I was asked. I said I didn't have the foggiest idea. 'We can't order tyres until we know the size and speed rating.' 'It's just a Ford Ranger truck,' I said. 'Aren't they all the same?' 'Oh no, sir. Not at all.' (I lied about the 'sir'. No one ever says 'sir' any more.) I protested. 'I bought it from your garage. Don't you know how big the wheels are on the biggest selling truck in the world?' No. Of course they don't. It's as difficult to find a competent person working in a garage or car dealership as it would be to find the Holy Grail or an 18-year-old virgin nurse. (At least I know how to spell 'competent'. I have a cutting in my vast silly cuttings file which carries the headline: 'Competant Person Wanted'. The advertisement was, of course, inserted by a Government department and paid for by taxpayers.)

I had to walk two hundred yards to where I'd left the truck, crouch down in the mud and examine the tyres. I've never looked at tyres much before. But they're covered with numbers and letters. There are as many numbers and letters on a tyre as there are in a telephone book. I wrote down the ones I thought seemed most promising. When I got back to the house, I rang the garage again. 'Those aren't the right numbers,' said the man in charge of the tyre department. So I had to trek back to the truck and write down some more numbers. 'Those are the ones,' he said. 'That's what I thought it would be.'

I tried to take a modest pension which I've been paying into for nearly half a century. It seems that it will pay me an 11% guaranteed annuity. I thought I'd just have to fill in a form and they'd start sending me the money. So far it has taken me three months of letter writing and telephoning to get nowhere. Scottish Life keep finding new ways to delay. There's this form. And that form. It's like trying to make an insurance claim after an accident. And now they have decided they wanted more identification. Do I walk away from the crap? Just living, simply surviving, is to relive the ordeals of Sisyphus. As soon as I satisfy one regulation another comes along. And although I do what I am supposed to do as quickly as I can they do not. I really need what celebrities call 'people' to deal with this stuff. A national newspaper editor once told me that the best bit of his job was having a chauffeur driven car at his disposal 24 hours a day. Another confessed that for him the main perk was having a Personal Assistant to pay his bills and deal with all those daily nonsenses which make life miserable for the rest of us.

It annoys me because my life is being frittered away on trivia and whether I sweat it or not the time will be wasted.

I have had so much trouble persuading South West Water that I am not using any water at Publishing House (and that they should, therefore, stop sending me estimated bills) that I am now trying to persuade them to do what they keep threatening to do - cut off the water supply. Threatening letters are, of course, the default position for Government departments, utilities and companies with Head Offices, twitter accounts and stock exchange quotations. Death, taxes and threatening letters from utility companies are, together with a steady deterioration in the quality of public services, now the four inevitabilities of life. I am so old that I always feel that I need to reply to these absurdities and so I wrote back to them attempting, yet again, to explain the situation. Naturally, they ignored me. I telephoned them. They responded by sending me estimated bills and threatening to take me court. I wrote again begging them to cut off the water supply. They threatened to take me to court and to cut off the water supply. I sent them a time and a date to do the cutting off and they wrote again threatening to sue me. Kafka would be proud.

None of this is unusual. This stuff happens all the time. Hours are wasted on crap. I am heartily sick of being threatened and bullied by government departments and large companies which behave like government departments. I am particularly irritated by the fact that most of the zombies working for these damned organisations will never accept any responsibility or make any attempt to help. They hide behind the skirts of the organisation and never for one moment remember that they too are simply pawns and that they too will be harassed and bewildered and angered and frustrated when they come, in turn, to deal with similar organisations. Give a man (or woman) a title, a badge and some sort of uniform and you create a monster. Moreover, because they have been told by the eurocrats that they cannot be bullied or threatened in any way they have taken that to mean that anyone questioning their authority or attitude must be a dangerous criminal. Saatchi's law is that satisfaction equals performance minus expectation. The theory used to be that it was always best to under-promise and over-perform. These days all Government departments, all utilities, the Royal Mail, post offices and most major companies seem to believe that they are doing customers a favour by allowing them to buy their products or services.

I have found that the only way to make any progress is to insist on making a formal complaint right at the very beginning. The zombies are afraid of formal complaints. They have to fill in paperwork and their decisions are studied and analysed. A zombie's career can be destroyed by an official complaint.

I long ago decided that I would resist the temptation to spread myself too wide; I decided I would not fight dozens of small battles which exhaust me and use up all my resources. But are these small battles? I don't know any more.

Either my capacity for dealing with crap has deteriorated or the amount of crap - the background level of crap - has reached levels that are utterly unacceptable. Life is like being nibbled to death by piranhas. The crap expands to fill the time available. The things which matter most should not be at the mercy of things which matter least and yet too often it is the things which really matter which are put off so that the petty irrelevances can be dealt with.

Because we want to get rid of it we always deal with the crap first so it gets priority and there is never time for the good stuff (the fun stuff and the really important stuff). The crap tends to demand to be dealt with first, because it comes from people with the power to have no patience. I have this nightmare. I am dead. 'What did he do with his life?' asks someone. 'He filled in lots of forms and dealt with a lot of crap.'

Has the crapstorm got worse or am I more sensitive to it? As I get older I realise that the world makes less and less sense. If I open a newspaper I see people in their 40s announcing new discoveries which I know to be two decades old. Does no one ever learn anything? Do people under 50 years of age know nothing? Why do doctors, scientists, economists and politicians insist on rediscovering the wonders of the wheel?

Tolstoy, writing to his son, said that the aim of a good man should be to bring love and truth into the world. He didn't tell him what he should do if the world didn't much fancy love and truth.

I don't much care for the world in which we live. I bear it because I have my love, The Princess, by my side. I tolerate the lunacies of the Cleggs and the Cables because she and I give each other strength. We are all frightened creatures, surviving in an increasingly alien world. Only the comfort of knowing you have someone loyal by your side to love and cherish, to protect and defend you, can overcome the fear. (Occasionally, some physical release is required. The Princes and I both have large bags full of rubber bands next to our chairs. Every time Clegg or Cable appear on TV we let them have one on the nose. We have become very accurate. It makes us feel much better, though it takes us ten minutes to pick up the rubber bands before we go to bed each evening.)

And I receive strength from the kind support of the many readers who still buy and read my books and who share our aims and our inspirations and our frustrations. Bless them all. Every one of them.

19.

We arrived at our new offices after dark. We were planning to have a quick meal and then pack a lot of books into padded envelopes but when we walked through the door we found ourselves wading in an inch or so of water. This, of course, is never a good sign. We remained resolutely cheerful and waded around in a heavy shower as water continued to pour down through the ceiling light fittings. Fortunately, we had noticed the water before either of us had turned on the lights. We managed to deal with the water leak but there was so much water on the first floor that it continued to pour through the ceiling. Having mopped up as much as we could upstairs we went back downstairs and found a dry corner where we could sit for a moment. 'Let's have a sandwich and a cup of tea,' I suggested. We couldn't cook anything because the cooker was underneath the deluge. 'We can plug the kettle into a socket in another room and find a couple of dry chairs.'

'We'd be better off eating outside,' The Princess pointed out. 'It's not raining as hard outside as it is indoors. And someone on the council must be having a street party because the council has inadvertently turned on the street lights.'

We considered eating our marmalade sandwiches on the pavement but eventually decided that we would be prime targets for muggers so we found a dry corner and had an indoors picnic. Then we found a mop and a broom and swept a few thousand gallons of water out through the back door. Fortunately, there are steps outside the back door and the water could travel downhill without any difficulty. As I looked out I realised that our hedge needs cutting again. I am beginning to hate that hedge. Two years ago I spent the best part of a day cutting it. When I'd finished I stood and looked at my handiwork. A stranger walked by and joined me. 'Did you do that?' he asked. I said I had. 'You've made a terrible job of it,' he said. Last year I telephoned a man who had put a card through our door. He agreed to come and look at the hedge. 'How am I going to cut that?' he demanded. 'I will need a powered hedge trimmer and a ladder.' I muttered something about my having assumed he would have these. 'And where am I going to put the clippings?' he demanded. 'I was hoping you might take them away,' I said. He snorted, gave me a pitying look and walked to his car.

When we'd finished playing Mr and Mrs Canute, The Princess stuffed books into padded envelopes and I stuck on stamps. It was early morning when we'd finished.

'You never told me that publishing was such a glamorous business,' said The Princess as we fell into bed. I just about remembered to switch on the alarm clock so that we could wake up in time to catch our early train to London.

20.

My collection of eaves-droppings is growing rapidly. Here's the most recent assortment:

1. 'I had such a restful time that my self-winding watch stopped.'
2. 'The sign says they've opened a brassiere. But the coffee is very good.'
3. 'People turn out differently. Hitler and Michelangelo both started out as house painters.'
4. 'There's more to life than being happy.'
5. 'People who get to be 100 without a criminal record should be allowed one free crime of their choice.' 'I think I'd bring it in at 80.'
6. 'I feel like an old person.' 'I don't know where we can find one at this time of night. Why don't you have a sandwich?'
7. 'He calls his bicycle Brenda after a shorthand typist he once knew.'
8. 'Who wants to live to be 90?' 'Me. I'm 89.'
9. 'He speaks five languages.' 'Yes, but I've never heard him say anything interesting in any of them.'
10. 'What were you like when you were little?' 'Oh, much the same but smaller.'
11. 'The terrifying thing is that in a few years' time these will be the good old days.'
12. 'The only thing he's ever done is grow old. And he took a long time to do that.'
13. 'I wish they'd bring back nostalgia.'
14. 'How come soap doesn't get dirty?'
15. 'Infertility runs in their family. They've all got it.'

16. 'He got six months. He says the worst thing was that the police and the magistrate made him feel like a criminal.'
17. 'When she was out I took a good look round her kitchen. It was obviously one of those places that is very difficult to keep clean.'
18. 'Halloween is on my birthday this year.'
19. 'I quite like some foreigners. Some of them are just like us.'
20. 'Anyone over the age of 70 who doesn't believe in God is a fool.'

21.

Shopkeepers in Paris tend to specialise. There is a shop near the Pont d'Alma which sells nothing but pistachio nuts. There is an estate agent in Montmartre which specialises in selling Parisian bakery shops. I know a shop near the Palais Royale which sells only pipes (no cigars or cigarettes - just pipes). And it is possible to find shops which specialise in selling olive oil, mustard, vacuum cleaners or white blouses for women.

Occasionally there are shops which reflect the eclectic tastes of the owner. And so there is, for example, an ironmongery shop near L'Ecole Militaire which also sells fancy hats and fascinators.

But things are changing. The economic crisis and the flood of new laws from Brussels mean that many of the most interesting shops have closed. Paris is still full of shops selling models of the Eiffel Tower, expensive lingerie, wine (cheap and expensive), shoes and tobacco but recently our street has lost two picture-framers, a cobbler and a mattress maker who used to sit in the window making mattresses and scowling at flaneurs who dared to stare. My favourite stationery store has gone too. I love beautiful stationery and notebooks. To me a black mark on beautiful thick, white paper is a thing of beauty. I love pens and pencils and crayons and this was a treasure trove of such delights. But now it's boarded up. Two out of three local toy shops have closed too. (Though that is probably more a result of the global trend than a local phenomenon. All the toy shops in the world are closing as children turn away from proper toys and towards computer game downloads.) Only the pharmacies, the hairdressers and the cake shops seem to be thriving.

One of our favourite cafés has closed and my favourite penknife shop is permanently shuttered. I have never before seen so many empty shops. They look so sad and so much the same. There is invariably a sad looking pile of scattered mail inside the doorway, accompanying the detritus of abandoned dreams.

Thanks to the EU, Paris is virtually shut now at the weekends. And the cafés and shops which don't close on Saturday and Sunday do so on Monday. The absurd working time directive has resulted in the mass closure of small owner run businesses and a dramatic reduction in the quality of life. Entrepreneurs who still manage to build businesses in Europe do so despite the best efforts of the bureaucrats of the European Union.

One or two new shops have opened, but these seem to reflect the new austerity. There is a shop nearby which is called 'Je Repare Tout'. A man sits in the window, surrounded by bits and pieces of electrical equipment, wires and lots of chunks of wood. He doesn't seem to have many tools: a couple of screwdrivers, a chisel, a hammer and a soldering iron. I can't wait for something to break down so that I can take it in to him.

All this became of practical importance today because our fridge freezer finally gave up the ghost. It must be nearly 20 years old and so it has served us well. But the motor was whining loudly and the food inside was melting. This is not a good time to be without a fridge. The temperature in Paris is well into the 30s.

I could not for the life of me remember where I had seen a shop selling refrigerators. I pulled out the telephone book, found the address of the nearest electromanegerie and decided to walk around to see what they'd got. When, after a twenty minute brisk walk, I found the address I discovered that the shop now sells only mobile telephones. There seem to be a thousand hairdressers for every Parisian but fridge shops are in short supply. I decided to ask the man who sells me my newspapers if he knew of somewhere suitable. He is a nice fellow and, being a typical Parisian, he is always smartly scruffy. Like Serge Gainsbourg he probably spends an hour and a half every morning making sure that he looks as if he has just clambered out of bed. He thought for a moment, apparently rehearsing his reply in his mind before exposing it to public scrutiny. 'Go straight ahead for two hundred metres, turn left at what used to be the cobblers, but which is now another mobile telephone shop,' he shuddered at this revelation, and halted temporarily to regroup and regain his strength before finding the energy to continue. Paris is, like most other towns and cities, now awash with shops selling mobile telephones. 'Then go on for three hundred metres, past the pastry shop which was burnt to the ground during the War and is now an office block for an insurance company, then take the second, no, I tell a lie, the third on the left and the second on the right and just before you get to the florists on the corner - which is run by a lovely lady called who used to be a dancer in the Folies

Bergere and still has a beautiful complexion - you will see a little café run by my old friend Jacques. Call into the café and ask for Jacques. He knows everyone and everything. If the café is closed go into the bread shop next door and ask for Marie. She will know because her brother works in the Mayor's office.'

I thanked him profusely, bought a couple of magazines, and went back to the apartment where The Princess and I opted for the last resort. We started looking on the internet. And gave up straight away when we found ourselves directed to some hick town in Texas. To the Americans, who run the internet, Paris is a town in Texas not the capital of France. And, believe me, Americans who live there need never worry about finding a replacement if their fridge should ever stop working.

I went out again and started wandering the streets. As I walked I passed 'Je Repare Tout'. The owner was in there doing something to a broken chair. He said he could help. He said he would come back to the flat with me. He talked incessantly as we walked. He was, he told me, the only fat person in Europe who doesn't have problems with genes, hormones or glands. 'I eat too much,' he explained. 'I like food very much.' He also told me that he was worried about going bald. 'My father is bald,' he said. 'So for a while I thought that I must go bald too. And then I learned that the man I think of as my father is not my father at all. My father is a man I thought was my uncle. He has a full head of hair. So maybe I am not going bald after all.' He grimaced. 'But, nevertheless, every time I wash my hair some of it leaves home and never returns.' He shrugged in the Gallic way.

I wanted him to say: 'It's the outlet ice valve coordinating widget that's gone. I can repair that. It will take five minutes and cost you 10 euros including parts, labour and tax.' But I feared that he would say: 'It's not worth repairing. It's 20 years old and kaput. It'll cost 300 euros to take away the old one and 700 euros for a replacement. I can do you a deal for 1500 euros.'

He tapped the back of the fridge rather like a doctor might percuss a congested lung and announced, with great gravity, that the machine had died and was no longer of any value in its chosen sphere. He said that since we were friends he could provide us with a new machine for 599 euros. He promised that the machine would be delivered and the old one taken away within two hours.

And to our delight and mild astonishment this is exactly what happened. Our new friend and a companion arrived at the top of our stairs with our new fridge freezer. They were exhausted but proud. They then spent some time setting up the new machine and, with patience and uncommon courtesy, explaining how everything worked. Once this had been done, and a cheque handed over, they departed, carrying our old machine down five flights of stairs. (The lift in our building is just about big enough to hold two people if one of them is anorexic and the other breathes in and, can hold their breath for the minute and a half it takes to reach the top floor. It is, in short, impossible for two people to enter the lift and leave still strangers. There is certainly no room in it for a fridge.) What a contrast with England where the dealers wouldn't even make an effort to deliver a fridge to our new house because the approach road is a trifle narrow.

22.

We had lunch with a fellow whom I will call Ambrose Cuthbertson because that isn't his name or, indeed, anything like it. He has had a spacious apartment in Paris for 40 years and believed that he had mastered the language when he had learned to say 'mercy buckets' and 'silver plate'. He spends four months of the year in France, four in Switzerland and four in Spain. The advantage of this arrangement is that he is not resident in any of these countries and is, therefore, excused income taxes. Having a substantial private income he is also excused employment. He carries a small copy of Molière in his pocket. It is an old, battered book, in English, printed on bible paper and with a blue leather binding. He reads it all the time and even read bits out occasionally. It wasn't until I'd known him for a couple of years that I discovered that he had learnt little bits of the book by heart. Apart from the two phrases I've already mentioned he cannot read or speak a word of French. It doesn't seem to cause him any inconvenience. If someone doesn't understand what he's saying he just raises his voice until they do. Surprisingly, it seems to work.

Ambrose spent much of our time together giving us a short lecture on foreigners. He has a very refreshing view on the subject and says that he is working himself up towards writing a book which will, he insists, help a good many people understand how the world works.

'Foreigners like to think they are different,' he said. 'They divide themselves up into little groups: Americans, French, Somalians and so on. The fact is that these are all rather superficial divisions. Anyone who isn't English is foreign and that's really all there is to it. I always feel sorry for foreigners. After all, they all come from abroad where they are accustomed to dodgy plumbing, dodgy food, dodgy water, predictable weather and, worst of all, living among lots of other foreigners. It is no wonder they are all a bit odd.'

Ambrose went on to say that he always treats the best foreigners, the ones who try hardest, as though they are honorary English people and he insists that they are always proud and pleased about that. I think he would probably like to give them beads and blankets.

23.

For years I have had my hair cut at a hairdressing salon just a few doors away from our apartment. The salon is run by a couple from the South of France.

This morning I wandered out to buy a paper and, as I approached the salon, caught sight of myself reflected in a shop window. I decided I needed a haircut and said to myself that if the salon was quiet I would pop in for a quick trim. But even twenty yards away I could hear them. They were having a huge row. There were no customers in the salon but he was threatening her with one of those brushes they use for flicking the bits of hair off the customers' shoulders and she was threatening him with a pair of electrical clippers. I walked past, tottered up the road and bought my paper, a baguette and some cheese. By the time I got back the black clouds had gone. She was fussing over the hair of an old woman and he was standing in the doorway, smiling and nodding benevolently to everyone who passed by. Neither of them is the sort of person who is tortured by the thought: 'What will people think?'

I went in and asked for my usual trim.

24.

One of our neighbours, a female artist in her fifties, is moving out of the building. Jeanette lives on the fourth floor and because the lift is small and the stairs steep she has hired a firm who move stuff out through the window rather than the door. They use a long ladder with a motorised ramp and whizz furniture and boxes up and down very efficiently.

She told us, rather sadly, that she is moving back to live with her elderly mother in Tours because she is broke. Her lover, a medium level civil servant who had a small apartment in the nearby Rue de Grenelle, died a couple of months ago and it was only after his death that Jeanette discovered that she has not been as successful as she had believed. For years she's been selling her paintings through a gallery in the 5th arrondissement and for years she's been getting good prices. Ten or so years ago she gave up her job as a teacher in a nearby infant school and devoted herself to painting full time.

When her lover died his brother, in the absence of a will the sole beneficiary, found a huge cache of our neighbour's paintings stored in the cellar of his apartment building. They were all still wrapped in the brown paper and string in which they had been delivered. The brother contacted the gallery from which they had been bought to ask them for a valuation and found, to his dismay, they were worth very little. It turned out that the lover had been buying up every painting the gallery had acquired. He had instructed the gallery owner not to reveal his identity to the artist and he paid considerably more than their market price. It had been his way of making Jeanette happy and enabling her to paint full time. For a decade she had remained blissfully unaware that her paintings were not commercially successful and that every picture which she had sold had been bought by the same person – her benefactor.

So now Jeanette is broke. She had never saved any of her earnings because she had assumed that her brushes and her talent would feed her for life. But now she knows that the paintings she has in her apartment are virtually worthless and that her career is hardly glittering. When we told her how sorry we were to learn of her misfortune she smiled and told us that she was not sad at all.

'I never knew how much he loved me,' she told us. 'Just imagine how much he must have cared for me to do this. He spent all his money to keep my dream alive. I had ten glorious years.'

She is going back to Tours to care for her elderly mother. 'I will have somewhere to live and my mother has enough money to feed the two of us,' she said.

'And you will keep on painting!' said The Princess.

'Oh no,' said Jeanette, shaking her head. 'The painting is over. They were wonderful years, those years when I thought I was a successful artist. Now, I come back to the real world. But without regrets. How can I have regrets? I have such wonderful memories.' She paused for a moment and wiped her eyes with a small, white linen handkerchief. 'What love!' she whispered.

'He truly must have loved you with all his heart,' agreed The Princess.

25.

The moment I got into the bath the telephone rang. For a while I lay in the water and let it ring. It didn't stop. After a while the damned thing had acquired a rhythm which seemed to me to suggest that the person at the other end was never going to give up. Relaxation, the only reason to take a bath as opposed to a shower, was impossible. And The Princess had popped out to the supermarket to buy essential, life-giving supplies of ice cream.

Knowing that the chances were high that the moment I stood up and climbed out of the bath the caller would give up and the telephone would stop ringing, I nevertheless put down my book and pushed myself to my feet. I had been in the warm bath too long and much of my blood was in my skin. I stood up too quickly and felt dizzy. I dropped my book into the bath and grabbed at the sink for support. My remaining blood supplies had all rushed to my feet. Actually, for all the good it was doing me it may well have rushed to Barcelona. I steadied myself, picked my soggy book out of the water, reached for the towel and padded out of the bathroom, leaving behind a trail of drips and soggy footprints. Now keen to answer the damned phone before it stopped ringing I moved quickly. I suddenly had a premonition that it would, after all, be a wrong number. When the telephone rings at an inconvenient time it usually is.

'Hello?' I said.

It wasn't a wrong number.

'You took your time!' said my friend Thumper Robinson.

'I was in the bath. Relaxing. Reading.'

'Oh well, never mind. You're out now.'

'Did you want anything in particular?'

'Are you in France?'

'Yes. You rang me in France.'

'I just wanted to see if it worked.'

'What?'

'My new telephone. I've got a new mobile phone. It takes pictures and plays music. I've put your number into the memory thing and I wanted to see if it worked.' Thumper is still struggling to escape from the 1970s, where he has been happily ensconced for some time.

'Well, it does.'

'Good. That's OK then. Must go. I want to see if I can change the ring tone to something a bit brighter. Patchy and I are going to visit Frank in hospital.' Frank is the landlord of my favourite pub, the Duck and Puddle. 'I've got to get him a bottle of wine.'

'Aren't you supposed to take hospital patients the grapes before they press them?' I asked him.

'He can't eat grapes. Too acidic. Just wine. Nice to talk to you. Bye.'

I replaced the receiver and tiptoed back to the bathroom. The water was tepid and the mood had gone. I pulled out the plug and decided to wait for The Princess to return with the ice cream.

26.

We heard of the deaths of two very old friends who lived in Australia.

They were both seriously ill and had been in a bad way for some considerable time. He had heart disease, and had had a stroke, and she had cancer which had spread throughout her body. They were both constantly in pain and there was little joy in their lives.

Two days ago they drove down to their small cabin cruiser, moored in a marina on the coast, and clambered aboard. They carried with them several bottles of their favourite whisky and a picnic hamper packed with all their favourite foods. They set off in late afternoon and several locals who knew them were surprised to see them set out because it was a bitterly cold day and the forecast was for a really cold night.

They anchored just outside the harbour, ate their picnic and they drank the whisky they'd taken with them. And then they lay in each other's arms, with just a rug over them, and waited for the cold to do its work.

They were found the following day, still in each other's arms. The empty whisky bottles were neatly stacked in the empty picnic hamper, along with the food wrappings they'd carefully collected together. They'd even rinsed the plates they'd used.

They died, of course, of hypothermia.

27.

My collection of eaves-droppings expands virtually every time I leave the apartment. Almost every visit to a café results in my jotting down another oddity. Here's the pick of the latest batch:

1. 'Why do we try so hard to make foreigners feel at home? If they had wanted to feel at home they'd have stayed where they were.'
2. 'The more I learn, the less I want to know.'
3. 'What would Napoleon do now?' 'I think it would be more helpful to ask: 'What would Harpo Marx do now?''
4. 'I can remember when the big question in life was whether to buy a bottle of Vimto or a bottle of Dandelion and Burdock.' 'There was a penny back on the bottle with the Dandelion and Burdock. I always thought of it as a sort of savings plan.'
5. 'I don't want to blink, I might miss something.'
6. 'This sauce is very rich and thick.' 'You make it sound like a footballer.'
7. 'I put women on a pedestal.' 'Only so that you can look up their skirts.'
8. 'He is insensitive and uncaring.' 'Is he American?'
9. 'I don't want to be famous. Famous people are always dying. The obituary columns are full of famous people who've just died.'
10. 'What would a smart person do, I asked myself.'
11. 'Why don't you give me the room you're going to give me when I come back downstairs in two minutes and complain about the room you're about to give me now?' (This was overheard at a hotel reception desk.)
12. 'I've got an F in maths but I'm going to tell my parents it stands for 'fantastic'.'
13. 'Dreams never come true so you might as well dream big.'
14. 'Come on, cheer up. It could be worse. How's your dad?' 'I'm afraid he died two days ago.'
15. 'Does this phone take French speaking?'
16. 'Why do you always have to stay in five star hotels?' 'Because there aren't any six star hotels.'
17. 'He's taken a job as front end lead at a multi-channel system inte-grator and subservice cloud management unit.' 'Oh, that's nice.'
18. 'He is driving me sane!'
19. 'The truth always prevails but by then it's generally too late.'
20. 'I wish I'd known he was on TV. I'd have made a point of not watching it.' 'But you didn't watch it!' 'I know. But I didn't watch it by accident. I would have liked to have not watched it on purpose.'

28.

Reading through a book I obtained from the American Library in Paris (which often has a bookcase outside containing unwanted books which can be picked up free by passers-by) I discovered this wonderful quote from W. C. Fields: 'If at first you don't succeed, try, try again. Then quit. There's no point in being a damned fool about it.'

29.

A woman who lives in the building next to us here in Paris has two sons. I discovered that they are twins though they look nothing like one another. Talking to an old woman who knows everything that goes on in our street, The Princess discovered that the two boys have different fathers. This can happen occasionally. It is, of course, a constant reminder to the world of the mother's generous nature.

30.

We travelled back to England on Eurostar as usual. A small businessman spent the first forty minutes making very loud telephone calls. (When I say 'small' I am referring to his size. I have no idea whether or not his enterprise might be classified as small, medium or large.) He was speaking so loudly that it was impossible to think or to read.

Eventually, as he finished one call and started another, I leant across the aisle towards him. 'This is a quiet carriage,' I reminded him.

'I know,' he replied impatiently, dialling a fresh number. 'But it is very noisy in the other carriage. Too many people making calls.'

He reminded me of Auberon Waugh.

Waugh was an enthusiastic smoker but back in the days when smoking was allowed in designated railway carriages he objected strongly to being forced to sit in a smoking compartment.

'It's full of smoke in there!' he complained angrily.

31.

I collected several sacks full of mail from Royal Mail. When she had handed me all the sacks the clerk produced an unstamped letter. Sending something in an unstamped envelope is far, far more secure than sending anything by registered mail or special delivery. The Royal Mail takes good care of unstamped letters. And the postmen, assuming that they are of little value, don't bother to steal them. 'You have to pay £1.50 for this,' she said.

I looked at the letter and turned it over. There was no return address on the back. They let you look at the envelope but they don't let you open it. 'Maybe someone stamped it,' I said. 'The stamp could have fallen off.'

The clerk examined the envelope and shrugged. 'You have to pay £1.50 if you want it.'

'What happens if I refuse to pay?'

'We send the letter to Belfast.'

'What happens to it in Belfast?'

'Someone opens it and then returns it.'

'That must cost Royal Mail more than £1.50.'

She thought about this for a moment. 'Yes, I suppose it would.'

I handed her the envelope. 'So, send it to Belfast.'

JUNE

1.

I've written a short 'pome' which I intend to offer to the European Union.
They have a flag and an anthem so now they need a poet laureate.

I am the EU president
I'm held in great esteem
I'm really not the plonker
Some people say I seem

2.

The Princess spent a glum morning at The Post Office. She had nearly 50
parcels to post off. The zombie behind the counter complained bitterly
about every parcel. 'Have you got many more of these?' she sighed after
she'd weighed and stamped three of them. She was obviously much happier handing out money to benefit claimants than dealing with the needs
of a very small business. The people who work in Post Offices don't have
any financial interest in the shop's success and are too dim to realise that
their wages might be vulnerable if the business goes bust. There is much
public discussion about whether or not prisoners should be allowed to
vote. Personally, I am just as concerned about the fact that Post Office
employees are allowed to vote.

3.

We have a new toaster. After sterling service our old one gave up the
ghost and browned its last slice of bread. It now sits in our black rubbish

sack, hidden under old tins and jars. I am, I have no doubt, breaking several EU laws in putting it there but if the clapperdogeons in Brussels think I am going to drive to the local toaster recycling centre (and burn up a gallon of diesel in so doing) they are further out of their tiny minds than I already think they are. Our new machine is a splendid looking beast, packed with chromium plated features and finished in metallic paint. It looks as though it could, with the right pilot, travel to the moon and back. It fails to satisfy only in the making of toast for which it is, I fear, woefully ill-fitted. This morning, when I arrived in the kitchen, I put a piece of bread into the toaster. I then sliced a grapefruit into halves, put one half in the fridge and the other half on the table. I poured out fruit juice. I made a cup of lemon tea for myself and a mug of hot chocolate for The Princess. I took the hot chocolate upstairs to The Princess's dressing room. I went back downstairs. And waited. And then, eventually, with obvious reluctance, a piece of lightly browned bread popped up in the toaster. If I left the bread out in the sun it would toast quicker.

4.

My book *Moneypower* has proved far more successful than I hoped or imagined. A reader has asked for an update on my investment advice. I told him that the principles expressed in *Moneypower* are still valid and will, I believe, be up-to-date indefinitely.

The combined efforts of the Federal Reserve in America, the Bank of England, the Bank of Japan and the dolts running the European Union will ruin the world and produce the greatest depression ever known. The result will be that currencies will collapse and unemployment will soar. Sadly, I suspect that in few (if any) countries will the depression be deeper and run longer than in England. The so-called Austrian school of economics (which espouses sound money, freedom for the people and small government) has become unfashionable. Our Government has been in denial for years and as a result we are now heading for a multi-generational decline. The future will be defined by a massive deleveraging by governments, companies and individuals. Inflation, devaluation, low interest rates, rising taxes and falling property prices will mean that there will be a massive transfer of wealth from the middle classes to the poor and to the rich. The value of almost every paper currency will fall and so pensions and benefits of all sorts will slump in purchasing power (just as the value of houses has slumped far more than most people realise).

I offered the following thoughts:

1. It is essential to question everything and to assume that everyone in power is corrupt, immoral and selfish and that the decisions they make will be at best self-serving and at worse dangerously destructive. Since I started to follow this sceptical philosophy I have been delightfully successful as an investor. Ignore the old adage 'Look after the pennies and the pounds will look after themselves' and adopt my new one 'Look after the pounds and you won't have to worry about the pennies'.

2. Don't allow your finances to become too complex. W. C. Fields had 200 bank accounts under fake names because he was worried about losing his money. Sadly when he got old and needed the money he couldn't remember the towns, the banks or the names he had used.

3. The only sound money is gold. Imagine. You are going to put something into a box, bury it and leave it for your grandchild to dig up in fifty years. It's a pension plan. What do you choose? A thick wad of fivers? Share certificates for Apple? Or a few handfuls of sovereigns? You'd be barking if you chose anything other than the sovereigns. The fivers will (if sterling still exists by then) buy your grandchild an ice-cream. The Apple shares will probably be worthless (since Apple will have long since gone bust). But the gold coins will still be gold coins and they will make a very welcome legacy. Critics point out that gold pays no interest. True. But there is no better way to preserve capital. A century ago ten sovereigns would have been a very good week's income. Today they are still a very good week's income. Today 0.6% of global financial assets are in gold. In 1980 the figure was 3%. That hardly suggests that we are currently experiencing a bubble. Indeed, the only people who call it a bubble are those who missed investing in gold when it was much cheaper and those who have a financial interest in promoting paper alternatives (that's just about everyone, and certainly includes all politicians, all bankers and all economists).

4. Control your money yourself. Financial advisers charge up to £250 an hour for advice which can only be described as pathetic. New regulations (doubtless straight from Brussels) mean that financial advisers must pass qualifications equivalent to the first year of an undergraduate degree course before they can advise clients about

investments and pensions. Well bully for them. I don't want a first year undergraduate deciding where I should invest my money. As far as I can remember that's the year when most students learn to drink lots of beer and chat up the opposite sex.

5. Last year Standard Life told pension holders who thought that they had invested in a gilt fund that the money had, by mistake, been invested in equities. If people who are paid hundreds of thousands a year can't tell the difference between equities and gilts they really ought to be doing something else for a living. Don't trust the 'experts'.

6. I recently read an interview with a flash investment fund manager who boasted that he took no notice at all of macroeconomics. He said this with the sort of dare devil insolence of a dangerous sports participant eschewing elbow pads. Macroeconomics is unimportant if you don't think the prices of oil and food are likely to have any impact on inflation and if you feel that the value of sterling will remain unaffected by geopolitical issues. I think I may organise an investment course called the Macroeconomic And Geopolitical Investment Course. I rather like the acronym: MAGIC.

7. Never trust an auditor's report. Auditors are either incompetent or crooked. A total of 180 European banks had to be rescued during or after the financial crisis which started in 2007. All 180 of those banks had previously been given clean audit reports. In other words the auditors failed to spot that any of those banks were facing problems, were badly managed or were likely to fail.

5.

I stood in the Post Office for fifty three minutes waiting to post 40 parcels. The staff who work there have been on an unofficial go slow since 1958. I had the parcels in a large sack and every time the queue moved forward a foot or so I had to drag the sack with me. When I got close to the front of the queue I found that the man behind the counter was busy chatting to the customer ahead of me. I don't know what language they were talking but it wasn't English. Indeed, it wasn't a language I recognised. They chatted for ages. I coughed and harrumphed and did all those things one does to draw attention to one's existence but they took no notice. Eventually, the customer left and I shuffled forward. 'I have some parcels to post,' I said. The man turned his head slightly to look at the clock (it required more effort than anything else he'd done for nearly an hour) and then shook it. 'Closed now,' he said. 'But I've been waiting...' I began but he had pulled down the blind on his little hatch and he had gone, showing a surprising burst of speed. I had to drag the sack back to the car and take all the parcels back home. It was not a good moment for a Romanian seller of the *Big Issue* to accost me.

6.

The average individual in the UK spends more than four hours a day watching television. That doesn't include the time they spend watching DVDs or playing with the internet. That's the time they spend watching television. And since there are not a few of us who watch little or no television there are clearly a good many people out there watching a damned sight more than four hours a day. Many of them are children and teenagers. And that is scary.

It's scary because television destroys the imagination and natural sense of wonder and replaces these joy-giving glories with a constant sense of inadequacy, a whole armoury of anxieties and fears and, as an over-rich topping, a strange streak of superiority and arrogance.

I caught a programme called *Dragons Den* on the BBC today and was appalled by the smug, smirking bullies who make up the panel. Who the hell are these people? I've never heard of any of them. Why do people want to parade their wealth and arrogance and nastiness in this very public way? It is a foul and pointless show which seems to me to have been designed, like much on television in general, and on the BBC in particular, to entertain through humiliation.

7.

I saw a packet of a variety of crisps called Hula Hoops which warned: 'May contain milk, soya, gluten, mustard.' Don't they have any idea what their products contain? Do they just throw in whatever they can get hold of? The Princess bought a packet of crisps which had, printed on the packet, a warning saying 'May contain mustard '. How can they possibly not know whether or not their crisps contain mustard? Does mustard just invade crisp factories? Don't they clean their machinery? I never knew that mustard was quite so dangerously invasive. It sounds more deadly than Dutch elm disease and more virulent than anthrax.

Anyone who is genuinely allergic to nuts or mustard or even both must either starve to death or buy their own raw materials and prepare all their food themselves. Even bread is now apparently 'made in a factory where nuts are used and may therefore contain traces of nut'. Don't bakeries clean anything any more? Packets of sweets are sold with a warning that they have been: 'Packed in a factory which also handles nuts. May contain nuts.'

There is, of course, a hidden question here: how did so many people acquire nut allergies? Or could it merely be yet another side effect of those advertisements promising untold wealth if you fall off a ladder or burn yourself drinking a cup of coffee that is too hot?

8.

The post office has returned a book we posted off. The parcel has 'No Longer At This Address' written on the outside. When I opened the parcel I was surprised to find that it was posted on 24th January 2007. So it took nearly five years for Royal Mail to fail to deliver it. That must be a record. I see that at that time we were charging £1 for postage and packing of books. How times change.

9.

I had my eyes tested at an opticians. 'Macular degeneration must be starting,' I said to myself when the teenage boy in charge of the machine conducted an examination of my visual fields. 'Can I do it again?' I asked. Generously, he said I could. I wiped the screen with a paper handkerchief and did the test again. This time all was well. When medical equipment is not cleaned and calibrated the consequences can be fearful.

10.

Sorting through a box of papers I found a large brown envelope containing bits and pieces I'd collected from my parents' bureau when my father died. One of the documents was a Mortgage Account book taken out when they bought their first house in November 1952. The purchase price of the house, a fairly large detached house with a good garden, two greenhouses and backing onto a splendid arboretum, was £2,300. We moved there, I remember, from one of those freezing cold pre-fabricated buildings. The monthly payments to the Cooperative Society started off at fourteen pounds, five shillings and seven pence though in later years my parents paid £16 a month and occasionally a little more. The mortgage was paid off in June 1964, just under twelve years after it had been taken out. I remember going with my parents to pick up the deeds from the building society. The three of us were ushered into the manager's office and with great ceremony he handed my father a very large envelope containing the deeds to the house. I had never seen my parents so proud as they were that day. The house, the garden, the greenhouses and the rose bushes were all theirs. The day is marked with a brown two and a half penny stamp, franked with a bold, blue rubber stamp confirming that the final payment had been made. Two things occur to me. First, I wonder how many young couples will be able to purchase such a house and pay off the mortgage, out of a fairly modest salary, in less than twelve years. We had motor cars, holidays and all the usual stuff. The mortgage was paid off out of an ordinary middle class income. Second, how sad it is that today's house buyers will never be presented with the deeds to their property. The extraordinary rise in house prices means that most will probably never pay off their mortgage at all. And the ones that do will, if they are lucky, merely receive a letter confirming that there are no more payments to be made. The Land Registry now records all property transactions on computer. No more deeds. No more parchment histories, filled with wonderful detail. (The absurdity of house prices is illustrated by the fact that around the world it is generally agreed that a house is worth buying if the purchase price is ten times the rent and a house should be sold if the price is twenty times the rent. In England, as I write, the average purchase price is around thirty times the rent.)

11.

We were in a car park in Barnstaple when a smartly dressed young man approached us rather diffidently. 'I'm terribly sorry to bother you,' he began, and he did look terribly sorry. He told us a long, complicated story about his car breaking down and him needing to catch a bus and having no money for bus fare. He was, he said, in a real hurry. He apologised again and again for having to ask us for help but said we looked kindly folk. The story was packed with detail. The Princess emptied her purse and I emptied my pocket and we gave him about £5 in change. 'Is there any way I can let you have the money back?' he asked. We said there was no need. He smiled and thanked us. And then hurried off in exactly the opposite direction to the bus station.

'There was, perhaps, rather too much detail,' said The Princess.

12.

I received quite a bundle of odd letters this afternoon. (The mail delivery used to be at 8.30 a.m. and then it was delayed to around 12 noon. I assume that this was done in order to save the environment. It has now been put back until around 4.00 p.m., presumably to prevent money laundering and to discourage terrorists.)

The first letter was from a reader who tells me that she responded to a knock on her door to find the postman standing there holding three parcels which were held together with tightly stretched red rubber bands. The postman told her that he had had to knock on her door because the parcels were too big to fit through her letterbox. However, when my reader removed the rubber bands she found that the three individual parcels passed through her letterbox quite easily. Maybe postmen aren't all malicious. Maybe some of them are just plain stupid.

The second curious letter came from a reader who demanded, rather snottily, that she be removed from our mailing list because we have addressed her as 'Miss' when she should have been addressed as 'Ms'. 'Because of this I shall not be buying any more of your books,' she writes pompously. What a silly woman. I wrote back: 'The member of staff who made the terrible and unforgiveable mistake relating to your title is elderly, partially sighted and although suffering from the early stages of Alzheimer's disease she has been struggling to work on because, since her husband's death, she has had difficulty in paying fuel and food bills. You will be pleased to know that on your behalf I have fired her for making such an egregious mistake.'

Next, I opened a letter from a reader who is an accountant who wrote to tell me that according to a 1997 court case it was ruled that accountants may be liable for damages if they fail to inform clients on how to structure their affairs in a tax efficient manner. He is puzzled because the Government is now cracking down on accountants who help their clients to structure their affairs in a tax efficient manner.

A reader sent me a cutting from a Scottish newspaper reporting that a woman has just won her fight to prove that she was made deaf by a vaccination she received when she was 15 months old. But a medical assessment panel has ruled that the woman (now aged 21) will not receive any compensation because she is not considered to be disabled enough. Officials at the Vaccine Damage Payment Unit accepted that the vaccine was the likely cause of her hearing problem but they ruled that since she is 'only' partially disabled she can't have any compensation.

I received a wonderful letter from a pharmacist in response to a piece in my book *Diary of a Disgruntled Man* asking why 93% of pharmacists are so bloody snotty. 'The two main reasons, in my case,' he wrote, 'are that 93% of the general public got right up my nose with their demanding demeanour and their unreasonable expectations. Secondly, when I went to be a pharmacist I entered my course full of enthusiasm with the naive intention of becoming a helpful member of the medical services of the nation. I soon learned that the ability to produce liquid extracts of vegetable matter, roll a good rhubarb pill and make an acceptable suppository were among the skills I learned which were totally superfluous, as was approximately 99% of the knowledge I had gained. I soon found that the only way I could make any kind of living was to write a label, stick it on a box or bottle and hand it out to one of the aforementioned general public. Endlessly. And you think you are disgruntled.' To my relief he goes on to say how very much he is enjoying the diary. 'There are parts which have even made me laugh out loud, something that rarely happens to me.'

Finally a reader wants my advice for her grandson. She wants to know if he should go into the sixth form or get an apprenticeship. I sent this reply: 'I really do find it difficult to give any sort of advice - it gets harder the older I become and the more I know (and realise I don't know). I do know, however, that we live in a world where education accompanied by certificates is considered (by the authorities) to be far more worthwhile than any other sort. We now live by certificates and licences and I can't see that ever changing. Bits of paper (though probably digitalised) rule our lives. It's daft but it's the way of the world. So, in a way, the more bits of worthwhile paper (including a degree) the better. On the other hand I can't see the jobs market improving for quite a while. And in that environment a real skill of any sort is invaluable. There will always be a market for plumbers and electricians whereas degrees in media studies are of very little value. What really matters, of course, is the aptitude of the student concerned. Some enjoy studying and find it agreeable. Others hate it and will always find it a struggle. The latter should probably choose education allied with practical apprenticeships if they're going to be happy. Horses for courses, as they say. And of course there is the cost. A degree is now going to cost a fortune and many who 'buy' them will not find them financially worthwhile. One other thought: the most useful thing I ever learned was how to type. I have yards of certificates. But to learn typing I taught myself. No certificate. But it's a most valuable skill.'

13.

The postman brought several angry letters. The first writer said: 'I have heard about you. I don't like what you say or how you say it. I work for an environmentalist group. I have not read any of your books and I do not intend to do so but you are a dangerous person. I intend to go onto every website and give your books bad reviews and the lowest rating I can.' This didn't surprise me at all. Climate change fanatics are largely the same people who advocated biofuels with such ignorant enthusiasm, who claim to care much for the world but who care nothing for their own country's history or heritage, who are always unable to put anything in context and who talk glibly of hectares and kilometres instead of acres and miles. They are also, invariably, meat eaters who refuse to recognise that it is impossible to be a meat eater and to care about the environment. And they profess to worry about polar bears without giving a damn for animals caged in laboratories or farm animals crowded for days into animal transporters.

The second letter (which came unstamped) contained one of our mailed-out catalogues with the words 'This is a waste of resources' scrawled across the front. The catalogue has been deliberately crumpled up so that we cannot reuse it. All the catalogues were sent to people who had previously bought our books so I'm not sure why this reader was so upset.

Third, a reader writes to say that he has read my book *Moneypower*, and has found it of interest, but that he doesn't want to keep it on his shelves and so he wants a full refund. He says, presumably as a sweetener, that he liked the book so much that he will buy more books of mine in the future. I have written back to point out that we do not run a library book lending service. We always give refunds if we send the wrong book or if a reader doesn't like the look of a book for some reason when it arrives. But if we are now to be forced to give refunds for books which have been read 'with interest' then I think I will give up. I wonder how WHSmith would deal with a customer who walked in, announced that he read a book but didn't want to keep it and so wanted a refund. The curious thing is that I half suspect there may well be a law shortly which will insist that I do give refunds to such customers. It will, of course, be devised by EU bureaucrats who have never done a day's proper work in their lives. They will, presumably, also force cake shops to give refunds to customers who have eaten and enjoyed their produce but don't want to eat it again.

A reader has complained about my book *2020* (a book predicting what will happen by the year 2020), claiming that it is full of predictions and opinions and was written before 'the reshaping of Britain could be evaluated'. She also complains that the book is not balanced and that I have relied very heavily on my own viewpoint of the world.

Two weeks ago a reader wrote in and wanted me to publish his book. I sent him a note wishing him luck and explaining that I only publish my own books. Today I received another letter from him. He has written back complaining that this is unfair and that I have an obligation to publish his book too. His beef seems to be that it is unfair that my books should be published while his remain cooped up in his computer.

A 70-year-old woman wrote to tell me that she had been fired by her employer (her local council) on the grounds that she is too old to do her job properly. 'I cannot survive on the old age pension,' she says. 'But I'm not allowed to work because I'm considered too old.' A reader wrote to tell me that her 86-year-old mother was told by her surgery that she couldn't attend for a blood pressure check unless she also had a flu vaccination. A woman returned a copy of *England's Glory* because it contains no pictures. (The book is in excellent condition and we can resell it so I sent her a refund cheque with a note suggesting that if she wanted books with pictures she either look for books described as 'illustrated' or choose books intended for children.) A reader in Spain has written ordering a book. He tells us that it must arrive at his home on the 16th or 17th of next month. He clearly has more faith in the postal services than I have. I'll be content if the book gets where it's going. A producer wants to turn my Bilbury novels into a television series. But he insists that the doctor hero must be black. (This is, of course, in response to the usual, perverse political correctness which now pervades every aspect of our world. I wonder how many Devon villages had black doctors in the 1970s? And, while on the subject, why do advertisers pander to the vigilantes in our society by always including a mixed couple in advertisements and always ensuring that the man is black and the woman is white and never the other way round?) A reader points out that since schools were originally introduced to keep children occupied while their parents were working (and to train children for the daily drudge of employment) it makes no sense to waste money running schools in Scotland. 'Since nine out of ten Scots are parasites, dependent upon English taxpayers for their daily kippers and haggis, they will be better prepared for a life on the dole or working for the civil service if they merely stay at home and watch daytime television.' A reader tells me that his computer deletes articles from my website before they can be read and downloaded. And another reader points out that Muslims will be taking over within a decade or so. He predicts that under Muslim rule, all dogs which roam free will be rounded up and shot, gays will not be allowed to marry ('Try forcing Muslims to accept gay marriage and see where it gets you') and that Harriet Harman will have to wear a burqa and walk some distance behind Mr Harman.

And we've also received a letter from the local council asking us if we would like to contribute to the debate about school holiday timing. Adding up the suggested holiday periods I see that local schools will be open for 195 days next year. Teachers and pupils will have 170 days a year off. This is part time working for teachers since it means that on average they work 3.75 days a week.

I don't know what the rest of the mail contains. I stopped opening envelopes for the day. I wonder if it's too late to get a job as a teacher.

14.

For years now British employers have been complaining about the European Working Directive, which limits the number of hours employees are allowed to work each week. The Directive has been widely blamed for the fact that hospital doctors now work very restricted shifts (endangering the lives of patients) and for the fact that general practitioners no longer work nights and weekends. But today I discovered that the UK had originally obtained an official 'opt out' from this legislation. We do not have to restrict working hours. A previous government must have decided to ignore the opt out and to introduce the legislation despite knowing how much damage it would do. My bet is that we can blame Blair and Brown for this. Even if I'm wrong I think I'll blame them anyway. Dumb and Dumber have done so much damage to England that they might as well accept this extra chunk of blame.

15.

The Princess and I met an Irishman in a bar this evening. When I asked him what he did for a living he told me that he was a liar. I told him that I was impressed by his honesty. He seemed confused. After a few minutes of conversation which left us both bewildered I realised that he meant that he was a lawyer. When spoken in a gentle Irish brogue the two words do sound rather similar. He was a decent fellow, for a lawyer. He told us that whenever he is in London he stays at the Ritz because he thinks the name is rather appropriate for a man in his profession. He told me something I will never forget. 'People often say that you don't need a lawyer if you haven't done anything wrong,' he said. 'But that is dangerous nonsense. It is when you are innocent that you do need a lawyer.'

16.

We met one of our new neighbours. I call him a neighbour but he lives two or three miles away from us. We met because his car was blocking the lane.

'Sorry about this,' he said. He was small and rather round. He was wearing a blue fisherman's smock, orange trousers that were too short for him and bright yellow socks. 'Can you help me push this thing off the road? It seems to have stopped.'

While The Princess steered he and I pushed his car onto the parking area next to what I assumed was his cottage.

'It's the carburettor,' he said.

I nodded as though I understood all about the vagaries, inconsistencies and unreliability of carburettors.

'Or the gearbox. Or maybe something in the engine.'

'It won't go?'

'That's it exactly,' he said. 'Are you good with cars?'

'Not in the slightest.'

'I used to sell garage doors,' he told us. 'But I've never been good with cars. I'll have to call the garage. That would be best, don't you think?'

I agreed with him that calling the garage would probably be favourite option.

'I started off life wanting to change the world and found myself selling garage doors,' he said. 'Those things that roll up and disappear into the ceiling. You press a button and they roll up and you press another button and they roll down again.'

'I've seen them,' said The Princess.

'To be honest I never had much faith in them,' he said. 'Too much to go wrong. I preferred the old-fashioned wooden doors you open and close by hand.'

'But you don't sell them anymore?'

'No. I gave it all up. I lived in Sheffield. Horrible little house on an estate. My wife was a social worker. She had Ambitions. She enjoyed our life but I hated it. I wanted to give up the garage doors and become a painter but she wouldn't consider the idea. She said we needed the money. I said I didn't see why we needed the money. I've always had simple enough tastes. Much of the money I was making was spent on sustaining a lifestyle I hated. Two cars, grey suits, white shirts, ties and dinner parties with upwardly mobile couples every Saturday evening. We used to argue about it all the time. Then one Wednesday morning she told me she was going to live with a man who works for the council. Half of one of the couples we had dinner with on Saturdays. So I gave up my job, put a few things in the car and came down to the Cotswolds. I was in Bourton-on-the-Water by tea time. I rented a room over an estate agency, bought some paints and started painting. My name is Pettigrew by the way.'

We introduced ourselves. 'Is that what you do now?' I asked. 'Paint?'

He nodded. 'I paint countryside scenes of the Cotswolds. Watercolours. I'll never be in the Damien Hirst bracket but I make a living. I frame them, take them to the tourist shops and they sell them for me. We split the proceeds.' He looked at his watch. 'Must get on. You're not going near Cirencester are you?'

I said I was.

'Could you give me a lift do you think? I promised to take a couple of paintings in to a shop in town.'

The Princess said we could.

'With my bicycle? So that I can get back afterwards?'

I put half of his bicycle into the boot and left the other half hanging out. Clutching two framed pictures our new friend climbed into the back seat and we drove him into the town.

'May I look?' asked The Princess, as we drove.

Mr Pettigrew showed her his pictures and before we dropped him off had commissioned him to paint a picture of our new home.

'A truly serendipitous breakdown!' he said, as he left us, beaming broadly. 'What a wonderful day this has been.'

He is, without a shadow of a doubt, the nicest neighbour we've met.

17.

I spent the morning trying to do the accounts and found myself stumbling over the new paperwork the utility companies are sending and the new statements the bank is mailing.

I am fed up to the back teeth with progress. I've had enough of it. Progress has given us bookshops staffed with reject shelf stackers from Tesco rather than with booksellers. We used to have newspapers written by journalists old enough to shave and when television programmes ended at the end of the evening the National Anthem was played. Postmen used to deliver the mail twice a day (including Sundays before Christmas). Progress has given us deserted High Streets, darkened suburbs and bankrupt banks.

In the bad old days we lived near to an old-fashioned ironmonger. The man who owned the shop (who ran it with his wife and a 'boy' who was in his fifties) had a thingy board upon which was screwed, glued or otherwise fastened an example of every type of screw, washer and fitting. I would point to the thingamajig I wanted and within seconds he would produce it. He would put it into a brown paper bag and ring up the purchase price on an old-fashioned cash register. Today, the ironmonger has been replaced by a chain store where the staff hardly know the name of the town where they are working, let alone where to find the department where ironmongery bits and pieces are to be found. And so, thanks to progress, I spend half an hour peering into plastic packs and eventually I find something that looks as if it might be the right thing. I want one but I buy twelve, because they come in blister packs of twelve. When I get home I have to slash open the pack (an adventure in itself) to find out if the thingy is the right thingy. And when it isn't, which I know it won't be, I cannot take back the blister pack because I have opened it.

Everything is constantly changing in the name of progress. Am I, I wonder, the only person who doesn't know what or how or why the telephone company charges me whatever it does, the only person who prefers paper bills to electronic ones, the only person who wishes the bank would just do what it is supposed to do instead of forever offering me services no sane person would buy? Every change means upheaval, time wasting and confusion. None of them makes my life easier; most of them are designed simply to cut costs and improve efficiency at the expense of quality of service. These things are changes. But they aren't progress.

When the Government forced us to watch digital television we found we needed three pieces of electrical equipment (instead of one) to watch television. The incomprehensible brochure which came with one of them informed us that we had to leave it on all night on standby (something we have been told we shouldn't do because it threatens the planet's very existence.) All were complicated to set up and more difficult to operate than the system we had before. Every piece of progress seems to mean that I have less control over, or understanding of, my life than I had yesterday. Good ideas seem to be abandoned simply because they can be described as old-fashioned. My first small mobile telephone, which I had in the late 1980s and which wasn't much bigger than the one I have now, could, in an emergency, be operated with two AA batteries. That was immensely useful. I used it to edit a column while sitting in Café Sperl in Vienna, to buy shares while sitting in Deux Magots in St Germain and to buy advertising while sitting on a cliff-top in Devon. I know of no modern phone which can be battery operated. (And where are the clockwork phones which would make life so much easier?)

We have a richer heritage than all our predecessors because we have all they knew and more. But our problem is overload. We are constantly struggling to sift the wheat from the chaff; to separate the music from the noise of modern life. I am not against change but I am against change without purpose. There seems to be a myth that before anything new can be created everything old must be destroyed. This is nonsense, of course. But it's an example of newstyle thinking. Traditions are sneered at not because they are irrelevant or irrational but simply because they are old. We all depend on one another more than ever but we have been encouraged (indeed forced) to be ever more selfish. People are so self-centred these days they no longer have friends; these days they have support systems. Here's a truth I have discovered: the more technology promises the less it is likely to do what it promises and the more effort you will have to waste trying to make it work.

We bought a shed. It was the best we could find. The walls are so thin that I could probably push my fist through the wall. We bought a CD player but before we could get it to work we had to connect two bare wires.

We all need daily rituals. They comfort us. Routine, predictability, habit, reliability - all are comforting. But the rules and regulations change daily. And so life becomes ever more tiring and stressful. The lack of stability and the increase in uncertainty mean that our stress levels soar and our health and productivity decline. Too much freedom in little things is exhausting because it leaves us needing to make too many decisions. That's why we allow ourselves to develop habits. We tend to eat the same thing for breakfast every morning and we tend to follow the same route when we go to work. In shops we queue so that we don't have to remember who is in front of us and who is behind us. But while the state is trying to get rid of all our important freedoms, taking control of the big decisions for us, it is also making life more complicated by making it impossible for us to deal with the little things in life by following routines; we are constantly unsettled and fearful without really knowing why. And so we happily allow the bureaucrats to tell us how to live our lives because we suspect that our inability to cope with daily problems must also mean that we will be incapable of coping with the big dilemmas.

Politicians are crooked or completely out of touch or a mixture of both. They are in love with progress. The Government wants to spend billions on building a new railway line so that trains will travel a few minutes faster. Is that really what people want? I don't think so. I suspect that most people would rather have more frequent trains, more reliable trains, cheaper tickets and a bit more leg room.

The whole of our society has crumbled in the face of progress. In the bad old days a family would have a doctor, a solicitor and probably an accountant whom they could trust. Reliable motor mechanics and gardeners could be found if you needed them. Today? Ha! The Princess and I trust no one. I know that if I go for an eye test, the optician will try to sell me something. He won't be content to charge for testing my eyes. He will want to sell me new spectacles or some pills to stop me going blind. If I take the car to a garage I will have to pretend that I know what a carburettor is and that I like to spend my evenings taking apart gearboxes, oiling them and putting them back together again. If I give any hint that I am not au fait with the niceties of motor car construction I will be ripped off. The standards in all areas of life have fallen consistently. We are awash with self-righteous police chiefs who stand up and scream when anyone dares criticise a policemen, despite the fact that they must surely know that today's policemen lie routinely and with just as much fluency as politicians. And the village policeman, the one real person in an authoritarian world, now lives 40 miles away from the village he polices.

I've been with the same clearing bank for decades. But it's a one-sided loyalty. Every month I find simple transactions ever more difficult to manage. I used to receive statements every week. Now, in the name of progress, they come once a month. If I pay in cheques the teller just wants to sell me insurance, an ISA, or a new deposit account. Even the lowest employee receives bonuses and incentives - those two corrosive and destructive inventions. I am a constant victim of institutionalised deceit.

Life is stressful because of the incessant and usually unnecessary changes, and the confusions created as a result.

One of our banks was recently taken over. The mess produced by this seems unending. We pay the price. Another bank has written to say that our account is (for our convenience, of course) being moved to a virtual bank. Our account number has, inevitably, changed. And so everything that was set up with the original bank account also has to be changed. The potential for disaster is vast. And inevitable. Another bank wrote to tell me that a deed box they were storing for me was being moved to a branch in Glasgow. They gave us three days' notice.

And always the Government gets bigger. Civil servants now run the NHS, the BBC, two of the nation's largest banks and many of the biggest and best known home and car insurance companies. None of the staff understands the meaning of hard work or thrift.

Many years ago I used to work as a consultant for several Trading Standards offices. I remember that two men in cheap suits would drive 200 miles to bring me documents to sign. They would then have a pleasant lunch in the pub, remove their jackets and sit on the beach before driving back. When I suggested that they might save themselves considerable trouble and expense by putting the documents in the post (the Royal Mail was more reliable in those days and it was heard of for mail to reach its destination within days of being posted) the senior of the two men explained that if they drove they could claim all their expenses, plus a very generous mileage allowance.

Thoreau's motto: 'Simplify! Simplify!' is clearly not popular with politicians (particularly Chancellors). The only sensible change is change for the sake of improvement or making us feel better. But we don't have that sort of change. We have the change-for-the-sake-of-change sort of change. And we have the change because it's more-profitable-for-some-one-else sort of change.

18.

I tottered to a pharmacy to buy an Epipen. Now that there is no longer much of a health service in the United Kingdom I always like to have one of these handy. One of the few things doctors can do in an emergency is to inject adrenaline to deal with an anaphylactic shock. I carry one not just for The Princess and myself but for any emergency. Carrying an Epipen is easier than carrying adrenaline ampoules, a syringe and a needle.

After about five minutes of searching, the pharmacist, a foreign woman, came to me holding an Epipen. 'Is this what you want?' she asked.

'Perfect!' I said. I took a piece of paper out of my pocket, wrote out a private prescription and handed it to her. 'It will be ready in 20 minutes,' said the woman. 'But you've got it!' I protested. 'You're holding it. I can take it now.' The Epipen was inches from my grasp. I thought about throwing down a £20 note, snatching up the pen and running.

'Twenty minutes,' insisted the woman. 'We have to put a label on it and put it into a bag. Those are the rules.'

'It's already in a box,' I pointed out. 'I don't need a label or a bag.'

'Haven't you ever been to a pharmacy before?' she demanded, rather rudely I thought.

'Yes,' I replied. 'But they didn't keep me waiting for 20 minutes while they stuck a pointless label on a box.'

I left, wasted 17 minutes walking around the shopping centre, and went back to the pharmacy.

Five assistants were standing round doing nothing.

'Is my Epipen ready?' I asked.

'The 20 minutes is not up', said another foreigner. I asked if she had trained in the USSR but she didn't understand me.

After another three minutes I looked at my watch again and wondered why it is that everyone in England with any power at all has to use it as a default. After exactly 20 minutes, a self-important missy brought the Epipen. It still had no label and no bag. The pharmacist I'd spoken to first stuck on the label and put the labelled Epipen in a bag. I gave her the money. She handed me the bag and my change.

I took the Epipen out of the bag, and handed her the bag. 'I don't need this,' I said. I then peeled the 'As directed by a physician' label off the Epipen box and handed her that. 'I don't need that either,' I said, and wandered off.

Another jolly shopping experience in England.

19.

We visited a friend in Wiltshire and were surprised when we arrived to find the house empty but the front door wide open.

'Oh, I never lock the doors,' he said. 'Around here it's not necessary. There are very few strangers around and the locals all know I don't own anything worth stealing.'

'What about at night?' asked The Princess. 'Don't you lock up when you go to bed?'

'No,' replied our friend. 'I keep a double barrelled shotgun under the bed. If anyone comes into my house uninvited I'll shoot him with the first barrel and put the second barrel load into the ceiling.'

We both looked at him, puzzled.

'The one into the ceiling was the warning shot,' he explained with a grin.

20.

We arrived in Paris and when I emptied our mailbox I found, among all the letters, advertising leaflets and magazines a small piece of carefully folded white paper. When I opened the paper I found that it contained a small quantity of white powder. I immediately poured the powder down the lavatory, threw the piece of paper into the communal dustbins and washed my hands. The Princess and I spent quite a while puzzling over how the package got into our mailbox. We can only assume that it was either intended for another apartment, and was dropped into our mailbox by mistake, or that someone who was carrying the package panicked for some reason and dropped it into our mailbox to get rid of it. Why do really odd things always happen to us?

21.

The man who runs a newspaper kiosk near to our apartment, and who knows that I am medically qualified, asked me whether I could name five members of the animal kingdom who are known to live longer than human beings. I could manage only two – parrots and tortoise. The other three are carp, pike and crocodile.

22.

I tried to send a text message to wish a friend 'Happy Birthday'. I had great difficulty in coping with the tiny keyboard on my mobile telephone. (My first mobile phone, purchased around 25 years ago was the size and weight of a brick and much easier to handle.) I blame the minute keys, not my clumsiness, for the fact that the text which was received at the other end of its ethereal journey read 'gapqy biqtgdaz' and was wrongly assumed, for some time, to be a message in code.

23.

'Who lives in the apartment at the front of the first floor?' I asked our neighbour Henri 'I've never seen anyone go in or out but I've heard noises and I've seen a light at the window so I know someone lives there.'

Henri explained that the man who lives there lives alone and is 'un ermite' (a hermit). 'For years he was just a hypochondriac, nothing unusual in France, but gradually things got worse. He read first that most people die in their sleep and so at night he did not go to bed at all. He napped in a chair through the night. Then he read that most people who are murdered are killed by people they know and so he refused to leave his apartment in the day time. He goes out only at night. Twice a week he rushes to the supermarket at the top of Rue Cler which is open 24 hours a day. He buys what he needs and rushes home again.'

24.

I'm always interested in finding out medical customs in other countries. For example, when I wrote my book *The Story of Medicine* I was delighted to discover that in ancient China it was the custom for patients to pay their doctors only when they were well and to stop paying for the duration of any illnesses they suffered.

Today, I learned from a German picture framer who has a shop in our street that it always used to be customary for German doctors to offer a glass of champagne to patients they could not cure, and to whom they could offer no hope. If the doctor had to give bad news he would attempt to ease the moment by opening a bottle of something bubbly.

25.

The salon where I've had my hair cut for years is closed. The husband and wife team who ran it have presumably divided up the scissors and the combs and gone their separate ways. I am not surprised. They had been arguing for years, sometimes on the street.

So, instead I went to a fellow with a small shop nearby. There was no one waiting and this should have alarmed me because waiting is now so popular that whole rooms are put aside for it in many buildings. The barber ushered me straight into the chair. It was only when he tried to throw the cloth around my neck in that skilful, debonair way barbers have that I spotted that he had Parkinson's disease.

It was an interesting thirty minutes.

He cut my hair by holding the scissors in two hands and making sudden lunges at my head but all things considered he made a pretty good job of things. He told me that the electric razor was too heavy for him to hold and so he used a cut throat razor for trimming my neck hairs. Once again he held it in both hands.

Sitting in that chair, and letting him cut my hair, was one of the bravest things I've done for ages. 'If I get out of this alive,' I thought, 'and with my ears and eyes intact, I don't care what my hair looks like.'

'Congratulations!' he said, when he had finished. 'You are my first customer of the day.'

I handed him a note in payment. He dropped it and then dropped the change. I smiled weakly and thanked him.

'Your hair looks good,' said The Princess. 'Did you go to the usual place?'

26.

We went to 'Printemps', one of the biggest stores in Paris, hoping to find one of those things you lay across the bath to hold soap, nail brushes and books. I don't know the name in English so couldn't even look up the word in my dictionary. Eventually, after spending an hour or so riding on escalators we found the bathroom fittings department and, after a little miming and much talk of reading in the bath, purchased a device designed to be held up by two suckers fastened to the tiles alongside the bath. Not as good as a thing to lay across the bath but it was all we could find. 'Shall we have two?' I suggested to A, as the assistant dug one out of the cupboard. She held up the box for my approval. 'How much is it?' I asked. 'Sixty five euros.' I looked at The Princess. Nearly sixty quid for a soap dish seemed a lot. 'I think one will be enough,' I said firmly though I did purchase a box of 44 tiles. (We have one cracked tile in the bathroom but the shop only sold tiles in boxes of 44. We now have 43 spares.) When we got back to the apartment I spent three hours trying to fix the damned thing to the wall. The suckers wouldn't stick. It is, it seems, impossible to buy quality these days. Over sixty quid for a useless, and it seemed to me rather cheaply made, bathroom fitting.

After Printemps we went to FNAC to spend the 200 euro vouchers we'd obtained with our Eurostar frequent traveller points. It feels like party time whenever we spend our free vouchers. It's an annual delight. We each chose an armful of CDs that added up to just short of 200 euros. When we got to the counter the assistant pointed out that most of mine were on special offer and, therefore, could not be purchased with the vouchers.

When we got home I opened a Harry Nilsson album and the cheap plastic case broke. The Nilsson album contains two of his most unforgettable tracks: *You're breaking my heart, so fuck you* and *I'd rather be dead than wet my bed* (sung together with the Senior Citizens of the Stepney and Pinner Choir Club No 6). A real musical curiosity.

27.

We started to walk along the river this afternoon.

'My shoes are pinching,' I said, after we'd gone a mile or so. It was a beautiful, warm afternoon.

'There's a bench just here,' said The Princess.

'Oh, is there?' I said, feigning surprise. 'Gosh. So there is.'

We sat in the sunshine. I took out an old orange Penguin Wodehouse I was re-reading for the umpteenth time. Pelham Grenville Wodehouse created sentences with the skill and care that Georges Auguste Escoffier created soufflés. The Princess took out an improving book. And occasionally we watched as the world tottered by. There was a children's playground not far away and we could hear the shouts and laughter of the children playing. Playgrounds in Paris are marvellous; full of colour and originality. In England all the playgrounds are rubberised and sanitised and utterly boring; there is no opportunity for creative play or even the slightest bit of danger. We used to have adventure playgrounds which

VERNON COLEMAN

consisted of planks of wood, scaffolding, piles of mud and rope. They are long gone. Banished to a world of memories.

After an hour or so The Princess closed her book and looked at me. 'How are your shoes?' she asked. 'I thought we could go back for tea and buns, if you can walk.'

'Oh, I think I'll manage,' I said bravely. 'What a pity our walk was spoiled.'

The Princess smiled.

She always knows.

28.

Sorting through a cupboard full of my own books I found one which carried a photograph of me leaning up against a pillar in Covent Garden. The picture was taken for a Pan paperback by a photographer called Jerry Bauer who specialises in taking portraits of authors. I was wearing, I noticed, a sports jacket which I remember buying from Austin Reed in Regent Street some 40 years ago. It looked smart in the picture and for a moment I wondered what had happened to it. And then I realised that I was wearing it. The lining has worn through in a couple of places but the jacket is still going strong and still looks good. It has, to be honest, worn better than I have.

29.

We visited our favourite church, St Clothilde, which is near to Les Invalides. The organist was practising and we sat and listened to him for a while. We lit candles for the friends we have lost in the last year or two and then spoke to one of the priests. He had a beautiful smile; a smile that was in his eyes as well as on his lips.

'It is very quiet in here,' said The Princess. 'I don't suppose very much ever happens.'

'Oh you are wrong,' he said. 'Things do happen here.' And he told us a story. He said that one of his tasks is to open the wooden boxes which are placed around the church next to the candles which visitors can buy and light. The boxes don't often contain very much, usually just a few euro coins and occasionally a small denomination note.

'Two weeks ago,' he said, 'I opened one of the boxes and found inside it a ring wrapped in a piece of paper torn from an envelope. There was a note on the paper, written in what was clearly a child's handwriting, apologising. The writer said that she had lit a candle and then realised that she had no money with her to pay for it. All she had of value was her ring and so she was putting that into the box instead of the fee of two euros.'

'The ring was not a valuable one,' said the priest. 'In fact it was worthless in monetary terms. It was made of plastic and probably from a Christmas cracker or something similar. But I had a feeling that it meant a good deal to the child who had given it to us and so I put it aside. I hoped that one day I might be able to return it to its owner.'

'And did you?' asked The Princess, desperate to know the outcome.

'Ah,' said the priest with a smile. 'You are intrigued too!' He nodded. 'Yes,' he said. 'A week later I was on duty in the confessional boxes but business was quiet. There was no one with sins to confess and so I was standing in the church just thinking quietly to myself. And then I saw a young girl come into the church. She was about seven years old. She had long hair; she was quite a thin little thing. I could tell from her clothes that she came from quite a poor family. She had very cheap shoes that were too big for her.'

'I waited a while before I did anything. I don't know why. But I waited. She walked up to the place where the candles are displayed and she took one from the storage shelf, carefully lit it from one of the candles which was already alight, and then placed it on the rack above. Then she reached into the pocket of her dress, took out a coin and dropped it into the wooden box. It was a two euro coin. I have heard so many coins fall into those boxes that I can tell you the value of any coin that I hear drop. It must have been the world to her. Perhaps her pocket money for a week, a month, who knows.'

'And then I approached her. I took the ring out of my pocket and I held it out to her. I asked her if the ring was hers. She had tears in her eyes when she saw it. She nodded. She did not say anything. She just nodded. She could not trust herself to speak because she was crying. And besides I am a priest and I think she was frightened a little. Perhaps she had never spoken to a priest before. And I think that maybe she was frightened that she would be in trouble for putting the ring into the box instead of two euros.'

'Please take it back,' I said to her. 'God was pleased to borrow your ring. It was kind of you to lend it to Him. But now He returns it to you with His thanks.' The girl took the ring and put it into her pocket. She did not put it onto her finger. I think perhaps it was too big for her.'

'She asked me if God was not cross with her and I told her that He most certainly was not. The loan of the ring was, I said, worth far more than two euros to Him. She thanked me and she made a strange gesture, a sort of curtsey I think. And then she walked away. She did not run. Little girls do not run in church. She walked. And just when she got to the door, before she left, she turned and she waved to me. Like this.' He waved a little girl sort of wave.

'Do you know who she was lighting the candles for?' I asked.

'Oh no,' said the priest. 'That is between her and God.' He smiled. And he bowed to us, and then he walked slowly away.

Priests do not even walk quickly in church.

30.

I received a telephone call from a man who, a century or two ago, used to be my dentist. I hadn't heard from him for years but was pleased to hear his voice, particularly as he wasn't telling me that I needed a filling. He was, he told me, in Nice attending a dental course. It was his first time abroad and he was terribly excited about the fact that people were driving on the wrong side of the road and eating bread rolls with chocolate in them for breakfast. Just as some people are excited by the word 'sea-front', and others drool when the words 'immensely' and 'rich' are placed in the same sentence, so our former dentist was excited by the idea of anything foreign and romantic. (These tax deductible courses are always held in places like Nice. Presumably there is never any hotel accommodation available in Wolverhampton.) I don't know what the course was about, something to do with better pliers for yanking out resistant teeth I suppose, but my erstwhile jaw breaker had got himself into rather a complicated situation in the dull evening hours when he and his chums weren't purring over shiny bits of dental equipment. He had met a young lady in his hotel with whom he had developed what can best be described as a close relationship. She was, he said, 18-years-old, five foot ten inches tall, blonde, willowy but well-endowed and Russian, and she had told him that she was trying to escape from the Russian Mafia. He said that despite being a virgin she was incredible in bed and that anyone who'd seen her in action and didn't know her would not have believed that she'd only ever once kissed a boy before meeting him. My dentist friend, being probably the most naïve person on the planet, had believed her story and, after giving one the receptionists a huge tip, had secretly moved her into his hotel room so that the bad guys couldn't find her and force her to do unspeakable things to, for and with dentists attending courses in tooth extraction techniques. He had also given her a considerable sum of money so that she could buy new clothes to replace the ones she didn't dare go back and collect. 'She wants to escape to England,' he told me, 'so I need money for her to buy a new passport. She knows someone who can help her but she needs 5,000 euros.' He told me that although he'd known her for less than 24 hours, and hadn't been able to exchange more than two words with her, since she didn't speak English and he didn't speak Russian, he was in love with her and when she arrived in England he was going to leave his family and move into a flat with her. I asked him how he knew all these things when they didn't share a language and he told me that the kind-hearted Russian waiter who had introduced them had been very helpful. At no point had it occurred to my friend that this beautiful young Russian girl was in another branch of the 'lie back and open wide' business. The bottom line to this bizarre but entirely true story was that the dentist hadn't got as much cash as his new friend needed and didn't know where he could find it and wondered if I could help, either by sending him the money or by sending him The Princess's passport so that the girl could use it to travel to London. I told him that I didn't think the passport switch was going to work terribly well and that if things went wrong we would all end up hoping that the makers of 'soap on a rope' were still in business. I tentatively and delicately tried to suggest that the girl might, perhaps, not be telling him the complete truth but I obviously wasn't tentative or delicate enough because he became quite indignant and told me that he thought I'd understand because I'm married to a younger woman. He then slammed down the telephone.

JULY

1.

The title of my book *People Push Bottles Up Peaceniks* was inspired by the headline *British Army Push Bottles Up Germans* which appeared in the *Daily Mirror* during the Second World War. Knowing this a reader has written to remind me that when Michael Foot, then the leader of the Labour Party, was chairman of a European Parliament lobby group formed with the aim of getting rid of the nuclear bomb, a newspaper ran the headline *Foot Heads Arms Body*. He also told me that a newspaper in Essex ran a story about spending cuts for local libraries with the headline *Book Lack In Ongar*.

My other favourite newspaper headlines include: *Lawyers give poor free legal advice, March planned for next August, Lingerie shipment hijacked-thief gives police the slip, LA voters approve urban renewal by landslide, Patient at death's door - doctors pull him through, Headless body in topless bar, Teachers strikes idle kids* and *Antique stripper to display wares at store.*

I spent most of the day replying to this and other mail which had accumulated and we were just sitting down to watch a DVD which The Princess had bought me when the telephone rang. It was my dentist friend. He was distraught. He had popped out of a lecture on new ways to make holes in teeth in the hope that he could see his new love and had spotted her canoodling with an orthodontist from Idaho. He seemed particularly upset about the fact that he was an orthodontist though I don't think the fact that he was from Idaho bothered him too much. There had, apparently, been quite a scene which had ended only when the girl had telephoned for help and a burly Russian pimp with tattoos had turned up in a Mercedes coupé and adjudicated in favour of the man from Idaho who had apparently produced a well filled wallet as a character witness.

'I've been such a fool,' said my former dentist. 'How could I be such an idiot?'

'Don't feel so bad,' I said. 'It was the sort of mistake anyone could make.'

2.

'I'd like to buy some stamps,' I told the Post Office counter clerk.

'What do you want?'

'Five hundred of your excellent 20p stamps please.'

She shook her head. 'I can't let you have those. The manager says we have to keep them for customers, they're very difficult to get hold of.'

'I need them because quite a number of packets and parcels need 20p stamps on them.'

'The 20p stamps are very popular.'

I said I knew that and that I'd been to three other Post Offices trying to buy them. 'Do you have any in the safe?'

The Princess has also tried to buy 20p stamps. They are, literally, rarer than penny blacks. Every post office counter clerk admits that there is a huge demand for them but that they can't get supplies.

'Yes, but the manager says we can't touch those because we need them for customers.'

'I am a customer. Why are you saving them?'

'Because they're difficult to get hold of and customers need them.'

'But I'm a customer.'

'Why do you want so many 20p stamps? Why not just buy £1 stamps?'

'Because it costs £2.20 to post a book weighing up to 750 grams and £1.40 to post small packets,' I explained. 'It's 20p stamps I need. But I'll take some £1 stamps while I'm here.'

'I can let you have some 10p stamps. But I haven't got any £1 stamps. There's a shortage.'

'If I buy 10p stamps I've got to stick on twice as many stamps,' I sighed.

'Why don't you get a franking machine?'

'Because we can only rent them and the forms drive me mad.'

'You can always bring your parcels in so that we can weigh them and put our postage stickers on them.'

'But you go mad if we bring in more than 10 parcels at a time. And the people in the queue behind start rioting. Do you have any 40p stamps?'

She looked at me as though I were potty. 'There isn't a 40p stamp.'

'Why not? There should be.'

She shrugged. 'Do you want the 10p stamps?'

'How many do you have?'

She opened her folder and found the 10p stamps.

'I can let you have 12.'

'Just 12?'

'That's all I can let you have.'

'What about some 20p stamps?'

'I can't let you have those.'

'But you have 20p stamps! I saw some when you flicked through your folder.'

'Those are for customers.'

'I am a customer.'

'I can let you have one.'

'One is no good!'

'OK. You can have two. But I can't let you have more.'

At this point the youth behind me punched me in the back. 'Hurry up, mate,' he said. 'I want to collect my money.'

I turned round. The youth who had punched me was in his early twenties. He had bits of metal attached to his nose and both ears and numerous tattoos. He wore a Burberry cap and a dirty singlet. His pupils were as big as black tiddlywinks and his head was bobbing from side to side. I turned back to the counter clerk.

'Do you have any 50p stamps?'

'There isn't a 50p stamp.'

'Yes there is.'

'No there isn't.'

'It's the stamp for a second class letter.'

'Oh. A second class stamp.'

'It's worth 50p so it's a 50p stamp. If I put two of those on a parcel they count as £1.'

So I bought £300 worth of second class stamps. And as I left I heard her complaining to the next customer, the youth collecting his money.

'Did you hear all that?' she demanded. 'We get some awfully difficult customers in here.'

Eventually, in order to purchase the stamps I needed I had to visit five separate post offices. At each establishment I was received with the same arrogant, unhelpful manner. And burglars should take note: post offices carry very little stamp stock these days.

3.

I received a letter this morning giving me the news that Archie, once a general practitioner, had died. I only knew him slightly but his was the saddest of sad stories.

Fifteen years ago he was a partner in a well-established two man medical practice. He was a good doctor, well-liked by his patients and well respected by his colleagues. He was also a keen musician, regularly playing the saxophone in a jazz band and able to play over a dozen different instruments.

Archie and his partner looked after their patients themselves. They worked alternate nights and alternate weekends and when one of them was away on holiday the other worked 168 hour weeks. They had once tried using a locum but they found that it caused more problems than it solved.

One dark December evening Archie, who was not on duty, was sitting with his wife watching a film on television. He and his wife had drunk a bottle of wine with their dinner and Archie was sipping a brandy. At ten o'clock he received a telephone call to tell him that his partner had been injured in a motor car accident on the way back from visiting a patient. He wasn't seriously ill but he was obviously unable to look after the practice. And so Archie had to take over looking after the night time emergency calls.

Just after midnight Archie was called to see a patient who had had a suspected heart attack. Knowing that he had been drinking Archie tried to get a taxi but couldn't find one. The local taxi firms couldn't help him for half an hour. And so Archie had to drive himself. Racing through the town he was stopped by a police patrol and, because one of the policemen smelt alcohol on his breath, he was breathalysed.

That was the point at which the nightmare started.

Archie's breath sample was positive and so was a blood sample. He was convicted of driving while under the influence of alcohol and he lost his driving licence. More crucially the police sent a routine report to the

General Medical Council and Archie was struck off the medical register. His career was in ruins.

Without an income he and his wife couldn't pay the mortgage. Archie was in his early forties and the couple had two young children at a local private school. They had huge outgoings and no income. Archie could only get a low paid administrative job. His wife resumed her career as a nurse but they were no longer earning enough to pay their bills. Within a year they had to take their children out of their schools and they were forced to sell their home. They moved into a small flat and sold most of their furniture. They struggled on but Archie, who felt that their disaster was entirely his fault, started drinking heavily. And two years later he and his wife split up.

In the years which followed Archie became a tramp and lived on the street. He earned money for alcohol, and a little food, by playing a penny whistle outside the local railway station. His former patients would sometimes recognise him and give him money.

And now he's dead.

When I first heard this tragic story I couldn't help thinking that the courts and the General Medical Council had been unthinkingly unsympathetic. Was there no one in authority with the imagination to remember the words 'There but for the grace of God'?

I still feel the same.

A kind and good-hearted man was crucified by society for trying to do his duty.

4.

The National Trust shop in Wells is selling Christmas cards. I asked the assistant if the cards were left over from last year or being sold early for this year. The entirely unembarrassed assistant told me that they were on sale for American customers. I said that in my ignorance I had always assumed that the Americans, for all their idiosyncrasies, celebrated Christmas on the same day as us. She looked at me sharply and then looked away.

I'm no great fan of the National Trust. When my parents died I wanted to pay for a bench to be put in the garden at one of the National Trust properties where they had both worked for many years as volunteers. I said I thought a bench around a tree might be rather jolly. But I was told that it couldn't be done. In what I thought was a rather pompous reply I was told that the National Trust wants its houses to look like normal homes. I replied that I don't know many homes which have retired bank managers and other dignitaries sitting or standing in every room to protect the porcelain, making sure that no one runs off with a davenport and ensuring that no one steps over the ropes. Nor do I know many homes which have little signs designed to keep people moving in the right direction, 'Do Not Touch' signs on the furniture, and a shop in the conservatory selling overpriced chocolate.

We used to visit National Trust properties occasionally but we decided we won't visit them anymore. On the basis of this personal disappointment I have decided arbitrarily that National Trust properties are soulless, dispiriting morgues and that the people who run the organisation are small-minded bean counters.

We wandered around to the cathedral as we always do when we visit Wells. The cathedral was begun in the 12th century and finished in the 13th century. To be honest it hasn't lasted well for there are clear signs that the building is starting to age. It really isn't good enough that a building which is only 900 years old should be already showing signs of wear. There's a tombstone in the Cathedral which reads: 'Reader that shalt shortly die: what is thy hope?' We also visited the moated Bishop's Palace. George Gissing said that there was no more beautiful place in England for 'thinking' than the walk beside the Palace moat and I wouldn't want to argue with him.

And then, as the local schools emptied and the main street filled with unruly rashes of schoolgirls dressed like teenage hookers, we headed back towards the car park. The rampaging schoolchildren of Wells are far more of a menace than the genial tramps who live on the streets in the city. The Princess saw a middle aged woman rummaging in a rubbish bin in the main street, looking for something to eat. The Princess was so upset she opened her handbag, took out her purse and handed everything in it, about £30, to the woman. We wandered into the Swan hotel for afternoon tea. In the lounge a member of staff was talking with a very loud woman from a local rubbish company about whether or not the hotel's bins should be padlocked. This occupied them for longer than one might have imagined possible. When they'd gone, two salesmen equipped with laptops and telephones sat down and started ringing up their customers and conducting conference calls with distant managers. We left. Outside, the city was quiet, except for the tramps. The unfriendly car parking regime means that visitors are discouraged. But the tramps, who don't have cars, don't mind. It occurred to me that tramps may well flock to Wells because it is one of the few places in England which still has decent public lavatories. Most other towns and cities have closed all their conveniences and are, consequently, woefully inconvenient for visitors. I cannot understand why councils which can no longer afford to run public loos do not do as the French do and auction off the right to run the loos to a local matron. The French have done this for years. All over Paris women rent the lavatories from the council and then make their living by charging a modest fee for the use of the facilities - which they invariably keep spotlessly clean.

5.

I read that employees can claim tax relief if they give their employees flowers on their birthdays. Since The Princess is employed by me and it is her birthday next month I am terribly tempted to try this out. Maybe this year I could try it out with a posy of something restrained, discreet and inhibited and then, if all goes well, I could go for the indulgent, ostentatious, extravagant tax deductible gesture next year.

6.

Yesterday I spent four hours strimming the orchard while The Princess mowed the lawn. Today I feel knackered although I admit that being old is considerably better than being dead. Still, there are privileges. I can give unsolicited advice to people who don't want it and don't know what to do with it. And there are some advantages to being older. Now that I am fairly aged I can always pretend to be senile. 'You're in the wrong seat!' snapped an angry young businessman on the train the other day. If he hadn't shouted and looked such a prig I would have moved. He was holding a laptop computer bag and an iPad and looked the sort of witless idiot who might well work for a bank so, instead of moving, I settled still further into the seat, looked up at him and smiled benevolently. 'Do I want a cup of tea? No thank you. But that is very kind of you, young man.' I reached into my jacket pocket. 'Do you want to see my ticket?'

Being old can even be useful. When the boiler engineer wouldn't come out to repair our heating system I told him that I am an old aged pensioner and talked of cold, death, coroners and responsibility. 'I'm just making a note that you are refusing to come out,' I said. 'In case I die.'

This ploy doesn't work with doctors, they no longer give a damn, but it works with heating engineers.

I must have become someone else. I cannot be this old. I keep thinking of all the missed opportunities. I have wasted far too much of my life dealing with crap. I have not yet come to terms with being so damned old. Still, I mustn't moan. At least I didn't die very young.

I remembered an old story about an old king who was challenged to a duel by a young pretender. The winner, said the pretender, will take the throne. 'OK,' said the king. But the duel won't be with swords. The weapons will be two cakes on a plate. One will be poisoned. The protagonists will each take a cake and eat it. The winner, who lives, will keep or take the throne.

The young pretender refused the duel and had to leave.

7.

Looking through a pile of old medical magazines I see that in 1994 I was invited to write a paper putting my point of view about animal experimentation for the journal *Cardiovascular Research* (published by the *British Medical Journal*). I wrote, as invited, a simple, one page denunciation of animal experiments. When the journal appeared I was astonished to see that the editors had been so worried by my paper that in addition to publishing an editorial opposing my view, and a rebuttal article opposing what I had written, they had also sent a copy of my article to no less than 13 eminent medical experts and had, as a result, printed just under 14 pages of letters defending vivisection. I was not given sight of any of these letters and so had no opportunity to respond. And that, believe it or not, was the best offer I ever had from a medical journal to discuss vivisection. And even that was a damned sight better than anything ever offered by a broadsheet newspaper, any magazine or the BBC. (It is widely accepted that the subject of the holocaust is now closed for discussion but I suspect that many people don't realise just how many other subjects are also regarded as unsuitable for discussion on the BBC. When it comes to AIDS, global warming, genetic engineering, the European Union, vaccination, vivisection and a host of other crucial issues, only the official view is acceptable to the BBC. Alternative, or critical, views are simply not aired.)

I first started to campaign against vivisection when I was a first year medical student at Birmingham University. A friend of mine met a technician who worked in the basement where cats were kept for experimental work. The technician had boasted that he had won money by entering a competition which was being run by the manufacturers of a well- known brand of cat food. The university was buying cat food by the case load and enabling the technician to collect labels at a wholesale rate. My friend and I somehow managed to get into the basement to see what was happening there. We were appalled to find scores of unhappy looking cats kept in cages. I wrote a news story about what we had found for one of the Sunday newspapers. From that moment on I was pretty much a marked man.

A few months later I walked into a class to discover that I was expected to dissect a live rabbit. There seemed to me to be no real point to this. I walked out and went to the canteen where I drank coffee with equally outraged students. None of us returned to the class. None failed (which gives you an idea of just how crucial the experiment was considered to be). Later I cut up my medical school tie on television as a protest against the vivisection experiments being conducted in Birmingham.

It truly isn't difficult to demolish the arguments in favour of vivisection. For one thing all vivisectors readily admit that at least half of their experiments produce unreliable results. But they don't know which half. Under those circumstances it is pretty clear that you can't possibly rely upon the results of any experiments performed on animals. For another thing I can name over 50 regularly prescribed drugs which cause cancer and other serious problems when given to animals. Drug companies (and the Government) ignore results which are inconvenient, arguing that animals are different to people and so the results really don't matter. Every disastrously dangerous drug introduced in the last century has been thoroughly tested on animals. I once offered vivisectors £250,000 to produce a single patient who had been saved as a direct result of animal experiments. The offer was widely publicised but there were no takers. A House of Lords enquiry into animal experimentation invited me to assess the pro-vivisection evidence produced by the Department of Health. It was not difficult to destroy the evidence on purely scientific grounds. But no one took any notice. In the old days (when I was allowed to debate vivisection on television and radio) I debated many times with leading vivisectionists. I won every public vote afterwards. These days the vivisectionists refuse to debate with me simply because they always lose. When the vivisectors found that I was booked to take part in a debate at Oxford University they refused to attend and Oxford University, to its eternal shame, bowed down and recruited someone else to take my place.

Despite the evidence vivisection continues because those who support it have far more money and clout than those who oppose it.

Part of the problem is that those who oppose vivisection tend to be enthusiastic but amateurish whereas those who support vivisection are ruthless and exceedingly professional. The anti-vivisectionists imagine that they can get away with gentle, reasoned, intelligent debate. This doesn't work because the other side (funded by drug companies) lie and cheat very efficiently. They know that the first rule of propaganda is that if you tell a lie enough times to enough people it will eventually become the accepted truth. And the vivisectionists have succeeded in controlling the establishment quite firmly. So, for example, animal charities in the UK are not allowed to campaign against vivisection. The Charities Commission is a Government department and they won't allow any charity to oppose animal experiments. The big animal charities will not oppose vivisection because those who run them are frightened of losing their charitable status. Similarly, lottery money cannot be given to charities campaigning on behalf of animals.

Moreover, it is my experience that whenever one fights hard for something, the people who will provide the most potent opposition will not be those who hold opposing views, but those who claim to hold similar views but who do so from a slightly different vantage point. They may, for example, be members of an organisation of which you are not a member. This opposition is inspired by jealousy and a feeling that their territory has been threatened, and it is infinitely more toxic than the kind of opposition inspired by simple disagreement. The result is that anti-vivisectionists spend more time, money and effort fighting one another than they spend fighting vivisectionists. Some years ago I tried to persuade all anti-vivisection groups to work together. The refusal was unanimous. I suspect that too many groups saw themselves in competition with one another, rather than partnership.

Meanwhile, the pro-vivisection propaganda continues unabated. And we do what we can to oppose it.

A few years ago we sent copies of all my books on animal experimentation to every school in the country. One or two school librarians sent the books back on the grounds that they did not approve of their students reading such material but the vast majority was delighted and many librarians asked for more copies. These days we put copies of the same books onto the shelves in public libraries and bookshops which refuse to stock them. This probably causes some confusion at stocktaking ('Who ordered six copies of *Why Animal Experiments Must Stop?*) but it does allow readers to see what is available.

After speaking at a rally in Oxford I was taken to the railway station by an enthusiastic animal rights campaigner who turned out to have a jemmy and other laboratory breaking tools in her car boot. We were stopped by several van loads of policemen on the way to the station but I managed to intimidate the policemen by photographing and recording their every move, and even though they searched the car thoroughly they didn't notice the jemmy or any of the other equipment. (I found out later that the person driving the car had previously been arrested before for breaking and entering.)

8.

Many things in life genuinely confuse me. During the last week alone I've jotted down the following small mysteries:

1. In films people tear up handkerchiefs and shirts to make bandages. How do they do this? I once tried to rip up a shirt and found it quite impossible. I could probably manage to rip up a paper handkerchief but I don't believe a circus strong man could tear a linen handkerchief with hemmed edges into strips.
2. Why do people never give luck any credit ('I owe everything to good luck') but are always quick to blame luck when things go wrong?
3. Why do we say paintings are wonderful if they look like photographs and that photographs are wonderful if they are like paintings?
4. Why do parents say to children who want to follow the herd: 'Why do you have to do what everyone else does?' and then, when they try to do something different: 'Why can't you do what other people do?'
5. Why does the Government spend money telling people to go hospital at the first sign of a stroke (because speedy action is vital) when they know that the average waiting time in a hospital casualty department is between four and five hours?
6. Why do parents receive compensation if their child dies? The family isn't losing any money unless they were going to sell the child or send him up chimneys.
7. Why should we automatically respect someone who is rich and titled when everyone knows this is probably because one or more of his/her ancestors was a thief or a whore?

8. Why do school teachers have their training day during school time when they only work part-time and could easily fit their training into one of their many long holidays?

9. Why do so many people dress according to what the weather ought to be rather than according to what it is?

10. Why do motor racing trophies look like the bits which are left behind when a new central heating system has been installed?

11. Why do workmen always have a radio blaring as loudly as they can so that there is no peace even when they are not hammering and banging?

12. Why do rail companies force customers to buy car park tickets which tell thieves precisely how long each car will be left unattended?

13. What happens if a nobleman becomes a transsexual? If an earl had a sex change would he become a countess? If an earl had a son and daughter, and the daughter were older and she had a sex change and becomes a man, would she then become the viscount instead of the younger brother?

14. Why do people keep their best crockery (and everything else) for strangers, the next best stuff for friends and the worst stuff for loved ones?

15. Why are train and aeroplane designers allowed to discriminate against tall people by making the distance between seats so small that there is no room for legs which are longer than average? If I travel in anything other than first class I have to sit with my legs sticking out into the aisle, where they are constantly attacked by trolleys and bags. Fat people get special treatment when travelling but whereas most fat people are fat by choice I cannot help being tall. Travellers above a certain height should be allowed to travel first class at a reduced price. I gave up flying some years ago and although this was partly because of all the rules and regulations (they insisted on taking my Swiss Army Penknife from me) it was also a result of the fact that the seats are always crammed too close together. I have, in the past, been invited to speak in America, Australia, Sri Lanka and Israel but have, in the end, always declined because I simply couldn't face the thought of spending more than an hour on an aeroplane.)

16. Why do rich people buy so-called art that everyone else knows is rubbish? (When I was at medical school a friend and I produced

a piece of art rubbish and entered it into a prestigious local art competition. Our effort was highly commended by the judges.)

17. Who first discovered that yak droppings could be used to light a fire? How would you even think that might be the case? What did his chums say when he suggested it?

18. Nine out of ten men over 50 are bald or balding but nine out of ten rock stars have a full head of hair. How can this be? There are only two explanations: either most rock stars are women masquerading as men or else they are wearing wigs.

19. Why do tags and leaflets say: 'Do not remove' and 'Retain for future reference'. Why would I want to keep the tags which decorate bed linen, furniture and just about everything else I buy? And why do people decorate their homes with large signs which say HOME? Don't they know where they are? And why do shops sell doormats with 'Welcome' or 'Home' woven into them? The last time we bought a doormat The Princess had to physically restrain me from asking for one with 'Fuck Off!' woven into the coconut fibre.

20. Why are manuals always written by foreigners who can't speak English?

21. On television programmes where viewers are invited to phone in to vote for something why do the presenters always say: 'Do not call after the lines are closed. Your vote will not be counted but you may still be charged.' Why don't they just turn the machine off? There's a special device for doing this. It's called a switch.

22. Estate agents often describe homes as having two and a half bathrooms. But how can you have half a bathroom. Does it contain half a bath? And what does half a bath look like? And why do estate agents insist on offering customers completely inappropriate properties? During our last property search one agent offered us a house with duck and grouse doors which was cornered between a busy dual carriageway and a pig farm. Mind you, to be fair, the estate agent seemed genuinely grateful when I told him that it wasn't quite what we were looking for but that it might well suit a deaf dwarf with no sense of smell.

23. Why don't bills ever get lost in the post?

24. Why do people hire 19-year-old life coaches and 20-year-old management consultants? Don't they realise how amazingly stupid this is? Our world is full of 20-year-old management consultants who know everything about nothing and nothing about everything.

9.

I received a letter telling me that in May 2012 the English Democratic candidate for Liverpool Mayor, Paul Rimmer, went into a police station in Liverpool to ask why they were flying a striped flag outside the station. He was told that it was 'the gay flag'. Mr Rimmer asked why the station was flying a gay rights flag rather than the Union Jack or the Cross of St George. He quoted from the Old Testament and left the police station but shortly afterwards he was arrested for a hate crime. He was duly photographed, finger printed and had his DNA taken. He was held for six hours. He was then told that the Police were dropping any charges. Meanwhile, Liverpool City Council had confirmed that Merseyside Police had allegedly not obtained permission under the Town and Country Planning Regulations to fly a gay rights flag. And since the flag was being flown at 42 police stations across Merseyside the police have been accused of committing 42 criminal offences. (I am always fascinated by the way that words change over time. The word 'gay' was used in Victorian times as a synonym for prostitute.)

10.

The Princess had to visit a doctor. She went with great reluctance. Her past experiences with the medical profession have not filled her with confidence.

'You're not VERNON Coleman are you?' demanded the doctor looking at her surname and glowering at me. The chill over the consulting room was palpable.

I confessed.

'He's the doctor who writes nasty books about doctors?' he said.

'Yes,' whispered The Princess. We left. We won't be going back to see him again.

11.

I am an idiot. We have two outside taps, one near our back door and the other inside the greenhouse and I have been using those taps and carrying water all over the garden in buckets and watering cans. Today, I realised, belatedly, that it is much easier to take water from the stream and, since the stream meanders from the top to the bottom of the garden, and there are several small bridges, there is nowhere in the garden very far from running water.

12.

A woman working at a garage we use saw the title 'Doctor' on my cheque book. 'Oh, I'm in the health care business too,' she said excitedly. 'I'm just working here temporarily.' She waved a hand around the garage and pulling a face to show how little she liked it. 'My real job is as a chiropodist.' I made appropriate noises of admiration and approval. 'I did a correspondence course,' she said. 'It was some years ago now, but I still do a little corn paring to keep my hand in.' It occurred to me, but I did not say, that the first patient who visits a chiropodist who has trained by mail order must be a brave patient.

13.

In London we popped into Boots the chemist (I can no longer remember why) where a man approached me and complained that he couldn't find the nail clippers. I don't know why he told me about it. Presumably, Boots employees are getting older and more decrepit looking than in happier, healthier times. I sympathised with him and suggested that he go somewhere else and buy a box of crackers. When he looked puzzled by this advice I pointed out that most boxes of crackers contain at least one pair of nail clippers. 'I doubt if you'll have to pull more than half a dozen crackers before you find one,' I assured him. 'You can throw away the silly metal puzzle, the shoehorn and the revolting metal egg cup.' He seemed surprisingly grateful for this information and hurried off to find a shop selling Christmas crackers. It's so satisfying to be able to help complete strangers in this way. As I left the shop I was assailed by the stench of stale animal fat which pervades this area of the city and is presumably a consequence of one of the fast food outlets. I wonder if it is possible to develop coronary artery disease by inhaling fat? The unfortunate souls working here must constantly suffer from nausea.

Then, while standing waiting in another shop, I picked up a packet of something called Fritos. Printed on the packet was a notice telling prospective purchasers: 'You could be a winner! No purchase necessary. Details inside.' I told the hobbledehoy behind the counter that I didn't want to buy the packet but that I wanted to study the details. I asked if it would be all right for me to open the packet, find the relevant document, and then put the packet back on the rack. The woman, who had clearly been fully trained to work in a Post Office, looked at me very firmly and told me in a voice that was full of hidden menace that if I opened the packet and didn't buy it she would call the police and have me arrested. I pointed out that if I didn't eat any of the Fritos I wouldn't have stolen anything and I wasn't sure I would have committed an offence. She said she would think of something. The outcome of this potentially informative experience remains hidden in uncertainty for The Princess then pulled at my sleeve and told me that we needed to be at the railway station.

14.

There's quite a row going on in our nearest village. One householder, who operates a small bed and breakfast establishment, has put up a sign claiming that Gloucestershire's most famous son, the Victorian cricketer W. G. Grace, once slept in the house. They are even offering tourists the chance to sleep in 'W. G.'s bedroom'. Although it doesn't seem to me likely that this offer is likely to draw holidaymakers and thrill seekers from afar the claim has aroused considerable antagonism. The village pub has a picture of W. G. Grace in its snug and has long claimed, in a fairly low key sort of way, that the cricketer stayed there on numerous occasions. I only hope the rising bad feeling doesn't end up with the protagonists waving cricket bats at dawn. The Princess wonders where it will end. Maybe there will be fights over the identity of the pub where Cotswold poemstress Pam Ayres enjoyed a bowl of soup and a bread roll.

15.

My parents had a wonderful canteen of cutlery that was given to my father as a leaving present in the 1960s, after many years working at a firm called Crabtree in Walsall. The cutlery, in a beautiful wooden box, had never been used. They were keeping it, each piece still wrapped in tissue paper, for some special occasion. And whatever the special occasion was it never came. Silver wedding, golden wedding, ruby wedding - all passed by and the cutlery remained in its box. It has been ours for a year or two now and today we opened the box and decided to use it. I noticed immediately that one of the knives had a little rust on it. The others are just as bad. There is a clear lesson. Use it or lose it doesn't just refer to muscles and brainpower.

16.

The landlord at our local public house is trying hard to attract publicity. His bar menu now includes garlic mushrooms with butterscotch sauce and a strawberry and fried egg sandwich. I think he must have been watching too many cookery programmes on television.

17.

Queen Elizabeth II's father, George V1, was a smoker who died of lung cancer while still in his fifties. It occurred to me that if he hadn't smoked the second Elizabethan age might have been considerably shorter. What difference would this have made to our world?

18.

I read that Arnold Schwarzenegger decided to run for Governor of California pretty much as a joke. Arnold was promoting a film on the Jay Leno show when Leno asked what he was going to do next. Trying to find something zippy to say, for fun, the film star apparently said that he intended to run for Governor. And thus it was and came to be. When he made the claim, Schwarzenegger had no staff and no plans. Two months later he was Governor.

19.

The Princess and I were in our front garden when a woman walked past our gate. She had three dogs with her. Naturally, they were not on leads (although this is an offence). She stopped for a moment to chat. 'The boy is so naughty,' she said, simpering. 'He chases the deer and sometimes,' she looked around and lowered her voice,' 'sometimes he kills the young ones.'

We both stared at her in horror.

'Isn't he a naughty boy?' She pretended to be critical but clearly was rather proud of her damned dog.

Neither of us could think of anything to say. I could think of lots of things to shout. But nothing to say.

20.

We visited a couple who have built a house using hand cut oak beams fastened together with wooden pegs. He doesn't seem to have any nerves and when they were still building the house we regularly saw him walking across a narrow beam without any sort of safety harness. She says whatever comes into her mouth without using her brain to filter the words. We call them Frank and Fearless. They admitted that when the wind blows their whole house moves and creaks like a sailing ship. As we left The Princess and I agreed that we prefer a house to stay still and silent.

21.

Pablo Picasso wanted a new wardrobe making. He met a carpenter in a café and drew a picture of the wardrobe he wanted. 'How much will it be?' he asked the carpenter, handing him the sketch. 'Just sign the drawing,' was the reply.

22.

I've been trying to grow tomatoes in our wonderful Victorian greenhouse and it has not been a great success. At the beginning of the year we spent £2,000 having broken glass and rotten timbers replaced and I then spent several hundred pounds restoring and equipping the interior of the greenhouse. I bought seeds for a variety called 'Moneymaker', but they ought to have been called 'Moneyloser' because although I spent hours watering and staking and feeding and tending the growing trusses the flowers refused to turn into fruit. So far our numerous plants have, between them, produced just three, small, green tomatoes. One of them has acquired a slightly orange tint on one side and I constantly examine it to see if the colour is spreading. It isn't. My mother used to make chutney with green tomatoes but I can't remember the recipe and I doubt if three very small green tomatoes would have filled many jars. It's a good job I don't grow tomatoes for a living. I gather that farmers everywhere are having a terrible year. The endless rain and the lack of sunshine mean that nothing is growing. Only the slugs are flourishing.

23.

We met our friend Thumper Robinson for lunch. We met him in the Duck and Puddle public house. (The sign hanging outside shows a duck and a poodle because the artist misheard the commission when it was given to him. The owners of the pub decided they liked the sign and hung it anyway.)

'I won't say no,' said Thumper, when I offered him another pint. 'You don't think this stuff could be habit forming, do you?'

'Only if you drink it regularly,' I assured him.

24.

Reading an old copy of *Country Life* magazine I found this quote: 'It is in our nature to hunt and fish and shoot.'

What nonsense!

It is no more in our nature to hunt and fish and shoot than it is in our nature to put wode on our faces and run around wearing animal skins and waving wooden clubs. The people who still hunt are primitive, under-developed and quite uncivilised. Their attempts to justify their bloody thirsty habit are really rather sad.

25.

A friend of ours is making a television programme in the wilds some-where. He will appear on camera by himself and the publicity will no doubt make a great fuss of the fact that he is making his journey alone.

I teased him about this. 'You're not properly alone,' I pointed out. 'You have a cameraman, sound man, director, producer, research assistant and location manager with you.'

'I'm near as damnit on my own!' he protested. 'We aren't even taking hair and make-up with us.'

26.

While waiting to cross a busy road in London I noticed a small child aged about six or seven standing beside me. It's a road I'm always worried about crossing and I couldn't help worrying about the child. Where on earth were her parents? I wanted to take her hand and make sure she got to the other side safely but I didn't dare. Instead I just prayed that she would cross when I did and follow me across the road. Thankfully she did so. The biggest danger to children doesn't come from evil strangers but from stupid parents.

27.

Thumper rang me to tell me that a mutual friend has gone insane.

'How do you know?' I asked, laughing.

'He's applied for a job with a council and started cleaning his car on Sunday mornings,' replied Thumper.

28.

We visited Charles Dickens' house in Doughty Street in London. We both found it rather sad, soulless and dispiriting. They have an old chair of the Great Man's but at some time or other a vandal has reupholstered it! What, pray, was the point of that? I reached out to touch the chair and set off an alarm.

We also visited the fake rooms of Sherlock Holmes in Baker Street and they were much, much more fun. I took a photograph of The Princess together with a sturdy gentlemen dressed as Dr Watson.

29.

Sitting in the garden, looking at the dandelions and wondering how long it will be before they take over the world, I found myself looking through the retrospectoscope. I thought of all the times I'd done things I shouldn't have done and of all the times I'd said 'I wish I'd done that'. And I realised that the regrets for the latter outweighed the former by far. I suspect it is true of most people. We regret much of what we do, but we regret more of what we don't do. We still all have some choices, though sometimes we don't stop to consider what they all are but simply pick the easy option. But we do have choices. And sometimes we are too conscious of the downside; of what might happen to us if we do what might turn out to be the wrong thing for us; what might in some way prove to be uncomfortable. The truth is that the seminal moments in life are only obvious retrospectively. (The only advantage of taking away choice is that you do at least take away all possibility of regret.)

I once had a contract to commentate on cricket matches. I pulled out and have regretted it ever since. I pulled out because the touring Test side were from the West Indies and most of them were cricketers I'd never seen play. When I looked at their photographs I had a cold sweat. I knew, just knew, that I would never be able to identify them. What a fool I would have looked mixing up the players. But I should have tried it. It would have been fun. They'd have sacked me if I'd screwed up, but what the hell.

And I once got very close to publishing a magazine called *Dr Vernon Coleman Monthly* or some such thing. I panicked when I realised that I was going to have to proof read the whole thing - as well as write and edit most of the material myself. I was already writing two weekly columns, one of 3,000 words and one of 1500 words, running my publishing business and writing and editing a monthly newsletter. The pal I'd hired as production manager was a heavy drinker and although he was supposed to proof read the magazine he was drinking too much gin to do the job properly. I knew I couldn't rely on him and so I panicked. I abandoned the project and he was so cross he never spoke to me again. I have huge regrets about that. 'Might have been' is one of the saddest phrases in the English language. Never to have lost or been disappointed is a result of not trying enough. It is the excursions and diversions and asides which make life fun.

30.

Our neighbours are really excelling themselves. The Princess met one of them in our lane and was appalled when she was told that our home has always been an unhappy place. 'It's haunted by evil spirits,' said a woman who really ought to be placed in a ducking stool and submerged until she confesses that she is a witch. The neighbour who complained about our hedge, and who is not the brightest log on the fire, has complained because our builder has to rebuild a stone archway. He swore at the builders and even when they explained that the archway is crumbling, dangerous and about to collapse he still accused us of being vandals. We've also received two anonymous letters in our letterbox. One warned us that excrement will be placed in our letterbox if we do not take down our fence. The other warned us that our cars will be sabotaged if we stay in the area and continue to refuse to allow dogs to roam free across our land. We don't really know who sent the anonymous letters, of course, but we have a pretty good idea of the identity of the devious little cretin who is responsible. It's always a mistake to write anonymous letters on the back of envelopes addressed to yourself. Just crossing out the name and address with a felt tipped pen doesn't do the job well enough. We could go the police, I suppose, but it would be good to lance this boil sooner rather than later and the only way to deal with such cruel individuals effectively is to attack them in a way they don't expect. As the author of *The Art of War* pointed out: 'To fail to take the battle to the enemy when your back is against the wall is to perish.'

31.

A foreign friend who cannot be expected to know better since he is foreign complained that women aren't encouraged to play sport seriously in England. This is a foul calumny. The English have led the way in encouraging women to take part in sport. For example, it is now well established that women play a vital part in village cricket. Many make the teas (producing vast quantities of sponge cake and cucumber sandwiches) and most are responsible for washing the whites belonging to their spouse or boyfriend. Women have welcomed this opportunity to take an active part in the game and there are even stories of girls and women being allowed to adjust the numbers on the score board (though naturally this is only allowed under the strictest of supervision). In the light of all this evidence those who complain that the English gentleman can be sexist and politically incorrect should think carefully before repeating their slanderous remarks.

AUGUST

1.

If you ever want to taste eternity try telephoning Royal Mail. Almost any of their numbers will do but I particularly recommend ringing your local sorting office where it is almost certain that no one will ever answer the damned telephone. Maybe they don't know what it is. They hear it ringing (just above the sound of the television) but aren't sure what they're hearing. It's easier to get hold of MI6 than it is to contact the local sorting office. They make GPs surgeries look accessible.

2.

I was driving slowly back home, enjoying a few moments of unexpected summer sunshine that had presumably landed on our shores in error, when I approached the local garage. The proprietor was standing on his forecourt while a tall stranger wearing green Bermuda shorts, a pale blue short sleeved shirt and a Panama hat with a yellow band around it was waving a finger at him. I tried not to look, hoping that I could drive past without getting involved but when the stranger heard my car he turned away and stood in the road so that I had to stop.

'This man is a crook,' he said, loudly.

'You're probably right,' I agreed. Behind him I could see the proprietor grinning broadly.

'There's a sign that clearly says 'Cars repaired while you wait' complained the tourist. He pointed to the sign as Exhibit One. 'We've been waiting since 9 o'clock this morning and there's no sign of anyone starting to do anything to our car...and as for finishing it!' Only when he'd finished his complaint did it register that I had agreed with him. 'You say he's a crook?'

'No,' I said. 'I didn't say he's a crook. You said he's a crook. I said you're probably right.'

'I don't open up 'till ten,' the proprietor said. In the winter it's later.

'It says 'Cars repaired while you wait'!' the exasperated tourist shouted, pointing to the sign.

'Shouting at me ain't going to get your car mended sooner,' said the proprietor. 'If I'm listening to you I ain't mending your car is I?'

'I think that there has perhaps been a bit of a misunderstanding,' I suggested, trying to turn a potential crisis into a mere disappointment.

'Cars mended while you wait,' said the tourist. 'It seems simple enough to me.' He was getting very red and it wasn't that hot. 'And we've been waiting,' said the tourist. 'We've met our part of the bargain. But the car still isn't mended.'

'Don't say how long you have to wait,' said the proprietor. 'We had a fellow last month who waited four days. He didn't complain. He did his waiting down at the Duck and Puddle and I fetched him when his car were ready. He said he'd had the best time he'd had in years and that he'd be coming back next year to break down again.'

3.

The Princess and I have birthdays always on the same day of the week. I have a beautiful brass 50 year calendar which shows that on whatever year you select, our birthdays will be on the same day of the week each year. Not even leap years disturb this pattern.

4.

Here are a dozen more not entirely useful things I've learned during the last few days:

1. The horse chestnut tree got its name because there are marks resembling horse shoes on its trunk and branches.
2. I heard a man from Bomber Command talking on the wireless. He said that when he first joined he was told by his station commander that he would have to do 30 flights before he could have a break. 'How long will that take?' he asked. The station commander said he didn't know because no one had ever completed that many.

3. When Empress Catherine the Great, the dictator of Russia, planned to visit the newly conquered Crimea there were worries about her seeing shivering people huddling in cold, shanty towns and so her chief minister, Potemkin, sent carpenters, plasterers and painters to build a fake town of clean, smart cottages. They were instructed to fill them with smiling peasants who were told to wave from the windows as Catherine went by. The short-sighted old queen was delighted by the fake rural bliss which, after she had gone, was dismantled. The deceptions were called Potemkin villages. Much the same happens when our Queen travels around the country. (It is not unknown for houses due for demolition to be painted if they are on the route the Queen's car will take.)

4. The father of W. G. Grace, the cricketer, once drove a kite-drawn carriage from Bristol to London. He also used box kites to suspend his wife above the Cheddar Gorge.

5. Dylan Thomas, the great Welsh literary god, wrote exclusively in English. Any versions of his work in Welsh have been translated from the English.

6. When he was a young boy Charlie Chaplin was looked after by a woman called Mrs O'Shea. She made him his first pair of long trousers and made them without pockets so that he wouldn't stand and slouch. She also thought it would teach him how to use his hands when standing. But Charlie made two slits in the sides of the new trousers and sewed in a pair of socks to use as pockets. Most of the iconic pictures of Chaplin show him with his hands in his pockets.

7. In 1957, when Spanish nobleman Francisco Godia-Sales drove in the German Grand Prix, his valet stepped forward when he pulled into the pits for mechanics to refuel his Maserati 250F. The valet placed an enamel bowl, warm water and a towel on the pit counter. After the nobleman had washed, the valet held out a silver tray with a glass of champagne. By the time that was drained the mechanics had finished and were shouting 'Avanti!' The driver moved to get in and then hesitated, looked back at his valet and the champagne glass. 'No,' he said. 'I'll have another glass first.' And he did.

8. When he was dying the economist John Maynard Keynes was asked what he regretted most. He said that he wished he had drunk more champagne.

9. When Andy Warhol was shot, and thought to be dying, in June 1968, the artist was put into an ambulance, bleeding. A friend, Mario Amaya, an art critic, was with him. He had also been shot. The ambulance driver looked at Mario and said: 'If we sound the siren, it'll cost five dollars extra'. Mario said they would pay the extra five dollars.

10. Cary Grant insisted on signing cheques for everything under $50. Grant explained that his autograph was sold for $50 and so no one cashed cheques he wrote for under $50 because the signature was worth more than the cheque.

11. On August 18th 1914, with the Germans still two hundred miles away in Brussels, the Banque de France set in motion its emergency plan. Paris had, after all, fallen three times in the previous hundred years. The bank's gold reserves, (38,800 gold ingots and bags of coins weighing some 1,300 tons) were secretly shipped to hiding places in central and southern France. The train carrying the gold was derailed at Clermont-Ferrand. Around 500 men were needed to get the train back on track, to collect up the spilt coins and to keep people away.

12. During the early part of the First World War, *The Times* ran a column on preparing for the hostilities which included this practical advice: 'Instruct your keeper immediately to stop feeding your pheasants with maize or corn.' (This rather reminded me of the barrister who prosecuted Penguin, the publishers of *Lady Chatterly's Lover,* and infamously asked the jury to consider whether they would allow their servants to read the book.)

5.

'You are very old-fashioned', said an acquaintance. I thanked him. He looked at me strangely and I realised that the fool had meant it as an insult.

6.

We received a letter saying: 'I recently ordered three books by Vernon Coleman and am pleased to report their condition on arrival at my house was excellent. I decided to start by reading *The Diary of a Disgruntled Man* and have hardly put the book down since opening it. When I got round to removing the address label from the packaging I noticed that the postage stamps had no franking marks on them to show they had been used. I decided to forward the stamps to Publishing House. If the Post Office can't be bothered to frank the stamps why not reuse them?'

Over the last few months we have received a good many letters like this one. It seems that the Royal Mail doesn't bother franking stamps any more. I suspect that we are pretty well the only people in the country still sticking real stamps on parcels. A reader in Northern Ireland simply stuck an address label over his address and used the jiffy bag to post something to me. I then reused the same envelope (and the same stamps) to send something to him. And so on and so on. This is called recycling and is, of course, helping to save the planet and mankind. The same stamps have now been used seven times which may well be some sort of a record.

7.

Listening to the news I'm reminded that statistics are used with ruthless efficiency by politicians and lobbyists. And they are used to mislead as much as to inform. For example, if I say that 500,000 walkers die in England and Wales every year it sounds as though walking must be a dangerous activity. But although the statistic is true (most of the 500,000 people who die each year have done some walking) it is egregiously misleading.

8.

I've had another standard letter from the General Medical Council (the GMC) asking me to let them know who my employer is and who will be responsible for handling my revalidation paperwork. I am, apparently, required to provide details of my designated body.

The GMC's entirely daft new scheme requires anyone who wishes to remain registered and licensed to practice medicine to find an establishment approved doctor prepared to assess them and to check that they have managed to find the requisite number of doctors and patients prepared to confirm that they are 'satisfied' with a doctor's competence. The last time I looked the revalidation programme required each doctor to find 15 other doctors and 35 patients to stand up and be counted on their behalf. Now, Harold Shipman would doubtless have been able to find all these supporters but I don't think I've known that many doctors in my entire life. The revalidation programme exists to exist; it will, without doubt, make life worse for both doctors and patients. It will provide a good deal of pointless employment for arrogant bureaucrats but the quality of medical care will decline still further. Even the Government admits that no one really knows whether there will be any benefits. A programme of red tape, intrusive paperwork and pointless interfering, which will cost many billions and waste millions of doctor-hours, is being introduced to satisfy the egos of a bunch of self-important nonentities. The revalidation programme will not protect patients from bad medical practices and nor will it prevent the remorseless slide in medical ethics - a process which is being orchestrated by the wretched GMC.

The whole revalidation process seems arrogant, disorganised, unprincipled and designed to remove creative, thoughtful, original doctors who vary from the 'norm' (whatever that may be). But then what can we expect from an organisation which has apparently decided that the Hippocratic Oath is out of date and unnecessary and which now seems to approve of doctors killing their patients where this is deemed appropriate and necessary (for which read 'a useful cost-saving procedure')?

The revalidation scheme is poorly designed administrative rubbish which will eradicate originality and imagination and promote and preserve the worst aspects of modern medicine. The manipulative, the superficial, the ruthless, the commercial, the hypocritical and the greedy will thrive. The thoughtful, the caring, the sensitive and the original will struggle to survive. The absurdly overcomplicated scheme will result in doctors having even less time for patients and there will, consequently, be more complaints than ever. The process as approved by the GMC and the medical establishment and the Department of Health is chaotic and will, I believe, do far more harm than good.

The General Medical Council, like so many organisations these days, seems to exist to exist. A recent GMC budget shows that the organisation had an income of nearly £100 million and spent over half of that on staff and lawyers. They spent vast amounts of money on premises and office costs and something called 'purchase of assets'. Just 6% of their budget went on providing professional advice to doctors. In other words the main purpose of the GMC seems to me to be, like all professional bureaucracies and quangos, to exist.

And as a final irony the GMC buys and pays for private medical insurance for many of its staff - presumably because it reckons that the quality of health care provided by the NHS just isn't good enough for the people whose jobs consist of protecting the quality of care provided by doctors. The GMC is not unusual in this regard, of course. Most NHS employees wouldn't be seen dead in an NHS hospital bed.

The Department of Health, the GMC and the medical establishment have, together, lost touch with what patients really want and need. And the General Medical Council has completely lost touch with what doctors need. A plague on all their houses. My biggest fear these days is that The Princess or I will one day be taken into an NHS hospital. The last time I was in one the doctors tried to rip out one of my perfectly healthy kidneys. I believe that both my parents were killed by the NHS. And the 'treatment' my Princess received in one of the nation's most eminent medical facilities would have disgraced a country veterinary practice.

9.

The Tory led coalition Government has announced that it wants to redistribute wealth and to ensure that the middle classes pay their fair share of the nation's tax bill. I thought at first that this was a joke put about by Ed Balls but to my astonishment I discovered that it was real.

This absurdity stinks of Clegg and Cable, the evil fiscal twins. Other than foreigners and bankers there is no honest, working person in the UK who does not pay more than their fair share. Indeed, the phrase annoys me just as much as the phrase 'unearned income' when used to refer to investment income. I earn, I save, I invest. And any income I receive from my labours is unearned. In what way is it unearned?

Socialists want to pull people down to equality, true Tories want to pull people up to equality but the Liberals just want everyone to suffer and feel bad about everyone else. Their dream is universal resentment, their style sanctimonious hypocrisy. The curious thing is that it is the Liberals who have given us a world dominated by and run for scroungers, skivers and shirkers who are driven to spend their lives buying stuff they don't need with money they haven't earned. It is their ill-based, obsession with caring for people (in a remarkably patronising way) that has created our absurd and unaffordable welfare based society. It is sometimes mistakenly thought that it was communism which has given us this world of hand outs and 21st century soup kitchens. Not a bit of it. Lenin and his chums would not have tolerated the lazy and the expectant for a second. They believed that everyone had to work, and work hard.

And yet the Liberals are irredeemably totalitarian in many ways. In the world of the Cleggs and Cables everyone is entitled to an opinion as long as it matches the party line. Clegg and company chunter on about the wealthy having to pay their fair share when the whole point of our taxation system is that the indigenous wealthy always pay more than their fair share. Do they not understand this or do they not want to understand it? Or do they simply believe that if you hand out vast amounts of other people's money then the recipients of your largesse will always vote for you?

I have no doubt that with the nation's economy in a complete mess the Government will soon start introducing far more taxes. Indeed, I have been predicting wealth taxes for some time now. No one in Government cares a damn that wealth taxes, inheritance taxes, taxes on so-called unearned income and capital gains tax are all vindictive taxes which are morally and fiscally indefensible.

Our tax system is a bad joke. My favourite absurdity is the fact that if you win a prize that involves no work or skill it is tax free but if you win a prize that involves work and skill it is taxable. That pretty well sums up the whole philosophy of the politicians and the malicious, spite-inspired half-wits who work at HMRC. And my favourite example of their complete lack of understanding is the fact that they always seem to think that I will know how much I am going to earn in the forthcoming year. At the beginning of each tax year I have no more idea of my income during the coming twelve months than I have of the weather we will enjoy. But tax inspectors, never having done a proper day's work in their lives, simply don't understand.

Still, the next time I am picked out 'at random' by tax inspectors determined to waste my time I will have the joy of handing them a cheap notebook. When the staff member who used to manage my accounts retired I decided not to hire a replacement but to manage the books myself. Since I can't make head nor tail of the accounting packages that fit computers (and since they don't seem to bear any resemblance to the requirements of the tax form) I now run my accounts in an A4 notebook.

And if things get too bad I think I will do what an acquaintance of mine did a year or two ago. He went abroad, renounced his British citizenship and came back as a foreigner. He now lives in England, pays a modest premium to the Government so that they won't send in the thugs, and never has to fill in a tax form at all.

10.

Our telephone went at 5.30 a.m. A woman whom The Princess knows very slightly was on the other end of the line. The Princess had given her the telephone number in a moment of uncharacteristic weakness. The woman wanted to know if we could recommend a hotel in Paris.

'It's half past five!' said The Princess.

'Best time of the day!' I heard the woman say. 'I can never sleep well at this time of the year.'

'We'll ring you later,' said The Princess. 'When tomorrow has properly started.'

Naturally, neither of us could get back to sleep. We lay in bed for a while and then the birds started singing and that was that.

There are, I think, two sorts of people in the world: those who think 5.30 a.m. is early in the morning and those who think it's very late at night.

11.

One of our builders is in a bad mood. He visited his income tax inspector yesterday and things did not go well.

'Do you ever use your van for private purposes?' asked the inspector.

'No,' said the builder. 'I've got a car for private use.'

'You don't ever use the van to carry things around for your wife or your children?'

'Oh, no!'

'Do you ever stop off on the way home and do any errands?'

'Well, last week I did stop off at the chip shop and buy some fish and chips. My wife was out so I thought I'd save myself the bother of making tea for myself and the kids.'

The inspector from Her Majesty's Revenue and Customs leapt on this admission and told the builder that he was disallowing fifty per cent of the cost of running his van. This was particularly galling since the van is one of those scruffy, battered vehicles that is full of old paint cans and empty cement bags.

'Why on earth did you go to the meeting?' I asked. 'They always try to trick people who meet them face to face.'

'The inspector said he wanted a meeting,' said the builder. 'My accountant said I had to go.'

'You have to answer their letters but you don't have to go to meetings with them,' I told him.

'He would never have got that out of me in a letter,' said the builder.

'Exactly.'

That visit to the inspector's office has cost our builder several thousand pounds a year. And it will cost him that money every year for as long as he remains in business.

12.

The sunset of our lives should be a time of contentment. We should be allowed to approach old age with a warm expectation of peace, the knowledge that we will have the time to savour delights previously passed by in the hurry of daily work. The elderly have the right to expect to be respected for the work they have done in their lives and the wisdom they have accumulated.

And yet today's elderly (and the problem is becoming greater by the year) face uncertainty, fear, disillusion and abuse.

We in England could learn a great deal from how the people of the East still treat their elderly. Our culture places an increasingly large premium on youth. Everything in our society is geared towards helping the young, and improving their lot. In China, the first question an official asks (after enquiring about name) is 'What is your glorious age?'

If the reply is anything over 50 then the caller responds with increased humility and respect. The 51st birthday is welcomed with enthusiasm. It means that the individual can rejoice on reaching his half century. And birthdays after that are, increasingly, regarded a reason to rejoice. Someone who reaches 61 will be prouder still. And anyone who reaches his 80s can expect to be revered.

Not so in England today.

In England we kill our old people.

Officially.

Hospitals are instructed to kill off the elderly to empty beds and to save money. They are told to do it by withholding food and water from old, infirm patients. Let them starve to death or die through dehydration. And it happens. I've seen it happening. No wonder medical schools and the General Medical Council consider the Hippocratic Oath to be out-of-date. You can't have doctors being taught to care for their patients when you know damned well that they are going to be instructed to kill them.

What a bloody country.

13.

We drove a few miles to the west and met a friend of ours in a hotel in Cirencester. He has been enormously successful. He's a member of a rock band and a multi-millionaire. When we came out of the hotel the vegetable and flower market in the town's high street was closing down. One of the traders, trying to attract the attention of another, put his fingers into his mouth and whistled. It was loud and piercing.

'I've always wanted to be able to do that,' said the rock star rather wistfully. 'I really envy that fellow.' And he clearly meant it too.

It seemed curious. The fellow we were with was rich beyond dreams. He has three lavish homes and more sports cars than he can possibly drive. He is envied by millions. The object of his envy sells vegetables on a market stall.

14.

We have two local councillors living nearby. Both are women. One, whom we call Ebb, is in charge of highways and the other, whom we refer to as Flo, is in charge of amenities. Collectively they are known as the Tide sisters. Since we don't have much in the way of highways or amenities in our district the former is responsible for making sure that the grit bins are kept filled for the winter (and is therefore known locally as the Minister of Snow) while the latter is responsible for ensuring that someone cuts the small area of grass around the war memorial (and is, consequently, known as the Minister of Grass). Neither of them actually does either of these things, of course, but both are particularly adept at using their telephones. They use them in the same way that jousting knights in the Middle Ages used their lances.

There is, perhaps inevitably, some tension between these two important political figures. One, the elder of the two, is the only person I know who is both thick and thin at the same time (though I have no doubt that there are many models who would also fit that description) while the younger, who has one of the most luxuriant moustaches in Gloucestershire, is an emotionally blowsy woman. It is doubtless rude and politically incorrect to say that any woman has an oversized derriere these days but it is sufficient to postulate that both these women would have sat comfortably alongside those ladies who, in the days when bustles were popular, were accustomed to magnifying the delights with which God had endowed them with the assistance of artificial aids. In the vernacular, both had bums which followed them round like faithful, if slightly arthritic, Labradors. If measured on an intellectual scale both women would sit comfortably a rung or two below the fungi. Ebb is the sort of person who campaigns to have Noddy books banned from the libraries on the grounds that Noddy sleeps with Big Ears who is not only clearly a paedophile but also cursed with a name drawing attention to a physical deformity. Flo sends toasters to characters in television soaps when they get married.

Despite their differences of opinion (which are many and varied), Ebb and Flo sometimes operate as a duo, possibly believing (quite erroneously) that this gives them greater clout.

And today they came round to see us to tell us that there had been a complaint about our hedge.

'One of your neighbours is very upset because one of your brambly bits sticks out,' said Ebb.

'He has to drive past it every day and it brushes against his paint work,' said Flo.

'I wonder who that could be,' I said.

'We can't possibly tell you that,' they said in unison, clearly unable to differentiate between a question and an ironic comment.

'Shall we take a look at the errant bramble?' I suggested.

They thought this a terrific idea so we walked a hundred yards up the lane until we found it.

'There it is,' said Ebb, pointing to a piece of bramble which was dangling down menacingly.

'It's clearly over the highway,' said Flo.

I took out my penknife, cut off the piece of bramble and threw it over the hedge into our garden.

Ebb looked at Flo.

Flo looked at Ebb.

They were clearly nonplussed by this. They had expected that the Saga of the Bramble might be worth at least three committee meetings, a report and possibly even a council inquiry. It had not occurred to them or to the complainant that the problem might be dealt with in such a simple way.

'Phew,' I said. 'Another deadly menace has been over-come.'

They looked at each other.

I closed my penknife, turned round and went back home. This is life in the Cotswolds in the 21st century.

15.

We visited Roddy and Molly, friends of The Princess, who live just out-side Chepstow. When we arrived I was surprised to see a large 'Beware Of The Dog' sign fastened to the gate. There were rubber toys and a large well chewed bone on the front lawn. We opened the gate cautiously, keep-ing it open behind us so that we could, if necessary, make a quick retreat. 'I'll telephone and tell them we're here,' said The Princess sensibly.

'We don't actually have a dog,' admitted Roddy as he led us into the house.

'But the rubber dog toys and the bone...,' I began.

'All just window dressing,' replied Roddy. 'Makes the house look unattractive to hawkers, Jehovah's Witnesses, Mormons, burglars, tax inspectors and busy bodies from the council.'

Breathing audible sighs of relief we relaxed.

'Do you have any pets?' asked The Princess.

'We've got a black and white cat called Minstrel, and the kids have got a tortoise and two goldfish,' said Roddy. 'But none of them has bitten anyone yet.'

16.

The widespread availability of better methods of transport has changed the world dramatically. To a man or woman today a journey of 10,000 miles is as common as a journey of 1,000 miles was to their fathers, 100 miles to their grandfathers and 10 miles to their great-grandfathers. I was reminded of this truth when we met an old couple just outside Lynton in North Devon. He is 92 and she is 87 and they have never been out of Devon. Indeed, they have never been out of North Devon. To them a trip to Barnstaple has always been a great adventure. And although their grandchildren travel the world they find it difficult to contemplate travel-ling as far as Taunton or Exeter.

17.

I read of a transsexual who was given an operation on the NHS to replace her penis with a vagina. When this had been completed the local health authority apparently told her that they couldn't afford to give her any breasts. So they left her in limbo - a man above the waist and a woman below the waist.

My first thought was that the hapless transsexual should pray to St Agatha, the patron saint of breasts. But maybe she should also pray to St Dympna, the patron saint of insanity.

The NHS was created to provide free medical care for the genuinely sick and I don't believe the NHS should pay for sex change operations (or for cosmetic surgery or infertility treatment) but what sort of wicked human beings would do this? Only the sort of nameless, faceless, brainless halfwits who sit on committees could be so ruthlessly cruel.

And then I read about a ten-year-old boy who became a girl. When he returned to school after the holidays, wearing a dress instead of trousers, other parents complained that they should have been consulted and then stood at the school gates hurling abuse at the ten-year-old. It was, note, parents not children who hurled abuse. I'd horsewhip the lot of them. And why do parents have to collect their kids from school? I remember walking two miles home quite merrily at the age of six. If my mum was out I knew where the key was kept. The paedophilia mania and overcautious parenting has ruined the lives of an entire generation.

18.

The squirrels have stripped the bark from a number of our beech trees and in so doing they have destroyed their own habitat. Several trees are now so unsafe that they need to be felled. There is no little irony in the fact that there is a dray at the top of one of the doomed beech trees.

19.

Like many authors I keep a cuttings file of strange news items. Here are just a few of the items I've collected in the last month or so.

1. The Home Office has admitted that two million people in the UK have disappeared. They don't appear to have died, they don't pay tax and, horror of horrors, the authorities and the police do not know where they are. I think this probably shows that there are two million people in the UK who are brighter than the rest of us.

2. The ambulance service estimates that 500 lives are lost because of slower response times as a result of sleeping policemen - which are backbreaking and car busting. In some areas ambulance drivers have to take the long way round in order to avoid these

horrors. In other areas they have no choice but to slow down and then accelerate again - causing more noise and pollution and using more fuel. These damned sleeping policemen (aka speed bumps) cause massive damage to backs and motor cars. And the number of potholes in our roads make the sleeping policemen quite superfluous.

3. A woman refused to move her car which was blocking in an ambulance. The patient in the ambulance subsequently died. The woman was fined just £500.

4. University staff are now given sabbaticals every two or three years. Apparently they find it too exhausting to have to wait seven years.

5. It has been announced that the NHS plans to make Caesarian section deliveries available to healthy women when there is no medical need. Women will have an automatic right to demand that their baby is delivered by surgery - instead of naturally. This will cost the NHS a fortune and it will result in many unnecessary deaths. Caesarians cost at least £800 more than natural births. The decision to make Caesarians available to all was made by the same bunch of half-wits who decide which drugs will or will not be available to dying patients.

6. The no touching rule at lap dancing clubs has been waived for visually challenged members. (I rather suspect that such clubs will receive a good many more applications from men turning up carrying white sticks and leading the family dog.)

7. According to a free copy of *The Economist* which I picked up on Eurostar, the male hippopotamus flings its faeces to impress the ladies, and flatworms have penis jousting contests to demonstrate their fitness and virility. These are the only items of useful news I have ever read in *The Economist*.

8. A new company is selling statues of Lady Hamilton. They do not advertise them as such but it seems to me that these could most properly be described as whore memorials.

9. Internet addiction is now being treated online.

10. Products sold within the EU now use 'UK' as abbreviation for Ukraine, not the United Kingdom. The abbreviation for all things British is EN. That should delight the Scots.

11. There are apparently just two football teams on the Scilly Isles. They only ever play each other and they only have one pitch. I am

told that the teams play each other 22 times a year in their own league but also play for an annual cup. Each year the winner of the cup plays the winner of the league and if one team wins both, then the winner plays the runner up.

12. Financial traders with the longest ring fingers make more than three times as much money as their less well-endowed colleagues. The length of the ring finger is a measure of prenatal exposure to male sex hormones, which boost the concentration and reflexes. The traders with the longest ring fingers earned on average £828,000 over 20 months while the men with the shortest fingers made £154,000. Other research has shown that finger length is linked to fertility, sporting ability, increased confidence and faster reaction times.

13. William Morris wallpaper has been found in a house in the West Country. The wallpaper is believed to be worth more than the house and experts are looking at ways to remove the paper so that it can be taken to London and put into a more expensive property.

14. Scientists have worked out that if the earth were divided up and shared out we would all get around 1 trillion tons each.

15. There is a report that the brain function of civil servants starts to decline at the age of 45. My immediate question is: how does one measure brain function in a civil servant? Is there anything to measure? Most have never done anything worth doing, made anything worth owning or written anything worth reading. And most have never had an original thought.

16. Research has shown that 25% of men who think they are fathers are not the fathers of the children they call their own.

17. McDonalds, the fast food people, has lost a lengthy court battle to stop the 'Mc' prefix being used by a Malaysian restaurant. Malaysia's highest court decided that a privately owned Kuala Lumpur restaurant could call itself McCurry. I gather that McDonalds, being American, do this quite often. In the mid-1990s McDonalds stopped a Seattle coffee shop from using the name McCoffee, a name under which the café had operated for 17 years. But McDonalds have failed in Canada to prevent the use of the name McBeans. I have written to McDonalds to ask if they have any objections to my plans to open a chain of restaurants called McCrap. I have told them that since my restaurants will sell only fatty junk food and I will pay minimum wages they cannot possibly argue that I will be

a competitor. Our advertisements will proudly claim: "We sell the cheapest, crappiest food on the planet. McCrap burgers will give you bigger heart attacks because they contain more fat than anyone else's - with extra gristle!"

18. After council workers (including teachers) went on strike one employee asked for a day off in lieu because he was off sick when the strike took place.

19. A man was stopped by the police in Italy for driving a Lamborghini too slowly. They told him he was being an embarrassment.

20. A female celebrity with footballing connections is reported to travel with an eyebrow architect and nail technician (in addition to the usual entourage of hairdresser, bodyguards, make-up specialist and so on).

21. More than a quarter of all births in England are to foreign born mothers, who are breeding far faster than home-grown mothers.

22. The authorities have decided that those without homes may now use a park bench as an official address. Is this because the authorities feel that they must make an attempt to register the homeless or is it because they fear that they will need to keep track of the people losing their homes through foreclosure?

23. Film bosses say that modern film fans like lots of noise and action. The studio owners say that cinema goers don't give a bruised gooseberry who appears in a film, or even if it is in focus, as long as it is noisy and fast moving. Film producers also admit that they now try to keep sex out of their films (so that young film goers will be able to get in to see them) but that there are no limits on violence. Films are aimed at teenagers because they are the patrons who buy the most popcorn and cola - and that is where the profits are.

24. A recent survey showed that the vast majority of people don't want to pay more tax or give more money to the Government. The BBC's (self-serving) conclusion was that people have become selfish. There was no suggestion that perhaps, just maybe, people didn't want to give more money to the Government because they didn't like the way their money was being spent, and are beginning to understand that the Government is always the problem and never the solution.

25. I read that another well-known couple are naming their baby after the place where they think he was conceived. But such couples are often making a huge mistake. Sperm and egg don't get

together until around 12 hours after intercourse took place and so most babies are actually conceived on public transport or in offices or shops. And the baby named after the place where his parents thought he was conceived is quite likely to have been conceivèd somewhere else. The baby named 'Ritz' should, in reality, be known as 'Harrods'. Or 'Tesco Express'.

20.

The Princess spoke to a woman in Cirencester. Within 90 seconds of the conversation starting the woman had told her that she and her husband owned two houses. 'I'm a houseswife!' she announced.

21.

It is alleged that a man who used to live in the East of the Cotswolds (and who died recently) was fired from his position as Master of the Queen's Bedchamber when he was found in flagrante in the bedchamber itself. His paramour was one of the Queen's Ladies In Waiting who had clearly decided not to wait any longer. I suspect that this is merely a scurrilous and unfounded rumour. But it is, nevertheless, rather glorious.

22.

A man I met in the nearby village shop (and whom The Princess and I refer to as Archibald the Grim) told me that he likes to go for a walk at 6.00 a.m. every morning. When I expressed surprise at this he told me that he liked to get out and breathe the air before it has been breathed by others and become second-hand and stale. Since he lives at least a mile from anyone else this seems to me to be rather excessively cautious.

23.

I was walking back from the post-box when I saw a man lying on his back on his garden lawn. He had his legs in the air and was shaking them from side to side. He seemed quite anguished. I asked him if he needed help. 'A bee went up my trouser leg,' he explained, clearly in some distress. 'They always try to fly upwards so I'm giving him the opportunity to leave in peace.' And moments later a bee emerged from his left trouser leg and flew away.

24.

Apart from the incident with the bee up the trouser leg it has been a quiet week. A leaf falling off a tree three days ago was pretty much the only other highlight.

25.

There has been much excitement in the next village. When a cat was reported as having been stuck up a tree for two hours the fire brigade sent an engine, the police sent two squad cars and an animal charity sent a small white van. The council sent two clip-board carrying youths in cheap suits, the local newspaper sent a reporter and a photographer and the local independent television station sent a crew. There was no one there from any of the local radio stations and I hope that questions will be asked at a managerial level. It turned out that the story was not so much the cat as the identity of the owner who turns out to be someone who regularly appears on our television screens. We were passing when the excitement was at its peak and we stopped to observe.

'There seems to be a lot of talking going on,' pointed out The Princess. 'But very little rescuing.'

She was right, as usual.

Representatives of the emergency services were giving lengthy interviews and posing for endless photographs and when the reporters and cameramen had finished interviewing them they began interviewing one another. An elderly local resident told us that the owner of the cat, a black and white moggie, was away doing whatever television celebrities do but that she was believed to be rushing back home either to try to persuade the cat to come down or to be interviewed or both.

'I don't know why they make so much fuss,' said the elderly local resident. 'No-one has ever found a cat skeleton in a tree. He'll come down when he's hungry but he's not going to come down with all these people here is he? Besides, cats like being the centre of attention. He's probably having a great time up there.'

The Princess and I decided that the elderly local resident was probably right and so we climbed back into the car and drove away. We did so just in the nick of time for as we left a flashy Japanese sports car came screeching to a halt next to the television crew and a distraught looking young woman leapt out. 'Not until I've done my hair!' she screeched at the television cameraman.

Neither of us recognised her but since we rarely watch television this was not surprising. Nevertheless, excitement of this nature is rare in our part of the world. For a few brief moments we felt we were at the centre of the universe.

26.

My eavesdropping has been going well. It's a glorious hobby. You can do it sitting down or standing up, indoors or outdoors and while you're doing something else. There is no closed season. All you need is a notebook and pencil. Here are some of my favourite recent additions to the collection:

1. 'The difference between plump and Rubenesque is all in the mind.'
2. 'I'm not even a has-been.'
3. 'What's the point of learning geography? Everything I learn this year will be out of date by next year. Why don't I wait and learn everything then?'
4. 'I had to fuck a lot of frogs before I found a prince.'
5. 'The male ballet dancer looked as if he had a bag of plumbing tools down the front of his tights. I didn't know where to look.'
6. 'You don't have to be rich enough to do everything you want to do, just rich enough not to have to do things you don't want to do.'
7. 'I have a theory about why old people can remember stuff that happened to them fifty years ago but can't remember what happened yesterday. I think memory is like a bucket. When it's full it's full and there isn't any room for new stuff. If doctors could get in there and clear out all the old, unnecessary memories people would be able to remember more recent stuff.'
8. 'When things look tickety there is always some boo waiting.'
9. 'My husband thinks women should all wear white.' 'Oh, that's romantic. Like brides?' 'No, so that they blend in with the domestic appliances.'
10. 'What exactly is a loose woman?' 'I think it's one who has had lots of kids.'
11. 'Apart from my teeth, bowels, stomach and feet I'm not in bad condition for a man of 89.' 'How old are you?' 'I'll be 47 next birthday.'

12. 'Old people all look the same to me; grey hair, wrinkles, beige clothes and sensible shopping bags. They limp, smell of wintergreen and wear too many clothes for the weather.'
13. 'I have too much trouble with life before death to worry about life after death.'
14. 'What does your husband do now?' 'I suspect he's still decomposing.'
15. 'Every morning a stream of people run past our house. And it's the same people every morning. I can't understand why they don't get up a bit earlier so that they can just walk to work.'
16. 'I'm going to put my husband's ashes into an egg timer. It'll be the first useful work he's ever done.'
17. 'She said she had nothing to wear and he didn't believe her so she turned up to the dinner wearing nothing but a coat and a pair of shoes.'
18. 'She called the police and told them he kept trying to touch her.' 'Did they arrest him?' 'No, he said he was only trying to steal her handbag so they let him off with a caution.'
19. 'If you can't get the cap off it's a good glue.'
20. 'When the gorse is yellow it means that it was a mild winter or a harsh one. Or that it will be a warm summer or a bad one. It's one of those. I can't remember.'

27.

A local farmer died. He was working in the fields when his elderly tractor toppled over. There was no safety cage and he was crushed underneath it and must have died instantly. The farmer was a well-known character who was often seen riding a black stallion along the local lanes. He used to ride it bareback, without reins or any of the usual paraphernalia. He gripped the horse's flanks with his knees and held on tight to its mane with his hands. He was a regular in all the local pubs where his favourite evening meal was a plate of chips and a bottle of champagne. He used to call it 'fizz and chips'.

28.

There is a small hall and a sharp, blind bend near to our house. Three young children on bicycles were racing down the hill as fast as they could. Sometimes they got round the bend and sometimes they crashed into the ditch which runs beside it. It was a dangerous game to play but my main fear was that as they came racing round the corner they would collide head on with a vehicle coming in the opposite direction. I went out to warn them of the danger, thinking that perhaps they did not realise that cars often travel quickly along the lane. The three children, two boys and a girl, listened to me as I spoke, as though taking notice of my warning. And then the biggest, and presumably the eldest, replied, looking me straight in the eye as he did so. 'Fork off,' he said, in a sneery, posh, public school accent. The supercilious little brat will doubtless find employment in the police force if he lives long enough to grow up. The three of them then turned away and continued their dangerous game.

29.

I decided to watch some cricket and so The Princess and I drove to Taunton. It's a town that we both love though it is fading fast and becomes scruffier and sadder every time we visit. While The Princess went shopping I took out a mortgage on an entrance ticket and settled down on a bench. To my surprise I saw Mr Pettigrew sitting in the row in front of me. He wore a mustard coloured blazer, a sky blue shirt, plum coloured corduroy trousers and black patent leather dancing pumps. He looked like a misshape out of a bag of liquorice allsorts. At the end of the over I wandered over to where he was settled and said good morning. He seemed to be enjoying himself enormously. There are some men who take a scorebook with them to cricket grounds so that they can record the result of every ball bowled (the same men who go to concerts with a copy of the score, so that they can follow every note) but Mr Pettigrew was clearly not one of those. He was reading a novel by Laurence Block, and sipping from a large tumbler which clearly still contained a good deal of whisky. He was smiling and looked very content. 'I didn't know you liked cricket,' I said.

'Mrs Pettigrew said I should have a hobby,' said Mr Pettigrew. He put the whisky glass down on the bench beside him, marked his place in the book with a finger and closed it. 'She read in a magazine that there are definite health benefits to both partners if a man has a hobby.'

'Ah!' I said. 'I didn't know there was a Mrs Pettigrew.'

'Indeed there is,' he told me proudly. 'We met two years ago. She makes cushions. Very splendid cushions. When she suggested that I ought to find a hobby I looked at various possibilities,' he said. 'Cycling, stamp collecting, bell ringing, orchid growing, flower arranging, fishing, darts, collecting beer mats...' he waved an arm to suggest that the list he had considered had been much longer.

'And in the end you chose cricket?'

He looked puzzled. 'Oh no,' he said. 'Not cricket. In the end I decided I would drink in public houses. A very traditional hobby. The bar here is very nice. They serve a good cheese sandwich. I come here, I go to Gloucester and so on.' He held up his glass. 'And I've found a way to save the planet and contribute to the environment too,' he said.

'Marvellous,' I said. My heart always sinks when I hear this. Everything is done with the excuse that it's to save the planet. The gas company wants me to pay by direct debit to save the planet. They send me letters regularly inviting me to do this; as does just about every company I do business with. In France, the phone company wants me to manage my account on the internet to save the planet. But at the same time everything you can think of is wrapped and double wrapped and triple wrapped in a complicated wrapping melange of plastic and cardboard, held together with staples and wire. I've seen plastic toys fastened into their cardboard containers with enough wire to fence a ten acre paddock.

'I help the water shortage by drinking my whisky neat,' he said with a big smile.

I couldn't help smiling back. 'Do you enjoy the cricket?'

'I like it best when the sun goes in and the players go back to their dressing room,' he said. 'Everything is more peaceful then. I like to watch the groundsmen. They are so busy, there is so much to watch. They drag on those huge tarpaulins even though it is not raining. They brush the grass and mess around with sticks and poles and buckets and wheelbarrows. They do all sorts of things. It is much more interesting than the cricket. And there is no clapping so it is quiet so I can enjoy my book.'

'That won't last you the rest of the day,' I pointed out. He only had about 50 pages to go.

'Oh, I have two more books with me,' he said contentedly. He pointed to a bag on the ground by his feet. It contained a box of sandwiches and a couple of books. 'Tell me,' he said, 'why do so many people bring cushions with them?'

'The wooden benches can get a bit uncomfortable after eight hours or so,' I explained.

'Ah, I don't think that will be a problem for me,' smiled Mr Petti-grew. 'I have a very large bottom. Lots of natural padding.'

'Do you like the one day matches?' I asked.

He shook his head. 'I watched one on the television,' he said, with a shudder. 'I saw no point in it. Instant cricket. Instant everything. How much longer will it be before football matches consist only of penalty shootouts? They could call it 'Penaltyball' and replace those tedious 90 minute matches with the penalty shootouts previously used to find a decider in drawn matches.'

The fielders had, by now, settled into their new positions for the fresh over and the bowler had walked back to start his run. 'I'd better get back to my seat,' I whispered. Mr Pettigrew looked up. 'Oh yes,' he said rather sadly. 'They are going to play again.' He nodded goodbye, took his finger out of his book and resumed reading the novel he had brought with him.

If the authorities did a head count that day they would have probably put him down as a cricket supporter. And, in a way, I suppose he was.

When I got back to my seat I looked around. At least a quarter of the spectators were reading books, magazines or newspapers. A quarter were chatting to their neighbours. And another quarter were busy eating or drinking. None of these was keeping more than half an eye on the cricket.

I took a book out of my pocket and settled back to enjoy an hour or two at the cricket. A moment later something happened on the pitch. There was a good deal of shouting. By the time I looked up the shouting had stopped. There was some talking but I couldn't hear what was being said. I realised I didn't know the identity of the team Somerset was play-ing. I decided that I'd perhaps buy a score card during the tea interval so that I could find out. I could perhaps buy a cup of tea too. I went back to my book. I used to follow cricket very keenly. But I'm older now. I have an old man's habits, an old man's preferences. When I was younger I often used to think 'I'll do that when I'm older'. Now there are just regrets and an acceptance that it is too late to take up competitive skiing, scuba diving or even club cricket.

The cricket ground at Taunton is almost unique in being in the centre of the town, and during the tea interval I visited a couple of nearby char-ity shops. I bought original 19th century cast recordings of *The Mikado* and *The Gondoliers* made by the D'Oyly Carte company under the super-vision of Rupert D'Oyly Carte. The records came in huge cases which I could hardly carry. I paid £5 for the lot and wondered how we were going to play them. When I met The Princess later she was carrying a huge cardboard box which turned out to contain a 19th century wind up gramophone. I couldn't believe it. She'd bought the gramophone for just £50 from a small antique shop she'd found. Serendipity rules today.

30.

The Princess bought me a copy of *The Dandy* comic. I was terribly disappointed to see that Desperate Dan has been changed beyond all recognition. He has lost his gun and his spurs and a good deal of weight. He now looks like a cartoon version of a local authority recycling collection consultant. He no longer eats cow pie and when he is frightened he cries. The old comics, the ones published half a century ago, used to contain wonderful messages. For example, I have a copy of *The Beano* dated December 5th 1959 in which Biffo the bear hides a bottle of pop so that his friends won't see it. In the final frame of the sequence Biffo finds a secret place to drink his hoarded lemonade. But in hiding it he has shaken it so much that the pop fizzes out and is lost. The message, printed in a bubble above his head, is: 'That'll teach you not to be so greedy'.

The politically correct have destroyed children's comics in general and Desperate Dan in particular, just as they have made their mark on all other aspects of our lives. Books by Kipling, Buchan, Sapper, Dornford Yates and even Enid Blyton are now considered politically incorrect by the scrofulous, ever whingeing literary censors who patrol our schools, libraries and bookshops, and books by the first four are hardly ever available in public. Even Dickens and Shakespeare are out of favour. The smarmy, whey faced commissars who stalk our libraries no longer approve of *Oliver Twist* or the *Merchant of Venice* because the authors who invented Fagin and Shylock are considered to be unacceptably anti-Semitic. When you start banning authors because you don't like the characters they have created then you are in a dark, bad place. Well, yah boo sucks to the lot of them. May their gums rot, their teeth fall out and they spend their lives watching endless loops of television programmes made by Simon Cowell.

Aggressive Jews have frequently attacked me (and successfully campaigned to have my books banned) for daring to criticise warmongering American policies. That's political censorship and although I find it dangerous and offensive I understand it. But to try to ban Shakespeare and Dickens because you don't like a character they have created shows a single-mindedness that should frighten the rest of us to death.

31.

I found a copy of an old newspaper interview with someone called David Maude-Roxby-Montalto Di Fragnito. What a wonderful name. I once heard of a fellow called Cecil John Edward d'Orellana Plantaganet Tollemache Manning which I thought was pretty good though my personal favourite name is Coplestone Warre Bampfylde (the soldier and artist who created Hestercombe). And Sir Ranulph Twistleton-Fynnes is pretty impressive.

Names matter an awful lot.

I once heard of a woman doctor who refused to marry the father of her children because his name was Nutter. She was a psychiatrist and preferred to live in sin rather than be Dr Nutter.

And would Prince William have married Kate Middleton if her name had been Tracey Ramsbotham and she'd had a sister called Sharon, a brother called Elvis and parents called Stan and Ethel?

SEPTEMBER

1.

The BBC continues to annoy me by using metric measurements when-ever a measurement is necessary. The BBC is, in my view, unpatriotic to the point of treachery, but this absurd allegiance to all things fascist is deeply irritating. England (and, as far as I know, the rest of our island) still uses proper measurements for all official purposes. Speed limits are measured in miles per hour and cricket pitches are measured in yards. But a growing number of government departments (and I think it is fair enough to include the BBC in this wide category) insist on using foreign measurements. Do these people not realise that metric measurements were devised by activists during the French Revolution? Don't they realise that they needed decimalised measurements because the revolting peasants were all innumerate? Don't they realise that even today the French still measure many things in feet and inches and that when they weigh stuff they still sell it by the livre?

All this damned metrication causes enormous confusion. Car speeds are measured in miles per hour but the Highway Code measures stopping distances in metres and most signposts now fail to include distances at all, presumably so that the authorities don't have to bother changing miles into kilometres when the EU deems it appropriate to make the change. Fuel consumption is measured in miles per gallon but fuel is sold by the litre.

Still, things could be worse. A fellow we know is a pilot and he tells us that airspeed is measured in knots per hour, altitude is measured in feet, but occasionally in metres, distances are in nautical miles, visibility is in kilometres and barometric pressure in either inches of mercury or hectopascals, which until recently were known as millibars.

How much simpler and safer life would be for everyone if the entire world went back to using proper measurements: feet, inches, yards and miles and pints and gallons. You know where you are with a mile or a pint.

2.

Looking around I am constantly bewildered and disappointed by the attitudes of the young. Life for many is over by the time they reach the age of twenty. Most of them won't be buried for another sixty years or more, but they are already dead in mind and spirit. For millions there is nothing ahead but a smorgasbord of wasted days and missed opportunities and in the end, expectations and perceived entitlements will be turned into resentments and what remains of life will become an unmanageable burden of cares, responsibilities, commitments, debts and nightmares. Anger and resentment will burn holes in their souls. It is bad enough to die in vain, but worse to live in vain.

My generation, and my parents' generation, had real purpose. Today, the young seem to have only a meagre, mean, selfish sort of purpose. Too many expect to become rich and famous without having to do anything. My generation, and my parent's generation, had an ingrained desire to do something that would make the world a better place. But this sense of public service, of duty (oh, how that word is out of date) has been largely drummed out of today's generation by rapacious politicians, greedy corporations and a numbing sense of entitlement. Millions watch life drift by, never grasping their destiny or taking control of any aspect of their lives. Thoreau, one of my favourite authors, famously wrote that 'the mass of men lead lives of quiet desperation' and he was never more right than he is now. By the time people are old enough to have acquired the wit and cunning to do something about the ideas they had when they were young, they have lost those ideals and the passion that fed them. The worst sin of modern man is obedience wrote Trevor Dudley Smith (aka Adam Hall) in *The Quiller Memorandum* and he was right. Time and time again I see people being advised to keep a low profile, keep their heads down and keep their powder dry. The sensible argument is that if you follow this advice you will avoid career and life damaging confrontations with the 'authorities'. But what's the point of living if you do that? Ships are safest in the harbour but that's not what they're for. My approach has always been quite different.

But I do try to be offensive to everyone in authority so that no one can accuse me of favouritism.

'Being potty is the only thing that keeps me sane in this world,' said The Princess this afternoon. As usual, she is absolutely right.

3.

We're off to an auction in deepest Somerset. We like to buy furniture at auctions. We don't buy old things because they are old but because they tend to be better made than new things. In the simple old days workmen made things with care, attention, love and skill. There's a financial advantage too. If you buy a brand new piece of modern furniture it becomes worthless junk the minute you've paid for it. If you buy an antique the chances are good that you are investing rather than spending.

Both The Princess and I love going to auctions though I confess, it is the people as much as the stuff for sale that I find fascinating.

First, of course, there are the dealers. You can always tell a dealer. They still wear sheepskin coats, drive Volvo estate cars and carry thick wads of twenty pound notes. They cluster together in groups, waking up and paying attention sporadically when the auctioneer reaches a lot one of them is interested in buying. They've all watched every episode of 'Lovejoy' and they bid with vague nods and flicks of the finger. Some of them are skilled. Some of them are chancers. Some can tell the difference between a chiffonier and a credenza. Some are just looking for brown furniture or something that looks as if it might be silver. They mostly know how to use strong tea, chicken shit and vinegar to make things look older than they are. And they all know that catalogues are written in a special language. 'Attributed to' probably means a work possibly by or partly by a particular artist. 'School of...' can mean that a picture is contemporary, with and showing the influence of a particular artist. 'In the manner of...' suggests that a painting is in the style of a particular artist but has a date later than his death. 'After...' probably means that it's a copy. And 'Bears the signature of...' suggests that a painting is probably a forgery. Bidding against dealers is, generally speaking, a wise move. They usually know what things are worth and if you pay a little more than they're prepared to fork out you will buy it at a cheaper price than you'd have paid in a shop.

Much of the stuff they buy is merely moving up a long chain and will probably never grace anyone's home. It is stuff for buying and selling rather than for doing anything with. The awful, uncomfortable looking furniture and the terrible paintings will eventually end up in auction rooms in New York and from there probably find their way to a private museum somewhere that no one can find on a map.

Sadly, things aren't as good as they used to be for dealers and with auctioneers charging huge commissions from both buyers and vendors I suspect that the only people making real money from auctions are the auctioneers. And internet bidding means that a private museum in the middle of the Arizona desert can bid directly for everything on offer in an English auction room. Once again the damned internet has taken the fun out of life. Potential buyers who have driven miles and braved the weather sit and shiver in cold auction rooms while unknown, unseen internet bidders do battle. Curiously, bidders who use the telephone don't seem to be cheating in quite the way that bidders who use the internet seem to be cheating. I don't understand why this should be but it is.

And, of course, there are the collectors. Most are there because they are dreamers. The book collectors live in hope of finding the MSS of *Cardenio,* Shakespeare's lost play, or the 6th Gutenberg bible. Or a copy of *Ulysses* with James Joyce's scribbles in the margin, or signed to Sylvia Beech. Or one of the handful of copies of the very first edition of *Alice in Wonderland* (most were destroyed because Tenniel didn't like the way the illustrations had turned out in Carroll's self- published edition). All dreams. The professionals know that real bargains are rarer than mare's nests.

Some are there because they have to be there and as the years go by they become enormously attached to their collections. Since they may have devoted many years of their lives to their obsessions this is hardly surprising. When I worked as a GP I knew a fellow who collected beer mats. He had a massive collection and in the last years of his life he wouldn't leave his house for fear that burglars would break in and steal them, or that there would be a fire which would consume them. In his final weeks on earth he worried incessantly about what would happen to his collection after he had died. Sadly, after he had died a nephew he had never seen inherited the house, the furniture and the beermats. The house and the furniture were sold and the beermats taken to the council refuse tip. It is extraordinary how often this happens. Artefacts which are of enormous importance to one man will be of no interest or value to anyone else. I once knew a man who had a vast collection of sporting trophies which he had collected. He hadn't won any of them. He'd bought them all in junk shops and jumble sales. They, too, were thrown away when he died. And I once knew a man who had a collection of oddly shaped vegetables. He kept them on his conservatory window sill. The trouble was that when they had dried, the vegetables had lost their shape and so he had to explain what they were supposed to look like. When he died his widow, who loathed them and had put up with them for nearly a quarter of a century, threw them all onto the compost heap. There is almost nothing that someone, somewhere will not collect. I know a transvestite who collects old bras, corsetry and other bits and pieces of lingerie. I suspect that the local charity shops are going to have quite a time sorting and selling that collection.

Whether it is stamps, train numbers or bits of old pewter it is usually, but not always, men who collect stuff. I did once know a woman who had a collection of 10,000 small glass animals, and my mother used to collect book matches which she picked up from all around the world. Not knowing what to do with them, and not sharing this particular collecting fetish I use them to light the fire. There will, I suspect, be enough matches to last us until 2087. Collecting is, I suppose, part of the 'hunter-gatherer' in us all. The specialists never show the slightest interest in anything other than the objects of their affection. But others, the generalists, have unstructured needs and will buy just about anything. A pal of mine, a GP, bought a bag full of old car keys. He paid 50 pence for them. For years afterwards, whenever he saw a traffic warden putting a ticket on a car he would stand, curse quietly, shake his head, take a set of keys out of his pocket and throw them to the warden. 'Here you are,' he would say. 'I'm fed up with cars. You have the damned thing.' He would then walk away, leaving the traffic warden to spend ages trying to get into the car with a key that didn't fit.

Another fellow I know used to buy old paintings of eminent looking folk. He hung them on his dining room walls. 'This is my great grandfather,' he would say, pointing with well-simulated pride at a cracked oil painting of a stern and stout man in uniform. We knew he was faking because we once saw a picture on his wall which we'd seen in a junk shop in Bideford. He liked to give the appearance that he came from a long, distinguished family. He wore a crested signet ring and had furniture which he claimed had been in his family for two hundred years.

When we buy at an auction (and we never go to an auction without buying heaps of things we didn't want when we first saw them and certainly don't want when we get them home) we always do best when we buy a mixed lot. This is wholesale, jackdaw style materialism. A box of bits and pieces. Box and contents is the usual technical term. Or, best of all, a large box of assorted books. We go to auctions these days not to look for bargains but to look for adventure and excitement and in the hope of finding something unusual. A box and contents may fetch between 50p and £10 and the glories are as unpredictable. They can be enormously disappointing or quite enchanting. At today's auction we bought two boxes of books, each costing the magnificent sum of £10 plus commission. The first box contained a number of first editions (including a splendid edition of Jerome K. Jerome's *My First Book*) and the second contained all eight volumes of the 1812 edition of *History of England* by Hume, a book of poems about ants and a variety of well looked after Victorian and Edwardian first editions.

The highlight of the day was the sale of a tray of kitchen ephemera: some EPNS cutlery, three wooden egg cups, a few chipped plates, an old, ugly brown jug and a broken toast rack. There wasn't a thing on the tray I wouldn't have thrown into the bin.

'Anyone give me 50 pence for this?'

'£1.'

'£1.50'

'£2.00'

At this point it became clear that something strange was happening. Two dealers were bidding for the tray of rubbish. And they were bidding seriously. Everyone in the room was looking at them. The two dealers looked at each other. One of them shrugged. '£100,' he said.

'£200.' countered the other.

The auctioneer, now a passenger in his own auction, could only stare in wonderment.

'£300.'

'£400.'

'I think we missed something,' said the auctioneer, with an embarrassed laugh.

We all stared at the tray and tried to work out what had been missed. The plates? The cutlery? Was the toast rack a rare piece of Georgian silver? Could it be the tray? It looked like a very plain wooden tray.

'£1,000,' said one of the dealers. The room had now gone silent.

'£1,100.'

'£1,200.'

'£1,500.'

The other dealer thought for a moment, looked hard at the tray and then slowly, regretfully, shook his head.

The winning dealer showed the auctioneer his number and made his way towards the tray. We watched as he reached over, picked up the ugly brown jug and walked away. 'You can put the rest back in at 50 pence,' he said to the auctioneer.

4.

I heard that Vivian Stanshall, the eccentric singer and raconteur, is being remembered at a Bonzo Dog revival concert with a one minute cacophony. Silence really just wouldn't have been appropriate, would it?

5.

We arrived in Paris in the early evening. Our route from the Gare du Nord usually takes us across La Place de La Concorde (unless the taxi driver is exceptionally imaginative and greedy) and, as always, it is there that we catch our first glimpse of the Eiffel Tower. Illuminated, as always, she looked wonderful. I cannot think of another man-made object, anywhere in the world, which is so instantly recognisable. And it is difficult to think of any man-made object which is admired so much. It seems strange to think that when M.Eiffel first erected his tower it was intended as a temporary structure and was greeted by the Parisians with boos and catcalls. The taxi driver who drove us must have learned to drive in dodgem cars in a fairground. How he managed to travel across Paris without actually hitting anything is a mystery. It is always good to arrive at the apartment. It's on the top floor and feels like a nest; secure, cosy and high above the travails of the world.

6.

We saw a motorcyclist in St Germain who had a face painted on the back of his helmet. He is playing a dangerous game. If he has an accident short-sighted doctors could well spend some time trying to turn his head round so that it faced the right way.

7.

A visit to Giverny, near the small town of Vernon reminded me that Monet was in his nineties when painting the famous lily ponds helped him create abstractionism. A little research among our books in Paris shows that he wasn't the only individual to have achieved great things after the age of 65. Doctors and nurses in England may want to kill off every citizen of pensionable age but the list of great achievements among the over 65s is impressive. Haydn wrote *Deutschland, Deutschland uber alles* when he was 65. Josephine Baker was dancing on the Broadway stage at 67 and Grandma Moses started her highly successful painting career at the same age. Ronald Reagan became president of the USA at the age of 69 and Gilbert White was the same age when he published *The Natural History of Selbourne*. Colette was 72 when she wrote *Gigi*, H. G. Wells successfully submitted a doctoral thesis at 78 and George Burns was 80 when he won an Oscar for *The Sunshine Boys*. Marc Chagall was still painting in his 90s, Benjamin Franklin was 81 when he helped write the American Constitution and Goethe was the same age when he wrote *Faust*. Stradivari was still making violins at 93 and P.G.Wodehouse was still writing novels in his nineties.

Suddenly, I don't feel quite so old.

8.

In a café today, The Princess and I overheard a Frenchman ordering an omelette. "Tell the chef I want it made with half a dozen eggs and plenty of cheese," he told the waiter. He turned to us and guessed that we'd overheard. "I feel like something light and healthy," he explained with an apologetic smile.

9.

A simple but insignificant truth occurred to me today. People in show business who use just one name (and I'm thinking of performers such as Bono, Madonna and Sting) invariably seem to me to be self-righteous, self-important and dull. I don't know why this is.

10.

An American friend of ours who lives in Thailand told us that a year ago a man he knows refused to have a wobbly kitten in his house. He said the kitten wouldn't live and he didn't want the unhappiness of seeing it die. It was given to a neighbour. And today the man, who a year ago seemed healthy and good for another three or four decades of life, is lying in a coffin while the kitten, which seemed so frail, is still alive and looks stronger than ever.

11.

The Women's Institute and the Churches' Legislation Advisory Service have advised their members that a new EU law makes it illegal to sell jam, marmalade or chutney in pre-used jars. The people who created this law hadn't been able to find anyone who has actually been injured, made ill or killed by jams or chutneys put into used jam jars but, hey, who said common sense had anything to do with EU life these days? The pitiless, brain-dead eurocrats have presumably stuck their dirty fingers into the used jam jar cottage industry in order to protect the manufacturers of jam jars and the official manufacturers of jams and chutneys. And just so that everyone knows that when the EU creates a law it means business the eurocrats have told us the penalties. Anyone who sells home-made strawberry jam or tomato chutney at a village fête will now be liable to a £5,000 fine and six months in prison. The eurocrats always deny that they are responsible for the daft laws with which we are encumbered. And it is illegal for ministers and civil servants to blame the EU for anything. But when the voters eventually learn just how many really stupid laws came from the eurocrats then the eurocrats' days of wine and roses will be finished. Any government's natural act is to grow. The EU, running a whole continent without any democratic control, has grown in authority and hubris, expanding its reach like hogweed or ground elder. The cost of this pointless bureaucratic extravaganza rises inexorably with salaries, perks and expenses soaring as though the EU and its employees were immune to the problems of the real world. Their idea of cost saving is to limit themselves to two bottles of wine each for lunch. The organisation's constant and unerring aim is to protect the interests of industry, management and staff and damn the consequences for the consumer. The lunacy seems never ending. And there is always someone else to blame. When it became clear that the EU's Common Fisheries Policy had resulted in a dramatic fall in fish stocks the eurocrats introduced a plan to slaughter thousands of seals and seabirds on the grounds that it was *their* fault that there would soon be no more fish in our seas. When the EU falls, it will be dramatic, noisy and a real delight to watch.

The fascists and socialists who run the EU argue that individual liberty has to be shelved until collective liberty can be made secure (which, of course, it never will be). It will all end in tears and, of course, it's all happened before. Rome had a socialist interlude under a bozo called Diocletian who created an expensive bureaucracy, payments for Romans who weren't working and taxes so high that men lost the incentive to work. Half the lawyers in Rome spent their days trying to find ways to evade taxes and the other half were busy closing the loopholes and creating new laws to prevent evasion. Lawyers and bureaucrats have always had hearts of flint and the morals of pirates. High taxes resulted in complaints from the hardworking that they were supporting the lazy and the incompetent. Golly. And in China in 100 BC exactly the same thing happened, and then happened again and again at intervals thereafter. In 11th century China the State took over the economy and gave benefits to anyone who wanted them. But the high taxes needed to pay for all the government employees and corrupt bureaucrats resulted in disaster. Human corruptibility and incompetence always make government control impractical. Oppressive, socialist states are always overthrown eventually and though communist, fascist governments exist for a while through a mixture of corruption, tyranny, bribery and suppression of individual freedom the result, in the end, is that the people always get fed up with the way things are. Too many rules, too much bureaucracy, too little individual freedom and too many taxes result in chaos, protest and the collapse of the economy.

We have a welfare state which ensures that wealth is distributed from those who work to those who do not. We have rules which are now patently absurd and the EU is being run by people who seem to be inextricably linked to the trilateral commission, the Bilderbergers and, of course, Goldman Sachs. In practice the EU consists of an army of bureaucrats who must spend their lives laughing hysterically at the absurdly silly rules they have made up. It is certainly true that anything that doesn't make sense came from the EU. The EU is what we would have if a committee was set up consisting of Marx (Karl), Hitler (Adolf), Marx (Groucho) and Attila (the Hun). Just who are the people who carry EU flags, put them on their cars or in their gardens or wave them at the Last Night of the Proms? There were even people at the last Olympics waving EU flags. Are they EU bureaucrats on an all-expenses paid day out or simply demented fascists?

The EU, fascist and dangerous, is the most absurd organisation created in history. I recently told a fellow I know that the EU had discussed plans to ban children from building sandcastles (because they were con-sidered to be too elitist) but had finally agreed to a compromise suggestion that for every castle built on the beach there should be five ordinary starter homes - made with just one bucket of sand with an EU flag on it. The chap to whom I told this nodded thoughtfully and not for one moment did he think that I was pulling his leg.

There are tears ahead.

12.

It has just been revealed that a best-selling British crime writer has used pseudonyms to write glowing reviews of his own books. He modestly described his own work as 'magnificent genius'. He has also apparently been writing reviews criticising his rivals. Sadly, I am not in the slightest bit surprised.

It is now a well-established truth that at least half of all the reviews on the Web are fake. They are either written to promote a product or service or they are written to attack a competitive product. Since over half of the reviews on the Web are worse than useless, because they are deliberately designed to mislead the reader, and since no one cannot pos-sibly know which reviews are real and which are fake, then all the reviews on the Web must be entirely worthless.

I don't really think things are quite that bad yet but I certainly believe that the majority of bad reviews should be ignored. The internet has cre-ated a society in which people feel entitled to pontificate without knowing any of the facts. The internet is a hunting ground for venomous cowards who, like HMRC snitches, attack anonymously. The problem with these cowardly, malignant nerds is that they know how to manipulate the search engines. They have no shame, no sense of responsibility and no personal pride. They are, it seems to me, often driven by anger, vengeance or jeal-ousy. There is an attack on my book *Oil Apocalypse* on the internet which was written by an individual who admitted that he had never even seen a copy of the book. Others encourage co-conspirators to add nasty reviews and comments to websites without bothering to buy or read the books they are attempting to destroy. Is it any wonder that an increasing number of people are turning away from the internet and want no more of it.

The internet is based on fakery, deceit, prejudice and self-interest. It is now possible to get a job as a 'fake review writer' (that's the official job description) and to write reviews of books you've never read or hotels you've never visited. The job pays $1 per 500 words so you can imagine how skilful the people are who do this work.

Now, it is a well-known fact that professional reviewers rarely ever read through a book they are sent to review. Arnold Bennett, probably the best known and best paid of all book critics, was quite open about it, pointing out that reviewers could not possibly earn a living if they actually had to read the books they reviewed. (Nor, incidentally, do publishers' readers bother to read the books they are sent.) And there is no doubt that much review space is effectively 'sold' to publishers by ambitious literary editors. Big publishers get most of the review coverage because they can afford to hire expensive publicity people to take literary editors out to lunch. I have sat through many of these lunches and they are, believe me, not about the author or his book but about the literary editor and his or her unpublished book. Since all literary editors are frustrated authors who have at least one book sitting waiting on their computer the relationship between big publisher and literary editor is a symbiotic one. The publisher gets review coverage (and useful quotes to use on the paperback) and after a year or two the literary editor gets his or her book published. (The book, being terrible, will sink without trace, but for the publisher the cost is a tax deductible and worthwhile expense.)

But the activities of reviewers on the internet are particularly absurd. I've seen books given bad reviews on the internet because a delivery arrived late or because the reviewer didn't like the author's looks. I've seen a book given the lowest possible rating on Amazon because a copy arrived with a slightly damaged cover. (Amazon will remove reviews which are obviously unfair or libellous but it is time-consuming to police the internet and I long ago gave up on this particular task.)

A pimply 16-year-old child can go on a family holiday to a seaside hotel and not like the soup. He can then write nasty reviews on a couple of websites and his uninspired hostility can destroy the hotel. Much of the stuff written on the internet is negative because it is written by self-important amateurs who are simply spiteful. Trolls are hecklers without style or substance. Much Web criticism is mischievous and designed to damage someone's reputation for no reason other than that the writer disagrees with something that an author has said or written in a previous book. The internet has given a loud voice to the crooked, dishonest, spiteful, prejudiced, vindictive and damned stupid. Thousands of honest folk now have to waste their time, money and energy fighting lies created by unemployed and unemployable semi-literates.

I moan about reviews on the internet but in reality I suppose things haven't changed all that much. Reviewers have always been a pretty seedy bunch. They are, for example, often automatically patronising about first novels and probably don't realise that *Pickwick Papers* was a first novel. *Wuthering Heights* was Emily Brontë's first novel. (Since she never wrote anything else it was also her last novel.) I was a reviewer of books and plays for *The Guardian, The Birmingham Post, The Times Educational Supplement, The Times Higher Educational Supplement, The Teacher* and many other important sounding publications when I was a teenager.

When I first started publishing my own books I used to receive quite a few reviews. *The Village Cricket Tour,* for example, received excellent reviews. But when reviewers found that I was self-publishing (and actually having the temerity to do it successfully), jealousy and industry pressure stepped in and the reviews stopped. One literary editor indignantly announced that he threw my books straight into his wastepaper basket because it wasn't right that an author should be able to make a success out of publishing his own work.

13.

We took the Metro to Pere Lachaise this afternoon. On the way to the station I picked up a copy of *L'Equipe* and found that it contained '10 regles d'or pour prevenir' - a guide to help sportsmen avoid heart trouble while exercising. My favourite was number seven which was 'Je ne fume jamais une heure avant, ni deux heures apres une practique sportive'. (I never smoke an hour before or within two hours after exercise.) How absolutely wonderful. Only the French. It has always been thus. I remember that back in the 1950s the French authorities used to display a health warning in all Paris Metro carriages. The warning showed a healthy, rosy cheeked workman upending a bottle of red wine. The caption on the poster was 'Jamais plus de deux litres par jour.' (Never more than two litres a day.) Another poster used at the same time contained the warning 'L'alcool tue lentement'. (Alcohol kills you slowly). Underneath someone had scrawled: 'Tant mieux. Nous ne sommes pas presses.' (Fine. We are not in a hurry.) And yet, despite the drinking, the smoking and the enthusiastic consumption of fatty food the French have an enviable life expectancy. One theory is that the Roquefort cheese keeps them alive. My theory is that they live long because they worry little and are far less susceptible to life's stresses and strains.

In foggy gloom we wandered around Pere Lachaise, and said hello to Jim Morrison, Lauren Fignon and the other heroes who now live there. Cemeteries always look much better in the mist. We spoke to a tramp who was sitting propped up against a gravestone. He had a bottle of claret in a brown paper bag.

He told us he sat there every day. 'I come because here I'm better off than anybody else,' he told us.

14.

There is a story in a French paper about a man who ran away from a circus to get a job in a bank. The man, who is 23-years-old, was born into a circus family but has tired of all the travelling and wants to settle down. He now has a job as a clerk in a bank in Paris.

15.

Preston Sturges, now almost forgotten, was one of the world's greatest screenwriters and film directors. ('Dialogue,' he once wrote, 'consists of the bright things you would have liked to have said, except you didn't think of them in time.') Sturges had a wonderful sense of fun and no great love for bureaucrats. I read today that the night before a meeting with the taxman he took all the receipts and papers which he had accumulated, placed them in a large cardboard box and mixed them up thoroughly. A wonderful recipe for chaos and, therefore, sound advice.

16.

We spent a very pleasant hour playing badminton in our apartment. Because we live in a loft apartment we have enormously high ceilings (when we painted them we had to tie brushes onto very long poles and stand on a very tall step ladder) and it's perfectly possible to play a decent game of badminton indoors. Afterwards we broke the law and risked the wrath of the Paris gendarmerie by feeding the pigeons on our windowsill. They are exceptionally civilised and health conscious pigeons and seem to be content with two meals a day: breakfast and afternoon tea.

17.

We went to St Clothilde, our favourite church in Paris, and lit a candle in memory of our friend C. J. Morris. He was one of my partners when I was a general practitioner, and the only one who dared to speak to me after I became a full time author and began to excoriate the medical establishment. I can remember many things about him but one incident in particular sticks in my mind and sums up his character perfectly.

John was a great cricket fan and particularly loved watching England play Australia. He and I were at a Test Match at Edgbaston one year and he had brought with him a friend whose name I have long since forgotten but whom I will call Derek. During the tea interval the friend disappeared for a while to get rid of some waste beer and John turned and told me that he was getting divorced. I expressed dismay and surprise and offered sympathy and whatever practical help I could. He told me that he didn't want a divorce but that his wife wanted to leave to set up home with another man.

'Anyone you know?' I asked.

'Derek,' said John.

I looked at him, aghast. 'Not the chap who has been sitting next to you all day?'

John nodded.

'But…,' I began, almost speechless. 'But your wife's having an affair with him, and leaving you to move in with him?'

John nodded. 'But it was months ago when I invited him to come with me to the Test Match,' he said. 'It wouldn't have been right to tell him he couldn't come. It wouldn't have been the decent thing to do.'

It was a gentleman's obligation and John was a gentleman.

18.

I bought a new swordstick today. I have always had rather a fancy for sticks which are more than sticks. There are excellent shops in both Paris and London which sell nothing but walking sticks equipped with swords, compasses and drinking vessels. I've seen one stick which comes complete with a pen and a bottle of ink hidden inside it.

It is, of course, illegal to carry the ones with swords inside them and a few years ago an unfortunate fellow in London was prosecuted and imprisoned for daring to defend himself against a gang of ruffians with a sword which he drew from his walking stick.

I bought my first swordstick when I was a medical student in Birmingham and I found it an enormous help when I ran a nightclub in my spare time. My club was called The Gallows and to help me run it I recruited a band of local miscreants who would, in other times, have been called street urchins. None of them had homes and they all lived in a loft above the club. Most of them carried knives and were not afraid to use them. My swordstick earned its price one evening when one of the youths was flashing a new knife he'd bought. It was, like Crocodile Dundee's, rather larger than the average sort of knife. The banter was rapidly turning rather nasty as the youths argued about whose knife was the biggest. To try to ease the situation (in my defence, I was only about 19 at the time) I pulled the sword half out of my swordstick. As the lights glinted on the blade there was a gasp of admiration. Mine was far bigger than anyone else's. The competition was over.

19.

In the old, far away days the post used to arrive in the morning and in the early afternoon. And then the bosses improved things and stopped the second delivery and the post arrived late in the morning or in the afternoon or sometimes not at all. The bosses all received huge bonuses for improving the service in this curious way.

Now the Royal Mail is going to dump mail with complete strangers. If you're not in and have a parcel which needs signing for, or which is too big to go through the letterbox, the postman can now dump your mail with a neighbour of his choice. Royal Mail won't tell you which neighbour because that would spoil their fun. Since one in six individuals in our wonderful country is now officially listed as a criminal this wonderful new scheme will undoubtedly have a dramatic effect on the amount of mail euphemistically getting lost ('lost' is the Royal Mail term for 'stolen').

This is, of course, the default option. Citizens who do not want their mail handed to criminals can apply for a small sticker to place on their letterbox instructing the postman to take undeliverable mail back to the sorting office. Postmen may, or may not, take any notice.

20.

Earlier in the year we tried to order some expensive office furniture from a well-known supplier. Knowing that their delivery lorry wouldn't be able to reach our house we offered to meet the lorry nearby and to bring the furniture the rest of the way in or on our truck. Inevitably, our offer was declined without hesitation. It isn't difficult to see why retail companies are having such a hard time these days.

The only alternative was to order from a company which uses a Luton van for its deliveries. Despite charging a substantial sum for delivery, and promising that we could decide when we wanted the furniture delivered, they gave us a date and told us that they would deliver sometime between 7.00 a.m. and 5.00 p.m.

We got up at 6.30 a.m. and by 8.30 a.m. I was fading fast. By midday I was cursing loudly. And at 4.40 p.m. the driver arrived. He complained endlessly about our lane, complained about his lorry, complained about his employer, complained about the roads, and complained about the weather. He dumped the furniture by our front gate and disappeared in a cloud of diesel smoke.

It took us nearly an hour to unwrap the stuff we'd bought but long before we'd finished it was apparent that we were expected to finish building the furniture ourselves. These days everything that is sold comes in a flat pack with a cheap Allen key and four tons of polystyrene packing.

Naturally, the holes weren't positioned in the right place and the sticky out bits didn't fit them. Everything was well wrapped in corrugated cardboard (as well as the polystyrene) but the shippers had somehow managed to damage just about everything.

'Do you want to send it all back?' I asked The Princess.

She thought about it for a moment.

'I don't think I can bear it,' she said. 'The telephone calls, the bad tempered driver coming back, the forms we'll have to fill in. And, then, we'll be left with no furniture and we'll have to start again.'

I agreed with her and so we decided to try to finish building the bits and pieces of desks and chairs that we'd bought. To be honest I must admit that when I say 'we' I really mean 'The Princess'. I am infamously short of patience and I never last long when faced with a boxful of bits and pieces of furniture. I usually end up throwing them all on the bonfire.

21.

The Princess has built one of the desks. At least, we are pretty certain that it is supposed to be a desk. Everything is so badly designed, and so badly made, that what she has made could easily be a wardrobe or a log box. I suspect that the manufacturers simply make a supply of bits, throw an assortment into each box and then stick a label on the outside. Since we know it is supposed to be a desk we are prepared to call it a desk. But to an outsider, unaware of its purpose, things would not be so clear.

22.

A friend of ours is suffering from intermittent claudication. He cannot walk more than a few hundred yards without getting a pain in his calves. He has no other symptoms. Surgeons have recommended major surgery to replace malfunctioning blood vessels in his legs. But our friend has said 'No' to the knife. Instead, he has solved his problem by buying a bicycle.

23.

We watched *My Week With Marilyn,* the enthralling story of the time third assistant director Colin Clarke spent with Marilyn Monroe as she struggled to make a movie with the ever-charmless Laurence Olivier. In one delightful scene Clarke dares to move a chair so that Dame Sybil Thorndyke can sit down for a moment and is confronted by a militant props man who threatens to close down the set.

Props men used to take their responsibilities very seriously and this immensely serious threat reminded me of a time back in the 1980s when I was making a television programme at Central TV studios in Birmingham. The programme was about tranquillisers and to illustrate the variety of drugs available I had taken with me a carrier bag full of bottles of pills. I'd given the bag to one of the presenters who had handed it to a props man to display on a table where he and I would sit.

Moments before the recording started I moved a couple of the bottles an inch or two so that I could see the labels more clearly. Before I'd finished there was a cry of outrage and the ominous sound of lights being switched off. A huge and very angry props man appeared from nowhere and glowered at me. 'If you want anything moving we'll move it!' he snarled. 'If you touch anything again we'll close this studio.'

Thankfully, my brain was having one of its rare operational days.

'These are my drugs,' I told him, inspired by fury at his arrogance and pomposity and doubtless emboldened by the fact that I genuinely didn't give a damn if he closed down every studio in the country. 'They are all prescription medicines and their distribution is controlled by Act of Parliament. I am a registered medical practitioner and I suspect that you are not. I am the only person here who is allowed to touch these bottles. If you try to move them in any way I will immediately telephone the police because you will be breaking the law.'

The props man, speechless, stared at me and stared at the pills, mumbled an apology and backed away. The lights were switched back on and the recording continued. When we'd finished the programme the presenter and the director insisted on taking me for a drink.

'That was a moment I will cherish all my life,' said the presenter who was positively aglow with delight.

'That uppity union bastard makes our life miserable,' explained the director.

And for a few moments I was a hero.

Alas, such moments come so infrequently. Why do the right words, the clever riposte, the smart response, usually come too late?

24.

I queued in Lloyds Bank in Cirencester and when I was eventually lucky enough to obtain an interview with a teller I asked if I might move some money from one of my current accounts to one of my deposit accounts. (I'm not sure whether they're called tellers or clerks or customer service executives or financial consultants but I refer to the unfortunate soul who sits behind the bullet proof glass). I gave her the two relevant account numbers and the bank sort code. The clerk asked if I had my passport or a driving licence with a photograph. I told her, regretfully, that I do not walk around carrying my passport and that my driving licence doesn't have my photograph. I showed her the usual bundle of plastic credit and bank guarantee cards and an official, police recognised press card which does carry my photograph. She said that none of this was acceptable. I playfully suggested that if she thought I had acquired the credit cards illegally then she should telephone the police. She said that there was no question of that but that she was following bank policy and that it was all done to protect me. I pointed out that I was merely trying to move my own money from one of my accounts to another of my accounts. I also pointed out that both accounts were in my sole name and that it is impossible to see how moving my own money from one of my accounts to another of my accounts could possibly put me at risk, be regarded as money laundering or be described as an activity conducive to terrorist activities. Moreover, the clerk agreed that I was trying to move money from a vulnerable account (a current account) to a less vulnerable account (a deposit account) and that I would hardly be doing that if my motives were dishonourable. At this point a manager was called. She agreed with the clerk, claiming that they were merely applying the bank's rules. It all seemed extraordinarily patronising. I asked again why they weren't calling the police. 'Either these cards are mine, and I am behaving quite properly, and you should do as I ask, or you doubt my authenticity and you should call the police.' 'Oh, there's no question of that,' said the managerial woman. 'We believe that you are who you say you are.' I pointed out that I was trying to move my money from one of my accounts to another of my accounts and that since the account I was trying to move it to would pay me interest it was difficult to see how I could possibly lose out. 'Would a thief move my money to a deposit account?' I asked. They agreed that this would seem unlikely but stood firm. I asked if they would telephone my branch and ask someone to identify me. They refused. The managerial person asked if I had access to internet banking. I said I didn't because I didn't believe it was safe. She looked alarmed, as though I had suddenly expressed doubt in the value of breathing or the sanctity of Fred Goodwin, and, after a pause, said that I was entitled to think that if I wanted to. It didn't seem to have occurred to her that when everyone does their banking online there will be little need for banks to have buildings, clerks or managers. I asked if she would look me up on the internet where, I explained, they would doubtless find photographs which would confirm to her that standing before her was the person I claimed to be. To my surprise, the manager said that the bank had no internet access. Feeling by now rather peeved I told her that I could see why Lloyds had gone damned near bankrupt and had required bailing out by taxpayers. 'You're just another civil servant,' I told her. She stared at me as though she'd never before seen anyone with steam coming out of their ears and backed away a foot or so, clearly concerned that I might explode and make a mess of her and the bank's fitted carpet. We parted company. Two people from different worlds.

After I left I rang my branch, spoke to someone to whom I had never spoken before and moved the money. The call, including polite chit chat, took three minutes.

This isn't the first time I've had difficulty moving my own money to another place.

'I know we all know you,' said a teller once when I was trying to do much the same thing at a branch I visit regularly. 'But we do this to protect you.' I pointed out that my passport, birth certificate and bank cards can all be stolen but that no one can steal my face and voice.

The truth, of course, is that none of this nonsense has anything to do with protecting my money or your money. All these absurd regulations are a result of laws brought in by the European Union to try to prevent money laundering. They don't prevent money laundering, of course, any more than confiscating nail files from old ladies prevents terrorism. The eurocrats have, as always, created a series of laws and regulations which simply make life difficult for honest, decent folk trying to go about their business with the minimum of fuss and time wasting. And, of course, the EU does absolutely nothing to stop the banks mis-selling interest rate swaps or payment protection insurance, nothing to stop them rigging interest rates and nothing to stop them supervising wholesale money laundering operations.

25.

A reader who works in a nursing home has written to tell me of a scam that, she says, is now extremely widely practised. When a resident dies, rings and other jewellery are routinely removed and are placed in an envelope. The resident's name is written on the envelope. The envelope is then put away somewhere and nothing is said about it. If the relatives notice that the rings are missing then the envelope will be produced and the jewellery handed over. But if no one notices, and no one asks for the jewellery, then it will be kept and, after the resident has been buried or cremated, quietly sold. 'Two women, both qualified nurses, who are employed at the nursing home where I work make several thousand pounds a year each out of this scam,' wrote my correspondent. 'I cannot expose the scam because there is never any proof. If the police were to come the nurses would simply produce the envelope containing the jewellery, and point to the name written on it.

26.

A friend of The Princess's called Molly was born in Wales but hates Welsh nationalists with a fervour. (Her real name is Glynis but she renamed herself Molly.) I asked The Princess if she knew why. 'When she was a little girl,' explained The Princess, 'Molly and a friend were playing at school when the friend fell over and hurt herself rather badly.

Molly ran to the headmaster who was in the playground and told him what had happened. But she told him in English. The headmaster was very cross. He told her off and before he would do anything he made her say it all again – in Welsh.'

27.

We met a friend who is a well-known press photographer. I've known him for years and although he, like me, is becoming rather frail and wobbly he still takes outstanding pictures. 'My problem is that I've always been a photographer who likes to move about a lot,' he said. 'Now that I'm a bit slow I find it difficult to jump around.' This reminded me of the time when he visited us and was asked to take photographs of a local girl who wanted to become a model. The first pictures he took were pretty ordinary (on two of them he cut her head off completely) and he was clearly becoming embarrassed. 'Do you mind if I move about a bit?' he asked eventually. He then leapt around taking pictures of her from all sorts of unexpected angles. The best picture was one he took after leaping out from behind a bush. He has, needless to say, earned a good portion of his living as what is known as a paparazzi photographer.

28.

The Princess and I were in the lounge of a pub in Somerset when a middle aged woman fainted. She did it very gracefully. I watched from a safe distance while the three people with her all did what people do under these circumstances. One picked up the woman's handbag and put it on a chair. A second unfastened the woman's coat (but, fortunately, went no further). And the third just ran round and round the room like a balloon that someone has blown up, failed to tie and then released. It was clear that there was nothing serious wrong and the faintee started to come round within a second or two. It isn't difficult to tell when someone is seriously ill and in desperate need of medical attention. She was neither. I was in the process of wandering over to offer comfort and professional solace when a woman in her twenties ran in from the bar. 'I'm the accredited health and safety officer for the hotel,' she shouted, elbowing me out of the way with all the finesse of a French front row forward. 'Bring me a glass of water!' she shouted to a waitress who had appeared in another doorway. She gave the impression of having been waiting many months for this moment. All those lectures she'd attended and all those regulations she'd learned were paying dividends. I watched in admiration as the health and safety officer took charge. She clearly didn't have the foggiest idea what to do but she did everything with great confidence and even if her first aid advice won no marks for substance she certainly deserved full marks for style. There was much flouncing and many irrelevant and pointless orders were given. She was the sort of woman who, in an earlier era, would have volunteered to work as a milk monitor. People were told to keep back so that the patient could have air to breathe. There was much talk of liability and insurance and we were all warned neither to give the faintee hot fluids nor to put a teaspoon into her mouth. I don't honestly think anyone had been planning to do either. Within a minute the waitress came rushing into the room carrying the glass of water which had been requested. She handed the water to the health and safety officer who took it from her, raised it to her lips and, apparently without knowing quite what she was doing, drained it. When the glass was empty she handed it back to the waitress and then, realising what she'd done, she blushed an impressive shade of crimson and ordered a replacement.

By this time the woman who'd fainted had fully recovered and was apologising profusely to everyone in the room. 'It's warm in here,' she explained. 'I've not had anything to eat since breakfast.' She seemed a trifle embarrassed.

29.

I walked into a Tourist Office to ask for the date of the local Carnival. The receptionist watched me walk up to the desk and, with exquisite timing, reached for her telephone just as I came to a halt. 'CouldyoupleasetellmethedateoftheCarnival?' I gabbled, before she could start to dial.

'I'm on the phone,' she said.

'You weren't when I arrived,' I pointed out.

'I am now,' she said.

'Not yet,' I said.

'I'm dialling,' she said snottily. She started to prod the buttons.

I glowered and bent over her with that crazed look I reserve for everyday encounters. 'The date of the carnival?' I demanded.

She told me. I thanked her and left.

30.

An old woman who lives in the next village, and who has always been poor, recently inherited a fortune from a rich brother who died. He had made his money out of a car dealership. She had never before had enough money to eat anything much more exciting than bread and cheese or to drink anything more exotic than weak tea. To celebrate her good fortune she invited everyone she knew to a local restaurant. On the day that the lawyers completed all the paperwork, and she took charge of the money and became a rich woman, they all enjoyed an expensive meal and drank a good deal of expensive wine. At the end of the evening the old woman staggered out into the street, drunk for the first time in her life. She fell into the path of a taxi and died instantly. There is a moral hiding there somewhere but I'm damned if I can find it. The story, a true one, is just too, too sad to be turned into a morality tale.

OCTOBER

1.

I realised that my Lloyds credit card is about to expire and that the new one hasn't yet arrived. I telephoned the 'help' number printed on the card, navigated the usual 'press one if you are living, press 2 if you died recently, press 3 if you died a long time ago' sequence and eventually spoke to a real, living Lloyds TSB employee. After confirming my identity with the usual idiotic security questions ('What's your name? How many legs do you have?') I had the following conversation.

'My new card hasn't arrived. Has it been posted?'

(After some delay). 'Yes.'

'Do you know when it was posted?'

(After some delay). 'Two weeks ago.'

'How do you send them these days?'

'By second class post.'

I am aware that the three secret numbers that can be used to confirm a telephone transaction will be printed on the back of my card so that anyone who steals the card can buy anything they like with it. The Passport Office won't trust Royal Mail to deliver passports but Lloyds trusts them to carry my credit card.

'Whose responsibility is it if the card is stolen?' I asked.

'Oh, it's yours. We don't take any responsibility if your card gets lost in the post. Once it leaves us it's yours.'

I cancelled the card and now must wait for them to send another.

I remember the staff at Lloyds in Cirencester and their irritating claims that their daft regulations are designed to protect me. The bank which won't allow me to control my own money, posts out a credit card by ordinary second class mail and if it gets lost it's my responsibility! The envelope might as well have *Contains A Credit Card* stamped on the outside in big red letters (in all European languages). Maybe *Please Steal Me* would be marginally clearer.

Why doesn't the bank send the cards to local branches where they can be collected?

2.

Around 2,000 copies of a new book of mine were delivered this afternoon. When we'd agreed the delivery date we had arranged for the lorry driver to help us unload but when the lorry arrived the driver refused to raise a finger. Despite the accompanying slip of paper confirming that he would help us with the unloading he stood and watched as a pensioner (me) and my wife (The Princess) moved all the books into what we rather grandly call our warehouse. While we struggled with the boxes of books he took time off from swigging something from a can to hand me a delivery note to sign. As my eyes flicked over it I noticed that it contained a phrase telling me that writing 'not checked' would have no validity. Since there was no way to check that the boxes all contained the books they were supposed to contain, or that the books were in a saleable condition, I refused to sign his bit of paper. The driver, extremely put out by this, telephoned his boss to find out what to do. Having some experience of situations like this I immediately ripped open the thick plastic which was wrapped around the boxes of books and rapidly unloaded all the boxes from the pallets. After a few minutes on the phone the lorry driver swaggered over to tell me his news. 'My boss says I'm to take the books back,' he announced with a sneer. Only then did he notice that the pallets were empty and that those boxes which hadn't been moved indoors were all piled up on the pavement. 'Best of luck,' I said. 'You can't go into our premises, of course. And if you want to load up the remaining books you'll have to do it yourself.' I then pointed out to him that he was parked on a double yellow line.' He jumped around, saw that I was right and then looked back at me. He had clearly not noticed the yellow lines before. 'There isn't anywhere else to park!' he said, as though this were my fault. 'No,' I agreed. 'There isn't is there?' 'Are you going to sign this?' he demanded, waving the delivery note under my nose. 'I don't think so,' I told him. 'I've lost my pen.' He mumbled something, crushed his can and dropped it into the gutter. He then climbed into his cab and drove off. He would, I suspect, have liked to leave with lots of noise and wheel spin but it's difficult to do that in a large lorry. As the cryptorchid, pustulent excrescence drove away a red admiral butterfly landed on one of the boxes of books. Beauty arrived as the beast left.

Just then our local street sweeper came by. He's a simple fellow but always has a smile for us. 'There are lots of leaves around,' he said. I agreed with him that there were. He looked around, as though trying to decide where the leaves had come from. And then he looked up. 'The trees don't help,' he said thoughtfully.' 'But they're lovely trees,' said The Princess. He thought about this for a moment. And then he smiled and nodded. 'I like this job,' he said. 'It's an outdoor job.'

'For every nasty person life delivers there's someone decent coming up just behind,' said The Princess.

3.

A recent article in the magazine *Country Life* stated categorically that badgers cause tuberculosis in cattle. This inaccuracy annoyed me so much I sent a short letter to the editor pointing out that there is no scientific evidence in support of this hypothesis. I added a postscript warning that if my letter were not published I would complain to the Press Complaints Committee. After some delay I received a note from the magazine confirming that my letter would be published. When it appeared they had included the threatening postscript. I suspect that they may have done this to assuage angry readers who might wonder why an animal rights campaigner should be given space in a pro-hunting magazine but if that was the idea then I fear it rather backfired. In printing the postscript they surely gave extra credence to my note and made it clear that what they printed was factually inaccurate.

Meanwhile, much to the delight of dairy farmers and other animal haters, the State-endorsed, State-funded annihilation of badgers is proceeding at quite a pace. It is a myth that badgers spread tuberculosis (TB) to cows. The evidence shows that cattle movements spread TB among cows. And it is cows that give TB to badgers - not the other way round. Killing badgers is just an excuse farmers make in order to avoid having to face the truth: modern farming methods are inhumane and unhealthy. Wild animals are often accused of spreading disease to 'farm' animals. Wild badgers are blamed for infecting cattle with tuberculosis, wild boar are persecuted for spreading classical swine fever to commercial pigs, deer have been killed lest they carry foot and mouth disease and bison are slaughtered lest they spread brucellosis to cattle. Even the hedgehog has been accused of carrying numerous dangerous diseases which might affect people or domesticated animals.

The belief that wild animals are the cause of illness and disease spread among domesticated and farm animals is a well-cultivated but unsubstantiated myth.

Farmers who perpetuate these myths invariably claim that the wild animal concerned has somehow acquired a natural immunity to the disease and is, therefore, able to remain symptom free while still being a threat to farmed animals. There is no scientific evidence to support these claims. And if the claim were true it would, of course, be scientifically illogical to kill the wild animals because they had successfully developed immunity to a disease.

Today's farmed animals are weak and susceptible to disease because of the confined, unnatural and stressful conditions in which they are kept and the poor and often unnatural diet they are given.

There is a lesson to be learnt from the fact that wild animals, who must fend for themselves and who are deprived of antibiotic cover and the other luxuries afforded domestic animals, are generally much healthier, and suffer far less disease, even though they are exposed to the same parasites and pathogens as domestic animals.

But it's not a lesson farmers are likely to learn. They claim to understand the countryside and to care for animals. Most don't understand nature very well and don't care a jot for animals - except as items on a balance sheet. (Why do farmers have tears in their eyes when they talk about orphan lambs? These are the same people who send lambs, just a few weeks old, to the slaughterhouse; tearing them from their mothers without a qualm.)

When wild animals fall ill in large numbers it is usually because of a violent, new problem - pollution, drought, overcrowding or the invasion of some new pathogen (usually introduced by human beings).

The bottom line is that farmed cattle are sickly and prone to tuberculosis because of the appalling conditions in which they are kept. Farmers who blame badgers when their cows fall ill are simply looking for an excuse; a scapegoat. (But don't tell them this. When farmers hear about a new animal they want to kill it. And so they'll start wandering around, guns blazing, in an attempt to kill all the scapegoats.) Killing badgers is mindless, pointless, politically convenient, commercially expedient brutality.

4.

In the *Financial Times* there is an article claiming that America 'has often surprised with inventions such as aircraft, automobiles and computers'. I was appalled by this. Don't they have sub editors or reference books at the *Financial Times?* Perhaps they're just being creepy to America, though I really cannot help wondering why there isn't someone there with more national pride. Journalists always fall for the American nonsense that they invented everything worthwhile. The truth, of course is very different. The first person to fly was George Cayley (1773-1857). Cayley was born in Brompton-by-Sawdon, near Scarborough in Yorkshire. He was thoroughly English and he was the founder of the science of aerodynamics, the pioneer of aerial navigation and the designer of the first modern aeroplane. He was the first person to understand the principles of flight and worked over half a century before people now often credited with inventing the aeroplane. (The Wright Brothers, often described by American writers as the first men to fly, did not get into the air with a heavier-than-air machine until 1903 - nearly half a century after Cayley's death). And there was also Sir Hiram Stevens Maxim (remembered today for his machine gun) who on 31st July 1894 at Baldwyn's Park flew ten years before the Wright Brothers got off the ground.

The first car was invented in England by Richard Trevithick in 1802. He also invented the bus in the same year. And then, because there were no roads suitable for his vehicles, he built rails and invented the train and the railways. The first mass production of cars was begun by Thomas Rickett in England in 1860. Karl Benz, the German, was laughably later in 1885 and by the time Henry Ford started experimenting with cars Trevithick's invention was nearly a century old.

And computers? Well, it was Charles Babbage (1791-1871), an employee of the Royal Mint and a Professor of Mathematics at Cambridge University, who invented the computer. Even the Americans (never good losers in the 'we were first' stakes) acknowledge that Charles Babbage was the first person to build a programmable calculating machine - a machine which had a programme of instructions which could be stored in a memory and used at will.

I'm not surprised that the *Financial Times* got this so wrong. The Americans are always at it. For example, they regularly claim that their man Edison invented the electric lightbulb though. The truth is that the lightbulb was invented by another Englishman, Joseph Swan (1828-1914). He managed it twenty years before Thomas Edison.

The Americans think (and claim) that they invented just about everything. Actually, the poor sods didn't invent anything very much. To give them full credit where it is due, they did invent barbed wire (though I've never understood the point of barbed wire which doesn't do anything other wires don't do except damage animals), pantyhose, a horseshoe manufacturing machine, the cash register and the revolving pistol. They've also given us grey squirrels, harlequin ladybirds (which kill our traditional ladybirds), the banjo and the vaginal deodorant spray. That is pretty much the total contribution the U.S.A. has made to world culture. Not terribly impressive. With the best will in the world it is difficult to think of very much else. After racking our brains The Princess and I came up with bubble-gum, Donald Duck, nasal hair clippers, parking meters, supermarket trolleys, the cheeseburger and breast enlargement surgery. Those are all useful and have no doubt made their mark in some areas of life. But. The Americans claim the brassiere but that isn't theirs either. And they always claim that Henry Ford invented the production line but the Venetians had a boat building factory with a production line in the 15th century. The Americans spent millions inventing a pen that would work in space but the Russians just took pencils.

England is, as you might imagine, the gold standard when it comes to discoveries, achievements and inventions.

Other countries have, considering their limitations, done quite well and certainly better than the Americans. The French have given us meringue, berets, cirrhosis, feather boas, cigarettes which smell of intestinal gases and long thin loaves of bread that cannot be properly wrapped. The Scots have given us tartan trews, the Tam o'Shanter, the sporran, skirts for men, haggis and bagpipes. The Germans gave us some sausages, the goose step, and plastic that looks like plastic to anyone except Germans, and which is used instead of wood to decorate the dashboards of expensive motor cars. (I have, over the years, learned three things about the Germans. First, their humour always involves someone else's misfortune. Comedy for German adults, otherwise known as 'groan ups' involves men losing their trousers and being chased by buxom women. Only once have I come across an exception. I once met a German publisher in London and asked him if he had been to the city before. 'I have been many times,' he said, 'but never made welcome.' 'I'm sorry about that,' I said. 'Don't worry,' he replied with a mischievous grin. 'I was bombing it at the time.' Second, they always obey all the rules. At the end of the First World War shots were fired at a crowd near the Berliner Schloss. There was mass panic as thousands ran for their lives. Every one of them obeyed the signs to keep off the grass. Third, the Germans cannot do anything by themselves. They have to do things together, preferably by numbers. This explains the success of those sex clubs in Hamburg and Frankfurt where strapping Teutonic matrons give instructions to platoons of fat but enthusiastic German businessmen.)

The Chinese gave the world chopsticks (despite being given plenty of opportunities to follow our example they still haven't caught on to the advantages of the knife and fork), the laundry mark, restaurant menus with numbers, crispy duck, jackets with little collars suitable for wearing without ties, long walls and rice pudding. The Swiss are rather like the Germans, except that they do not have their sense of humour or their joie de vivre. I once asked a Swiss friend to tell me the funniest thing the Swiss do. He told me, in all seriousness, that when young people start to work at Swiss banks they are told to go into the vault and polish the gold. 'Pretty funny, eh?' he said. Moreover, the Swiss do not always take their sense of humour with them when they get out of bed in the morning. Sometimes, they leave it under the pillow, sometimes they leave it safely locked in their safe deposit box and sometimes they simply cannot remember where they last saw it. To understand the Swiss you have to know that Swiss men wear white socks and think nothing of it. They do not even seem to be embarrassed about it. As Harry Lime pointed out they gave us the cuckoo clock and expensive chocolate but very little else.

The Spanish, who are not terribly bright and whose favourite colour is black, are a masochistic people who spend most of their free time being chased by bulls. It is not surprising that they have never had the time to invent anything except a variation on the cheap package holiday. (A concept which was devised by Thomas Cook, an Englishman.) The Italians have produced some great artists, some wonderful food and some magnificent motorcars. They have proved, beyond doubt, that politicians should never be taken seriously and they have acquired a vocabulary of gestures and a passion which enable them to make 'Isn't it a nice day?' sound so exciting that it could easily be a declaration of war. The Greeks have produced nothing whatsoever and do very little work. As a result all the buildings in Greece are falling down and in ruins. This is good for the Greeks because lots of people visit the country just to look at the ruins, some of which were built as long ago as the

1960s. The Greek people are friendly but very lazy. They spend most of their time sitting or lying down. They do their sitting in cafés or on boats and their lying down in bed or on the beaches. They drink a lot of furniture polish and can afford to do this because they do not pay any taxes and are kept by rich Germans who visit once a year and bring them beach towels. And, finally, the Australians gave us the boomerang, ostrich skin handbags and hats decorated with corks.

These are all valuable commercial and cultural additions to the world's inventory of useful bits and bobs but none of these countries has come close to contributing the sort of wonders that Englishmen have produced. All have simply done their best and all have added a little special something to the smorgasbord of tat which make junk shops, charity shops and eBay so fascinating.

The *Financial Times,* and all those who adore America and sneer at England should know that the English were responsible for inventing many things usually credited to other nations. The electric lamp, the internal combustion engine, the cinema, the steam engine, the car, anaesthetics, the first manned flight, champagne, photography, the guillotine, the first railway, the electric telegraph - all these are usually credited elsewhere but were, in truth the inventions of Englishmen. Adam Smith's economic theories were first propagated by Englishman William Petty a whole century earlier. Englishmen gave the world the first police force and the first postal service. We do not have to put England on our stamps since we invented them. Other less significant countries (such as France, Russia, the Falkland Islands, Vatican City and the United States of America) must identify their stamps by printing their name on them. England invented free trade and parliamentary democracy and was the first country to recognise that every man has a right to a fair and free trial before his peers. Countless sailors around the world have good reason to be grateful to Samuel Plimsoll, who helped overcome resistance to the Merchant Shipping Act which brought in such reforms as a loading limit for cargo ships. A Plimsoll line was marked on the hull of every cargo ship, showing the maximum depth to which the ship could be safely loaded. This practice, started in England, spread around the world. Francis Crick, an Englishman, was co-discoverer of the double helix structure of deoxyribonucleic acid (DNA), the basic building block of all living cells. And it was, I must not forget, an Englishman, Tim Berners-Lee, who invented the World Wide Web which gave us the internet.

The English were the first to invent the free press and modern democratic government. The English invented the jet engine, hovercraft, steam engine, the telephone and television, lawnmower, nuclear physics, postboxes, buses, satellites, submarines, knitting machines, the flushing toilet, the slide rule, the syringe, matches, the seed drill, the tuning fork, the diving bell, the jigsaw puzzle, carbonated water and the universal joint, the pencil eraser, the fire extinguisher, the electromagnet, dynamo, computer software, plastic, traffic lights, the light bulb, steam turbine, vacuum cleaner, crossword puzzle, mass spectrometer, polythene, cat's eyes in the middle of the road, liquid crystal display (LCD) and digital music player. It was Englishmen who discovered the circulation of the blood, the existence of red blood cells, binary stars, the laws of gravity and motion, orbiting comets, hydrogen, atomic theory, chemical electrolysis, the law of conservation of energy, diamagnetism, planet Neptune, absolute zero temperature, the theory of evolution by natural selection, the existence of electrons and neutrons, hormones, concrete, sewing machines, tarmac and radar. If you are beginning to think that doesn't leave much for the citizens of any other nation to invent, you're absolutely right. Over the last 250 years, English scientists and engineers have been responsible for around four out of every five major inventions, discoveries and new technologies.

To all that must be added the fact that the English have invented more sports than the citizens of all the other nations in the world put together. Indeed, all sports worth playing or watching were invented by Englishmen. But although the English love inventing sports, and playing them, they don't care much about winning. The English make the best losers because when it really comes down to it they would rather lose than win. Winners have social obligations which the English find embarrassing. It is much easier for an Englishman to be a good loser (to show appreciation for the winner and to be a 'good sport') than it is to be a good winner. And it is bad form to beat one's guests or visitors. The decent thing is to allow them to win (without, of course, realising that they have been allowed to win) and to then congratulate them heartily.

It is hardly surprising that the citizens of other countries dislike the English. They must all have massive inferiority complexes.

In addition, of course, the French hate us because we twice saved them from the Germans, the Germans hate us because we beat them twice and the Americans hate us because they aren't English, because they feel guilty for spending years sitting on their backsides while we fought two World Wars by ourselves and because they have never managed to build an empire like ours.

5.

I went to the Post Office to buy stamps. It is a chore I always dread, partly because of the inevitable queues and partly because the staff are so hostile and unhelpful that virtually every encounter is an unpleasant experience. I read a report recently which showed that 20% of our nation is functionally illiterate. The report didn't say this but I strongly suspect that they all work for the Post Office. And they aren't just benignly stupid. They are genuinely malignant. I am undecided about whether Post Offices give rudeness lessons to prospective employees or simply hire people who are already rude. Perhaps Post Offices pre-select cretins who are then sent away on special courses where they are taught to do everything at half speed, to ignore common sense and to regard their customers as the enemy.

I tried to stay calm as I watched the assistants handing out money to an apparently endless series of State subsidised supplicants. Why don't they have one queue for people who are taking money out (and who are in absolutely no hurry) and another, fast track, queue for people who are struggling to make a living so that they can pay taxes and subsidise the people who are queuing to take money out? The Government means test virtually everything these days and those on benefits are swamped with official breaks and goodwill. Just the other day, I received a note from Royal Mail informing me that if I am on benefits I will be able to buy cheap stamps this Christmas. So it doesn't seem unreasonable to ask that the Government bends over the other way a degree or two for a change. Few things the Government could do would help small businesses more than providing them with shorter Post Office queues.

The woman in front of me was sending Christmas cards to friends in Spain and France. The cards were identical. And they were all going to people within the European Union. But the counter assistant insisted on weighing every one before printing out those hideous, dull labels they use instead of stamps. These days the only people who buy real stamps are collectors (who mistakenly believe that they are investing in their pension fund) and people like The Princess and I running small mail order businesses. Since we turned Publishing House into a small, kitchen table enterprise we've found that the biggest problems we have are acquiring stamps and finding somewhere to put the stamped parcels.

Eventually I got to the front of the queue and found myself face to face with the day's zombie of choice.

'Two hundred one pound stamps and two hundred fifty pence stamps please.'

'Haven't got any,' said the zombie with a big smile. 'We're right out of stamps.' He was clearly delighted to be able to tell me this.

'What do you mean?' I asked stupidly, looking around to make sure that I hadn't entered a fish and chip emporium by mistake.

'We've run out of stamps,' he chortled. I don't think I've ever seen anyone chortle before but he was definitely chortling. A chortle is like a snort - difficult to describe but impossible to miss. 'We ran out a couple of days ago. We're waiting for a delivery.'

As I left, empty-handed, I found that I couldn't leave the Post Office. Two hugely fat women were standing talking in the doorway. They were blocking the exit. They would have blocked the entrance to St Paul's Cathedral. 'Excuse me,' I said more politely than I felt. 'Could I come through, please.'

The women ignored me.

I repeated my request.

One of the women turned her head slightly and glared at me. 'Can't you see we're busy talking,' she said.

It was one of those days.

6.

Wandering through a local graveyard we found a stone carrying this rhyme:

He squandered health in search of wealth,

To gold became a slave;

Then spent his wealth in search of health,

But only found a grave.

7.

The eavesdropping collection came along quite quickly last week. Here's a small selection:

1. 'I've got a gent here who wants to know what we can do for his piles?' (White coated assistant shouting across to the pharmacist.)
2. 'You can't hoard fun. So let's go out and spend some while we've got the chance.'

3. 'Blood may be thicker than water, but it ain't as thick as pus.'

4. 'There's an eclipse next week.' 'I'll catch it next time round.' 'There won't be another for 100 years!' 'I'm in no hurry.'

5. 'Women are like horses. They need to be given a good workout every day.'

6. 'I know more than you do, kid. I know what it's like to be young but I also know what it's like to be old.'

7. 'If he ever gets to heaven he will immediately start arguing with God about whether or not He exists.'

8. 'Working for the council is excellent preparation for retirement.'

9. 'I enjoy widowhood very much. I can have all the male companionship I like without ever having to darn socks or iron shirts. I wish I'd become a widow sooner. It's just a pity that a woman can't become a widow without having to find a husband and then get rid of him.'

10. 'I suppose all that traffic will be going somewhere.'

11. 'You think too much, and to be honest, thinking isn't your strong suit.'

12. 'If I'm not wanted you only have to say so.' 'You're not wanted.' 'If you want me to go away just say and I'll go away.' 'Go away.' 'I'm a man who believes in straight talking. I don't want to hang around somewhere I'm not wanted.'

13. 'He has a special benefits outfit which he wears when he claims his money. He wears an old worn suit, mismatched jacket and trousers, and a pair of shoes with a detached sole that flaps about as he walks.'

14. 'Women and children should always have priority.' 'What about Lucrezia Borgia and Myra Hindley?'

15. 'I've had a brilliant day and now I'm going to go home and celebrate by cracking open a bottle of white medicine. I think I'm getting old.'

16. 'What do you think is the worst disease?' 'The one you've got.'

17. 'When I was young people were always asking me questions. I didn't know anything but that didn't stop them asking me questions. Now that I'm older and I know a few things no one ever asks me anything.'

18. 'He has no luck at all. When he had a heart attack the ambulance had a puncture on the way to the hospital.'

8.

We are receiving more than our fair share of wrong numbers these days. This is probably the fault of Special Branch. I expect one of their in-house communication experts mixed up a bundle of wires when wobbling about on the top of a ladder recently. I have now started answering the telephone by telling callers that they have rung the vicarage. Moments ago I had a call from a man who wanted to speak to the chiropodist. 'Oh no my son,' I told him, in my best vicar voice. 'I'm afraid you have tele-phoned the vicarage in error. But may God go with you and may your feet always be healthy.' Apart from the fun this provides I rather like the idea of someone at MI5's GCHQ spending merry hours trying to work out if this was some sort of coded message.

9.

The European Union has won the Nobel Peace prize. Since Warmonger and Assassin in Chief Obama was another recent winner of this absurd prize one can hardly be surprised by this. The irony, of course, is that the EU could well be the cause of World War III.

The world is awash with serious geopolitical problems. The Israelis are desperate to bomb the sand out of Iran and the Middle East in general is about as stable as wet gelignite. There's a real possibility of a war between Japan and China, and America is stuffed to the coasts with idiots who want to start a war with China. (If they can't afford a bloody war a cold one will do nicely.)

But it's Europe that is most unstable. Selfish politicians defending their much beloved euro have deliberately ruined the lives of millions and caused massive unemployment. Will they be forgiven when the news gets out? The growing greed of bankers, company bosses, senior civil servants and politicians mean that there is a huge divide between the haves and the have-nots. The politicians are trying to solve Europe's economic problems without annoying the rich and the resultant austerity programmes, linked with high taxes for the middle classes, mean that the only people not ready to go onto the streets in anger are Russian billion-aires and hedge fund crooks (who've bought the politicians with huge bribes and neutralised them with lawyers).

The determination to save the euro (a fake currency which was created as a quiet route to a federal Europe) has resulted in high unemployment - focussed among the young and the old - in most European countries. And the continuing economic problems produced by this nonsense mean that pensions are being battered into submission for all those who aren't employed by governments or the European Union itself. And, finally, the policies espoused by the lovers of the euro mean that hyperinflation is pretty much a certainty. And with the Americans deliberately destroying their own currency the prices of basic commodities are bound to soar.

The euro was created by a process known as groupthink and it survives by groupthink. In this phenomenon ideas or views which originate outside a powerful group are not even considered. The result is that terrible decisions which are made for all the wrong reasons are sustained simply because a small but powerful group of people won't even contemplate the idea that they could be wrong, or that there could be a better way. As times goes by the chances of the groupthink conclusion being questioned become increasingly unlikely.

Will there be a war in Europe during the next five years? I wouldn't bet against it. History shows that nation states everywhere fail when the people are first encouraged and then forced to kowtow to the bureaucracy and the functionaries of the State. The functionaries do not have the charisma required for leadership and so the next stage is mass resentment against what is perceived as oppression. We live in a world where the masses want everything but aren't prepared to pay for anything: resentment is never very far from the surface; it's always there, simmering away. The EU bureaucrats are too stupid to realise it but they are, through their fascist and undemocratic ways, creating an inevitable revolution.

10.

My replacement Lloyds bank card has struggled through. (The stolen one is by now doubtless in the hands of crooks in Delaware or Islamabad who have yet to discover that their prize is about as useful as a dead leaf). Endless brave postmen and postwomen have valiantly resisted temptation and the piece of plastic without which there can be little life for any of us has finally dropped onto the doormat. The card does have to be activated before I can use it and the procedure has clearly been designed to foil the cleverest of crooks. I have to key in the card number (which is on the card), the expiry date (which is on the card), the three security numbers (which are on the back of the card) and my birth date (which is about as good a security question as asking which month comes after January). Still, I have my card and can now once again seek out rare print delicacies on Amazon, the demon website.

11.

Max Hastings, the former editor of the *Daily Telegraph,* has promised to leave the country if Boris Johnson ever becomes Prime Minister. Hastings says that he has known Johnson for 20 years and he is a 'gold medal egomaniac'. 'I would not trust him with my wife, nor with my wallet,' he says. 'He is manically disorganised about everything except the carefully crafted chaos of his public image, and he is far more ruthless and nasty than the public appreciates.'

I have long thought the same.

When Johnson was editor of *The Spectator,* the magazine ran full page advertisements for my book *Rogue Nation* (an attack on the USA and its illegal war on Iraq). Johnson then hired his sister to write a profile of me. The unpleasant (and, I thought, patronising) piece was not accurate and the magazine printed a long letter from me in rebuttal. All my advertisements were subsequently rejected by *The Spectator.*

Despite his carefully crafted image as a quintessential Englishman, a sort of Bertie Wooster type buffoon, Johnson was, of course, born in America and in my book that makes him an American and, therefore, doubly unfit to be Prime Minister of England.

There was a time when our politicians were serious minded and had genuine beliefs. Remember Enoch Powell? Johnson would make a good host of a cheap game show. He is about as well designed for political power as Tony Blair, Gordon Brown or David Cameron.

12.

We were in one of those excellent antique markets which are scattered throughout the Cotswolds. A few dozen local dealers rent stands and display their wares in small alcoves. They then take it turns to man the desk and the till at the front of the shop. 'Look at this!' said the Princess, drawing my attention to a small mahogany cupboard. 'It'll be perfect for the living room. Just the thing for my reading lamp. And there's room for a cup of tea, too.' She bent down and examined it more closely. 'And look,' she said. 'There's a handy little cupboard for magazines and books. It's really unusual. It opens forwards - just like the cupboard for music in my piano stool.'

'That's the space for the chamber pot,' I pointed out.

The Princess squealed, shut the door quickly and jumped away.

We moved on.

13.

We went to Stroud and picked up a few magazines and a bad bout of depression. It is said that old hippies go to Stroud to die. I can see why. Stroud is the sort of town where anyone would feel ready to die. There isn't any point to it. It is ugly and has no redeeming features whatsoever, except for the fact that it is on a main railway line and, with the station right in the centre of the town, residents can get away quite easily. The town council must be composed entirely of dead people. We have been there several times and have yet to spot anyone smiling. The whole place is full of gloom. It's the sort of place that would be good for organising funerals because there would be no chance of anyone showing any inappropriate signs of levity. We were told by a mechanic who works in a nearby garage that he once attended a wedding in Stroud where the best man made a long speech about all the dead people who would have liked to attend the ceremony if they had been alive. He talked at great length about these individuals, their lives, their relationship to the bride and the groom and the great sadness which everyone felt at their not being available for the fixture. By the time he had finished, everyone there was in tears. The bride's make-up had all run and her mother was sobbing hysterically. That's the sort of place Stroud is.

Architecturally, Glumsville, as the locals call it, is a tribute to bad taste. There is an indoor market which isn't as interesting as a 1950's bring and buy sale and, with the exception of an acceptable music shop, we haven't found one acceptable commercial establishment in the place. There are, however, a couple of decent advertising signs in the town. There is a curry house run by a man called Singh which has a large notice up which proclaims: 'Singh for your Supper'. And a shop selling clothes for ladies has a sign on the window announcing: 'Our bikinis are exciting – they are simply the tops!' Despite these delights, if I had to describe Stroud in two words I would choose 'pustulent' and 'excrescence'.

14.

In my book *Stuffed!* I argued that the way we run our State is now unsustainable. I have been warning for nearly a quarter of a century that we will, by 2020, reach the point where the number of people dependent upon the State will exceed the number of taxpayers supporting them. And for several years now I have warned that our governments are elected by the takers not the makers. There are a good many people in our country who now believe that they are entitled to live at everyone else's expense. A new study from the Centre for Policy Studies recently showed that 53% of households now receive more in benefits than they pay in tax. In Scotland, the figure is 88%. It is difficult to believe but just 12% of the people in a country whose politicians are fighting for independence pay more tax than they receive in benefits. (Incidentally, if Scotland does become independent, who is going to pay for the rebuilding of Hadrian's Wall? There will obviously have to be a wall because if there isn't, millions of illegal immigrants will be pouring into all the twee Scottish ports and then screaming south across the borders in order to claim their English benefits. They obviously won't want to stay in an impoverished Scotland which will be struggling to survive on the sale of kilts and silly Tam o'Shanter hats to easily beguiled American tourists.)

We now have a bigger State sector than China. During an average lifetime, a British citizen hands over two thirds of a million pounds to pay for government services. That means that the average working man and woman pay more, over their lifetimes, for oppressive legislation and interfering State financed busy bodies than they pay for houses, pensions and cars combined.

I have quoted 19th century historian Alexis de Tocqueville on many previous occasions but one of the things he wrote suggests that we are now running out of time: 'A democracy cannot exist as a permanent form of government. It can only exist until the voters discover that they can vote themselves largesse from the public treasury. The majority always votes for the candidates promising the most benefits. A democracy always collapses over loose fiscal policy. The average age of the world's greatest civilisations has been 200 years.'

For the moment, we are left living in a fascist superstate where freedom is regarded as a disposable luxury and where laws and regulations are produced with glee by fecund administrators. Still, the plethora of rules created by the system can be turned against the bureaucrats themselves.

The Princess and I have discovered that whereas large companies and government departments may not give a fig for us, their employees do have their weak spots and they respond with terror to a nice mixture of refined, pompous, aggressive, gleefully offensive, patronising, threatening abuse, and spirited, targeted vituperation, served with a formal complaint and a quotation from a vaguely relevant section of the Human Rights Act. Those who live by the pointless regulation must also die by it.

What a sad world. It is difficult to believe that ours is a nation which gave us, and the world Cecil Rhodes and Sir Stamford Raffles.

15.

We were driving along in our latest motor car, a four wheel drive BMW, when suddenly all the warning lights came on, producing a dashboard extravaganza which would have delighted any aficionado of seaside illuminations. I obeyed the instructions, pulled over and stopped immediately. When I telephoned the dealer from whom we'd bought the car I was offered a service appointment for the following week. BMW's emergency service engineer came out and looked at the car but was baffled. So we ignored the pretty lights and drove on. After a while they all went out.

16.

The council sent round a skilled and trained team of arboreal specialists to prune the trees near a friend's house. The team came equipped with helmets and other safety equipment but no ladders and no saws. They contented themselves with reaching up and breaking off the lower, smaller branches and twigs. They then went away, leaving debris on the pavement.

17.

A reader who comes from Leeds (but spells it Leed's) wants to know why my books are now often priced at £50. She complains that the price of my books is too high and goes on: 'I can buy a book packed with insights by the statesman Tony Blair for £12.50 and he will not get a penny.' She also complained that my books 'seem to tumble out of the author's own head'.

Putting aside the slightly puzzling 'tumbling out of my head' criticism I replied saying that she was entitled to believe that Blair was a statesman and quite right in asserting that she can buy books more cheaply. I pointed out that I am told that the latest volume from the writer with a surgically enhanced bosom known as Jordan is quite reasonably priced. I explained that I now limit the print runs for my books and that I do this partly because it is impossible to persuade bookshops to stock self-published books in serious numbers and partly because I want to restrict the information I offer to a relatively small and loyal group of readers. In the old days (when we had staff at Publishing House and we were printing and selling hundreds of thousands of books we could keep the prices low and still make enough money to survive. It was not unusual for us to print 5,000 to 10,000 copies at a time of a big-selling book. Large print runs mean much lower costs per book.)

What I didn't bother to point out in my reply is that although my books have a cover price of £50 I usually sell them to my regular readers at a much lower price.

The reason for this is simple.

If a book buyer decides to order one of my books through a wholesaler or a bookshop I will be expected to offer a huge discount. It is not uncommon for wholesalers to demand that they be allowed to buy the book with a 50% discount. And they do not pay the cost of packing and posting the book to them.

The sums are easy to do.

If a book has a retail cost of £20 and I give a £10 discount I am left with £10. (In order to receive this money I may have to send half a dozen invoices and wait a year. There's a good chance I will never be paid.)

Out of the £10 I have to pay for the printing of the book and for packing and posting it. Some of my books cost £3.50 to post within the UK and over £12 to post abroad. The padded bags we use can cost up to £1 each. Then there are labels and sticky tape and so on. Because my print runs are low and I insist that my books look and feel good the setting and printing costs are high. It is not unusual for me to pay £6 to £7 for copies of my books. Obviously, I don't receive any money for the books which don't sell. I have to pay the printers before the books are sold and I have to pay for the cost of transporting and storing the books somewhere dry.

And so I now price my books at £50 so that when a bookshop or wholesaler orders a copy I can fulfil the order without making a huge loss. Readers who order directly (from my catalogue) can buy books at a much lower price.

The truth is that many publishers now lose vast amounts of money. And many small publishers and self-publishers struggle to break even - let alone survive commercially.

For a variety of reasons, proper, printed books have come down in price dramatically in recent years (and prices are falling even faster now that eBooks are being sold). I have on my shelves many books that cost £20 or more when I bought them ten or twenty years ago. Meanwhile, print costs, paper costs and storage costs have all soared. A few years ago it was possible to print and bind a book for less than £2. Today you would have a job to print anything other than a catalogue (or a mass market book) for that sort of price.

In those old days it was usual for a publisher to price a book at around five or ten times the printing costs. And that is exactly what I would like to do now. The rest of the price would include the cost of overheads (offices, warehouse, council taxes, electricity, heating, telephone and so on). The problem is that the cost of setting and printing a book has risen so much that I paid over £8 per copy to produce *Stuffed!*, my last book. The cost would have been higher but I collected the books from the printer myself. And, of course, there is the cost of marketing and advertising. Simply printing a catalogue can result in a four figure bill. And it costs at least 50p to buy the stamp to post off each copy.

Finally, of course, there is the question of unsold books and returns. No publisher can predict precisely how many copies a particular title will sell. If you print too few you will annoy potential customers and lose sales. If you print too many you will end up with hundreds or thousands of unsold books cluttering up the place. However well I try to estimate a print run I will get it wrong sometimes. All publishers do. (That's why bookshops so often have piles of books being sold at very low prices.) In America around a third of all published hardbound books are returned unsold. Most of these books cannot be resold and unless they can find a home on the remainder tables they are simply destroyed. Astonishingly high returns (in excess of 50%) are by no means unknown and in the world of paperback publishing are fairly commonplace.

So, that's why I now price my books so high. I'm not profiteering. I don't accept advertisements in my books or on my website so my only income (apart from my investments and the old age pension which the Government puts into my bank account each month) comes from selling books.

18.

We were unloading boxes of books at our new offices when I saw an elderly neighbour confronting two council workmen. He asked them, politely, not to lean their heavy equipment up against his fence. (They were doing something messy, pointless and expensive to the kerbs.)

'We'll lean our stuff where we want to lean it!' snarled the foreman. And they did.

'It cost me £400 to have it repaired last time,' said the old man, close to tears.

'That's your problem,' said the foreman.

I had a similar experience when workmen were digging a channel to bury television cables. They dug so close to our elderly but solid stone garden wall that part of it fell down. When I remonstrated a very belligerent man in ugly boots said the wall was in a poor state anyway.

Workmen don't give a damn when folk complain because they know that little or nothing will happen to them. And if they are fired they will receive generous benefits from the State.

19.

The Princess was reading a magazine.

'Why do nurses and barristers always talk about 'us' when they mean 'you'?' she asked.

I looked at her.

'Nurses always say things like 'Have we had our bowels opened?' when they're not talking about *their* bowel movements. And barristers always say things like: 'We're going down for three to five I'm afraid.' Why do they do it?'

'I have no idea,' I admitted.

'You're a doctor!'

'It doesn't alter anything. I still have no idea.'

The Princess sighed and put down her magazine. 'Would you like a cup of tea?'

20.

It is impossible to pick up a newspaper or turn on the television without hearing the name Jimmy Savile. The disc jockey and television presenter has been demonised. He was probably the best interviewer of all his peers (never patronising or maudlin) and tireless in his efforts for charity. But the wolves have sharpened their teeth and his reputation lies in tatters. His name has been linked to the Yorkshire Ripper killings and, for all I know, he is probably being blamed for the outbreak of World War II, the demise of Clinton Cards and the late arrival of the number 27 bus from Wolverhampton last Thursday.

I have no idea how much truth there is in the allegations but it is true that people working for the BBC treated him as a god-like figure. I remember once going into a Radio 1 studio to record an interview and finding that the whole studio was thick with cigar smoke. A huge cigar butt lay in a cheap metal ashtray on the studio desk. 'Sorry about this,' apologised the producer. 'Jimmy has been recording in here.' I was astonished. Smoking had long been banned in recording studios. No one else would have dared to light up. No one else would have got away with it. I know why. I felt strangely privileged to gasp and wheeze my way through the recording because the smoke was Jimmy's.

But now journalists, police, politicians and lawyers seem obsessed with the sexual proclivities of the dead disc jockey. Journalists because throwing dirt at the memory of a dead celebrity avoids any danger of ending up on the wrong end of a libel suit and lawyers because there may be a possibility of gouging compensation for anyone who was travelling on the number 27 bus last Thursday. The hysteria has been orchestrated by editors leaping at the chance to stick knives into a celebrity who can't defend himself or sue and by lawyers leaping at the chance to represent litigants who can. The hysteria will merely drag up old memories. The only people who will make money will be the lawyers. So what good has been done? And what harm? Can these finger pointing critics really see no serious problems in our society which need their attention?

Meanwhile, our nation is falling apart. Crooked politicians, crooked bankers, crooked financiers and barking eurocrats have ruined England. But nothing, it seems, matters more than Mr Savile's habits. The end result of the self-righteous drum beating will be that a number of Savile's charities will close and the people who would have been helped won't be helped. I doubt if the people beating the drums will be setting up any charities of their own. Another great result for the politically correct social vigilante movement. Maybe next they can turn their attentions to Lewis Carroll and Mark Twain (both of whom liked the company of young girls), J. M. Barrie who liked playing with small boys and Edgar Allan Poe (who married his 12-year-old cousin). And Degas who loved painting all those little ballet dancers. I bought a perfectly respectable, entirely innocent book recently which happened to have a picture which included a young girl in school uniform and plaits on the cover. A nervous bookseller had stuck a large white label over the whole photograph. Sheer bloody lunacy. I bet the value of all those Degas bronzes is collapsing by the minute.

21.

Some doctors are now apparently telling patients that they can only discuss one problem per consultation. This is utterly absurd. Any doctor who only allows patients to discuss one problem per consultation should, in my view, be reported to the General Medical Council for incompetence and struck off the medical register. It is a basic principle of medicine that one disease may produce many different symptoms and signs. Diabetes, for example, may produce a whole host of different problems - which may appear unrelated. Only when the symptoms and signs are presented together will the diagnosis be clear. Are patients who turn up at the surgery complaining of diarrhoea now to be expected to come back the next day to mention the vomiting?

Moreover, any doctor with experience knows that when patients say 'While I'm here, doctor...' or 'There's one other thing...', they're introducing into the conversation the sign or the symptom that really took them into the surgery in the first place. Embarrassment may have prevented them from mentioning the thing that has really been worrying them. Receptionists now often demand to know why a patient is making an appointment and patients who have rectal bleeding, for example, may prefer to mention something more mundane such as a small skin rash in order to get into the surgery.

Any good doctor ends every consultation with the words: 'Is there anything else?' because he knows that patients are often too shy or embarrassed or frightened to mention the symptoms which really matter.

22.

The Princess and I went to Malmesbury and parted for an hour so that we could both do some shopping. When we met in the art gallery café near to the car-park we compared purchases. 'And I bought this from a woman in the car park,' I said, pulling a thin paperback entitled *Composting Through The Ages* from my pocket. 'I bought it from a woman who approached me when I was buying the car-park ticket.

'I have one of those too!' said The Princess. 'She caught me a minute ago as I came back.'

The paperback is self-published and packed with photographs of compost bins and compost. The printing is a little idiosyncratic, as is the spelling, but the book was clearly written with great passion.

'She said sales were going very well,' The Princess told me. 'She says she doesn't let anyone into her home unless they buy one. She even sold one to the man who came to read her electricity meter and he apparently lives in a flat.'

23.

The Princess met an old lady in a charity shop today. The old lady told The Princess that she had lived alone for over half a century. She had been married for just six weeks when the Second World War started. Her new husband was in the army and he was captured by the Japanese. He was in a Prisoner of War camp for three years. When he arrived back home for the first time his wife had, rather unthinkingly perhaps, made him a rice pudding for desert. When she placed it on the table he got up, put on his coat and walked out. Neither she nor anyone else ever saw or heard from him again. I think it's one of the saddest stories I've ever heard.

24.

All the emergency warning lights came on in our BMW for the second time. It's quite alarming when it happens. But this time the lights clearly came on when we drove over, or into, a pothole. I suspect there must be some sort of electronic fault hidden deep within the car's innards. When I stopped the car, and allowed it to have a little rest to calm itself, all the lights disappeared. I'm contemplating covering the area of the dashboard where the little lights appear with sticking plaster.

25.

A third of all England's trees could disappear in the next year or two. There are around 80 million ash trees in our forests and woodlands. A disease which has been devastating ash trees on continental Europe (and which started in Poland twenty years ago) finally reached England in February 2012. Amazingly, unbelievably, it was not until the very end of

August that Government officials put down the coffee cups and the biscuits and launched a 'consultation' review to decide what to do about the impending disaster. Why were they thumb twiddling for so long? Were they deliberately waiting for the situation to get bad enough to need action? I just hope that the responsible civil servants have their bonuses trimmed this year. Thinking about this it occurred to me that one of my great sadnesses is that I did not plant more trees when I was a young man. I planted a few dozen, here and there, but what a joy it would be now to be able to go back and look at acres of deciduous woodland where once there had been nothing but fields. The great and now largely forgotten novelist and essayist Compton Mackenzie once wrote of the joy of going back to see trees he'd planted as a boy. I envy him that.

26.

The news that hospitals are deliberately killing off elderly patients in order to empty blocked beds and reduce health service costs came as no surprise. I exposed this some time ago in one of my books on medicine. But the revival of the story has hit the headlines. I stood in the newsagents alongside a man of about my own age who looked aghast as he read the front page of the *Daily Mail*.

'The Government made a mistake when they put Dr Shipman in prison,' I said.

The man looked at me, puzzled.

'They should have made him Minister of Health,' I pointed out. 'He'd have done all the necessary killing for nothing. The National Homicide Service would have saved a fortune. He'd have got rid of patients humanely and cheaply.'

The man laughed loudly and then, when he realised that what I had said made too much sense, he stopped laughing and looked very sombre. He nodded, once, looked at me, said 'Yes' very softly and walked away.

27.

We met Mr Pettigrew. He was looking very pleased with himself; as though he'd been freed from some great burden.

'We had relatives to stay,' he said. 'It's always the same with visitors. For the first two days it's good to have them around. They're a bit of a change. They're polite and helpful and we have fun. 'We must go,' they say. 'We don't want to be a burden.' 'Oh no,' we say stupidly. 'You must stay.' And so they stay. And then suddenly everything goes bad. After four days it has all become very tiring. We have to tip toe when we move about because they're still in bed. They want breakfast at ten o'clock. They leave all the towels damp in the bathroom. They wander about the house in the middle of the night and we think they're burglars.'

We nodded and made sympathetic noises.

'So then we have to use our trick to get rid of them,' said Mr Pettigrew.

'Please tell us,' said The Princess.

'Well, all our visitors like going for walks across the fields,' he explained. 'And at this time of year it's becoming a bit chilly. And it rains occasionally. So we lend them yellow anoraks.'

We both looked at him and frowned.

'Yellow anoraks attract all the midges and mites and bees and wasps,' explained Mr Pettigrew. 'There are still a few around even at this time of the year. Our visitors come back covered in bites and very fed up. And although we tell them how much we like having them with us, and beg them to stay, they go home the next morning.'

28.

Thanks to a few hundred Scottish farmers, afternoons in England have suddenly become much darker. I spent an hour this morning putting the clocks an hour forward and another hour putting them two hours back. This is more than a biannual waste of time. Insurance companies have shown that there is a significant increase in the number of road traffic accidents every time the clocks change. And there is clear evidence that changing our sleep patterns affects our already delicate mental health. According to researchers at Stockholm's Karonlinska Institute, our risk of having a heart attack goes up by 5% every time we change the clocks.

As far as I can make out the only people who benefit are a few hundred farmers in the north of Scotland who moan that if we don't change the clocks they'll have to get up in the dark to milk their cows. They are presumably frightened that there might be ghoulies and beasties hiding in the shadowy corners of their darkened barns. So, why don't we buy them all torches or install electricity on their farms? Alternatively, we could let Scotland have its own time zone. Hadrian, bless him, had the right idea. He just didn't build the damned wall high enough.

29.

The world is, it seems, now full of very sensitive individuals. A few weeks ago the nation was gripped by the saga of the senior politician who had allegedly called two policemen 'plebs' and who had decorated his verbal attack with a fairly traditional expletive ending in the word 'off'. Allegedly. Numerous pompous policemen and defenders of the force complained that in disputing the allegation the politician was suggesting that policemen might not always tell the truth, the whole truth and nothing but the truth. Their indignation was diluted somewhat by the fact that an enquiry into the Hillsborough Disaster concluded, just a day or two earlier, that policemen in Yorkshire had been lying more vigorously than they had been drinking tea. In the eyes of too many it is, it seems perfectly acceptable for policemen to shoot, bully and push innocent members of the public but it is not acceptable for elected ministers to say rude things to them. I think I must have been the only citizen who thought that the politician would have been better served if he admitted that he'd sworn at the coppers and called them 'plebs' because they deserved it. (The policemen had allegedly refused to open the gate for him and allegedly forced him to climb off his bicycle and allegedly push it through the pedestrian gate. Allegedly.) In the end I thought the politician showed a lack of back bone by resigning. (Although the policemen alleged that the politician had sworn at them, they did not arrest him and so it will presumably be in order for me to swear at a policeman next time I see one out in public. They can hardly arrest me for the same offence. My problem is that since I don't live or work in Downing Street the only policemen I ever see are the ones sitting in cars on motorway bridges, and shouting abuse while driving underneath them at 69 mph is unlikely to produce much of a response.)

And now the news is dominated by the story of a professional football referee who is allegedly accused of calling a footballer a Spanish twit. (He may have called him something else if the asterisk was there to replace another vowel in the daily newspaper reports.) I gather that the complaint here is that in describing the Spanish footballer as 'Spanish' the referee was being racist. The uproar is vast. I have little doubt that if we still had a Home Guard they would have been mobilised. The Cleggs and Cables of this world speak of little else. I am, I confess, a little puzzled by this, though I am, I regret to say, not in the slightest bit surprised. What puzzles me is how commentators at the next international sporting event are going to describe competitors if they cannot say which country they represent. Commentaries at the Olympics should be interesting.

It seems to me that the world is now populated almost entirely by hypersensitive, self-righteous prigs who regard any sort of passionate comment as racist or improper. We have become absurdly tolerant of small things in public life but at the same time we have become absurdly intolerant of the big things. A politician who is alleged to have called a couple of policemen plebs feels forced to resign from office but politicians who take us into illegal wars are allowed to sit in the back of chauffeur driven cars and tell the rest of us how we must and must not live our lives.

30.

Just about everything I do these days seems to involve my breaking the law. The Princess and I have been working hard packing books and putting them into grey Royal Mail sacks. Earlier today we filled the truck with ten sacks and took them into the local sorting office. When I returned with another truck full of sacks the Royal Mail employee who accepted the sacks glowered at me and asked if I had weighed the sacks before delivering them. I confessed that I hadn't. (Our postage scales weigh only up to 1 kg). 'You're only allowed to put 11.5 kg into one sack,' he snarled. (Like most public institutions everything done by Royal Mail is weighed in EU friendly figures rather than proper, traditional and perfectly legal British measurements.) He proceeded to instruct me that our sacks were too full and that the postmen had had to take out some of the parcels before the sacks could be moved. All this was done not in a friendly sort of way but in a 'State Functionary reprimanding a peasant' sort of way. The truth is that these bloody rules may well apply within their four walls but they do not apply to us. But, nevertheless, if we want the bastards to accept our sacks The Princess and I will, in future, have to try and estimate 11.5 kg worth of parcels when filling sacks. It seems an awful feeble load - under two stones in proper measurements. The Princess and I carried our over-laden sacks two at a time without difficulty. What unthinking, milquetoast, namby pamby zombies the Royal Mail now employs. We have become a nation of overregulated wimps and wusses, terrified to open our mouths in case we inadvertently offend someone and find ourselves in court and frightened to death that if we ever actually do something we will find ourselves in breach of one of the gazillion regulations which now control our every move. And what seems to me worse than all the rules, and the damned rule-makers, is that there are legions of big girls' blouses out there who are so empty-headed and incapable of rational thought that they enthusiastically, officiously and efficiently obey the latest regulation and make damned sure that everyone else also obeys. What a world we have created. The sad truth is that most people and Royal Mail employees (not necessary the same thing) will happily do bad things if they're told to do them. Researchers have shown that one in two individuals will merrily shock strangers to the death if they are instructed to do so. We have a resigned and apathetic population, exhausted by the chicanery and craven behaviour of a seemingly endless stream of self-serving, greedy, rancid, political pirates. Cant and political correctness are commonplace. The bottom line is that the people are responsible for the mess we are in because most have never protested about the idiotic rules. They haven't spoken up and they have continued to vote for the same lying psychopaths. Is it any wonder that we now live in a cesspit of debt with home owners, banks and nation all bankrupt when the Government deals with our financial problems by printing money and using it to buy gilts? And this, they seem to believe, is a solution. For our Government to try to spend its way out of a recession is like someone who can't afford to pay their mortgage saying that they'll deal with the problem by buying a new car. We are surrounded by lunatics. Do the people put up with all the stupid regulations because they are brainwashed into thinking that the daft ideas are good ideas or because they are frightened to say anything? Or is it because they never bother to find out what is happening but, instead, just immerse themselves in the goings on of television soap characters. And, perhaps, they have forgotten how to be truly shocked because they are constantly pseudo-shocked by the never ending supply of bad and scary news about bad and scary behaviour by our crooked politicians, incompetent civil servants and cheating, dishonest, drug and bribe soaked sporting heroes. Maybe I'm being too hard on the people and the Royal Mail employees. Maybe their skulls are stuffed with tapioca pudding instead of brain. Maybe I should just blame the politicians who have grabbed far too much power for themselves. It was Thomas Jefferson who wrote: 'My reading of history convinces me that much bad government comes from too much government.' And it was one my heroes, the late, lamented and sadly mislaid Ambrose Bierce, hero to all sensible men and women, who claimed to disapprove of all forms of government and of most laws. Wise man.

I do feel so much better after writing all that.

31.

A week ago I spent the best part of a day clearing leaves away from our car parking space. The damned things had already turned into a three inch thick mulch. Running out of space to put them I moved a few hundred-weight of leaves onto a piece of our garden. I received a letter from the council telling me that they were intending to prosecute me for fly tipping. The only person who saw me moving the leaves was Mrs Baskerville who was out walking her damned dog at the time and who marched past pretending to be interested in the toes of her Wellington boots so that she didn't have to notice me. I have written back to the council pointing out that the leaves I moved did not belong to me but came from trees which are public property. Furthermore, I explained that they had arrived on our land uninvited and that in the interests of health and safety I had moved them onto another piece of our land. I enclosed an invoice for £500 for the time I had spent moving their leaves around. I also pointed out that the only person who had seen me moving the leaves was at the time walking her dog. 'The dog was not on a lead,' I wrote, 'and the owner was therefore in breach of the law which states that dogs should be kept on leads when walking on public roads.' I also pointed out that since the dog owner was returning from the woods but was not carrying a doggy bag it seemed entirely possible that her hound had emptied its capacious bowels on public land and that the owner had failed to collect her dog's droppings as prescribed by law. That should keep the snotty bastards at the council busy for a few months. With any luck at all, the criminal Mrs Baskerville will be carted off to Holloway Jail.

NOVEMBER

1.

We arrived at our offices to find that the doorbell had been ripped out of the door frame and the knocker wrenched off the front door. Both were thrown down on the mat. In addition someone had scrawled all over the paintwork with an indelible marker pen.

'Who on earth would do all that?' I wondered out loud.

'Trick or treaters,' said The Princess. 'It was Halloween last night and we weren't here to hand out sweets and money.'

I'm convinced she's right. Several neighbouring buildings had the same treatment. It seems that today's youngsters are learning the protection racket at any early age.

2.

For nearly 20 years now I've managed my own pension fund through a SIPP. The firm which runs the fund is supposed to send me a statement twice a year. They never do. When I ring up to remind them of this small obligation I am always told that the statement was posted and must have got lost. This happens twice a year as regularly as the clocks go forwards and backwards. 'Would you please send me another copy,' I ask. They say they will. And a few days later the statement arrives. How odd it is that the first statement always gets lost in the mail while the second statement always arrives safely.

3.

Councils all over the country are now turning on the street lights at dusk and then turning them off again as soon as it gets really dark. There has been much boasting recently about the amount of money this saves. One council announced that it had saved £300,000 by not turning on street lights at all in areas of the town where no council employees had parked their cars. A quick look at the accounts showed that the £300,000 would enable a team of administrative assistants to go on a fact finding mission to attend a conference held in the South of France, though without also turning off the traffic lights there would not be any money with which to do anything with their conclusions. None of this matters very much to The Princess and me. Our nearest street lights are four miles away as the crow flies and considerably further as we mortals must travel. (When the council didn't bother to mend faulty street lights near our offices I rang twice without success but on the third occasion I pointed out that drunks frequently wandered into the road because there were no lights. 'There will be an accident, and probably a death,' I warned. 'I've now told you about this three times. Could I have your name please?' Since no bureaucrat ever likes the idea of taking responsibility, or finding themselves in a coroner's court, the lights were mended within 24 hours.

4.

Here are three animal stories I've discovered recently. All are absolutely true.

1. During the Second World War the Americans tried to use bloodsucking insects to detect hidden enemy troops. The idea was that the insects would be released and would bite the enemy. When the enemy soldiers jumped up and down scratching, the American soldiers could shoot them. The plot didn't work because the insects refused to stay where they were released or to bite the intended targets.
2. In 1860, a pig almost started a war between England and America. The pig, which was Canadian, kept crossing the border between Canada and the USA so that it could eat American potatoes. When an American farmer shot the pig, a British warship was dispatched to deal with the miscreant. The Americans sent a unit of 60 soldiers to defend their countryman. The War of the Pig was averted only when the commanders of the two sides agreed to stand down.
3. When Paris was under siege in 1870 a war correspondent called Henry Labouchere claimed to have eaten cats and kittens. 'A cat is something between a rabbit and a squirrel, with a flavour of its

own,' he wrote afterwards. 'It is delicious. Don't drown your kittens, eat them.' He described a dish of kittens in onion ragout as simply 'excellent'. During the same siege Labouchere also claimed to have eaten spaniel slices (which he said weren't bad and tasted rather like lamb) and donkey steaks (which he wasn't terribly keen on, saying they tasted rather like mutton). During this siege the Parisians ate every horse, dog, cat and rat they could find. When they'd finished they descended on the zoo and served themselves a banquet of boiled bison, slices of elephant's ears, stewed monkey, baboon on a stick and roast macaw. The French will eat anything as long as it is cooked and served nicely.

5.

The Princess and I have made a guy to sit on our bonfire. We haven't bought any fireworks because we don't want to scare the animals who live in the wood but we're having a bonfire, a guy and baked potatoes.

Our guy is a splendid looking fellow, about six feet tall and plump. After a voting exercise which we based on the proportional representation system so popular with politicians who can't win anything by fairer means we have decided to name our guy 'Vince'. It seems apt. After all, Vince Cable must surely be the most dangerous man in England. If Scotland Yard published a list of public enemies he ought to be Number 1.

I'm much looking forward to tonight's entertainment but bonfires are not just a once a year delight in our household. One of the main advantages of a garden is being able to have regular bonfires - not piddling little things in tinny incinerators but proper, raging fires with flames leaping thirty feet into the sky. There are always plenty of clippings, prunings, fallen leaves and so on to be burnt and these, of course, provide the framework for our burning of all the waste paper which one naturally accumulates and which would otherwise take up too much of our meagre allocated rubbish allowance. I have been going through my old files and burning letters and documents relating to old battles. I've burnt old libel actions, old complaints and old cuttings. I found scores of old interviews I can't remember giving. And I added to the burning pile details of a publicity tour I made for my book *Bodysense*. I travelled for three weeks, averaged 36 towns and cities a week and did literally hundreds of television, radio and newspaper interviews. It made me feel tired just to read the itinerary. A bonfire gets rid of confidential waste far more effectively than a shredder - and with less ecological damage. It is also a visual and olfactory joy. I adore the smell of a garden bonfire. Kyril Bonfiglioli, writing in his acidic, gloriously anarchic novel *Don't Point That Thing At Me,* described bonfires having a smell which is 'at once wild and homely' and he was precisely right.

I've also used our massive, stone walled bonfire site (a professional quality bonfire site if ever I saw one) to rid the garden of infected leaves. Our horse chestnut tree is infected with the accursed leaf mining moth and the only way to break the cycle is to burn the discoloured leaves wherein lie buried the larvae. An expert from 'Trees'R'Us' ('branches everywhere') tells us that the disease is not supposed to harm the tree or prevent the production of conkers but it does. We have had no fruit at all this year. Not one conker. This is truly sad. Even The Princess (who is not quite as taken with the fruit of the horse chestnut as a former third form conkers champion must be) is saddened by this. She collects conkers too because she knows that if you spread them around the house they will keep spiders away. (The only other truly effective method involves turning up the heat very high. Spiders don't much like hot, dry houses. But nor do we.) For some unfathomable reason spiders don't like anything to do with the horse chestnut. A man I know once had a home made entirely with chestnut wood. He never had a single spider in the house.

I couldn't help wondering if the disease could have been started, or at least spread, by the spoilsports who want conker trees chopped down to stop small boys risking bruised knuckles. There is apparently a therapeutic chemical you can spray onto the tree to get rid of the disease. But how the hell do I spray a tree which is sixty, seventy feet high in the middle of a small woodland?

And so I rake up every leaf I can find and burn them all.

The horse chestnut is also threatened by something called bleeding canker. Elm trees have been decimated by Dutch elm disease. Sweet-chestnut trees are being threatened by sweet-chestnut blight. Larch trees, camellia and rhododendron have all been destroyed by a fungus like disease. Oak trees are dying of something called acute oak decline and plane trees are attacked by their own infection. And now ash trees are under attack. The Princess fears that the biggest threat to us all could well be the apocalypse of the trees. Without them we cannot survive. I agree with her. But nobody in power seems to care much. They probably don't realise how much we depend upon our trees and how long it takes a tree to grow.

Several of our apple trees are threatened by something nasty too. I've been busy with the pruning saw. Only our scores of beech trees, huge willow and tree sized hazel bushes seem clean and healthy. Oh, and the firs and holly bushes look pretty good.

As a result of all this disease my bonfires have been particularly large and smoky this autumn.

In addition to their aesthetic qualities bonfires have other uses. There is, for example, no better way to destroy hard drives and old computer disks than in the heat of a raging bonfire. A computer contact of mine once boasted that whatever I did to a hard drive he would still be able to read whatever was written on it. Two days later I gave him a hard drive which had sat for three hours at the heart of a raging bonfire. The whole thing had melted into an unrecognisable shape. It did not, indeed, look man made, but had smooth surfaces and more resembled something that wind and rain had carved. I don't know how hot it was in the middle of that fire but old manuals and telephone directories were bursting into flame upon being thrown into the heart of it and so the temperature must have been well over 451 degrees Fahrenheit.

'What the hell is this?' he demanded, holding the still warm relic.

'It's my old hard drive,' I told him.

He examined it carefully, grudgingly admitted that it looked as if it could have been a hard drive and admitted without further ado that he had about as much chance of extracting information from it as I have of being recognised in the New Year's Honours list.

I have, over the years, acquired small skills at bonfire lighting and am, I suppose, a legal pyromaniac. With a cardboard box lain on its side and filled with crumpled broadsheet newspaper (the tabloids don't work anywhere near as well, and the *Daily Telegraph* is by far the most inflammatory publication I've ever known) I've burnt green and soggy clippings in the middle of a snowstorm. The trick is to lay the clippings carefully in layers so each layer smokes and then heats up while the top layer keeps out the snow.

But the forecast for tonight is cold and dry so there will be no need for heroics. A wind proof lighter, some old cuttings and a huge pile of hazel, beech, apple and sycamore prunings will be all I need.

Tonight our guy will burn and we will eat decent sized potatoes, pricked all over with a fork, carefully placed in the ash of the fire until they are powder soft on the inside and crisp on the outside, then seasoned with butter and salt and eaten with a fork. Who needs to scare the squirrels and the pheasant, the robins or the deer? Only a Philistine with no love for nature lights fireworks in the countryside. And yet, sadly, there are many of those. Yesterday one of our neighbours, a self-proclaimed tree hugger, an ethanol and windmill obsessive, a hypocritical nature loving boor with the sensitivities of a sarcastic fringehead fish and the imagination of an abandoned tree stump, invited a group of relatives from some far off metropolis and together they burst the silence of the night with an expensive barrage of display-quality bangs and flashes and the inevitable whoops of sad, middle aged delight. They dined al fresco on gallons of white wine spritzer and battalions of barbecue sausages stuffed in white finger rolls. The following morning our lawns and woodland were scarred with the rocket stick and burnt paper leftovers of their homage to a night in Beirut.

6.

Our postman dumped two handfuls of indiscriminate and irrelevant mailing rubbish through our letterbox this morning. When I went into town this afternoon I took the leaflets, brochures and catalogues with me and handed them in at the local Post Office. 'What are you giving me these for?' demanded the puzzled counter clerk. He had a mean, sharp face and looked as though he stole coat hooks from public lavatories as a hobby. 'The postman dropped them through our letterbox by mistake,' I explained. 'I thought you'd like them back.' I then walked swiftly away. I don't usually do this. Usually I put such unwanted rubbish into a red pillar box so that the postman can pick it up with the proper mail.

7.

The myrmidons at HMRC have written to warn me that from next April they are going to make my employer's tax form at least twelve times as complicated as it already is. Instead of filling in an online form once a year I will have to download special software, do unspeakable and unimaginably perverse things on their website and then complete an online form every month.

This is, of course, utter lunacy. I wrote a letter asking if their aim is to force all small businesses to close down. 'I know that the European Union does not like small businesses,' I wrote. 'And I understand this. After all, all fascist organisations prefer a world in which society is managed by a consortium of big companies working with the State. However, I do think that given the nation's current parlous economic condition you really ought to be destroying employers at a rather more sedate pace.'

I then realised that the letter I had received from HMRC did not include a mailing address, a telephone number, a fax number or an e-mail address.

I am not surprised that HMRC receives a constant barrage of complaints. My biggest wonder is that people know where to send their protests. Talking of complaints, I saw today that, according to research carried out for a legal firm, of the 58,000 complaints received by HMRC last year an amazing 57% were upheld by HMRC itself. Isn't that hysterical? The most common causes for complaint were mistakes, unreasonable delays and poor treatment by HMRC staff. And the Treasury recently announced that the average caller gave up waiting for someone to answer the tax helpline after five minutes and 45 seconds.

The corollary to the letter from HMRC that contains no mailing address, and no other way of getting in touch, is that taxpayers should never give government departments (such as HMRC) their home address, their private telephone number or their e-mail address. Anyone who does so is likely to be harassed so incessantly and so soundly that he or she will give in to whatever their demands might be simply to make them go away. In my experience it is far better to use a Post Office box or an accommodation address and to insist that the slimy bastards send all their communications through the mail.

It is also sensible to avoid attending meetings. Attending meetings with the HMRC is not yet compulsory and I always prefer to conduct negotiations by mail so that I have everything in writing. If they change the rules and I do ever have to attend a meeting with a tax inspector I will insist that it is held either underneath the Arc de Triomphe or in the Hard Rock café in Paris (the noisiest and busiest places I know). And I will wear a T-shirt emblazoned with the slogan: 'I pay your wages'.

8.

Three days ago we succumbed and decided to install broadband. The Government now insists that I fill in my VAT forms and some of my tax forms online. If I don't they will send me to prison. I have to register new books online because there is no other way.

And so I rang the telephone company and asked them to set up a broadband connection. They did it in seconds over the phone. Today, we received a largely incomprehensible letter from them telling us that they will be sending us something called a router and that we will need micro-filters attached to all our telephone sockets. I have no idea what a router is and I am afraid that we are completely out of micro-filters. I telephoned to find out what these things are. Apparently I can buy micro-filters from appropriate IT friendly stores. And a router is being sent to us by a carrier. I rang up to ask if the router could be sent with the postman who knows how to find the house. It cannot. It must be sent with a carrier. I suggested that the company give the carrier our telephone number so that he would be able to ring us when he gets lost. 'Our carrier drivers are very experienced,' said the snotty 12-year-old on the other end of the telephone. 'They will find your house without any problem.' The driver will get lost. The satellite navigation systems used by van drivers all take them to the wrong village. And most van drivers panic when they see the sequence of 'Road unsuitable for motor vehicle' signs which they have to ignore if they are to reach us.

9.

The gas and electricity people have for months been demanding access to Publishing House so that they can read the meters. They repeatedly inform me that we are obliged by law to allow them access to read the numbers on the little dials. Two weeks ago I at last took pity on them and gave them a date and a time that would be convenient to us. We may be obliged to let them view the meters (even though I have repeatedly told them that no gas or electricity is being used) but there is no law that says we have to let them in at a time convenient to them. So, today, at 12 noon promptly a man arrived. He had been given special permission to read both meters. The whole procedure took approximately a minute and a half and was quite painless. I suspect that many people spoil the utility companies by allowing them to dictate the date and time when the meters will be read.

10.

It took me several hours to open the mail. Someone has written trying to persuade me to store all my files on the 'cloud'. Idiots. This is not a new idea, of course. Ever since biorhythms and food combining were fashionable people have been trying to persuade me to store my confidential files on the internet so that they will be 'safe' and I can collect them from space wherever I am and with whatever device I am using. The people who use such a system are naive and stupid to the point of needing full time care. They are, without a doubt, the sort of people who go on holiday with their home addresses clearly visible on their luggage labels and then show genuine surprise when they arrive back a fortnight later and discover that they have been burgled.

A former education minister in a commonwealth country sent us his book. He has instructed us to publish his book or to find him another publisher. There isn't a single 'please' in the letter.' And a former bestselling author has sent his typescript 'for consideration'. More cheerily three proud readers have sent me copies of books which they published for themselves. It is a delight to see how many people are now self-publishing and showing courage, determination and single-mindedness in so doing. Dr Samuel Johnson once wrote: 'He would earn his bread writing books must have the assurance of a duke, the wit of a courtier and the guts of a burglar'. All this is doubly true for the author who also publishes.

To my astonishment three copies of my book on vaccination have been returned by newspaper editors to which they were sent for review. They (or, rather, their proprietors) paid good money to post the books back to me. It seems that the book is so 'hot' that they don't want to keep it on their premises, don't want to sell it on eBay and certainly don't want to review it. We have now sent out 300 review copies of this book. As far as I am aware there have been no reviews. In China, a newspaper for which I was working refused to print an article criticising vaccination and subsequently my publishers refused to reprint any of my books (which had been extremely successful there) or to print any of the books which they had asked for permission to publish.

A relative we haven't seen for decades, has written saying that she has just seen a copy of our new catalogue. She wants to know how she can obtain a copy of one of my books. She says she is particularly interested to read my latest book. So, in pure Dodgson style, we post her a copy of my book on vaccination.

A reader tells me that her husband, who has Alzheimer's, has had to re-sit his driving test. Much to her horror he has passed the test. 'He hardly knows who I am, he gets lost and confused just walking around the supermarket. But they've given him back his driving licence.' She has decided that the only solution is to sell the car. It means that they will have to go everywhere by bus.

When I went to Liverpool as a Community Service Volunteer in the 1960s the founder, Alec Dickson, described me as a catalyst - there to make things happen. (I spent a year persuading thousands of children and teenagers to do things like decorate old people's flats. I didn't tell them that they would be doing a good thing. I told them that the council, the police and the unions were all strongly opposed to what I wanted them to do.) I thought of that when I opened a lovely letter from America. I sent a reader over there a copy of one of my books on animal experimentation and he has written back to say that he is 43-years-old and that he intends to spend the rest of his life sending letters to senators and congressman based on my book. No writer can hope for more.

A reader has written to tell me that the council she works for pays £7.50 for each ream of copy paper which is used in its offices. She says that she can buy the same paper for £4.99 in a chain store. I'm not surprised. When, some years ago, I exposed the fact that the NHS was paying far more for stationery and other essentials than I would pay if I bought the same items from my local supermarket the NHS bosses were instructed by the Government to hold an inquiry. They did. But it wasn't an inquiry into why they were wasting so much money. It was an inquiry into how I'd found out.

And a kind reader has asked if I have any objections to him using phrases from my *Stress and Anxiety* audio tape in a song he is recording. I thought a sampler was an example of embroidery skills but it is apparently something quite different. I will tell him that I have no objections and that I hope it is the Christmas number 1. If they still have such things.

11.

There are many ways to annoy sanctimonious neighbours but I have found that one of the best methods is to light a bonfire. We have enormous piles of garden rubbish to burn (clippings, cuttings, dead branches and so on) and I have found that as soon as I start to burn garden rubbish one of our unpleasant neighbours walks along the lane coughing loudly. I think this is supposed to be a hint. I suspect I am supposed to dowse the fire immediately. However, our neighbours have been so unpleasant that I regard this as a sign of weakness on their part. I am now searching the house, the garage and the sheds looking for bits of old carpet and polystyrene to add to the next bonfire.

12.

I overheard this conversation in a pub today:

'Plans always look fool proof and then the unexpected comes along and screws things up.'

'That's why we plan; that's why we prepare for the unexpected.'

'You can't.'

'What do you mean?'

'You can only plan for the expected. You can never plan for the unexpected because, by definition, it's unexpected and, therefore, beyond planning.'

'Then we'll just have to keep our fingers crossed.'

'That's probably the best we can do.'

13.

The Princess has a friend called Lucky.

I asked her where he got the nickname.

'He's always lucky. Good things happen to him.'

'Give me an example.'

She thought for a moment. 'He lives in a smart neighbourhood but never bothers to cut his hedge. It's a scruffy mess. Terrible. The neighbours are always complaining about it. Then one day a man from an advertising agency knocked on his door and asked him if he'd let them cut his hedge. They were making an advertisement for a new hedge trimmer.'

'So they cut his hedge for him?'

'Yes.'

'That's pretty lucky.'

'You haven't heard it all.'

'Go on then.'

'They paid him £500 to let them film an actor cutting his hedge.'

'That's definitely lucky.'

14.

We were discussing people we know.

'I don't know anyone who's normal,' I said.

'I'm not sure there is any such thing as a 'normal' person,' said The Princess.

'Humphrey Todcaster,' I suggested. 'He's pretty normal.'

'Do you know anyone like him?'

'No. I don't suppose so. I don't suppose there is anyone like him.'

'So he can't be normal.'

'What about Bertie Warburton?'

'There's no one like Bertie! He's a bell ringer and he collects shells.'

'I can't think of anyone who's normal.'

Maybe no one is normal,' said The Princess.

And I'm sure she's right. As she always is.

15.

I learned of a new scam today. A man I met in the street told me about it. He was picking up receipts that had been dropped on the pavement and examining them all very carefully. He'd been drinking and was more talkative than he should have been. 'These are worth money,' he said, showing me a handful of receipts he'd picked up. I asked him why he thought old receipts could be worth money.

'Look at this one,' he said. 'It's a receipt for a blouse. Nearly £40. Nearly £40 for a blouse! They paid cash. What I do is I go into the shop and I find a blouse to match the receipt. Then I take it off the hanger and go to the till and hand it to the assistant. I say it doesn't fit or it's the wrong colour. And they give me the £40.' He grinned and breathed beery fumes over me. 'Of course it doesn't work when people pay by credit card,' he said. 'The receipt has to be for cash.'

'How often do you do this?'

He shrugged. 'Three or four times a day,' he said. 'You can only go in each shop once a day or so.' He smiled, very proud of himself. 'I thought it all up,' he said. He waved an arm around. 'And there are receipts everywhere! Too many for me to use by myself. Why don't you come in on it with me? With two of us we could hit twice as many shops!'

16.

I have often heard it said of people that they would be late for their own funeral. But today a local man called Nigel Harborough (known to his friends as 'Market') actually managed it. The hearse in which he was travelling was held up by road-works and did not arrive at the cemetery until forty five minutes after the allocated time. The star of the event was, therefore, the 'late' Mr Harborough in every sense of the word.

VERNON COLEMAN

17.

A friend of ours who has been holiday in Devon told us this story. A budding bridegroom, enjoying a three day stag party with some friends, was sitting by the side of the outdoor swimming pool. The men were all dressed in evening dress, ready for dinner, when one or two of the friends decided that it would improve the quality of their lives if they were to throw the would-be bridegroom into the pool.

'Wait!' he cried, as they grabbed his arms and legs and prepared to heave him into the pool.

Surprisingly, perhaps, they paused. And then they waited while the object of their interest removed an expensive looking wrist watch and placed it in his jacket pocket. 'A present from my fiancée,' he said.

And the watch was still in his pocket when they threw him into the pool five seconds later.

18.

I started to watch an international rugby match on television and was appalled at the fact that my eyes were constantly distracted by very intrusive advertising. Why on earth do the rugby people need to sell their souls? Why do they need so much money?

At most theatrical venues it is usual for the performing artist to split the take down the middle with the venue owner so it's fair to say that at a rugby ground or cricket ground the take is probably divided in a similar way. So, consider a rugby stadium where there are seats for 100,000 and the ticket prices average out at £50 each. That's a gross income of £5 million. (I am ignoring the profit from selling shirts, silly hats, hot dogs and beer although this sum must also be considerable.) Assume the teams receive £2.5 million as their share of the loot. And then assume that each player receives £5,000 for the match and that each team brings 20 players. That takes up £200,000. Now assume that providing the team with transport and training facilities and a manager to pick a team and make sure they all get to the ground on time costs another £100,000 a match. And let's take out another £200,000 for providing referees and linesmen, drinks at half time and free tickets for wives and girlfriends, and fresh jerseys and shorts, and hot water for baths afterwards. That leaves a neat £2 million in profit. And I still haven't counted the money paid by the television companies which will have paid a small fortune to show the match. So, why the hell do they need to sell advertising on the pitch, on annoying moving boards around the ground and on the players? It cannot be long before stretchers are emblazoned with tacky, inappropriate and annoying logos.

The answer to my own question is, of course, that they need the money to pay for a vast army of administrators and people hired to find yet more sponsorship. Rugby, like cricket, and every other professional sport, has been taken over by accountants and marketing specialists.

Actually, cricket is even worse than rugby. It is run by administrators, businessmen and politicians who seem to me to have lost any interest they might have ever had in the sport itself. The game, in their hands, has become a crude and charmless business; the sole purpose is to make money, though it is never quite clear why, or who will benefit. The passion, the sport, the honour have all been purged. The game would be in safer hands if it were run by cricket loving spectators, with no experience of anything but the patience to sit all day under an umbrella, eking out the tea and sandwiches in the small hope that there might, just might, be an over or two of cricket before the official close of play.

The modern team travels with doctors, analysts, bowling coaches, batting coaches, fielding coaches, psychologists, fitness gurus, dieticians, masseurs, physiotherapists, wives, girlfriends and probably mothers. To pay for all these unnecessary acolytes, cricket grounds are selling the naming rights to their grounds, and allowing sponsors to decorate the boards around the ground, the grass, the players, the umpires and the sightscreens. And despite all this pampering there are constant complaints about how hard the work is, though most cricketers have probably never worked down a mine or on a fishing boat and have very little idea of the meaning of the words 'hard work'. Cricketers are now so wimpy that they rush home mid-match if their wives or girlfriends have babies, headaches or menstrual cramps. Worse still is the fact that too many of the people concerned with the game from a professional perspective are so obsessed with money that corruption has spread widely among players and umpires. It is no longer possible to believe the results of any professional cricket match.

Life was much more fun for cricket fans in the 17th 18th and 19th centuries. Cricket matches were organised between teams of cripples and teams of women. Publicans put on games to attract beer buying customers and the local gentry made the bets. In the 19th century there was one glorious match played between 11 one-legged pensioners from Greenwich and

11 Greenwich pensioners who only had one arm each. The one-legged cricketers won, even though one of the batting side lost his false leg as he ran and a one-armed fielder seized the fallen limb and threw down the wicket with it. (The umpire gave the hopping batsman out, though heaven knows under what rule.)

I got so fed up with the advertisement drenched rugby on the television that I went out into the garden. I collected two buckets full of slugs which I deposited in the garden of one of our obnoxious dog-loving neighbours. I also buried around 200 old pre-decimal coins, pennies, threepenny bits, sixpences, shillings, florins and half crowns, which I recently found in a cupboard. They have very little value but in a few decades time a small boy will, I hope, dig them up and carry them into the house as 'treasure'.

19.

We have had a lot of trouble with our unpleasant, thoughtless, snooty and churlish neighbours during the last few months and the other day The Princess came up with a terrific idea.

We have printed an official looking notice headed *Regional Development Authority Planning Directive.* The rest of the notice contains details of approved plans for the conversion of our garage into a three story structure (with flat concrete roof). We have, the notice informs anyone who cares to read it, been given permission to erect 'light industrial manufacturing facilities for lathe metalworking and chemical spinning.' In addition, we have been granted permission by the Deputy Commercial Planning Director for the Region to convert a barn into a commercial recording studio to be known as *Loudsound Studios.* This will be made available for hire by rock bands from all EU countries. Our planning permission gives us the right to operate the studios between the hours of 08.00 a.m. and 23.30 p.m. At the bottom of the letter we have printed a good many official-looking names and references and a few vaguely accurate telephone numbers in Brussels. Naturally, no one there will be prepared to confirm or deny that any of these permissions has been given. The whole thing has been wrapped in plastic and pinned to the doors of our garage.

As we left to catch our Eurostar train to Paris this evening we spotted two neighbours studying the notice. And The Princess tells me that as we drove away she saw them both running back to their respective homes. There was, she says, a good deal of urgency in their movement.

20.

We met an Englishman on the train to Paris who has lived in France for thirty years. He misses only the cricket but has found a way to cure himself of this particular brand of homesickness. When the weather is cloudy and the sky overcast he takes an uncomfortable chair out into the garden and then fetches an umbrella, a newspaper, a flask of tea and a packet of sandwiches. He then holds the umbrella between his knees, opens the flask and the sandwiches and reads his paper. It is, he says, a surefire cure for homesickness.

21.

Another wretched organisation representing the gas fitters of France has written to us demanding access to the apartment. They say we are obliged to let them in so that they can check that we know how to turn on our gas by ourselves. We are told that we will be expected to show the technician our technique for gas tap turning. We are also told that we must be present in the apartment when we do this. (This is all so stupid that it is clearly a piece of EU nonsense.) The gas fitters have sent us an inconvenient appointment but stupidly and with delightful naivety they have printed their fax number on their letter heading. (Most well-run bureaucracies no longer print fax numbers or, indeed, addresses of any kind on their letter heading. HMRC in England, world masters at inconveniencing the general public, now send out letters which don't even have a telephone number or a website address.) I sent the gas fitters a letter, in English, cancelling their appointment and telling them the time and date when their man would be expected to arrive. He would, I added, be expected to remove his shoes or to bring with him a pair of clean plastic overshoes. When their man does not arrive I will make a formal complaint and our persecutors will immediately find themselves two sets down. There is no place for tender mercies when one is dealing with modern bureaucracies.

22.

Walking in a small park near the Trocadero I dived to catch a falling leaf and ricked my knee. Like all professional sportsmen I can now boast that I have a recurrence of an old injury. The Princess will give the unhappy joint some healing and I am confident that all will soon be well. Her healing hands should be an official national wonder.

My dive did not go unnoticed. The Princess later reported that several couples walking past eyed my antics with some surprise. And, out of the corner of one eye, I caught one elderly couple looking at me with ill-disguised contempt. They clearly thought me too old to be dancing around in a park. How absurd. I was determined to catch a falling leaf to give to The Princess as a good luck charm. They have always been hard to catch but there is no doubt that these days leaves are more elusive than ever. Moreover, their elusive nature seems to have coincided with a slight diminution in my own ability to move about with quite the catlike skills I possessed half a century ago. I suspect that this must all be another consequence of global warming, global cooling or some other global phenomenon.

Still, I eventually caught a very fine leaf. I placed it in a small, white paper bag I found in my pocket and wrote on The Princess's name, the place, the time and the date. It is something else for The Princess to keep I'm afraid. And it is always difficult to throw these things away.

23.

We were travelling on the number 69 bus which goes across Paris to St Germain, when there was quite a kerfuffle at the front of the vehicle, which was quite crowded. A woman of about 30, who was standing, suddenly turned and hit a man on the face with the flat of her hand. It was quite a slap. Not unnaturally the man, who was about the same age and who had been standing nearby, wanted to know why the woman had seen fit to attack him. 'You pinched me!' complained the woman. She pointed to her ample but smartly clothed derriere. 'I did not!' protested the man. He was saved by an elderly couple who were sitting next to the offended young woman. 'He did not touch you,' said the old woman. 'But I fear that when the bus rocked my umbrella might have caught you in that place.' The young woman, realising that she was in the wrong but not wishing to admit this in public, responded at first by blustering. But then, under intense public pressure, she apologised. 'It is not enough,' said the man, assuming the air of an aggrieved party. 'You must now allow me to commit the crime for which I have already been punished.' The woman stared at him uncomprehendingly. 'You have slapped me for pinching your bottom,' said the man. 'So now I am entitled to pinch your bottom.' Everyone laughed and it was generally agreed that this would be just. 'Alternatively,' continued the man. 'We will leave the bus and you will allow me to buy you coffee.' And so they left the bus at the next stop and there was much genial applause as they did so. The old woman looked particularly pleased with herself.

24.

The Princess and I were kept awake until 4.00 a.m. by music and singing in an apartment three floors below. We were invited but I'm afraid neither of us is keen on parties these days. The occupant, and party thrower, is a 55-year-old man who works as a teller in a bank on the Champs Elysee. Until recently he lived with his mother in the suburbs but when she died he sold her flat and bought a place in our building so that he could be in the heart of the city. When his mother was alive he obeyed her every command. He did not smoke or drink or eat meat or fatty food. He did not go out with girls, go dancing or frequent nightclubs. But now that she is in the family vault in Père Lachaise he is a changed man. He does all the things that he was not allowed to do when she was alive. He is living like a teenager enjoying a wild weekend while his parents are away. A young secretary from the bank has moved in with him and the two of them have become stalwarts of Parisian nightlife. He smiles a good deal and is quite charming. But in the morning I will have stern words with him about the noise. He will apologise profusely and bring flowers and chocolates for The Princess. I will tactfully remind him of his obligations to the other occupants of the building and he will promise not to do it again until the next time. (Making a lot of noise in an apartment building is a dangerous game to play. We know of a man in a nearby building who was so incensed by the noise made by his neighbour's parties that before he went away on his fortnight's holiday he turned on his television set and put the volume switch to 'high'. The guilty individual learned his lesson the hard way.)

25.

We spent the day indoors. Outside it was wet and miserable. Inside we were cosy. We read, painted and watched several movies. Thankfully, we have a good collection of our favourite films here. We also watched a couple of episodes from the Jeeves and Wooster series starring Hugh Laurie and Stephen Fry. I'm old enough to remember the series made in black and white starring the immortal duo of Ian Carmichael and Dennis Price but the Fry and Laurie series is exceptionally good and a delight for the eye and the ear.

26.

The Chinese Government gets a lot of criticism and much of it is well deserved. Personally, I don't much like the way they have succeeded in banning my books. But there are one or two things they do of which I approve. For example, the Chinese recently announced that people who use the internet must disclose their identity. The cowardly vipers who snipe at people from behind pseudonyms will, in future, be forced to reveal themselves. I'm all for that. I also rather liked the fact that during a deadly flu scare they announced that people who cough and sneeze in public without putting their hands over the mouths and noses will be punished. And I very much approved of their decision to execute corrupt civil servants who had endangered the health of the public. Who, apart from corrupt civil servants, could possibly object to that? But I'm still peeved that they banned my books. My books used to sell well in China.

27.

Our building in Paris was awash with heavy duty rumours this morning. On the second floor, the apartment at the back of the building is occupied by a couple who come from Nantes. He is a kind, warm-hearted fellow who always has a jolly word and a joke for everyone. He used to be an auctioneer and still talks like one with the result that both The Princess and I have to ask him to slow down every time he speaks to us. He thinks this is very funny and so he talks even faster. He has red cheeks, a purple nose and a huge, tobacco stained moustache of which he is extremely proud. Although he has lived in the city for decades his clothes smell of mould, sheep dip, diesel, whisky, pipe tobacco and damp Harris Tweed. His jackets are fitted with poachers' pockets (for hare, rabbits and pheasant) which he uses to carry a bottle of whisky around with him. He always enjoys good health. He is the sort of man who could eat six sausages, a pound and a half of bacon and three eggs without showing any signs of indigestion. She is a miserable, bad-tempered soul who responds to any remark with a tale of woe. Whenever anything bad happens to anyone she can always top it. Whenever anything good happens she can change the mood of a conversation in a second with a miserable account of someone's botched operation or failed lawsuit. She is an enthusiastic spreader of malicious gossip and a mean-spirited pessimist who always leaves everyone feeling more depressed than they were before they spoke to her.

No one has seen her for two days and the rumour is that Jean-Louis has done away with her. The problem is: what, if anything, should we do about it if he has. We are all better off without her. But is it our duty to tell the police and have Jean-Louis arrested?

It had been decided that we would all keep quiet when she returned. She had been to visit her mother who is dying again.

28.

We are using the tourist boat on the Seine in the same way that we once used buses and taxis. It is cheaper than using taxis, and more expensive than the ordinary bus. But it is more convenient than either, considerably more practical and far more fun. Since just about everything worth seeing in Paris is within a short walk of the Seine (the top part of Montmartre is, perhaps, an exception) the boat is an excellent way to move around. There are just enough stops to make it handy for most of the places we are likely to want to visit and not enough to make it too slow. And we avoid traffic jams and diesel fumes.

29.

A couple we vaguely know called us up and asked us to show them round Paris. We love showing people round the city but we really don't know this pair well enough (or like them enough) to devote a day of our life to taking them round. We're going back to England tomorrow and we have a lot we are planning to do. And we know, from past experience, that they will take advantage of us in every way possible (they will, for example, expect us to pay for absolutely everything). But we both find it difficult to say 'No', and so we agreed to meet them in a café at the bottom of the Champs Elysee.

When we left the apartment I took with me a copy of an excellent, lavishly illustrated guide book to Paris. The Princess raised an eyebrow. 'They'll want to borrow that,' she said.

'I know they will,' I replied.

'But it's your favourite guidebook!' she said, knowing how much I hate to lend my books to people.

I told her that there was method in my madness and that I knew what I was doing. When we met I took out the guidebook and used it to show them several places they ought to visit.

'Oh that looks a wonderful book!' said the wife, gazing at it as though she'd never seen a book before.

'Would you like to borrow it?' I asked. 'It's a new edition. It's got all the opening times, addresses and so on in it.'

They both leapt at the opportunity to borrow the book. The husband put the book in his rucksack before I could change my mind.

'We'll look after it for you,' they promised.

We bought them coffee and cakes and, after an hour or so, made our excuses and left.

'You won't see that book again,' said The Princess.

'Cheap at the price,' I told her. 'I can buy another.'

She looked at me.

'It's an idea I got from Oliver Goldsmith's *The Vicar of Wakefield,*' I admitted. 'If you have unwelcome visitors you lend them something that is of more value to them than to you. They won't want to return it and so they'll keep away so that they don't have to give it back.'

The Princess nodded and smiled. 'The cost of a new guidebook is much less than the cost of looking after them for a day.'

'Exactly!'

30.

A friend who lives in our building took us to the Gare du Nord. He drives rather wildly, even for a Parisian.

'Why don't drivers in Paris ever give any signals?' asked The Princess.

Our friend turned to her and shrugged in a typically Gallic way. 'We French are a very private people,' he said. 'It is no one else's business where we are going.'

DECEMBER

1.

I picked up a newspaper at the station as we headed back to England. Mark Carney, the new Governor of the Bank of England is an ex-Goldman Sachs employee so Goldman Sachs now pretty much controls the world. (Carney is also Canadian and it sometimes seems that the majority of important posts in England (in finance, administration, sport and media) are held by foreigners. Even the Mayor of London was born in America. This does not happen in other countries. In countries as dissimilar as France and the USA, for example, you simply won't find foreigners in positions of authority.) The rest of the news is equally dispiriting. People living in flooded areas of England have been told that they can only apply for sandbags only when flood water has already entered their homes. The Government is changing the rules about pensions yet again. (My SIPP managers sent me new rules last week. These are now already out-of-date.) And there is some discussion about the fact that NHS hospital staff are being paid bonuses if they kill off enough old people through a scheme named the Liverpool Care Pathway (a name straight out of Orwell). No one really seems to care terribly much about this, however. Even the laughably inept and stupid General Medical Council, which I discovered recently has reorganised itself as a charity, seems to approve of the mass slaughter of the elderly as long as there is Government funding involved. I wonder how much uproar there would be if hospitals started killing off everyone under the age of 20, or poor people, or the very badly and expensively injured, or civil servants or members of the railwaymen's union. In fact, of course, the Liverpool Care Pathway is quite unnecessary. Hospitals kill the elderly without being paid bonuses. Nurses refuse to feed patients because they consider it beneath them to do anything that doesn't involve a computer. And auxiliary workers aren't allowed to do anything that involves getting physically close to a patient or a mop.

In a second newspaper we picked up there was a story reporting that yet another bunch of scientists have claimed that there is a link between badgers with tuberculosis and cows with tuberculosis. The story makes it clear that it is not possible to tell whether cows give TB to badgers or badgers give TB to cows but the headline, with scant regard to the facts, announces: *Science blames badgers for TB.* I put away the newspaper and took out Bruce Lockhart's biography of Sidney Reilly, the British spy. Reilly was probably the only spy who really did nearly change history.

As soon as we arrived back at the house I sent a letter to the newspaper which printed the inaccurate badger headline, pointing out that their own story invalidated their own headline and that it would be just as accurate to have printed *Science blames cows for TB* and to call for a cull of cows. At the bottom of the letter I added a note telling the editor that if he doesn't print my letter I will make a formal complaint to the Press Complaints Commission. This invariably proves effective.

When I got round to opening the mail I found a letter from Scottish Life offering me compensation of £600 for behaving like a utility company.

2.

The weather has been so bad recently that a young roe deer has been visiting our garden at night to take some of the food which we put out for the birds. We now feed so many wild animals that their food bill is greater than our own. They repay us a million-fold with their presence.

3.

One of the squirrels which regularly visits our bird table and bird feeders is quite a bully. Whenever another squirrel approaches he leaves whatever he is doing and chases them away. Today, the bully was so busy gnawing nuts through the metal latticework of one of our feeders that a second, smaller squirrel managed to climb onto another feeder hanging from a nearby hazel bush, without being noticed. It is, of course, quite pointless to purchase 'squirrel proof' bird feeders. Make one out of riveted titanium and carbon fibre (assuming it is possible to rivet titanium and carbon fibre) and our squirrels would have it in bits and spread over three acres before we could get back into the house, so we have learned to sit back and enjoy them. However, to try to deter the squirrels, to slow them down for long enough to leave some nuts for the birds, I had hung this particular feeder from a very small and extremely flexible branch. The smaller squirrel, nervously looking over his shoulder to make sure that he hadn't been spotted, struggled so much to get at the nuts that the branch bounced up and down and the feeder slipped and fell onto the ground. For a few moments the squirrel couldn't understand what had happened. He looked around desperately. And then, suddenly, he spotted the feeder. The lid had come off when it had fallen and the nuts were now all spread on the ground around it. The squirrel launched himself into the nuts and started, literally, stuffing his face with them. Meanwhile, the bullying squirrel, who had seen nothing of this piece of good fortune, was still busily gnawing through the wire mesh of the feeder he was attacking and every so often managing to obtain a small piece of nut.

There was, I felt, a moral hiding in this incident. Aesop would have made something of it. The greedy squirrel was working hard for very little reward. The nervous squirrel, through a little determination, a good deal of courage and a lot of luck, was in nut heaven.

It's our 13th wedding anniversary and one of the days when we do our best to avoid all contact with the outside world. I remember that when Professor Albert Einstein and his wife were interviewed on their golden wedding anniversary they were asked to what they attributed the success of their marriage. Professor Einstein took his wife's hand and said: 'When we were married fifty years ago we made a pact that in our life together I would make all the big decisions and she would make all the little decisions. And we have kept to it for fifty years. That is I think the reason for the success of our marriage.' Then he thought for a moment before adding, 'The strange thing is that in fifty years there hasn't yet been one big decision.'

4.

The Princess and I decided that it might be fun to take our car to France and explore some of the countryside without having to bother with trains and taxis. But we have abandoned this idea. I discovered that in order to drive in France a driver must carry with him at all times his driving licence and his insurance documents, and he or his vehicle must be equipped with headlamp converters, a luminous vest, a warning triangle, a GB sticker and a breathalyser kit. And, of course, it is *very* illegal to carry in the car a device for warning about the presence of speed cameras (this includes carrying a satellite navigation system which offers this sort of facility). A fellow I know told me that when he last drove in France the storm-troopers stopped him and searched his car just for the hell of it. When they found his expensive satellite navigation device shut away in the glove compartment they threw it on the ground and stamped on it and then fined him the sort of sum usually only associated with serious bribery accusations. 'None of this worries me too much,' I told The Princess. 'But I refuse to have anything to do with luminous vests.'

5.

This is quite a day for mankind. I have defeated the squirrels.

Yesterday, I smeared some Vaseline around the metal poles of our two bird stations and put one of those collars which vets sell to stop dogs scratching their ears around the wooden post holding up the wooden bird table. The squirrels are bemused and thwarted. The Vaseline won't harm the squirrels (largely because having slid down the pole once they don't try a second time) and the collar has them stumped. I am pathetically pleased with myself. I have temporarily defeated half a dozen rodents.

6.

It is sad but true that Christmas is, for millions, the most miserable time of the year. It is a time full of forced joviality, of boredom, of excruciatingly dull television and of commercially organised theft in overcrowded shops. It is a time when people buy each other expensive gadgets and jumpers that no sensible person would actually want, and when they wrap bath salts, soap, slippers and tea towels and give them to maiden aunts who put them, unwrapped, onto the shop shelf of their wardrobes. It is a time when they send silly and expensive cards to people they never speak to and hardly remember, and eat and drink so much that they feel ill and have to spend the first three months of the following year dieting. Even supermarkets become unbearable as people panic buy when they discover that the shops may have reduced opening hours for a couple of days. It is a time when sadness seems more intense than in any other season. I know one fellow who puts up the same cards year after year in an attempt to disguise his lack of friends. And I know another who sends out the cards he received the year before. He crosses out the messages and writes new ones. Although quite wealthy he is so mean that he doesn't put stamps on the envelopes, claiming, quite wrongly, that the postmen will be far too busy to bother charging the postage and the penalty fee. Those unlucky enough to be on his Christmas card list have to spend two hours queuing at their local sorting office before picking up, and paying for, a second-hand card.

But for The Princess and me it is a joyful time. Since neither of us has any family to entertain we spend quiet Christmases indulging ourselves in peace and tranquillity. We do whatever we want to do. We do no real work. We make no courtesy visits. We neither make nor receive any telephone calls. We stock up with logs, good food, armfuls of books, a few toys and a good many old films.

We do, of course, have a well decorated tree. Although we once owned 30,000 real Christmas trees in a plantation (we sold them when thieves stole many and damaged more and when trespassing dog walkers just trampled down the younger trees) we use a tree we bought 12 years ago. We found it at Woolworths and we paid £9.99 for it. I wouldn't swap it for the Norwegian spruce that sits in Trafalgar Square. We have a fine collection of Victorian ornaments and we buy new lights each year so that we don't have to spend hours untangling last year's. (However carefully you put away the lights they will, by the following December, have become hopelessly entangled. There will be knots that even a sailor would look at with awe.) Most of our cards are ones we send each other, which may sound sad but isn't in the slightest. And, of course, we buy loads of crackers, though the people who make them (and who select the bits and pieces to put inside them) seem to have run out of imagination and style. I think the modern definition of the word 'disappointment' should be the feeling which follows the pulling of a Christmas cracker and finding a shoe horn, egg cup or nail clipper inside.

We won't get carol singers where we live and so when The Princess had finished decorating the tree (I keep away to minimise damage) I snuck outside and repeatedly sang the only chorus of *Oh Come All Ye Faithful* with which I am familiar. The Princess brought me a mince pie and a glass of the very best 18-year-old Laphroaig. I ate and drank the delights on the doorstep and then the lady of the house, with a promising twinkle in her eyes, kindly invited me to step inside. It looked as if additional benefits might be available and I did so with aclarity.

7.

There is much bleating on television from teenage economists arguing that pensioners are not being hit hard enough by the Government, as it struggles to repair the damage done by Brown and the Scottish banks. This, I fear, shows only how ignorant and stupid teenage economists can be. The truth (as if anyone is interested in that these days) is that pensioners who aren't former civil servants with massive inflation-proofed pensions, have been hit harder than any other group. Their pensions and savings have been devastated by absurdly low interest rates, deliberately lowered annuity rates and soaring real inflation. In our new world of debt and continuing recession anyone who has worked hard and saved hard is treated as a criminal. No one in England has suffered more than pensioners as a result of the fiscal chaos caused by the moronic Brown and the egregiously incompetent Scottish bankers.

8.

The Princess and I bumped into Ebb, one of the Tide sisters in the village shop.

She smiled sweetly at us and if we had been holding a baby she would have kissed it. She drew herself up to her full five foot one inch. The added height made her almost perfectly spherical.

'Am I right in thinking that you are in charge of snow?' I asked.

She frowned. 'I am,' she said. 'But we haven't had any yet this year.'

'Exactly!' I said, making sure that the exclamation point was clearly audible.

She looked very confused. 'I don't understand,' she said.

'My wife and I have bought a toboggan,' I said. 'We want to go sledging in our garden.'

She nodded and frowned again.

'We can't,' I said. 'There hasn't been any snow.'

'No,' she agreed. 'There hasn't been any snow. Not yet.'

'So when are you going to get us some snow?'

'I'm sorry,' she said, backing away. 'I'm only the parish councillor. I think you need to speak to someone at the District Council.' She turned and if she'd been capable of running she'd have run.

'You shouldn't tease her,' whispered The Princess. 'She takes herself very seriously.'

'That's why I tease her,' I said.

9.

Our modest stream has become a raging torrent. If it would promise to stay like this I would consider installing a turbine so that we can create our own electricity. I remember being very impressed many years ago when I saw the hydroelectric plant at Lynmouth in Devon. But I am confident that if I do this then it will never rain again and our stream will dry up completely.

The weather is so bad that we are now putting out food specifically for the squirrels. We've tied bags of nuts and two halves of coconut to one of the beech trees near their dray.

10.

A little while ago I had winter tyres fitted to our four wheel drive truck – just in case we had any bad weather this winter. Yesterday I managed to fry the clutch and had to take the truck to a nearby garage to be repaired. Today it started to snow. We spent an hour this morning refilling all our bird feeders and, as soon as the snow had stopped, putting down food for the ground feeders such as blackbirds and robins. Then we spent a couple of hours tobogganing on a slope at the top of the garden. As we walked back to the house I noticed that a group of adults and children from the nearby village were using the hilly part of the lane near to our house as a toboggan run. As a result the snow on the road, which is already impass-able to all motor vehicles, has been turned into ice. Inevitably, the ice on the road will remain there long after the snow has melted. More politely than I felt I pointed this out to one of the adults. 'There's a terrific slope in that field over there,' I said, pointing to a nearby meadow. 'I'm sure the farmer wouldn't mind if you tobogganed on the grass.'

'We've made a good run on the road now,' replied the man.

'But if you keep going the ice will be packed really hard and no one will be able to use that road for days.'

The man looked at me, thought for a brief moment and then glared. 'That's your problem then innit, mate.'

11.

The Princess and I spent another wonderful afternoon on the home-made toboggan run in our garden. She had never been tobogganing before but she took to it like a St Moritz regular. At one point, early in the afternoon,

I was giving her a push start when the toboggan suddenly stopped (it had caught on the rope at the front which had somehow got underneath the runners) and my momentum and weight carried me forwards at quite a speed. Not wanting to land on top of The Princess I managed to fly over her and got so much air (as I think the skiers say) that I cleared her head comfortably. I must have been flying at least four feet off the ground. I then landed ten to twelve feet in front of her, on my back. I was in the air so long that I was surprised not to have been offered a plastic sandwich and the chance to buy duty free spirits. Fortunately, I landed in a thick blanket of fluffy snow and, apart from losing my hat, my dignity and one glove, suffered no damage. We were both disappointed afterwards that we did not have a video of the incident to review at leisure.

12.

The snow has melted, quicker than expected. The ice created on the lane, by the activities of the thoughtless tobogganers, is still there. And since the forecast is for the cold weather to continue for several more days the ice is likely to remain a problem for a good while to come.

13.

Just after five o'clock this evening I heard what sounded like a strimmer in the lane outside. I looked out of the window and could not believe my eyes when I saw Mr Spick using a huge petrol driven leaf blower to remove leaves from the lane and to blow them into our garden. It was so dark outside that I could only see him because our exterior lights had all flicked on. It was also raining quite heavily. It occurred to me that he was probably the sort of fellow who, in suburbia, would voluntarily cut the roadside verge outside his house within half an inch of its life. My incredulity turned to outrage when I realised that he was blowing leaves from the lane through our garden gate. Since we already have enough dead leaves in our garden (and since I had recently spent most of a day clearing piles of them out of the way) I pulled on a coat and tottered outside to remonstrate with him. 'I'm just cleaning up the road a bit,' he explained. 'The leaves interfere with traction on the road.' He drives a gloriously inappropriate rear wheel drive sports car with so little ground clearance that two leaves piled one on top of the other probably stop it dead in its tracks. I once found him sobbing in the lane because six inches of errant bramble had scratched his paintwork. To someone who drives a variety of travelling dent exhibits such behaviour is difficult to understand. From the way he looked at me I just knew that he thought I would be certifiable if I did not understand. I think he wondered why I wasn't grateful to him for this selfless, public-spirited act. It was pitch dark outside and what he couldn't see was that behind him the wind, which was gaining strength, was blowing the leaves he'd moved back onto the road he'd cleared. Nature likes her dead leaves to be distributed where she wants to put them and she always wins.

I came back indoors and told The Princess that I thought Mr Spick had lost touch with reality. He is normally so uptight that if you put a piece of coal up his rear end you would have a diamond within a week or ten days at most, but blowing leaves off the battered, potholed, ice damaged tarmacadam of a single track country lane with grass growing in the middle of it seems to me to take nuttiness to an entirely new level. For another three quarters of an hour we could hear him continuing to clear the lane, using the earth's valuable petroleum reserves to enable him to blow leaves onto our land. I hope the leaves realise that they are supposed to stay where they've been put. I was tempted to take him a scrubbing brush and a bucket of soapy water but I resisted the temptation. I was worried that he would use them and knock on our door for constant refills.

14.

We received one of those annual round robin letters from friends who insisted on telling us what an absolutely wonderful year they'd had, and how tremendously successful all their marvellous children had been. Nauseating.

I sent them the following round robin describing our year and the wonderful successes of our fictional son Albert:

'Well, what a year it has been. It is difficult to believe that a whole twelve months have gone by since I wrote to you last. We hope that this seasonal missive finds you and yours healthy, wealthy and wise! We look forward to another Christmas of joy and a modicum of goodwill to all men.

As always this has been a very special year for us. Albert has painted some marvellous pictures. Sixteen of them have been accepted by the Royal Academy where they sold a whole bunch of old Masters to pay for his pictures to be nicely framed. His French horn concert at the Royal

Albert Hall was a tremendous success, as I'm sure you heard. I had to insist that they redid the ceiling in order to improve the acoustics but it was well worthwhile. The CD they made of his playing has been number 1 in 87 countries for the last 19 weeks. Oh, and I must tell you that his book on insect life has been chosen as the Booker Prize Winner and Albert himself is the favourite to win this year's Nobel Prize for Literature. All the critics loved the book and the Americans were particularly enthusiastic. Next year Albert will celebrate his eighth birthday and his skiing instructor tells us that several gold medals are a certainty at the winter Olympics.

I do hope that your own lives have not been too dull in comparison, and that your children do not sound too disappointing when compared with Albert. He is the most special little boy on the planet so your family is bound to appear unsuccessful in comparison. So the answer, my dear friends, is simple: don't bother to try to compare, just content yourselves with feeling inadequate and envious.

On that happy note we send you annual greetings and love.'

15.

In today's mail I've received three letters from people asking me to appear on television documentaries they are preparing. (I suspect they are all students and that I'm part of a college project). There is a letter from a woman wanting to know how to write a book, a letter from a man wanting to know how to sell the book he has self-published and a 46 page letter (together with X-rays and laboratory results) from someone wanting a second opinion. I have a letter allegedly from a cat, writing about my book *Secret Lives of Cats* and a copy of a diary allegedly written by another cat. A man wants to use chunks of my book *England Our England* in a leaflet he is writing and a woman wants to know how to patent mud. She also wants to know how to protect the mud around a lake at a secret location in South America. A woman wants me to tell her where she can buy organic food near her home, a man has written to tell me that he can show me how to be a successful publisher if I send him £147.50 and a reader tells me that Josef Mengele is alive and well. (He will be over 100-years-old if he is alive. Maybe he is now running the NHS.)

I've also received a four page colour leaflet from the Marylebone Cricket Club telling me what I must (and must not) wear when visiting

Lords. There is much advice on the type of clothing that is appropriate when visiting the pavilion on match days, when visiting the pavilion on days when there is no match and on visiting other parts of the ground. I am advised that certain types of garment are considered inappropriate and that The Princess is not allowed to wear dresses with straps unless she also wears a cardigan to cover up flesh that would otherwise drive members to distraction or worse.

And a man in Sunderland has sent me a long letter about his health problems. At the top of the letter he has written, in red ink: 'Please let me know if you don't get this letter.'

16.

We never fly these days. But we do travel a good deal. Here are my accumulated tips on travelling comfortably.

1. Never travel with luggage you cannot carry by yourself for half a mile. Porters and trolleys are, like steam trains, a thing of the past.
2. Don't expect any form of public transport to arrive at its destination on time. Always carry enough reading matter and food to last for at least a day more than your journey is scheduled to last.
3. Never miss an opportunity to go to the loo. You may not see the sense in this now. But the next time you are stuck in a taxi in a traffic jam in central London for 90 minutes the wisdom of this hint will glow like a beacon in your memory.
4. When packing always put the most fragile things right at the very bottom of your bag - without wrapping them. This will enable you to stop worrying about whether the delicate items which you have packed are going to get broken. You will know that they stand no chance of surviving the journey and you will find this strangely liberating.
5. Holiday brochure writers are trained by estate agents. Here are some of the terms you may come across - and their real meaning:
    a) Walking distance = you can save two taxi fares every day if you take hiking boots, thick socks and a compass.
    b) Friendly locals = if you are female the local men will have their hands on your bottom at least 60% of the time and if you are male the local men and women will have their hands in your wallet at least 98% of the time.

c) Unspoilt area = three and a half hours from the airport, no telephone, no television, no newspapers, undrinkable alcohol and food that is swimming in grease.

d) A local speciality = hideous concoction, not eaten by locals for a century and a half, which enables restaurants to charge double for bits of food which no one else wants to eat.

6. When you are shown into your room at the hotel do not unpack. Wait five minutes and then ring the receptionist and demand to be given a better room. (The chances are high that they will have put you into a room which is over the discotheque/next to the lift/above the fan outside the hotel kitchens. They will be counting on the fact that when you have unpacked you will not want to be bothered about changing your room.)

7. For the first two days of your trip tip the hotel staff generously and indiscriminately if they treat you with anything which could be vaguely described as courtesy. There is then no need to tip again. Waiting until the last day to tip the staff will do you no good at all.

8. Men should always wear a silly but expensive hat; a proper hat not a baseball cap. Wear a hat which makes you look like an English tourist. It should be something that will roll up or which can be crushed. Profiling at airports and railway stations mean that the best way to avoid attention is to look slightly absurd - like a tourist with bad taste. (But not an American tourist. They are loathed everywhere.) And the easiest way to do this is to wear an unfashionable hat. The added advantage of wearing a hat is that when you remove it your appearance and profile changes instantly. If you find yourself being chased by officials you can hide quite quickly simply by stuffing your hat into a bag.

9. Pack as few metal objects in your bag as you can. Border guards believe fervently in the power of metal detectors. (They have not yet realised that it is possible to buy guns made entirely of plastic.) Johannesburg airport used to have real life examples of things that you couldn't take on the plane fixed to the wall above the entrance door. I was particularly reassured by the fact that passengers were being actively discouraged to carry rocket launchers and landmines in their luggage.

10. If at all possible try travelling with a television camera crew in attendance. As Palin, Boorman et al will doubtless confirm it makes travel so much easier. Forget paying extra for first class

tickets. Use the money to take your own camera crew. If you can't manage a camera crew then at least take a movie camera of some kind and keep it running if you ever have trouble with officials.

17.

We went to Tetbury to buy provisions and magazines. As we walked back to the car I saw someone I thought I recognised. I nudged The Princess.

"Who's that?' I asked. 'I'm sure I recognise him. He's someone famous. He must be in films. I think he plays villains.'

She looked at him and then looked back at me. 'It's the chap who sold us our last car,' she told me.

18.

Parents and schoolchildren are demanding free iPads, free Wi-Fi and free home broadband connections. These are today's bread and circuses. You could start a religion that would sweep the world if you gave away free mobile telephones with free e-mail connection.

Young people used to fight for peace, freedom and democracy. Today, most don't even know those words exist and those who do don't know their meaning. In our new, fascist world we are ruled by eurocrats and the only things that matters are Twitter, Facebook and the digital revolution.

Half a lifetime ago Tom Wolfe wrote about the 'me' generation. Neither he nor anyone else could have forecast just how bad things would get. Our New World is broken and the people in it don't yet realise the price they are going to have to pay.

19.

I received a letter offering me help with the new regulations which Her Majesty's Revenue and Customs (HMRC) is introducing for employers. At the moment I have to fill in an employer's form once a year. (Naturally, I have to do this online, using HMRC's abysmal website.) From next April I will have to visit the damned website and fill in an online form once a month. This will, of course, increase my workload by a factor of twelve and the letter I received came from a firm of accountants who are offering to help me complete all these wretched forms. There will, of course, be a fee.

Just how all this extra 'paperwork' will help the nation escape from recession has not been explained but I'm prepared to guess that all this red tape comes to us courtesy of the European Union and with the enthusiastic support of the HMRC staff. Today, anyone who runs a business is used by the Government as a tax collector but, in contravention of the guaranteed minimum wage agreements brought in by the EU, the Government refuses to pay a penny for this work. Not only does the Government not pay for this work but it also imposes automatic fines on anyone who makes a mistake. And mistakes are, of course, almost inevitable since the tax systems which are in operation (both for employment taxes and for VAT) are so absurdly complicated that not even paid professionals understand them. Indeed, HMRC's own inspectors don't understand them either.

People who work for the Government don't have the foggiest idea how the real world works and they don't have any sympathy or understanding for anyone struggling to make a living or run a business.

According to a report commissioned by HMRC itself small companies now bear 80% of the burden of the nation's red tape. The average small businessman or woman now spends 28 hours a month filling in tax forms of one sort or another. (This means, of course, that they invariably end up in breach of the Working Time Directive.) On top of that he or she spends about a week filling in the annual tax form. And in addition there are endless enquiries to be dealt with. That's just HMRC. There are, of course, numerous other Government departments demanding that forms be completed, answers provided and regulations obeyed. Everything is made worse, much worse, by the fact that there is little or no consistency or continuity within the system and tax inspectors in one part of the country will interpret the legislation in quite a different way to tax inspectors in another area. The aim in some areas seems to be not to see that the taxpayer has paid the right amount of tax but to find something to disallow and, if nothing can be found, then to harass and bully the taxpayer until he simply hands over what is, in effect, no more than old-fashioned protection money. The assumption is that every taxpayer is cheating and the aim is to cause as much distress and inconvenience as possible so that the taxpayer despairs and abandons his search for justice. I doubt if I am alone in regarding HMRC as a corrupt organisation staffed by greedy, vindictive inadequates who use their positions to abuse honest people and who are, in the process, wrecking the nation's economy. Everything is made infinitely worse by the fact that today's HMRC employees are given bonuses if they gouge extra money out of taxpayers.

And on top of all that, the entrepreneur has to deal with the day to day problems created by the banks and the utility companies. It is the endless official and unofficial paperwork which is largely responsible for the fact that bankruptcies are rising at a phenomenal rate. I'm surprised that any real work ever gets done and that those who endeavour to deal with all these demands are not collapsing and dying in even greater numbers.

Our modern bureaucracy is also made worse by the fact that those in charge, and their underlings, seem convinced that everyone in the country is a crook. Politicians and civil servants lie, lie and lie again and so they assume that everyone else lies too. In a way I suppose this is hardly surprising. Since we have a Government which lies about everything to everyone, and which employs people who are encouraged, by example, to lie about everything to everyone, it is only to be expected that HMRC staff, who are, even if not civil, still our servants, should assume that taxpayers are similarly deficient in moral standards.

Moreover, although the principle that every man is expected to know the law (and that ignorance of a law could never be offered as an excuse for breaking it) was probably reasonable when the laws in existence were basic and straightforward it is now neither fair nor reasonable. The principle that a man is expected to know the law (and, indeed, all the laws) was fair when the laws were logical and easy to understand (and based, albeit rather loosely, on the Ten Commandments) but when the laws are incomprehensible, confusing, contradictory and constantly being altered both prospectively and retrospectively, and when even the experts in a particular area cannot keep up with what is right and what is wrong, then the principle no longer works and becomes contrary to good sense and to basic human rights.

My own experience convinces me that the HMRC is largely populated by individuals who are arrogant, pompous and patronising and who, moreover, don't even know their own rules and regulations. It seems hardly surprising that although vast numbers of immigrants are pouring into England (largely to take advantage of the over-generous benefits programme) around 500,000 hard-working taxpayers are leaving every year. Many, if not most, of these are the self-employed and those running small businesses – the very economic backbone of any country. It is usually argued that they are all going because of our weather but this, of course, is a lie. Most are leaving because they no longer feel that they belong; they feel that they are being over-taxed and they feel that the State expects them to take but never receive. Moreover, they are exhausted by the ever-growing demands of the nation's bureaucracy. (No one at the HMRC ever bothers to work out what all these emigrants cost the country in hard cash but it is clearly a sum well into the billions.)

'Taxes are the price we pay for a civilised society,' said Oliver Wendell Holmes, who has always been one of my heroes. And he was right, of course. But uncivilised tax demands, expectations and enquiries are too high a price and they threaten the fabric of our society. Government employees have created a world in which the divisions between the State and its functionaries on the one hand, and the citizens on the other hand, grow wider day by day. There is growing distrust and disappointment and anger and resentment among people who create the wealth which pays for the State. And without those people there will be no money and no State and no comfortable jobs for the functionaries. An over-aggressive, over-demanding HMRC does enormous damage to the economy and the nation's tax gatherers are destroying the nation's economy.

In the end those taxpayers who do not choose to emigrate will have to learn to defend themselves more aggressively. The millions who rely upon the State for their daily bread have become adept at manipulating and controlling the system. Taxpayers will have to learn to deal with England's vast army of apparatchiks in the same way.

Many have already learned the hard way that if they are picked out for an enquiry they have only two choices: kill themselves or prepare for war. They must forget the nonsense about there being nothing to worry about if they've done nothing wrong, and they must gird their loins and unsheathe their swords.

HMRC employees have been given the power to bug telephones (at home and at work). They have the power to intercept the mail (whether earthly or electronic) and to plant listening devices in cars and offices. Accountants are now legally obliged to share everything they know about their clients with the authorities. Nothing is private, nothing is confidential.

HMRC likes people who roll over and pay up quickly. Because HMRC staff now earn bonuses if they thug people into handing over extra cash they no longer like wasting their time on long drawn-out and unproductive enquiries. But because we all now have rights (not least those given to us by the Human Rights Act) our complaints must be taken seriously. HMRC staff don't like that either. The honest taxpayer has more control over the morons at Revenue and Customs than he thinks he has.

I always like to rant and rage about HMRC. It makes me feel better.

But meanwhile I have to decide what to do about the new monthly employer's forms. Many small employers will doubtless make their staff redundant. These new rules will be the straw that breaks many an employer's back. (Neither the Government nor HMRC has the intellectual capability to work out that this will push up the unemployment figures and increase the expenditure on benefits.) But I'm not going to make The Princess redundant so it seems I have two choices: either I hire someone to fill in these damned monthly forms (it will, I hope, be a tax deductible expense) or I devote yet another few hours a month to fighting HMRC's evil website. But maybe I can find a better solution.

20.

In Bilbury, our mail is delivered to a Post Office Box. However, the new postman occasionally delivers mail addressed to the previous owner, or simply to The Owner (most commonly mail from the TV licensing bandits). Whatever he delivers, the postman folds twice before half pushing it through the letterbox, leaving half the item poking out into the rain. There is no need for him to do this because the letterbox is big enough to accept an A4 envelope. When he has left the folded envelope sticking in the letterbox there is, inevitably, a large gap which allows cold air to enter the building. I left an envelope pinned to the door. The envelope was clearly marked *Christmas Tip For Postman.* Inside I included this note: 'My tip is that you get a job outside the service sector. Your total lack of concern for your customers makes you unsuitable for your present work. I enclose an alternative opportunity you might like to consider.' I pinned to the letter an advertisement requiring construction workers for a rebuilding project in Iraq. I do hope he found it helpful.

21.

We collected our P.O. Box mail from Royal Mail. There was a huge queue stretching out of the sorting office and for about thirty yards outside. Most of them did not know it but they were queuing to pay good money to collect Christmas cards which were too big for the standard postage rate. It was raining and they were all getting soaked. The old man in front of me was having a lengthy argument with the postman at the counter. 'I keep getting mail for my neighbours,' he complained. 'If it continues to happen I'll just throw it in in the bin.' He seemed exasperated, but not as exasperated as the huge queue behind him. 'Do you think you could perhaps sort this out after Christmas?' I suggested. 'There are a lot of people queuing in the rain.' He turned and stared at me as if I'd suggested he join the Foreign Legion. No one else said a word. No one else ever does. He turned back to the man on the other side of the counter. 'So, what do you suggest?' he demanded. 'I suggest you just throw the mail in the bin,' said the weary postman. 'It's probably just junk mail anyway.' 'Right,' said the angry customer. 'I will. I'll bin any more mail that isn't mine.'

And he left. He was gone before I dared to suggest that he might simply drop the mis-delivered mail into a post-box. I was appalled by the postman's response. I now understand why so much mail goes astray. The real problem, of course, is that many organisations (such as HMRC) consider that a letter posted is a letter received. If you don't pay a tax demand because you didn't receive it you will still have to pay the fine. To be fair, it isn't just the Royal Mail which seems to take a debonair attitude towards mail. I recently ordered a Christmas present through Amazon which the courier firm left at the local Post Office. I only found this out when I complained that the parcel hadn't arrived. 'It was left in a safe place,' I was told. 'It's not here,' I countered, only to be told that the courier had left the parcel for me to collect. Pity no one bothered to tell me. Even bigger pity they couldn't be bothered to deliver the damned parcel instead of expecting me to complete the final few miles of the delivery myself.

'I'd like to collect my P.O. Box mail,' I told the postman. I showed him the small cardboard card with the relevant P.O. Box details (we have a number of P.O. Boxes and picking out the wrong one can cause great confusion.) He stared at it and frowned. I had to explain what a P.O. Box is. He went away. It took him fifteen minutes to find the mail. My loathing and contempt for the Royal Mail grows with each day that passes. And I'm not alone. I see that a number of the few remaining mail order suppliers who still use the Royal Mail (and who once proudly offered delivery within two days) now warn their customers to allow up to 28 days for parcels sent by first class mail to arrive. I doubt if even the Italians have a postal service as bad as ours. It is, perhaps, hardly surprising that a growing number of people who buy stuff through the internet choose to collect the things they've bought from a local shop, rather than entrust them to carriers of any hue.

As we drove home, it occurred to me that I have just ten days to go to finish this book. I will be heartily miffed if the Mayans are right and the world ends today.

22.

Our Christmas groceries were delivered. 'Well, I won't see you again until after Christmas,' said the delivery driver. 'So I'll wish you a Happy Christmas.' He sighed. 'This will be the last time I see you until after the holidays.' I handed him the £20 note I had ready folded in my back pocket and wished him Happy Christmas. 'Oh I couldn't,' he said. 'I shouldn't. I mustn't. It really isn't allowed.' 'It's OK,' I said, 'we won't tell anyone.' 'Are you sure?' he said. They always say: 'Are you sure?' I hate it when they say 'Are you sure?' What do they think I'm going to say? Am I going to say: 'No, I'm not sure. It was a crazy idea. Give it back to me.'

I said I was sure. The £20 note disappeared. One minute it was there. The next minute it was gone. He should be in cabaret. *Mr Magic Makes Your £20 Note Disappear Before Your Very Eyes.*

When we unpacked the delivery we found they'd forgotten to include the damned parsnips. How can we have Christmas dinner without roast parsnips?

23.

Mr Pettigrew told us a wonderful, true story. He has a neighbour who is frail and elderly and who uses his dog to do the shopping for him. Every day he puts money and a shopping list into a basket and the dog carries the basket to the village shop. The shopkeeper puts the groceries and the change into the basket and the dog takes everything back to the old man. The old man always leaves his back door open, whatever the weather, so that the dog can get in and out easily. Two days ago the dog arrived at the shop carrying an empty basket. There was no shopping list and no money. Alarmed by this the shopkeeper drove round to the old man's house and found him lying on the bedroom floor with a broken leg. He was in a bad way but he is now making a good recovery in hospital and the dog is being looked after by the shopkeeper's family. If the dog hadn't gone to the shop, and the shopkeeper hadn't guessed that there was something wrong, the old man would have doubtless died. But the dog did go to the shop, the shopkeeper did guess that something must be wrong and the old man is fine. A wonderful piece of news for Christmas.

24.

We gave our friend Thumper his two presents. One we wrapped and one we did not wrap. The unwrapped present was a chain saw (his old one has been jamming a good deal recently). He opened the wrapped present in the way that a child would, tearing at the paper excitedly. I could tell that he was disappointed. He looked just how I felt when my parents took me to see the Da Vinci cartoon when I was a lad. I hadn't thought it at all funny and couldn't see what all the fuss was about.

'It's a book,' I said, unnecessarily.

'I've already got a book,' he said. Thumper never manages to avoid saying what is on his mind. Thumper is a practical fellow. He is the sort of chap who can build a cupboard, clean out a septic tank or tune a car without needing to buy a textbook or use a YouTube video to show him how.

'Not this one.'

He examined it carefully, as though seeing it for the first time. 'No,' he agreed. 'Not this one.'

'You don't have to read it,' I told him. Thumper can pick locks, tickle trout and start a car without a key. But he doesn't read much.

'We just thought you'd like to have one,' said The Princess. She took my arm. 'It's one we wrote together,' she told him.

Thumper looked at the names of the authors and smiled. He hugged the book to his chest and then stepped forward and embraced us, first individually and then together. When he moved away, a few moments later, there were tears in his eyes.

'I'll treasure it,' he said gruffly. 'Always.'

'If you want to give your new chain saw a bit of a run we've got a couple of trees that need taking down,' I told him.

His eyes lit up. 'Really?' he said.

25.

We watched two cartoons *Toy Story* and *The Snowman and the Snowdog.* One was witty, sharp and professional. The one about the snowman was predictable, badly written and dull. Both had something in common: the central human characters were a mother and a son. No father. Airbrushing dads out of stories for children seems fashionable. If they are there then they tend to be cruel, arrogant and distant. How sad.

26.

Among other wonderful goodies The Princess bought me a pile of old *Cricketer* magazines from the late 1940s and early 1950s. She found them on a stall in an antiques market in Cirencester.

I've been a huge cricket fan since the age of five but I have in recent years been enormously disillusioned by the way the game has been taken over by people who seem (and probably are) more interested in money than sport.

What a joy it is to be able to read about real cricketers and real cricket matches. I read with delight about the exploits of Denis Compton, Len Hutton, Godfrey Evans et al, pitting their skills and strengths against Keith Miller, Ray Lindwall and Don Bradman. There is no talk of tantrums or agents or coaches or television replays used to question the umpires' authority. I particularly enjoyed a reprinted article from the *Sydney Telegraph*. The article had been written at the end of the Ashes Tour of Australia in 1947. A slightly battered England had been destroyed by a powerful Australian side (and a good deal of bad luck) and the writer in the *Sydney Telegraph* concluded his piece with this paragraph: 'Australians who realise what mass bombing and doodlebugs and rationing can do to one's sense of fun and games would prefer Hammond (England's captain) to take the Ashes home - and to win them for Australia some other time when Englishmen are fitter and less tired.'

I think I shall spend a lot of time living in the distant past for a while. It's a highly recommended place to be. I shall abandon newspapers and magazines and, instead, immerse myself in reading about better times.

27.

A woman who works at one of the local supermarkets collapsed in the pub this morning. There was nothing wrong with her and it was generally agreed that she had probably drunk too much and slept too little.

'Don't suppose anyone has any smelling salts?' said the landlord's wife who attended a first aid course in 1958 and naturally considers herself an expert on matters medical.

No one had.

But Thumper removed his boot and tore off a sock. He then waved the sock under the woman's nose. She came round almost instantly.

'For heaven's sake don't anyone tell her what brought her round,' said the landlord's wife. 'Or she'll need counselling for years.'

28.

Here's what's wrong with our world: hopes and dreams have been replaced by demands and expectations. It's an incurable disease of the spirit.

29.

It has become impossible to run a mail order business in England. The Royal Mail is now so unreliable that it is not possible to offer anything remotely resembling a decent service. Orders coming in can take weeks to arrive. And the parcels which we send out seem to disappear with increasing frequency; when they do get through they sometimes arrive so late that the unhappy recipients send them back. We have, for the first time in our history, suffered from a spate of cancelled cheques as readers despair of ever receiving their books. One reader wondered if we were being targeted because of the political nature of some of my books. Not at all. Everyone involved in mail order seems to be suffering.

And, as if all that were not enough, the Royal Mail is now going to introduce a new barrier for those trying to run any sort of business. It will soon not be possible to post books abroad without taking the parcels to a Post Office, queuing for hours and answering a series of searching questions from one of their gestapo guards. There will have to be an inquiry about every parcel which is being posted. This reeks of a European Union directive. The aim, apparently, is to stop people sending explosives and body parts through the mail. There is no suggestion that people have actually been doing this; no gangs have been found sending sawn up grannies or landmines through the mail. But the new rule will make sure that they don't – unless, of course, the miscreants are naughty and lie to the inquisitors at their local Post Office.

Posting books abroad was already a commercial disaster. We put up our postage charges to £7 a book for those parts of the world outside Europe but that has proved woefully inadequate. A reader from the Cayman Islands ordered five books and, quite properly, sent £35 to cover postage. But the books actually cost nearly twice that much to post. So we lost money on the order. It took us 45 minutes just to stick on the stamps – which took up every available inch of space on the parcels. International postage prices have soared in the last year or so and the prices invariably require a complex combination of stamps. This latest absurd regulation will put an end to our selling books abroad.

I am, indeed, seriously depressed about our business. I can see no future for it. I loathe eBooks and Kindles. I love printed books. But I cannot see how we can continue printing and sending out books through the post. Our business model is doomed. I am saddened too when I realise that no author will ever again be able to run a commercially successful self-publishing business.

30.

The hound of the Baskervilles is still being allowed to roam free and has killed one of the pheasants which live in our garden. He succeeded in leaping a four foot high wall and today we found all that remains: a sad collection of feathers. A couple of weeks ago he killed a pair of loving and inseparable wood pigeons which had been living with us for months. Once again we found nothing more than a bunch of feathers; the birds were as inseparable in death as they had been in life. The tracks in the snow proved that it was the hound, and not a fox, which had done the killing.

31.

It has always seemed to me that the only route to follow is the precarious one of the independent thinker. As an iconoclast I have always exposed my ideas to the risk of ridicule and dismissal. I have always believed that all good new ideas sound crazy at first (if they don't then they are probably not very original) and I have always recognised that speaking my mind and eschewing conformity is bound to bring resentment and serious opposition. I have always understood that swimming against the current must mean that the journey will be wearing and depressing. I have always known that being original will mean being labelled controversial and that the conformists will dismiss me as a lunatic. I have always known that standing up, and being counted, is a dangerous thing to do. But I had not counted on being silenced, stifled, banned so very effectively. I underestimated the power of the establishment and now I understand what Herodotus meant when he wrote: 'Of all human troubles the most hateful is to feel you have the capacity for power and yet no field in which to practise it.' I can sympathise with H. G. Wells who, at the end of his life, cried out in real pain: 'Goddam you all. I told you so.'

How I wish I had been able to write the *Diary of a Gruntled Man.*

THE AUTHOR

By 'Patchy' Fogg

After working in Liverpool for a year, as a Community Service Volunteer, Vernon Coleman attended Birmingham Medical School back in the days when doctors and nurses regarded it as their duty to keep patients alive regardless of the demands of the State bureaucrats. When he arrived at the university he was told that he had to join the National Union of Students. He was told that it was compulsory and since he didn't much fancy joining something because he had to, he invoked the United Nation Charter and was allowed not to join. During his years as a medical student he ran a nightclub, reviewed plays and books for a number of national publications and wrote several columns. He qualified as a doctor in 1970 and has worked both in hospitals and as a GP. He is still registered and licensed to practise as a GP principal. He has founded and organised many campaigns concerning iatrogenesis, drug addiction and the abuse of animals and has given evidence to committees at the House of Commons and House of Lords.

Coleman resigned as a GP when he was fined for refusing to put diagnoses on sick notes. Patients asked him not to disclose details of their illnesses to their employers and he believed it was wrong that he should write diagnoses on bits of paper that would be seen by colleagues and employers. He was taken before a tribunal of what he calls 'faceless, nameless idiots' who demanded to know what his patients were suffering from. He refused to answer, telling them that their diagnoses were confidential and none of their business. They fined him £100 and threatened to keep fining him if he didn't start writing proper diagnoses on all his sick notes. His colleagues seemed utterly disinterested. Their view was that if the State wanted full diagnoses written on forms, then full diagnoses should be written on forms. Since no one else (and certainly no one from the British Medical Association or the General Medical Council) seemed interested in his stand he resigned and became a full time author.

He has worked as a columnist for numerous national newspapers including *The Sun, The Daily Star, The Sunday Express* and *The People.* He once wrote five columns at the same time for national papers (he wrote them under three different names, Dr Duncan Scott in *The Sunday People,* Dr James in *The Sun* and Dr Vernon Coleman in the *Daily Star, Sunday Scot* and the sadly short lived *Sunday Correspondent*). At the same time he was also writing weekly columns for the *Evening Times* in Glasgow. His syndicated columns have appeared in over 50 regional newspapers.

He says that he has never gone looking for trouble but that it has always had no difficulty in finding him. He hates being told what to do, loathes bureaucrats and dislikes compromise. He has been described as 'a rebel with too many causes'. Thanks largely to bits of paper awarded by foreigners his official title is Professor Dr Sir Vernon Coleman MB ChB DSc KStJ (KC). He now writes books which are printed in limited editions and could, therefore, be classified as 'rare books' before they start their lives.

Coleman is pathologically shy, sceptical and gullible and has, belatedly, discovered that kindness is often mistaken for weakness. He has no networking skills at all. On his one visit to Buckingham Palace he slipped out of a line of people waiting to be presented to HM and dodged Margaret Thatcher who was looking for someone to talk to. He describes himself as an outsider in the mould of Cobbett or Bierce and regards himself as a revolutionary anarchist. He has been told by the editor of one national newspaper that thanks to a decree from on high his name is now not allowed to appear in the media and although this sounds bizarre he suspects it might be true. His favourite mythical character is Cassandra, a Trojan princess who was cursed by Apollo to make accurate predictions that were disbelieved. His motto is: 'Why take the easy road when there are harder paths to follow?' He believes that he has a very special relationship with his readers and that when someone picks up a book a personal and private bond between author and reader can be established. He always tries to write sentences which encourage the reader to want to tell someone what they've just read. He knows that he would have been more successful as an author if he'd been sensible and stuck to writing the same book over and over again. (It's difficult to argue that a reader who liked *Rogue Nation* will enjoy *Alice's Diary*.) He says that his God loves all creatures equally and does not believe that a horse is better than an accountant or that a lawyer is better than a frog.

He can, at different times of day, be a cavalier and a roundhead, and is a rebellious traditionalist and a radical who hates change. He believes in the value of Old England and despises social engineering programmes such as political correctness, means-testing and multiculturalism. He believes that we all have a duty to stand up and speak out for those who have no voice.

Vernon Coleman and his wife have designed for themselves a unique world to sustain and nourish them in these dark and difficult times. The author is devoted to Donna Antoinette (The Princess) whom he describes as the kindest, sweetest, most sensitive and loyal woman a man could hope to meet. Whatever the season they can both often be found in a corner of The Duck and Puddle, and can always be relied upon to buy a round when it is their turn, and sometimes when it is not.